NOAH'S ARKIVE

Noah's Arkive

JEFFREY J. COHEN and JULIAN YATES

University of Minnesota Press
Minneapolis — London

The University of Minnesota Press gratefully acknowledges the generous assistance provided for the publication of this book by the Hamilton P. Traub University Press Fund.

Published by the University of Minnesota Press
111 Third Avenue South, Suite 290
Minneapolis, MN 55401-2520
http://www.upress.umn.edu

ISBN 978-1-5179-0423-4 (hc)
ISBN 978-1-5179-0424-1 (pb)

A Cataloging-in-Publication record for this book is available from the Library of Congress.

Printed in the United States of America on acid-free paper

32 31 30 29 28 27 26 25 24 23 10 9 8 7 6 5 4 3 2 1

CONTENTS

Aboard

A family takes shelter in a well-sealed home, having collected everything they need to begin life anew. Strong walls offer security against a world ravaged by meteorological calamity. The survival of this small community is made possible only through the exclusion of those who have been left to the rising sea, the humans and the animals they could not or simply did not include. At last the weather subsides, the waters retreat. A bright new day, sealed with a rainbow, portends a future they could hardly have imagined when the Earth was in flood.

This is the story of Noah and his ark, a tale of climate catastrophe and human endurance, of diminished safeties, wide disasters, and conservation at high price. It's also a narrative older than the Bible. *The Epic of Gilgamesh* contains a version in which the gods send the waters to drown the noise of ever-multiplying humans. The shipbuilder saves as many as he can fit aboard his vessel. But to Noah belongs the story of survival against deluge that we cannot stop telling, a myth undergirding how we imagine our own endurance within environments become hostile. A ship that sails the Flood easily becomes a starship, even Spaceship Earth, but it is still an ark that preserves a limited few. The biblical tale has become the structure of a recurring political tale, enacted by nations that imagine they can enclose themselves through border walls, as if continents could be parceled into gated communities. The story of the ark is enacted by every family privileged enough to draw down the boundaries of their home in response to the threat of viral infection. So many tiny arks, secure against viruses or immigrants or sea surge. So many little Noahs. For better or worse, the myth of Noah and his vessel of restricted preservation offers our most enduring narrative for how to survive life during climate change.

Everyone knows the story of the ark. Yet most of us recall details not from Genesis, where the narrative is elliptical and complicated, but from the simplified version we pass along in picture Bibles and entertainments for children. A bearded patriarch builds a mighty ship at divine command. Animals enter two by two, lions mingling with zebras and peacocks. As the rain falls, the chosen community sits snugly against the storm. The world is in flood. When the weather clears and the waves recede, all who were inside happily emerge. Those not admitted have vanished as if they never lived. The story ends with a dove, an olive branch, and a rainbow. It is hard not to fall in love with this ark and its promise of no future deluge, no catastrophes on the horizon, just landfall and a shimmering sky.

It is too easy to forget the stranger details of Genesis, such as the advent of giants as the story opens, or Noah's silence when God announces his destructive plans. Easy to forget that a rainbow is a weapon made of weather, a celestial armament, not the happy icon of stickers, emojis, Pride. Many of the animals admitted to the ark enter not two by two, but fourteen by fourteen. These are the clean beasts, the ones to be sacrificed and devoured after the ark finds its mountain. Like all the conserved creatures, they spend long months on the ship as messmates and companions of Noah and family, who before the voyage were (according to an enduring tradition) vegetarians. After the Flood, all clean animals may be offered to God or consumed by humans, changing forever their relation to those with whom they once shared a home. Genesis states bluntly that, henceforth, animals fear humans. For all we know, the dove (a clean beast) who brought back the olive branch is incinerated on the altar that Noah builds to celebrate the voyage's end.

Given the way the story concludes—a settler-colonist community founded on ritual slaughter, a brave new world in which Noah is soon to get so drunk that he passes out naked and wakes to curse one of his three children to eternal slavery, a story in which not a single woman bears a personal name and no one seems to remember the lives of those who perished beneath the waves—well, is it any wonder that, when released from the ark to reconnoiter the world, the raven never returns?

"Make yourself an ark." Let's discover what that sentence might mean, its costs, and the limits to its possibility. Let's remember the strangenesses to this familiar story and see what we can learn by way of ark thinking.

CHAPTER 1

How to Think like an Ark

Human activity holds weatherborne consequence. Storm clouds gather, portending disaster. "Make yourself an ark of gopher wood; make it an ark with compartments, and cover it inside and out with pitch," declares God (Genesis 6:14), and Noah sets to work.[1] In the face of anthropogenic climate change (the evil deeds of humankind are the divine trigger for the rising seas to come), he builds a vessel that will shelter some fragment of the imperiled world in the hope of beginning again. Today this injunction to construct a sealed, ordered, and exclusive architecture of conservation seems more likely to come from an environmental scientist, ecological activist, or writer of climate fiction. Ark-building is an almost inevitable response to the threats posed by a world in disarray.[2]

A space of sanctuary and preservation, an ark is built to convey some fragment of a turbulent present toward a better future. We stow in virtual arks sequences of DNA (The Frozen Ark charity) and upload images of endangered species into databases to preserve at least the memory of animal diversity from oblivion (National Geographic Society's *Photo Ark*). Sometimes we safeguard living creatures within physical structures christened with that name, carefully managing their reproductive habits to delay their extinction (The Amphibian Ark initiative). Plants have their own special version of an ark (Svalbard Global Seed Vault), as do the wealthy in a way (gated communities and other havens to exclude the tumults of the world). In speculative fiction, what was a boat for one family and their animal companions becomes a precarious enclave against a cyborg or zombie apocalypse, radioactive death, or viral infection. Every starship en route to a new Earth is an ark.

To ensure the security of the fragment he stowed, Noah shut his door against the world—safety at the price of severe loss. The stories we collect in this book often testify to something more promising.

They confirm that, within the frame of the ark, in its many iterations, it is possible always to pry hope loose from resignation and reduction, to find refuge not in a retreat inward, but by and through an active attention to what appears outside, past, and beyond. What the ark appears to exclude opens again by virtue of that very closure.[3] So, let's change tenses. Let's look to the future even if, all the time, we have to look backward: a cautious optative weighing of the possible in the face of a looming default pessimism. We are conditioned to build small arks against the menace of changed climate, internalizing parsimonious and austere architectures into lingering conditions of unkindness. But what would an unconditional refuge resemble? What does inaugurating an ark entail? How far will it get us? What practical, conceptual, affective, and political resources do arks offer?

The story of Noah and the Flood embeds a fundamental set of questions about the limits and possibilities of hospitality. With its announcement of reduced dimensions, the narrative constricts the capacity to shelter. *This* and *these* may be saved; *those* may not. When the ark reaches landfall, or just settles back down atop Mount Ararat, it functions as a foundation effect, annihilating all that came before it in order to terraform a new set of relations between animals, humans, and the divine. This is the "cleansed" world into which our colonist family settles.[4] And yet, this new world quickly turns out to be no better than the one that existed previously. Noah's story in Genesis continues long after a bow in the sky ratifies a new covenant and marks the Flood's terminus. His work was just beginning when God blessed his family and gave them the animals to eat. The lands were now theirs to populate, a chance to get right what Adam, Eve, and their children got wrong. Dry after drowning, the scoured Earth offered a hard reset, wiped clean of disobedience to the deity and all the stories that came with it: entanglement with snakes, the messiness of fratricide, the pollution of sexual crimes, the thriving of evil inclinations. The rainbow arrives not at the end of the tale but just as a second commencement is beginning to get underway, just as things are already about to go terribly wrong once again. No wonder that Noah's ark stands as a seemingly inevitable conveyance device for the tense present of our imaginations. Ark-building stands haunted, from its announcement, by everyone and everything that is to be lost. The story coordinates and occludes the relation between a series of contradictions: hope for a future enabled by catastrophe; refuge for those within premised on the despair and death of those without; inhospitable hospitality.[5]

Despite the insistence of biblical literalists, the Genesis narrative is far from straightforward. Our thesis, though, is pretty direct. The brute sketchiness of the biblical injunction "make yourself an ark" demands that its readers think hard about the difficulties of preserving a community against deluge, about who gets included and who excluded, about how the threat of the flood is experienced differently by varied groups of people and animals. Try to imagine what building an ark actually entails and the magnitude of the task, along with all the choices you would have to make in order to do so, crashing in on you. This is why, across the ages, the story invites retelling and reinvention. The ark narrative resists attempts to transform it into a one-size-fits-all, easy-to-assemble tale of how to weather catastrophe. The minimal scaffolding to the biblical narrative seems to autoproduce or proliferate a resistance to the trajectory it plots. The afterlife of the Genesis story offers a nonconsolatory, nonsalvific, open structure for wrestling with what it means to construct an inside and an out: boundaries, walls, and the costs of refuge for a restricted group. The worst thing you can do, we have learned, is to imagine that you are no longer on an ark.

The ark designates a generative textuality, a material-semiotic-rhetorical program or trope that makes stories and unfolds worlds. Each iteration, each repetition of the ark story, offers a chance for its constitutive elements and the ethical burdens they carry to recombine, err, fret, or stray, and so to turn out differently, under the pressure of their occasion or stowaways. Arks make regular appearances in our built worlds. They may show up with a sort of mundane but well-intentioned, suburban inevitability (the name of a daycare center, a petting zoo, a thrift shop, a dispiriting office building just outside London), courtesy of an irony that we may choose to attribute to fate, to chance, or to store-clerk ingenuity, microresistances in the wilds of retail space (see Figure 1). Then there are the more programmatic, even frightening instances. Arks that make arguments. Arks that rigidify worlds. Arks of despair, austerity, enmity, and cold futures. Perhaps it is time to pause, time to reread the story, to encounter its strangeness and its strange history, to rethink what is even meant by an ark. "Thinking like an ark" refers to the way the story of the ark continues: the way individual realizations localize competing

FIGURE 1. Irony in the wilds of retail space. Deals Store, Media PA, 2019. Authors' photograph.

narratives over what an ark is, what an ark means and how it asserts that meaning through what it collects and excludes; how the trope is deployed and unfolds.[6]

The book we are writing is therefore, also, a kind of ark.

Notes from the Field

Because we are building an ark, we decided to visit arks completed, abandoned, repurposed, and in process. When we first sketched the contours of *Noah's Arkive,* we knew that the project would arc from literary and artistic materials that predate the bible to contemporary speculative fiction (and manifold points between). But we wondered what would happen if we journeyed to some existing arks and got a feel for what it is like to experience a version—however eccentric, however limited—of ark-building. How do these realized arks imagine community? How do they order the world, and might that ordering challenge our premises? Although the COVID-19 pandemic severely interrupted our travel plans, in the course of our research we visited Ark Encounter in Kentucky (Figure 2), a modern Christian imagin-

FIGURE 2. "Everything fits" in the totalizing ark. Ark Encounter, Williamstown, Kentucky, 2018. Authors' photograph.

ing of the ark that insists on biblical literalism and yet is full of what its builders call "ark-tistic license"; Biosphere 2, an object lesson in the turbulence of closed systems and the afterlife of failed totalities (Figure 3); Arcosanti, an arcology or living-environment-dwelling as imagined by the archmodernist architect Paolo Soleri, now home to a mundane utopia, a financially precarious, intentional community, still experimenting with what community might become (Figure 4); the ruin ridiculously called Montezuma's Castle in Arizona, a lively complex of pueblo homes that long ago achieved what Soleri dreamed but whose architects seldom figure in stories told about building and imagining; and artist Eduardo Kac's studio-ark in Chicago, Illinois. Encountering each site has left its impress on our writing throughout this book. But no visit taught us more about how to think like an ark than our pilgrimage to the uncompleted and likely failed project called the Ark of Safety.

On November 16, 2016, we headed to Frostburg, Maryland, from Washington, D.C. The journey takes little more than two hours depending on traffic. It's easy to miss the roadside structure. Traveling west, you pass the ark quickly on your right as the highway skirts

FIGURE 3. Turbulence in a closed system. Biosphere 2, Pinal County, Arizona, 2019. Authors' photograph.

the town. The road bends and steel beams in the shape of an empty edifice stand, soaring skyward. "Noah's Ark Being Rebuilt Here!" announces a faded blue billboard (Plate 1). Farther on, tilted toward where the highway used to run, a taller advertisement announces, "Ark of Safety." This second sign reminded us of those we had passed along the way declaring Honda or Ford. The congregation had repurposed a defunct car dealership to house their place of worship. Anything can become an ark.

We had already conducted fairly extensive archival work. We could bore even the best of them with the particularities of arks and ark design through history, from the *Epic of Gilgamesh* and the ark floor plans of Josephus and Augustine to the failed domes of Margaret Atwood's *MaddAddam* trilogy, Jesmyn Ward's flooded home in *Salvage the Bones,* or Emily St. John Mandel's airport in *Station Eleven.* We knew that every ark manifests an ecology, that it comprehends a worldview, and that every ark invites as well as excludes. But what of this particular ark that grew up in Frostburg, a city of roads, bypassed when the flow of capital moved elsewhere? We knew that we had to take seriously the story that the congregation broadcasts to the world

FIGURE 4. A day of rain at Paolo Soleri's desert arcology. Arcosanti, Arizona, 2019. Authors' photograph.

through its blue highway billboard. "Noah's Ark Being Rebuilt Here" is a slogan that they do and do not share with us as we write this book on arks, refuge, and refusal. We did not want to conscript this ark to our worldview, nor did we want to be con-scripted into its own way of thinking. We are not sure that we rose to the occasion. But we did, we hope, allow this visit to become an occasion for the emergence of themes that animate the volume you are now reading.

We locked our car at the empty lot and surveyed the congregation's weathered place of worship. The wind was fresh. Crickets chirped in grass a few days past the need for mowing. No one was about. Perched on the hill above the small city, the landlocked and unfinished vessel looked a bit disappointing. Its bare steel beams beckoned all the same, so we climbed. At the top, expansive concrete slabs traced an immense rectangle, ghosting the shape of an architecture to come, an enormous Noah's ark in prospect. Laying a foundation according to the dimensions God delivers to Noah in Genesis, this ark's engineer clearly assumed a cubit must be eighteen inches in length, so that the concrete outline extended for about a football field and a half. We were impressed by the scale of the endeavor, a little overwhelmed. This ark in process, whether or not it ever finishes, had already created a lively little ecosystem: a noisy home for insects, squirrels, birds; a field full of weeds and wildflowers gone to seed; matted grass and mud, dried algae where rainwater pools and lingers. Wonder and curiosity are among the affects that an ark invites. And these dispositions would serve us well when we spoke to the man who had poured all that concrete, far more than is visible to the eye. For that is how foundations work: they compress, harden, render themselves invisible even as they subtend.

What happened next is hard to describe because we were trying to be open to encounter, trying not to fit the ark and its maker into an expected narrative.[7] We met Pastor Spence beside a metal building that the previous winter's snow had partially collapsed. He and a fellow congregant (whom we never met) were removing ceiling tiles and wall boards. His black jacket was white with dust and he was wearing a protective mask over his nose and mouth. We had written to Pastor Spence twice before our visit to Frostburg, to introduce ourselves, hoping he would be willing to speak with us about his Ark of Safety. Our requests had gone unanswered. We caught his attention, and he took the mask from his face, placed it above his head, greeted us, thanked us for our interest, but did not ask our names. We told him how impressed we were with the structure. He spoke happily of laying the concrete foundation many years ago. "I was an engineer at GM," he told us. "I drove here to build the ark." The ark was the vision of Pastor Greene, he emphasized, not his. He had inherited the project when that man left.

Pastor Spence warmed quickly to the opportunity to tell ark stories. We learned that a professional construction team had to be hired to erect the metal girders of the frame because no one in his congregation was licensed for that kind of work. So much time, so much pulverized stone, so much metal: Pastor Spence emphasized how deep the foundation plunges, invisible concrete set as anchor for a structure yet to be realized, a vision not yet made solid. Its construction had cost a great deal of money, but such is life. After the completion of the base and the partial metal frame a decade and a half ago, work on the ark ceased. Pastor Spence was not inclined to share why.

We asked Pastor Spence what the people living in the impressive new homes nearby thought of the ark. He spoke offhandedly of struggles: irate phone messages; demands that the steel structure be demolished; embarrassment at this white elephant; fears of devalued property. Arks are as likely to attract derision as they are to cultivate wonder. Would they prefer a vacant lot? Pastor Spence remained cheerful, but not hopeful. Wandering the site, we noticed places where the concrete was deteriorating, rebar exposed. The soaring girders that suggest the shape of the vessel to come have rusted. Although he would not say it, the window for completing this ark using the existing frame was closing, even had closed. Ruination is a form of renewal, but that process also erodes dreams. In the grand visions that inspire the completion of majestic arks abide a coldness and a closedness that this open, unfinished ark rebuffs. This landlocked ruin of a ship, never meant to sail, possesses an intensity that a larger architecture might not hold. Our sense of this productive incompleteness corresponds to Pastor Spence's own buoying sense that this ark endeavor, this refuge in Frostburg, still travels the globe as a story, bringing people to God and even curing the sick. For what else is a congregation other than an ongoing convocation, a shared conviviality? In that sense, this beached and failed ark *works*.

Pastor Spence told us that he had recently visited Ken Ham's Ark Encounter in Kentucky. He spoke with wonder of that ark's situation, its scale, its sheer monumentality. He admitted to crying when he first glimpsed Ham's achievement: a fully realized vessel built to a twenty-four-inch-cubit scale. Two years later, when we journeyed to Ark Encounter, we did so with his wonder and melancholy in mind. It would be a difficult visit. Ark Encounter is a powerfully scripted, precise, and total system. At first we were charmed, thrown off guard, by what seemed an embrace of fiction-making, by the creation of multiracial backstories for Noah's family, by the sheer massiveness of the structure, by the on-boarding of everything, even dinosaurs. But that inclusion comes at a steep price. Signs throughout the ark read, "Everything Fits." No matter how incongruous, every difference is transformed into sameness, the heterogeneity of the world reduced into boxed and ordered cargo. By its end, Ark Encounter struck us as a psychotic conversion machine able to absorb and assimilate anything into a comprehensive system without exterior. Throughout its structure we were greeted by avatars of ourselves modeled as scoffers, know-it-all academics, Jews, queers, all of whom perish during the flood, all of whom are damned. "Take Back the Rainbow" is Ark Encounter's self-proclaimed imperative. It is a project limned by psychological and spiritual violence. At the end of the visit, we sought sanctuary in the nearest public library.[8]

Back to Frostburg. Pastor Spence offered that his own congregation had gone about their project all backward. Ark Encounter had taken only six years to design, secure necessary land and funds, and then construct. But the Ark of Safety had been embarked on without a plan for raising the money needed for completion. We felt bad. We attempted to reassure Pastor Spence of what he had already accomplished, even if his ark is never going to be finished (the sign proclaiming "Noah's Ark Being Rebuilt Here" has since been taken down).

In retrospect we realize that our rush to sympathy did not allow the man to finish what he was saying. But arks do that, they close things off, and sometimes they lead you to invest your sympathy in the wrong places. All that labor, all that time and money, all that will to conserve—who would want to think it had gone to waste? Not that that was what Pastor Spence might have been going to say. Perhaps Pastor Spence had learned to dwell alongside his ark in its incompleteness, and that dwelling as a neighbor to a project forever ongoing was at this moment enough. From time to time, though, he would invoke a future in which the ark might be fully realized. He spoke of investors who had contacted him from distant places who would happily underwrite the project, if only they could find the time to visit. But just as the ark was about to launch on liquid capital flooding in, bearing the future along with it, the narrative would return to the congregation and their lives in the here and now, the ark offering a rather modest prospect.

What does it mean always to be working at ground level, aspiring to a view from the highest deck but suspecting that such a view will forever elude you? And there is so much of the ark below ground that you cannot see. Forever anchored to a hill in Allegany County, Maryland, unfaithful to the rules that God delivered to Noah, this ark is not the vessel of Genesis. Pastor Spence assured us that he believes in the literal truth of the Bible, that the Flood is a historical fact. But his structure has its own origins and remains the product of Pastor Greene's revelation. The congregation is not building Noah's ark, but rebuilding an ark for its own time and place. The Ark of Safety, Pastor Spence stressed, has extra "nonbiblical" space for his community, four floors rather than the Noachic three. His congregation wants room to meet, to pray, to work: an auditorium, some offices, elevators at each end for ease of access, especially for the disabled. "It was never meant to float." This ark is a house, not a boat. It doesn't necessarily expect a catastrophe different from the world that goes on around it each and every day. It exists for the congregation, and for anyone who exits the interstate and decides to remain.

"Noah's Ark Being Rebuilt Here!" It's easy to accustom yourself to that gerund: an act of building as a permanent condition. Most cars heedlessly pass the weathered sign and the ark's steel frame, continuing on to Hagerstown or Cumberland. A few do stop, drawn by what their passengers have noticed or by internet sites that detail the strangest roadside attractions you might glimpse as you travel the United States. As we ate lunch in downtown Frostburg and filled our notebooks with what was already becoming a memory of a visit, an encounter reducing itself into a narrative archive, we asked someone at the restaurant about the town's relation to the Ark of Safety. She related a different origin, heard from a friend, involving a man who sold his vision of the ark to the congregation, took their money, and vanished. She did not have an opinion on the ark; she was just reporting what her friends who had lived in Frostburg for a long time had told her as she studied at the nearby university.

Pastor Spence described a miracle to us, an event that unfolded in the time of Pastor Greene. A traveling salesman arrived in Frostburg driving a fancy car, wearing a five-hundred-dollar suit, intent on selling a security system for the worship building into which they had transformed the car dealership. Pastor Greene listened patiently to the pitch, noting how the salesman wriggled uncomfortably in his chair. He asked the man from out of town if he had a back problem and if he would like him to pray for him. The salesman was not interested. "I've listened to you talk for an hour about your security system," stated Pastor Greene, "let me tell you about mine for a few minutes." And so he did, and he prayed, and the man was healed. Pastor Greene suggested that the salesman donate a security system to the Ark of Safety, which he did. The salesman stopped traveling. He stayed and became a friend. He opted for the ark's invitation to remain safe. Pastor Spence told us that he had just come across this congregant's X-rays last week in the building he was now working on. Because the man did not want them returned, he had only just thrown them in the trash.

This little story wants to offer a tidy parable. A traveling salesman who sells security systems becomes secure in the Ark of Safety. His changed body speaks of his conversion and he stops moving: no more transiency of the road, no more writhing in his seat. The Ark of Safety, an ark in progress, offers a superior system of defense and foundation. Doubled in its reference both to the ark and to the congregation, the ark takes up a relation to the world premised on a profundity of faith that means something, that gives shelter, that encloses, that assimilates. The allegorical ark is a kind of machine that mandates that you stop, park your car, and join the rebuilding here; if you don't, you'll be on the wrong side of the gate when the flood comes rushing. Choose to stay, and eventually you toss away the image that shows the old, faulty support systems, the skeleton before it was properly aligned, because that past has been superseded. X-rays show what we cannot see with the naked eye. They diagnose. But true security lies in a deeper sense of system, a deeper way of understanding and responding to what goes unseen, a deeper sense of relation, an apparently truer truth. Arks within arks. Arkives.

We are interested in arks less because of what is stored within them than because of what they discard or exclude, the stories left to the rising water so that an ark's dimensions can appear to close. Pastor Spence wanted us to think like the salesman, to invest in the prospect of the perfect structure of the ark to come, a future that even he had to admit may or may not arrive. But, speaking with him, we also knew that we needed to think with all an ark might encompass, including the concrete support for the unbuilt ship, the part underneath the ground that you cannot see but that still exerts foundational force, and the strange little ecosystem that this ark fosters in adjacency. Pastor Spence's story of the miracle corroborated something of what we had come to Frostburg hoping to find: confirmation of our theory of arks as systems that close in on themselves, often violently. Even in Pastor Spence's story, admission proves costly, demanding. The tale of the discarded X-ray and the once transient salesman yields many of the themes we expect any ark to hold: the binding of selection, enclosure, and safety; the abandonment of most objects, people, and histories to a devalued outside; ark stories as mostly about men interacting with men (Noah's wife and the spouses of his sons are never named in Genesis); movement become stasis; story become architecture; waste become wonderfully generative. But Pastor Spence's parable also proves more complicated. Its narrative arc enables the security system that faith provides to comprehend, and thereby enclose, the knowledge that techniques like X-rays furnish. It does not deny the unseen. The traveling salesman's back hurt. The traveling salesman needed a home. Like a car, or a metaphor, or an ark, a parable enacts a movement or a transport. Like a rainbow, a parabola (originally the Latin word for a parable) is a curved plane, the warping of forward trajectories by gravity's relentless, invisible pull. One arkive encloses another, comprehends it, attempts to discard its remnants (the film) but not the information or the impetus it provides. A parable or a parabola or a rainbow is not a punctuation mark, not a period, but a *pull,* perhaps even toward escape velocity.

This same momentum, we hope, is true of our project of thinking with the Ark of Safety, an actual encounter that widened our horizons even as we condensed it into a parable of our own. Every ark collects affect, wonder, possibility. Every ark is a shared space that traverses history, gathering stories along the way, curving toward a certain predictability, perhaps, but never quite hitting a foreordained mark, never quite realizing a future known in advance. An ecology of refuge can quietly flourish beside a space of severe and demanding closure. In a moment of complete candor, Pastor Spence declared that we have no idea what the inside of Noah's ark was like. The Genesis story yields no specifics: no arrangement, no scheme, only a reference to lower, middle, and upper levels. In Kentucky, Ken Ham's Ark Encounter materializes the biblical narrative through complex technologies of watering and feeding that automate the labor of caring for all those animals taken aboard, a fully enclosed ecosystem—but that is an engineer's totalizing dream, not a system in any way present in the Book of Genesis. The biblical narrative offers a bewilderingly general blueprint for the structure's dimensions and tripartite division, but no instructions at all for how to live within an ark once complete. To fill an ark's space, to compartmentalize its vastness and populate its chambers with an archive of entities, is to authorize a series of irreversible paths, bypasses, and roads without roadside attractions. A finished ark almost always proves to be a disappointment: a suffocating space, too delimited, devoid of escape hatches. Refuge too easily yields to gated community (the kind that complains about nearby unrealized arks as property devaluation). We do not know what life on the ark was like, but in November 2016, the Ark of Safety asserted that we can discover what life near an ark can be, at least after thinking with the structure for a while.

"Noah's Ark Being Rebuilt Here!" is not an allegory for anything else. Pastor Spence is a person like no other. He is not a character or a type. Yet, as we drove home, we talked about Pastor Spence as Noah, in the sense of the ordinary medieval townsman who might be asked to play the role when the cycle play of "Noah's Flood" was being performed for the community each year. Everyone knew it was really just their neighbor in a costume, that Noah was a tradesman and father and maybe even a ne'er-do-well, rather than a perfect model of obedience to God. The ark in the drama where this man played at being Noah was a prop, easy to take apart and store for the next performance, lacking in one sense of depth, but still saturated in another. That ark would be no less beautiful for all its deficiency. As we embark on our book and, like it or not, rebuild our own ark, does that mean that we too are Noah, asking questions about security and transiency and conviviality and parables as we speed away from Frostburg, returning to our respective home-base bubbles in a safe little car? Can we offer an ark more humane than many of those that have set sail over the centuries?

Pastor Spence, the Ark of Safety, and Frostburg offered a hopeful way in a grim time for this project of thinking like an ark to set forth. Yet we also realized in retrospect that some of our momentum was enabled by leaving to silence some essential questions, likely because the answers would have been uncomfortable. Ruins can have that effect on people. When we looked at the ark, incomplete, half-built, we did not necessarily see what the congregation that raised its girders saw. The romanticism of formal openness does not equate to welcome. Were we allegorizing or activating this ark's literal inability to close? Had we queried Pastor Spence on his congregation's attitudes around racial justice, unevenly distributed impacts of climate change, environmental racism, or LGBTQIA+ inclusion, our conversation would likely have become more immediately difficult. Had we asked him for whom he had voted in the recently concluded presidential election, we might not have had a congenial language to describe our interactions. These are not minor points, and the remainder of this book dwells on them because, to be honest, had Pastor Spence ever been able to finish the Ark of Safety, it may well have become a version of Ken Ham's Ark Encounter in Kentucky: a fascistic total structure undergirded by the exclusion of those groups to whom we feel a close affinity. There are better ways to build a vessel of conservation and perseverance, modes of community that memorialize and interrogate rather than leave urgencies to silence. Our ark (this book) set sail limned already with so many of the failures, exclusions, and unasked questions on which arks are too often predicated. But thinking like an ark has taught us that, even though we will always ultimately fail, sometimes foundering and incompletion are the enablers of possibility. So we sail on, scrupulous in our avoidance of landfall. *Maybe the worst thing you can ever believe is that you are no longer on an ark.*

Thinking like an ark demands that we inquire into the linkages, porting, or interpenetrations of differing discourses, rival rhetorics, or in Charis Thompson's words, ontological choreographies that make our worlds.[9] The Genesis story functions as something like a "collectively producing" frame that convokes readers and viewers who then rework, collect, and recut relations among different story elements. As Donna Haraway offers, this capacity for surprise and change "is important for rehabilitation (making livable again) . . . amid porous tissues and open edges of damaged but still ongoing living worlds, like planet earth and its denizens in current times being called Anthropocene."[10] We agree. And to that end, the differently timed and located stories of Noah and his ark or the ark and its Noahs, animal passengers (human and otherwise), materials, and organizations that we assemble in this book offer a set of conceptual and affective resources for thinking salvage and refuge at cost. You might say then that our fieldworking, from the mundane, ironic, to the upsetting and bizarre, entails attempting to hold open the structure of the said to its saying. "Make yourself an ark"—how much is conveyed by that command![11]

Arks across the Millennia (against Origin Stories)

A powerfully enduring version of Noah's ark was elaborated by sixteenth- and seventeenth-century thinkers like John Wilkins, who described a vessel in which the use of every inch of space and its precise relation to other spaces is meticulously mapped. A world unto itself, this totalizing ark is delineated through cold calculus and founded on its own self-sufficiency. Wilkins believed that so scrupulous a plan could have come only from God, for if a human had designed the ship, then far too much would have been stowed aboard. The ark would founder.[12] Wilkins's ark is a rebuke to human extravagance, perhaps even to human compassion, because it is just big enough to hold what it must harbor and sustain, and no more. It grounds a reduced sense of community and enables the coming into being of a harsh polity, an economy of bare survival rather than an ecology of refuge. And yet, in dreaming a divinely precise, inhuman and inhumane architecture, Wilkins and his kind narrate a tale that runs contrary to a proliferative and joyfully imprecise tradition in the long history of ark-making, a countercurrent that overwhelms neat origins and tidy diagrams. When the very source of architecture is traced to such a biblically singular ark, one has to forget the built environment that was Paradise (a walled garden), or the city that exiled Cain, founded and named for his beloved Enoch, as well as the Tower of Babel to come and the rival arks of Sodom and Gomorrah. One also has to forget that Wilkins is a human designing an ark, though now happily undertaking that task as if he were God.

Too bad, then, that, at its continuous launchings as a particular vessel or trope, the ark keeps proving itself prone to leaks. Too bad the divine directions to Noah for building the structure only seem mathematical, but in fact leave far too much open to the imagination. Got gopher wood? No. Try pine, cedar, concrete, fiberglass. Any room for unicorns? Who in their right mind would leave unicorns off an ark? Did the individual members of Noah's family have stories worth telling? Were there stowaways? The ark is even bigger than it seems, and the calculus of its construction is in human practice seldom so parsimonious. Or, perhaps, not "too bad" at all, but all to the good or "just as well." The very structure that the ark sets in motion, the carving out of one space from another, refuses to allow its inhabitants to forget their excluded brothers and sisters. The ark keeps changing. It thinks, and remains caught up in thinking itself. No two arks are quite the same. Every ark makes solid only *a* world, not *the* world.

A fleet rather than a singular lockbox, the ark endures not because it is an epitome that can be realized (it is not at all clear that Genesis wants to offer anything like an ideal), but because it gathers under its name a flotilla of heterogeneous refuges that have long been navigating world history. Even when an aspirationally self-enclosed ark is placed into motion, its fate remains uncertain. After a dream of flood, the carpenter Johan Huibers created two ark replicas in the Netherlands, one at full scale and one at half. Huibers based the seven-story ships on biblical descriptions and began to stock them with domestic animals, from llamas to ponies and rabbits. Although Johan's Ark opened to the public in 2012, the project did not go according to plan. When Aad Peters purchased one of the ships to function as a traveling museum, he was compelled to replace the live beasts with wooden figurines. Peters told the *New York Times* that the animals caused "too many problems."[13] The same ark made the news in 2016 when it was being towed from the harbor in Oslo and collided with a Norwegian Coast Guard patrol vessel, opening a hole in its hull. As we write, the ark is stuck in port in Ipswich because it has been declared unseaworthy by British officials. No matter how tightly sealed an ark seems, the world impinges. Unexpected parables unfold. Arks seldom offer secure foundation.

The biblical story of the ark is attuned so much more to the people and animals that inhabit its limits than to the exploits of heroes. Noah is just an engineer, builder, collector, catalyst. He's been contracted to enable the story—a story that might just as well do without him. The philosopher Michel Serres writes that the biblical flood narrative warns of the impact of human actions on the order and balance of a world on which we depend for our survival. The peace, doves, and olive branches of Genesis stress a deep and abiding relation between human actions and the fragile endurance of earthly life: "Far from talking about guilt and moral interdictions, these scenes seem to warn that a certain global end turns us into objects that are dependent on our free acts as subjects: the sea rises."[14] Human endeavor and ecological consequence are powerfully intertwined. Noah's ark conserves a fragment of what would otherwise be wholly lost, thereby becoming a model for action when the climate becomes inimical. Because the ark of preservation in Genesis so well names, locates, and inhabits a fertile peculiarity within ongoing disaster, writers across the centuries construct a flotilla of such vessels.

The scale of ark thinking toggles back and forth constantly between the tiny, local, and mundane (here we are, sealed inside or excluded from this shelter against disaster), one the one hand, and the dizzying, capacious, and unplumbable, on the other (behold the origins of family, race, nation, species, planet; behold the disaster or disaster to come). There are at once too many and too few actors, too great and too limited a store of stories, as well as an overarching movement toward a well-sealed archive that erases a shipload of querulous alternatives. Through reduction into limited origin, an ark attempts to define and control the unimaginable, to place limits on the threat or the possibilities offered by climate change's successive deluges: floods of water, fire, viruses, information, displaced animals, and humans. All too often, arks come to love the very limits they draw, transforming boundaries of exclusion into ends in themselves, vain dreams of self-sufficiency. The threat of perishing in some undelineated outside becomes the occasion for the building of an actual, catastrophically singular vessel that floats into a fascist unfuture: the triumph of severely delimited climate control over hospitality, hap and hazard. At its worst, thinking like an ark tends to project the threat of flood into the future as well as the past, such that cataclysm becomes a perpetual state and the condition on which the ark's own permanence comes to rest.[15]

Shorn of their admonitions and prescriptive retributions, mythic tales of inundation make clear the ecological relation in which creatures come into being. Flood stories encode scalar shifts which reveal the way beings who may have seemed strangers have been companions all along. Aliens become intimates. Scenes of the Flood foreground perspectival habits of mind, habits from which worlds are built: the contested logics of species, race, gender, commensality, hospitality, value, difference. They hold these categories open for inspection, compel their contemplation, offer them to thinking, even if the arc of this thought (from ark to patri-arky, from kinship to hierarchies of difference) compels decision, generates finite concepts, closes on answers that close out thought. Terminus as well as origin, Noah's architecture of preservation stands haunted by what is lost, left behind, or destroyed, and haunted also by the realization that any past relegated to the sea is carried within reenacted memory, archived forward as unwanted.[16]

Paradoxically, an ark's drawing down of limits announces the intimacy of all that live. Panicked exclusion (the line that is drawn *somewhere* to prevent engulfment) testifies (against itself) to the fact of overwhelming community. This gathered multitude presses against the limits on which an ark is predicated. As closed totality and finite architecture, an ark may seek to preserve this or that group through the violent exclusion of others, but that cost remains structurally present, an archiving of severed connection that haunts the vessel long after the ocean bears it away. Salvation, fixed boundaries, mountaintop, and rainbow are only one possible destiny for an ark. The truth of an ark's story derives not from landfall so much as from the setting into motion of a consideration and management of both scale and suffering, the way its building project choreographs the realization of a structure in response to unequally shared collective risk. An ark's apparent self-enclosure testifies to the co-relation of all that lives, and the costs that come with forgetting that knowledge, with consigning worldly entanglement to the force of the rising sea.

The stories in which we find scenes of the Flood tend toward landfall, as in the case of Noah and Ararat, or toward a sovereign homelessness or homesickness, as in the case of Utanapishtim and his wife in *The Epic of Gilgamesh,* who are gifted with immortality in compensation for their survival.[17] Dry land marks the moment at which a certain kind of insight is lost, when thinking community at scale terminates, when a reduced and anthropocentric sense of things is reestablished, along with a renewed set of zoomorphic goods, forms of life we name: plants, animals, persons. Completion of the story means covenant and celebration, a melancholy sense of loss spliced with giddy relief. The ark that was built becomes a foundation, an infrastructure, a ground for all that follows. In Sarah Blake's retelling of the flood story in *Naamah,* Noah and family use the wood of the grounded ark for their first homes on dry land, and that recycling of the timbers seems better than pretending you can keep the ship pristine on its mountain for future pilgrims to discover, as if the present were not cobbled from the past. The story recedes into a history that is at bottom "arkival," a story stowed away for reuse, but which is in fact ongoing.

Landfall enables finite beings such as ourselves to think, to create stories that conclude. The finitude of plot mimics the finitude of person. That these assorted finitudes offer no finality is why, regardless of ending, of landfall, so many stories keep being told, keep talking too much. Landfall promises a brave new world but delivers more of the same. Rejecting landfall means holding on to hope—which, as Teresa Shewry so beautifully argues, belongs at sea: "Hope involves apprehension of the future in terms of openness, or uncertainty."[18] Hope arrives "on the verge of obliteration" (9) as a "mode of engagement that turns us toward the creativity and struggles that exist in the world" (25).

Ark thinking is both more and less than a human response to

events or practices that multiply feedback loops, moments when our magnitudinous co-relations with the great variety of others might seem to be lost, forgotten, or diminished to an extent that threatens all. Serres describes scientists who preserve viruses that they have otherwise eradicated from human populations as creating something like "a peace treaty, at least an armistice, in sum a Natural Contract."[19] This refusal to eradicate marks the apparent heights of human achievement, but also produces a perspectival shift enabling Serres to identify an alternative version of history, one in which what counts as an ark becomes unmoored from human agency. "Dream a bit," Serres encourages: "In the past, did this virus itself let a few humans survive, our fathers and mothers, in order to keep in its possession a stock of food and information?" Scientists perhaps now archive viruses only because viruses used human bodies to archive themselves. We invoke this long-ago potential arking of human bodies by viral Noahs not in order to insist on some kinship among parasites, but to wrest ark thinking away from conservation and landfall into the endless flood of relations to which it attests. Beings other than humans think the ark even as what is called thinking may differ for them from thinking for us. Every ark talks too much and dreams a bit. Every ark worlds.[20]

If the ark stands as both origin and expression, both allegory and rhetoric, a biopolitical crux or blueprint whose actualization decides everything, then what's important to remember is the way the skeletal frame of the Genesis story, replete with strangeness and contradiction, solicits so many countering responses from readers and listeners. Calling our book *Noah's Arkive* emphasizes the way the story operates as a failed or self-ruining totality, a chest or vessel that leaks, a collection of stories that play with and resist the familiar contours of the Noachic narrative vehicle as it continues to be routinely invoked. The story of Noah and his ark is a history of the minimal narrative framework of Genesis proliferating differing perspectives: life and death inside the ark; life and death upon landfall; life and death for those not on the ark; or *Not Wanted on the Voyage,* as the title to Timothy Findley's 1984 novel reads.[21] Positions shift. Differing perspectives are imagined, inhabited, and scripted as the story is read, remediated. The urge to dwell with and imagine the flood, to open the ark to what it leaves behind, to the animals and persons it remainders, proves a compelling and recurring haunt for artists. The ark cannot offer salvation or even consolation to many; it may however offer possibility, an ecology of refuge, even at times to those on the wrong side of its closed door. The afterlife of the Genesis story, when tuned to the difficult questions the story archives as the ark inexorably sails toward landfall, testifies to the ark as a structure to think with and through.

It's hard not to dwell here on a medieval illustration of Noah's ark that serves as an emblem for our later chapters. It's an image of the devil escaping through the hole he has drilled at the vessel's bottom, but he is careful to plug the opening as he departs underwater (Plate 2). Though a prince of havoc, why would he want to lose the ark-bound humans to the sea, since they are his source of schemes, information, and plots? What becomes of the devil without the human capacity for erring? Parasitism mandates preservation, and cunning Satan is as parasitic as any virus. Then so is God, saving some remnant of a disappointing species. Give them a covenant, a rainbow. See what happens next. Or try what the artist of the *Rylands Beatus* attempts (Plate 3), an all encompassing ark that overwhelms with its color and variety and flip-top lid for easily letting fly the dove. Stored within are insistently visible if sometimes inscrutable stories: a pot that signifies kitchen space and the labor of feeding; a baptismal font that bends the future into the past; a dove and raven lacking their mates; a proliferation of assorted other birds intertwined in the loveliest choreographies; apocalyptic beasts (stored for what purpose?); shy demons hiding their genitals; winged humanoid monsters that raise questions about sentience and intent; fancy privies at the very bottom to answer the question of what happens to all the shit produced aboard. Each of the colored squares of this seven-level ark are filled with exuberance, intensity: the ark has to work hard to contain its contents. Outside the dead float in a naked dance, the raven feasts on eyes (even as the eyes of the those who look on this sumptuous image feast upon its radiant expansiveness), the dove has found refuge in an olive tree to which the ark now seems tethered. The ark is a haven during disaster, but seems with its monstrous contents to bode catastrophes to come.

Against origins (is there anything less original than an ark?), the ark becomes the figure of our comaking with certain plants and animals. It testifies to ecological connection and the ways in which differently scaled structures produce different worlds, make up different kinds of humans, botanicals, and beasts.[22] Landfall in this sense refers to the stabilization of scales and lives that ark thinking can set into motion, the momentary security that grounds a planetary kinship—but never for long. The Book of Genesis marks the dissolution of animal–human kinship as "covenant." Once the ark has been emptied, God gives the animals over to Noah and his descendants not to preserve (that moment has passed), but to hunt, eat, and sacrifice. This changed relationship is signaled by a new emotion, terror: "The fear of you and the dread of you shall be upon all the beasts of the earth, and upon all the birds of the sky—everything with which the earth is astir—and upon all the fish of the sea" (Gen. 9:2). To think that these beasts and birds and fish used to be the world in its entirety, used to be *compagnons de voyage*. An ark can welcome, invite, invent. And yet to imagine life during an age of climate catastrophe, we habitually rely on the Noah story in a severely constricted form, an architecture of fear and dread. Every new beginning comes as someone else's beginning's end.[23]

The differently timed and located stories of Noah and his ark we assemble in this book offer a set of conceptual and affective resources for thinking salvage and refuge at cost. This soaked, fragile inquiry into the limits of hospitality is what Genesis *wants*. We load our book therefore with stories of ark-making and ark thinking sensitive to the way each invocation activates the trope and allows it to turn, and so we imagine possibilities latent to the Genesis narrative.[24] Every ark is an invitation, an opportunity to begin again the question of structure and origin, of past, present, and future, even as that gesture of beginning comes premised on the drawing down of limits, the closing of a door, and the making of landfall. Materializing spaces of circumscription and confinement, sorting the various and the volatile into fixity, an ark may function as a museum, as a chancery, as a seed vault, as a biosphere, as a starcraft, as a zoo, library, as a factory farm, as a slave ship, as a concentration camp, as a database, as a repository. Every ark preserves at cost. To engineer such a structure is to perform a gesture of despair and desire at once: despondency for an Earth not to be saved, confidence after disaster abates a better home is to come. Yet that "better" conveys a narrowness, begging the question of better for whom. An ark is not launched in the expectation of a more survivable or commodious world for all who dwelled on its lands before and within catastrophe. Selective and small, its spaces are closed against a cosmic diversity of humans and nonhumans, conserving meager community against general ruin. Arks easily become prisons.

Yet entangled within the closing of alternatives every ark attempts, the trajectories it sails will veer unexpectedly, will offer the unbolting of unforeseen possibilities, mundane utopias, defiant refuge. The same ark that reduces boisterous lives to sortable, storable units and attempts to regulate the plots of the stories it conveys inevitably opens the imagination to other possible worlds.

Envoy

In the beginning God created the heavens and the earth, but this act of origination did not start from nothing. The world was formless, clothed in darkness, and full of water. The breath of God or divine wind *(ruah elohim)* swept across the surface of the deep. After inaugurating night and day through the declaration of light, God parted these waters into an above and below, a celestial vault full of rain and an ever-restless sea. God ordered the cosmos into regions and time into days. Dry land was drawn from general flood. The firmament blazed. Earth and ocean were populated with all manner of creatures, including the first humans, lords of a walled garden. The world was full of life and it was good. God rested, the deepest rest.[25]

In the beginning of the beginning again, God opened the windows of the vault of heaven and unleashed the fountains of the deep, drowning the still young world. The creatures fashioned in God's own image had filled its lands with strife; all was in upheaval. Things had admittedly gone badly from the start. For their trespass, Adam and Eve were banished from Eden's enclosed perfection. Their descendants had built cities, engendered tumult, proliferated wrongdoing. The world was full of peril, and it was not good. As separated waters rushed into union, the force of flood obliterated the life that God had with such care fashioned, creatures that Adam had named and overseen. Yet, in an ark carefully constructed at God's command, obedient Noah preserved a representative selection of kin and beasts against the arrival of weatherborne catastrophe. After long months at sea, this meticulously curated archive came to rest atop a mountain. A new covenant was sealed with a rainbow, the promise of never again. Peace, doves, and olive branches: a second genesis. The work of repopulating the devastated Earth commenced. And yet the descendants of Noah again spread wrongdoing across the emptied lands.

The sea rises.

CHAPTER 2

No More Rainbows

The story of Noah and his ark is premised on the tripled security of landfall, covenant, and rainbow. During the deluge, the entirety of the world becomes coterminous with the ark itself, which does not sail so much as float, buoyed up by the flood so that when the waters recede it can come to rest on the mountaintop to which it seems almost tethered. Any movement the ark manages tends to be automatic, predirected, remote controlled. Come landfall, the ark's passengers are all, understandably, a little excited, apprehensive, expectant. Time to leave. Time for the whole beginning again *really* to get started. Perhaps that's the problem that the rainbow signals. *Maybe the worst thing we can do is to believe that we are no longer on an ark.* Come landfall, we turn our backs on the whole ark problem, on thinking like an ark, and cash in on the good fortune or immune privilege of having been saved because it's "just the way things are."[1]

Real danger lurks in this structure of arrival and disembarkation, in the whole business of contracting the limits of what may live within a finite structure built with discarded help, and then believing that this diminished world coincides exactly with an Earth that is now wholly for us (whatever collective that first-person plural pronoun delimits). So much momentum moves "us" forward, off the boat and into emptied landscapes. The elated, exhausted, panicked relief at landing proves almost irresistible. Noah and family turn their backs on the refuge that so long preserved them and head inland. That is when the trouble begins, or simply continues. For, nothing has been cleansed. The world just has fewer people, less life to it, fueling fantasies of elbow room for ark-mates or neocolonists to settle into, restricted notions of community, identity, and belonging that pass as universal, sealed by a parabola in the sky.[2]

But, the story does not have to be told this way. In truth (and this is what we have to keep remembering), it never really has been. We begin this chapter, then, at the end of the arc of the ark with triple signs of terminus that prove to be the story's most enduring, inevitable, and insufficient activation.

Cue rainbow.

Paper Promises: *Not Wanted on the Voyage*

As Timothy Findley's 1984 novel *Not Wanted on the Voyage* comes to its close, the rain has stopped and the sea is calm but the ark has yet to make landfall. The vessel remains afloat, above the drowned Earth. Doctor Noah Noyes (as the novel names him) stands on deck "with the raven on his arm" and tells his family "all about the new Covenant between himself and Yahweh: the promise that there would never be another flood; the decree that all should go forth and multiply . . . and that everything that lived and breathed and moved had . . . been delivered into their hands—*forever.*"[3] He shows them "the symbol of the Covenant" (338), a rainbow that one of the ark-mates pronounces "awfully pretty." But no one is fooled. "As pretty as a paper whale," answers Lucy, née Lucifer, the unexpected partner of Noah's son Ham. She and the others see the rainbow for what it is: a flimsy prop and an empty promise manufactured by Noah. They have experienced firsthand the severe law that his covenant intends to ratify. Noah sends forth the raven, which does not return. Nor, for that matter, do a succession of doves. A "better trained" dove does eventually make it home "with an olive branch in its beak" (338), but Mrs. Noyes thinks that the branch looks very much like the one the bird had perched upon in its cage, clipping the wings of Noah's divinely ordained signage.

That night Mrs. Noyes sits on deck with her beloved and blind cat Mottyl, her most constant companion throughout the novel and an animal she deeply loves. She gazes at the moon. No mountain has as yet appeared on the still sea that the Earth has become. She thinks all "about Noah's paper rainbow," the price of covenant, the repurposed olive branch that promises no peace—objects that want to become icons and allegories but remain, for now, just props. "The voyage will never, never end," she thinks; "and if it does . . ." (338). Mrs. Noyes does not complete the thought. Or its silent completion proves so terrible that it must not be voiced, but countered with an act that recalls the relationships of care that she and her ark-mates have forged against the depredations of the voyage, and particularly against the tyranny of her husband Noah Noyes. Come landfall, that tyranny will be underwritten by a new law that merely intensifies the old.

So it is that, on the eve of anticipated disembarkment, against a night sky that hosts no rainbow that anyone can see, Mrs. Noyes lays her hand on the head of her beloved animal companion and pauses:

> Here was this cat, whose sight had been taken by Doctor Noyes, and down below them all was the world that had been destroyed by Doctor Noyes (with some help from his illustrious Friend) and all that remained of that world was what, to all intents and purposes, had been seen by this old blind cat and by herself—sitting long ago and rocking on their porch above the valley. And now, Noah wanted another world and more cats to blind. Well—damn him, no, she thought.
>
> "No!" she said.
>
> Mottyl heard her—and stirred.
>
> Mrs. Noyes said; "I didn't mean to wake you. I'm sorry. Sorry—but not sorry. Watch with me, Motty—you blind and me with eyes, beneath the moon. We're here dear. No matter what—we're here. And—damn it all—I guess we're here to stay."
>
> Mrs. Noyes scanned the sky.
>
> Not one cloud.
>
> She prayed. But not to the absent God. Never, never again to the absent God, but to the absent clouds, she prayed. And to the empty sky.
>
> She prayed for rain. (339)

The novel ends: no rainbow but a paper simulacrum, no denouement but a resonant prayer for endless flood. Readers are left to wonder whether this conclusion in which nothing is concluded offers despair or a different kind of hope. The last word spoken in the book is given to Mrs. Noyes, and it is a refusal that seeks new futures, a resounding rebuff to landfall, covenant, and rainbow: "No!"[4]

In this chapter we linger with the rejection that ends Findley's novel, with Mrs. Noyes and her blind cat's rebuff of disembarkation. With them we recognize that the voyage continues despite the rainbow, that the whole business of ark thinking and refuge-making is something to be inhabited and interrogated, beyond the apparent closure of dry mountains and divine contracts. No more rainbows: what happens when we resist the lure and the price of landfall, the arc of the ark? Rejecting a future built on severe and divisive promises enables lingering on survival together in a catastrophe-limned *now,* in a climate-changed world, within a community that welcomes difference and disunion, despite or because of the relentlessness of the weather. We wrote this book in a time of floods and fires, when many have had great need of rainbows. We wrote as so many walls were being built, walls that shore up the monochrome immune privilege of narrowed national, racial, religious, and sexual identities, through the terror of exclusion and forced separation.

So many arks, so many little Noahs.[5]

A Prism in the Sky (Weapons and Promises)

Now, don't get us wrong. Our "hearts leap up when [we] . . . behold / A rainbow in the sky,"[6] or for that matter, a rainbow flag. Who doesn't love rainbows? Even Noah Noyes's paper bow was, as ark-mate Emma announced, "awfully pretty." The rainbow marks the end of the Flood. "I have set My bow in the clouds, and it shall serve as a sign of the covenant between Me and the earth" (Genesis 9:13).[7] This polychromatic promise means no more world-purging disasters, no more global devastations, no more washing of life from the land. The radiant curve in the heavens assures human and animal futurity, an invitation to start over, a lasting world to fill. "This is the sign that I set for the covenant between Me and you, and every living creature with you, for ages to come" (9:12). Sealed with a shimmer, the covenant extends to all who have exited the storm-safe shelter built at God's command. Adam's antediluvian era has drowned. Noah's Earth 2.0 begins.

The rainbow punctuates and periodizes. It marks the end of a troublesome epoch and the beginning of what portends to be a golden age. The rainbow marks an event. "I now establish My covenant with you and your offspring to come, and every living thing that is with you—birds, cattle, and every living beast as well—all that have come out of the ark" (Genesis 9–10). The gate of the vessel is thrown wide. Those humans and animals that once had trod the land together now tread it again as if for the first time. Beyond the ark, beneath the rainbow become gateway, a vacant Earth awaits division, cultivation, repopulation. Noah's sons and their wives go forth and multiply, the origin of all peoples (the Table of Nations in chapter 10 of Genesis). The animals do likewise, as the sources of all species. The rainbow offers history's arc itself, the connection between present and ancestral identities, between what was and what has come to be. Termination and commencement, the rainbow layers the loose strands of the past together to produce the appearance of an origin, a foundation, a beginning for the beginning again. It instructs its viewers to think back and look forward at once, skipping over a present rendered strangely indeterminate and fleeting by the rainbow's special effects and intense gravity. This rainbow signifies as promise, reminder, and guarantee.[8] It is also an ostentatiously placed divine mnemonic device: "I will remember My covenant between Me and you and every living creature among all flesh, so that the waters shall never again become a flood to destroy all flesh" (9:15).

A rainbow means that the time of bad futures, of no certain future, is past. The rain that once inundated now mediates and refracts the light of a sun that has returned. The weather is clearing. Looking ahead, the rainbow announces the stability or equilibrium of a continuously optimistic weather report. Whatever the season, whatever the local conditions, such rain that comes will pass and no longer universally obliterate. The rainbow's radiance, a localized trick of perspective, light refracted by water droplets visible to the human optical apparatus, signifies now the inconvenience of a local shower. The rainbow announces the new normal, the human–divine pact that will become second nature. Time to get moving. Time to get on. "A rainbow," repeats Noah approvingly, responding to a romance writer's suggestion of how to end a filmed version of his ark story in Jeanette Winterson's satirical retelling of Genesis, *Boating for Beginners*. "We go walking off all fresh and hopeful and we look up and see a rainbow," he continues, "We can pretend we didn't have them before. No one's going to argue, are they?" In response, Noah's scriptwriter, Bunny Mix, asserts: "If they've swallowed it this far, they'll love the rainbow."[9]

The problem is that the story of the Flood does not actually end with the rainbow. (Nor, for that matter, are rainbows always taken to be unproblematically positive or happy occurrences). The Book of Genesis keeps on beginning, an anthology of origins and initiations, of false starts, restarts, and continual starting over. Indeed, if Genesis teaches us anything, it is that origins are perilous and that it is very hard to remain started, to be said to have properly begun. Just as you get moving, just as you feel that you're getting somewhere, everything you thought you had left behind comes back or turns out to have been with you all along. Ark thinking triggers one version of the mechanism that Genesis keeps setting into motion. Eden, Babel, the Akedah, the exodus, and Sinai offer others. Throwing forward a story—a structure, primed by a speculative glee that all too quickly closes—enforces an end. But not really, for the story has to begin again all too soon.

Arcs make for poor punctuation. The curve of the rainbow enacts the tightening of a celestial armament: *qeshet* in Hebrew, *arcus* in Latin, and "bow" in English name a martial instrument as well as an atmospheric phenomenon. A rainbow is a weapon made of weather. In Babylonian mythology, the sky god Marduk hangs a bow in the clouds to commemorate his victory in battle against the water goddess Tiamat, the triumph perhaps of an ethereal masculine order over chaos coded as watery and feminine, culture over nature, spirit over body, form over unruly matter, and all those tired binarisms that attempt division of a roiled world.[10] The God of Genesis, on the other hand, declares that his rainbow (that is, his longbow made of rain) is neither a sign of triumph nor a yoke beneath which those who remain must bow their heads, but a reminder to himself of a promise he is making to all living creatures: "When I bring clouds over the earth, and the bow appears in the clouds, I will remember My covenant. . . . When the bow is in the clouds, I will see it and remember" (Genesis 9:14–16). God hangs up his weapon, transforms the rain that kills at a distance into a mnemonic device rather than a salute to self. But the possibility of deluge does not disappear exactly. Instead, the rainbow suspends the flood, archives its potential in the sky, inaugurating an order of sovereignty premised on eternal covenant. Sun and rain. Storm and sun. The rainbow curtails or catches up an inundation that might begin again if God were not to remember the promise. The rainbow testifies still to the possibility that its appearance forestalls.[11]

Already built into this celestial Post-it note is a curving of time, a transformation of the deluge into a perpetually reappearing symbol that wards off wet global catastrophe even as it suggests its ominous history, its foundational status. The rainbow functions as a parabola or double-sided souvenir that localizes two mutually constitutive but opposite perspectives: an immanent divinity who promises not to let his weather-making go too far; and the gratitude of humans who bear witness to that forbearance. A peace or pact has been concluded. Humans no longer risk destruction for their rowdiness, annoying the Gods as they did in Babylonian myth with their noise. God learns a difficult lesson: wiping out all life does not cleanse survivors of their evil impulse, and so inscribes the rainbow in the heavens. This pact formalizes an arrangement and reappears periodically as a reminder. The rainbow marks an accord. It prescribes a set of relations between human and divine that also resets relations between humans, animals, and plants.[12]

As one watchful observer of the skies puts it, "the goal of the story (God-Noah-the flood-the rainbow-the promise) is to force the mind to pass as rapidly as possible from the aesthetic state to the state of memory (of the story of human sinfulness)."[13] The always preread or preencountered or "paper" rainbow from Genesis programs a relation between meteorological phenomena and perception, between world and wonder, between the efficacy and the affect of a new covenant. It tells you what time it is and that it is time to start moving. Best, in fact, to keep moving. Don't dwell in the mountain or the desert or the garden of the here-and-now. Don't look back. For, it's by your moving, by not attending too long or too closely to the rainbow as weather, but instead by taking it as a predetermined signal, that God's memory device and the histories it memorializes remain in place. Covenants must be continuously recalled to maintain their sovereignty. The rainbow tells you that, because you still breathe, the world is now for you. Time resets. You have weathered the cleansing. The rainbow disembarks an entire prefabricated hierarchy of man, animal, and land. It is your job now to keep moving.

But, come rainbow, come landfall, what follows is not all that different from what comes before. In Genesis, the world after the ark finds its mountain is just as disappointing as the epoch lost to the retreating waters. The Flood is unleashed after God's observation of human wickedness, a counterbalance to the goodness he had beheld just after creation stopped beginning: "The Lord saw how great was man's wickedness on earth, and how every plan devised by his mind was nothing but evil all the time" (Genesis 6:5). Following the ark's landfall, God acknowledges through strikingly similar language that this evil impulse survives hydrous punishment: "Never again will I doom the earth because of man, since the devisings of man's mind are evil from his youth, nor will I ever again destroy every living being as I have done" (Genesis 8:21). *Yetzer hara*—inclination to evil: although the world will not be drowned a second time, nothing really changes after the oceans recede. Just after the rainbow is set in the heavens, Genesis continues beginning and next offers a story of drunkenness, naked humiliation, and a curse that transforms family into property. Animals henceforth fear their ark-mates, since they are now given over to them to consume and sacrifice. Noah and his family have to be reminded that they should not consume human flesh. And Genesis is only just getting started (again). Mrs. Noyes was right. Same kinds of sacrifice, same kinds of violence, just differently distributed or institutionalized.

What then do we gain by questioning this rainbow-promise, along with the arcing narratives it sets in place? The point here is not to refuse the divine or even to propose instead a multiplicity of divinities (the clouds, the rain to which Mrs. Noyes prays), so much as to refuse the emphatic singularity of *this* rainbow, the one that culminates the universal flood and only *seems* to end the story. When blind cat Mottyl keeps watch with Mrs. Noyes, their prayer constitutes not a pantheistic consolation so much as a pluralizing act of attention that scans the skies for alternate futures that would not overwrite, and so erase, the fragile present they have worked so hard to make, or the world they have lost, which now lives only through them. If, as Michel Serres writes, "meteorology is the repressed content of history (of narrative)," then Mottyl and Mrs. Noyes call on us to look to the weather for alternative resources that might offer a more capacious and hospitable refuge than landfall.[14] What the two refuse is not the rarity of a fleeting, unreduced, unweaponized rainbow, but the paper version that Noah lifts above the ark: the archival or stunt rainbow that seeks to colonize and direct their attention, that counsels inattention, in the name of moving on and getting ahead.

In *Not Wanted on the Voyage,* Noah's paper rainbow holds more menace than promise. It is directed toward humans and animals, rather than (as in Genesis) the God who sent the Flood as a reminder not to do that again, no matter how disappointed or angry he becomes. The Yahweh of Findley's novel perished in despair just after arranging for the waters that would sweep clean the Earth. Mrs. Noyes refuses a world in which the price of being safe on dry land is too brutal: the perpetual subjugation of women, the reduction of animal life to mere utility, walled communities over widened shelter, the cruel instantiation of a law that inscribes its violent hierarchies on all flesh. And this refusal, however mad, however fragile, however at risk from detractors, anchors possibility and renders the prospect of alternatives concrete, even as in the moment, here and now, resources may seem scarce and the danger mounts. Let's resist moving on, then, and linger with the refuge Mrs. Noyes and her cat Mottyl offer a little longer.

There are precedents for a more hospitable rendering of the rainbow, prismatic instances that seek to conserve or to hold divergent worlds together, rendering the rainbow something like an archival refuge. Robert Young asks us to recall the work of the early-twentieth-century linguist Nikolai Trubetzkoy, who, among others, proposed the idea of the *Sprachbund* ("linguistic alliance" or "language union") as a model opposing the implicitly biological basis of the *Sprachfamilie* and *Stammbaumtheorie* ("family tree") approaches to language.[15] In his 1923 essay "The Tower of Babel and the Confusion of Tongues," Trubetzkoy explicitly tropes the rainbow by way of the story of the Tower of Babel, refusing to allow the story of Noah and his sons to provide the grounding origin myth for languages keyed to family, homeland, nation, and racial identity:

> All the languages of the world form an uninterrupted network whose links merge into one another—something like a rainbow. Because this rainbowlike network is continuous and transitions within it are gradual, the overall system of the languages of the world, for all its motley variety, constitutes a whole, obvious though it may be only to the scholar.[16]

For Trubetzkoy, the rainbow functions not as sign so much as the shimmer of an order of belonging that may be approached only as multiplicity. The rainbow's colors fade into one another, a totality that is not fascist. Its colors are properly speaking *one,* the spectrum that is light refracted through interaction with a particular human sensorium. Although Trubetzkoy would deploy this nongenealogical model in the service of a still deeply problematic pan-Slavic, Eurasian nationalist fantasy, a deterritorialized rainbow offers an alternative strategy of organization that could refuse to allow apparent differences to confuse or divide a kinship, parceling out a phenomenon into what only seem like separate or opposed entities. As Young points out, awareness of connectedness extends to dead languages as well as to those declared still to be living; this rainbow-like network therefore unfolds across our time-bound notions of the living and the dead, gathering them into community.[17] The perspectival rootedness of the rainbow—no two people see the same one—registers how a multiplicity requires the presence of differently located, time-bound perspectives that necessarily disagree. What matters are the tools of translation we deploy as we seek to communicate the vastness of our (dis)agreements.[18]

"No More Rainbows," the title of our chapter, is not a disavowal, but registers a desire to dwell with the rainbow as a multivalent sign that offers neither transcendence nor conclusion, a search for a plurality of possibilities. We aim to restore the affective, aesthetic dimension to the rainbow's parabolic shimmer as an invitation to interrogate our decisions, to recall everything that ark-making has unmade, futures left to drown that still may be. Only one story ends in the rainbow, but many others continue regardless, and those stories constitute refuges for ideas that may still be turning, for affects worth recalling. In this chapter we tune into the way Genesis keeps on beginning, keeps on raising the question of origin or the way origins always seem so unoriginal, riven as the ark story is by castoff characters from before the flood, caught in an eternity of always coming back just when they ought to have been forgotten. To refuse the rainbow is, with blind Mottyl and defiant Mrs. Noyes, to scan the skies for other conditions of being (rain, light, air, and, yes, other rainbows, always plural and always fleeting), as we collectively inquire into the refuge they may offer.

Under the Rainbow (Genesis against the Rainbow)

You would be hard put to find a contemporary retelling of the Noah story that does not culminate in the ark resting on a mountain, the doors opened wide, the animals gathered happily beneath that bow in the sky. "Every animal, every creeping thing, and every bird, everything that stirs on earth came out of the ark by families" (Genesis 8:19). Such unity. Such promise. The assurance of the rainbow is that no waters will flood so generally again. So why not be merry? After so much storm-tossing, life at last goes on. But not for some of the clean beasts, the creatures who were loaded in their sevens rather than as pairs. Noah makes a selection "of every clean bird and of every clean animal" and ignites an animal offering on an altar. God inhales the pleasing scent of sacrifice and notes to himself that, while humans may not have changed much after the deluge, he will never again destroy all life. Day and night, seedtime and harvest, heat and cold will endure as long as the Earth: the difficult in perpetual cohabitation with the agreeable. As in humans, where the evil urge remains alongside the impulse to do good, the world will continue to be fraught, vexed, turbulent, even though it has been cleansed. This rhythm or pulse that keeps the world in movement makes life a storm (light to dark to light, heat to cold to heat, seed to harvest to winter): the advent of catastrophe become perpetual, but never again universal.

The blessing that God bestows upon Noah and his sons recalls the command he gave to their predecessors, Adam and Eve: "Be fertile and increase, and fill the earth" (Genesis 9:1). Something changes profoundly at this moment, however, compared with life in walled Eden. The beasts released from the ark, "everything with which the earth is now astir," are given over to humans as food: "Every creature that lives shall be yours to eat" (9:3). Birds, fish, and land animals shall therefore now "fear and dread" their former companions since they are "given into [their] hands" (9:2, 4), although with limitations when it comes to their consumption (no flesh to be eaten until after the lifeblood has drained). God also warns humans that they must not kill each other, since they alone are fashioned in the divine image. Human life is sharply differentiated from animal life. Whereas Cain was banished for his crime of killing his brother and preserved through a mark upon his head, the penalty for murder now becomes death (9:5–6). God then articulates his covenant or pact *(berith)* with Noah, his sons, their offspring through the generations, and "every living thing that is with you—birds, cattle, and every beast as well, every creature that has exited the ark" (9:9–10). This pledge applies to all forms of life and promises that "never again shall all flesh be cut off by the waters of a flood, and never again shall there be a flood to destroy the earth" (9:11). Covenant unites and divides at once. God's words to humans at the moment of sacrifice split the world that had been communalized aboard the ark, rendering some animals fit bodies for sacrifice and consumption, transforming their relationship through the advent of creaturely fear. The animals know what the humans will do to them. They know that their lives are not protected against killing as human lives are, and they tremble at what that change shall mean. Yet God's pledge also unites that sundered world, at least to a degree: animals and humans will struggle together, but in confidence that they will also survive together—more or less.

In *Not Wanted on the Voyage,* Timothy Findley registers this differentiation of human from animal life as a moment of trauma and loss. Lucy brings the bees topside. They seem to enjoy these outings. Mrs. Noyes does the same with her choir of sheep so "they could see the sky and breathe the air and maybe sing a song" (332). She decides it's time for the youngest lamb to learn to sing, and they embark on "Lamb of God," but instantly she regrets the choice, for "'Lamb of God' had taken on such a dreadful meaning." Instead, they embark on a rendition of "I'll Take You Home Again, Kathleen," which Mrs. Noyes "address[es] to the lamb in her arms." The sheep know all the words, of course, but no sooner do they begin than they begin to "Baaaa" (333). Mrs. Noyes laughs at the "curious sound" and tries a different song that she thinks will suit their mood better, "The Skye Boat Song" (333). But no sooner than the "bonnie boat" begins to "speed . . . / Like a bird on the wing," she notices that the sheep are not singing with her. "Aren't you going to sing it with me?," she asks, but the sheep only "Baaa" in reply. "Please sing . . . . *Please,*" she implores. Mrs. Noyes kneels before Daisy, who knows her whole repertoire and helped teach the other sheep to sing. "Not a word" (334). The scene ends with Mrs. Noyes watching "all the sheep and lambs—huddling together—excluding her. . . . No more songs and no more singing. . . . *Only* baaa" (334). Communication and commonality turn to static and exclusion. Translation stutters to nonsense. The burgeoning of a new covenant enshrines a common belonging on this cleansed Earth but does so by installing orders of creaturely difference. Nothing remains the same.

The biblical story of the ark concludes with an assurance that the deluge, this first drowning of the Earth, will also be the last, and the punctuation for this promise is the rainbow: "I have set My bow in the clouds, and it shall serve as a sign of a the covenant between Me and the earth" (Genesis 9:13). That last phrase is worth lingering over: not between God and humankind, but an everlasting pact between God and "every living creature . . . for all ages to come" (9:12). Beneath that rainbow, mundane life becomes a protected totality, just as upon the ark. But did anyone really get to leave? Were they not all already comprehended, their being rewritten by their time on the ark? Should tempests again threaten their fury, their gush of rain will compel the bow, and "I will remember my covenant" (9:14). Weather becomes a machine for generating historical memory, and thereby for ensuring survival during storm. Catastrophe's advent is a reminder that community will be cherished. The rainbow-become-heavenly-symbol, the weather weapon transformed into a mnemonic device, threatens (it appears only in perturbation) and allays (all further cataclysm is to be local; all creatures will, as a bounded set at least, endure). Covenant apportions the world into storm-tossed and struggling parts but also provides the metalanguage for thinking of the Earth as the totality of all its creaturely inhabitants. To strive against each other and to survive together become inextricable.

Scale and point of view in the Genesis narrative now shift. The doubled perspective of the rainbow (God looking down; ark-mates looking up) yields to the brothers Shem, Ham, and Japheth as they stride from the ark and behold emptied lands beckoning repopulation. Possibility seems suddenly unlimited. Freed from the constraints of the vessel and bequeathed a world to make their own, they can be kings. Everything starts afresh. Time to corral some animals, plow the land, and maybe even plant a vineyard. It would be difficult, after all, to celebrate a cleansed world and the open-endedness that catastrophe's wake has bestowed without a little wine to toast new prospects. It's a shame, then, that the fruits of that vineyard, the fruits of this plant–animal alliance, precipitate strife, pitting father against son, brothers against brother. It is this immediate and inevitable miscuing of action, here the intoxicating efficacy of wine, that signals the way Genesis inscribes a push and pull that drives and wrecks the story, a curving or bowing that ensures that, whatever else happens, we always get ahead of ourselves, and that the story must therefore keep on beginning.

After the Rainbow: *A History of the World in 10½ Chapters*

Genesis never names any mountain "Ararat," but uses the designation for a chain that spreads across Urartu (Turkey, Armenia, Iran, Iraq). "The mountains of Ararat" (Genesis 8:4) are a range, not a singular peak. Yet, come landfall, the place where the ark came to rest and where the rainbow came to shine keeps getting reduced to a solitary point. In Julian Barnes's short story "The Mountain," Amanda

Fergusson, Miss Logan, and their guide are climbing "the" Mount Ararat because life at its base has proven disappointing. The long pilgrimage to the mountain's summit begins shortly after Colonel Fergusson dies in his Dublin home. In the wake of her father's passing, Amanda finds herself in a perpetual argument with the difficult memories that are his patrimony. Whereas the colonel resolutely believed that every phenomenon has a natural explanation, that the world is full of "happy accidents," animal pleasures, technological marvels, and natural strife, his daughter found in religious pamphlets by writers like "Parson Noah" and "Parson Abraham" a compelling argument for a stern author behind the world's unfolding, as well as a unifying historical narrative.[19] The colonel's vision of mundane life centered on shared creaturely existence and a messy drive toward creation (sexual and aesthetic), with humans only a more sophisticated version of the beetles that dwell as unsought companions in the walls of his home. Against this convivial, chaotic, and often perilous bustle, Miss Fergusson believes all nature to be designed for human use, serving a singular and heavenly plan, an ordered story of hierarchy and justice narrated in Genesis and unchanged since that foundation. Father and daughter argued over the biblical Flood: "He began to rebuke her for a belief in the reality of Noah's Ark, which he referred to sarcastically as the Myth of the Deluge" (148). She held that the vessel was still to be found on the slopes of Ararat, not far from "where Noah returned to his agricultural labors after the Flood" (149), and that the very vines planted by the patriarch must continue to thrive at the foot of the mountain. After her father dies, Miss Fergusson sets off from Ireland to seek the monastic vineyard, so sacred that tradition prohibits the fermentation of its fruit: "Heaven has forbidden it, in memory of the fault into which the grapes betrayed the Patriarch" (149). Miss Fergusson insists that some geographies bear lessons so profound that history stills around them into enduring and unaltered testimony.

High on the slope of Mount Ararat, Miss Amanda Fergusson beholds with "prim pleasure" (168) the effects of an earthquake on the Monastery of Saint James, a site of commemoration and worship established amid the vineyards that Noah planted at the start of modern time. The sudden tremor reduces to rubble the church, its nearby buildings, and the village community. When her traveling companion Miss Logan asks whether they should not return to assist the survivors,

Miss Fergusson declares that there will be none, since the inhabitants are being punished for the sin of "fermenting the fruit of Noah's vine" (163), some of which was scandalously offered to Miss Fergusson during her brief stay at the monastery. Ararat, the mountain upon which Noah's ark came to rest after the Flood, is so holy a place that any transgression, no matter how small, will be punished at great magnitude.

The problem for Miss Fergusson is that her convictions for how life beside the ark should have unfolded after the rainbow are challenged throughout her journey by history's ongoingness and the flourishing of alternative tales. Changing circumstances spur adaptation and accommodation. Biblical memoryscapes are a poor guide to lived, quotidian realities. The archimandrite of the Monastery of Saint James welcomes Miss Fergusson to his home with a horned vessel full of wine pressed from the very fruit planted by "our great ancestor and forefather, parent of us all, Noah" (159). This gracious act of welcome seems to her blasphemy. Amanda Fergusson traveled to Ararat in search of the fruit of the purest vine, not the work of human hands. She departs the archimandrite's cell immediately to ascend the nearby mountain, hoping to purge "the sin of this world" with pure water from snow collected at the peak. The Flood repeats on a personal scale. Life lived at the foot of Ararat—everyday existence in sight of the halo that each day forms around the mountain where that ark is supposed to reside—irritates Amanda Fergusson with its hybridity, flux, and change (that is, with its ceaselessness, its refusal to freeze like snow after an ancient denouement). A world that ought to preserve stories in sacred perpetuity instead reveals too much unspooling mess. The animals still require feeding and the fields tending. The monastic rooms need a good cleaning, commerce impinges on pilgrimage, cultures unattested in the Bible proliferate, and humans do not conform to script.

When an earthquake jolts the mountain and Miss Fergusson looks down to witness the destruction of the monastery, her relief at being able to fit sin and punishment into an overarching narrative of catastrophe-as-cleansing is palpable. Yet, when she first beholds the daily rainbow of vapor that forms around Ararat's crown, she admits to her traveling companion Miss Logan that this radiance signals dual possibilities simultaneously: that the summit is holy, and that climatological conditions cyclically create the shimmering halo through atmospheric warming and cooling. "There were two explanations of everything," she allows, and "each required the exercise of faith" (168). The diurnal rainbow is a sign of timeless history or the indifferent result of time-bound weather, depending upon which narrative is allowed to spur its glow.

"The Mountain" ends with Miss Logan returning to Dublin alone. Miss Fergusson's companion never reads the Bible, but she doesn't mind its being read aloud to her. She is a traveler who enjoys a nice glass of wine from time to time and would not have said no to the archimandrite's hospitable offer. Badly injured in a fall, Miss Fergusson meanwhile has chosen to remain in a cave atop Ararat, provisioned with her bottles of pure snow and a bag of lemons, one ingredient short of being able to make lemonade. On that slope Amanda Fergusson will continue to argue with her father's ghost about the ephemeral beauty of human art against the eternal allure of the moon, a future full of science and changeable technologies or a future full of worship for the history that has passed. Her wound may or may not have been the result of an attempt at suicide. She topples down an incline where the footing is secure. Faced with the two explanations of "whether Miss Fergusson might not have been the instrument of her own precipitation, in order to achieve or confirm whatever it was she wanted to achieve or confirm" (167–68), the homebound Miss Logan chooses not one denouement over the other, but simply to dwell with the problem for "years to come." Miss Logan is, in other words, an astute reader of the narrative of "The Mountain," a story that refuses landfall and will not inscribe unwavering truths beneath the promise of some halo or rainbow over Ararat. Colonel and Amanda Fergusson present two modes of occupying the same dwelling, an Irish house where a clock ticks out the hours until death while a deathwatch beetle makes bumping noises that signal a desire to mate: "tick, tick, tick. Tock" (143). The rhythm or pulse of the world: light to dark to light, heat to cold to heat, seed to harvest to winter. Sometimes, Miss Logan realizes, the tempestuous middle spaces between explications and their clean culminations offer the most enduring possibilities.

Nor does Miss Fergusson's narrative *really* end with her abandonment along the mountain's slope. In "Project Ararat," a later story in *A History of the World in 10½ Chapters,* an astronaut on the moon hears a voice commanding him to "find Noah's Ark" (254). Upon his return to Earth, he discovers that he has outgrown the everyday life that attempts to swallow him back into its small stories and determines that he will fund an expedition to Ararat and follow the lunar injunction that haunts him. After traveling to Turkey in the company of a geologist–scuba diver, he arrives at the mountain but can uncover no trace of the gopher wood vessel. At last he comes upon a skeleton at the mouth of a cave, laid out as if the person died with eyes raised to Earth's luminous satellite, the place where his own quest began. "We found Noah," he tells his friend, "Praise the Lord!" (273). Disappointment at not locating the ark yields to joy in having come upon the remains of its builder. Yet upon his return to the United States lab, analysis reveals that the pieces of bone he has smuggled from the site belong to a woman who died only 150 years earlier (277–78). We readers know it must be Miss Fergusson of the snow and the lemon bag and the prim smile, even if her tale is inaccessible to him. The astronaut-turned-ark-seeker is last glimpsed attempting to fund Project Ararat Part Two. Quests for origin never end, since the origin keeps on beginning, an accumulation not a point, a mountain range not a singular peak.

In the Rainbow Archive: *Boating for Beginners*

Jeanette Winterson's *Boating for Beginners* stages a similarly looped and looping version of the ark narrative that makes explicit the story's archival peculiarity, its propensity to circle round into wide open middle spaces. "Just as a point of interest," chimes in the narrator, in a midbook metacritical interlude: "The Bible is probably the most anti-linear text we possess, which is why it's such a joy." Prefaced with an excerpt from a report (real or apocryphal) in *The Guardian* from "28.8.84" that "bags of rocks and chunks of Ararat, Turkey, that Biblical archaeologists believe are relics of Noah's Ark have been taken to the US for laboratory analysis," this comic novel concludes by interspersing quotations from the biblical story with two archaeologists discovering the ark's remains on Mount Ararat. Gardener and Soames turn up "gopher wood that showed clear signs of ancient wet-rot" (158), as well as all manner of impossible and apparently time-traveling flotsam and jetsam, such as "the barrel of a one-armed bandit" (159) and a "message in a bottle . . . written on parchment" that reads, "Hey girls, I made it," and is signed, "Doris." The following day, "Gardener found what looked like an ancient bottle dump—in fact it looked like a French farmer's back yard." Gardener also finds "a book, clearly thousands of years old, bound in a tough animal skin" (160). As "he turn[s] . . . the brittle pages—only a few left and most of them badly discoloured," he has "the terrible feeling that his mind was gone; . . . what he was reading now, while in a recognisable combination of languages, was quite ridiculous. If he hadn't known better he would have said it was part of a romantic novel" (160). Gardener keeps the book and the parchment note and brings them out at parties. Privately, however, as he "grows older and more esteemed the question comes back and back. 'Where did it come from? Who wrote it? And Doris, who was she?'" "God knows" is Gardener's only answer. Though, as readers of the novel can agree, the answers prove stranger still, deepening the archival looping to the story.

Noah, it turns out, "was an ordinary man, bored and fat, running a thriving little pleasure boat company called Boating for Beginners" (12) that took tourists up and down the Tigris and Euphrates. There he had been, going about his daily routine, when "a huge hand poked out of the sky, holding a leaflet. Trembling, Noah took it. It was yellow with black letters and it said, 'I Am That I Am, Yahweh the Unpronounceable'"—or at least "that's what Noah reported at the press conference" (13). People were understandably surprised by the revelation of the existence of a divine being. Noah takes advantage of their surprise to explain he and God have been "collaborating on a manuscript that would be a kind of global history from the beginnings of time showing how the Lord had always been there and always would be there and what a good thing this was" (14). The book will be written in installments, starting with a chapter entitled "Genesis, or How I Did It." After the media launch, Noah leads a "Glory Crusade" *cum* book tour, and their follow-up installment, "Exodus, or Your Way Lies There," does very very well (15), so much so that Noah and God decide "to dramatise the first two books, bringing in Bunny Mix [the acclaimed romance writer] to add legitimate spice and romantic interest" (20). Cast of thousands. Real animals. The show is "to tour the heathen places of the world, like York and Wakefield, in a gigantic ship built especially." The whole thing is to be filmed. The flood-to-come is intended to be a special effect, but God gets other ideas: "Why don't we do it for real? I'm fed up of this world and its whingeing scrounging pop-art people" (90–91). After all, then they could rerelease the book and boost sales, because "no one will know because they'll all be dead" (91). "Oh, except you lot," adds the Lord, "I wouldn't drown my own family, would I?"

Blood, by which we mean whipped cream and cherry jam, proves thicker than water. For it turns out that Noah also has a touch of Dr. Frankenstein and Mary Shelley about him. Deep in his library, there is a manuscript that describes how Noah "succeeded in discovering the cause of generation and life." "Searching for nourishment," Noah pulls "a slab of Black Forest Gâteau and a scoop of ice cream" from his fridge, "not noticing . . . that both were in a state of nauseating decomposition." Noah drops his cake in the trash can. Lightning strikes. "Then, before [his] . . . eyes, a curious, intoxicating motion rocked the plate back and forth" as "new life forms struggle their way to the surface of what had been vile slime." Noah is sickened by the limitations of his created beings; he grows to despise his freezer—which accounts for his general hatred of frozen food—and chronicles the evolution of one life-form into a "thing . . . dressed all in white, with a long white beard" (82–84). Months pass, and the "thing" takes "to living in a cloud." But it is proud. And Noah worries about regaining control. He confesses that it is only little things, such as the entity not "know[ing] which knife to use for pâté," that give him any "hold." The manuscript trails off. And, come flood, the "thing" no longer needs Noah. By then, Noah feels washed out and wishes he could "run away with Bunny Mix and a crate of gin" (127). "Maybe they'd live, maybe not"; after all, he's "been the best father he could" to his sons and "more than a mother to that chocolate sundae in the sky." "Well," he thinks, "he'd show them. First dry land and he'd plant a vineyard and get roaring drunk and stay drunk for the rest of his life," which apparently, so the archaeological evidence suggests, he did.

Meanwhile an orange demon "not bound by the vagaries of the plot" is out for recruits to what will amount to a counternarrative to the cataclysm. "God *will* flood the world, Noah *will* float away," he tells Gloria, Desi, and Marlene, "and unless you lot do your best to stay alive there won't be anyone left to spread the word about what really happened." Though, as far as the orange demon is concerned, "it doesn't . . . matter if you forget what really happened; if you need to, invent something else. The vital thing is to have an alternative so that people realise that there's no such thing as a true story" (123–24). After all, "history and literature down the centuries are depending on you," he insists; "are you willing to let that baldie and his mad family rewrite the world without any interruptions?" Noah's eighteen-year-old daughter Gloria has already been at work, smuggling her elephant Trebor aboard the ark. Gloria, Desi (Shem's wife), and Marlene, their transsexual friend, rise to the occasion with the help of Doris, who has been hired by Noah as a dog's body to help with the "arrangements." Doris is "still upset about having to be an unbelieving crone in what she thinks is Noah's film." The four of them weather the flood in the attic of a nine-story hotel, eating croissants (their last) and drinking coffee. Then they put on their waterproofs.

Strange and wonderful Winterson's archival satire may be, primed as it is by the need for counternarratives. But, like Miss Fergusson in "The Mountain," her characters and the events that make them turn are really no stranger than those in the Genesis story itself, and this is part of Winterson's point. And apparently, so we learn, Doris survives, as does Noah, obviously. Of landfall and rainbow we hear nothing, and we see less. Like Gardener and Soames, we are left to sift through the archival remains. Genesis becomes the ultimate frame narrative.

Blue Sky Thinking

Things would be different, of course, if only Noah's biblical story had in fact ended with the rainbow. But that is not the case, even though most ark retellings are mute about what happens next. Even Barnes's "The Mountain" is built around a post-deluge episode that his narrative cites only obliquely, embarrassedly: "The fault into which the grapes betrayed the Patriarch," as Miss Fergusson delicately states, only immediately to decrypt her euphemism on account of Miss Logan's obtuseness—"Drunkenness . . . Noah's drunkenness" (*A History of the World in 10½ Chapters,* 149). Noah's wine-induced intemperance has through the millennia discomfited biblical interpreters, especially because Genesis is so sparse in its account of the episode, and because the consequences of the binge will prove enduring, even if Winterson's version of the tale encourages us to read his lapse as the tired opting out of a parent who has had too much. The point, as Winterson understands only too well, is the antilinear or riven nature of this narrative, the way (appearances to the contrary) the strangenesses begin to begin again.

Back to Genesis. Just after the rainbow shimmers and the covenant is made clear, the sons of Noah exit the ark to start the work of founding new peoples. Of Ham, Shem, and Japheth we are told: "These three were the sons of Noah, and from these the whole world branched out" (Genesis 9:19). Their father meanwhile becomes the first vintner. Inebriated from the wine he has fermented, he blacks out, naked body prone on the tent floor: "Noah, the tiller of the soil, was the first to plant a vineyard. He drank of the wine and became drunk, and he uncovered himself within his tent" (9:20–21). Could the ark's captain be more reduced? Perhaps Noah did not realize (as some biblical commentators have argued) how fertile the ground would have been after the waters receded, imbuing his wine with a strength that overpowered him unawares. This potency might also help explain what seems to be a narrative fast-forward after departing the ark. "He planted it, drank thereof, and was humiliated all on one and the same day," suggests Rabbi Hiyya ben Ba in the midrash Genesis Rabbah (36.4), an extensive compilation of rabbinical interpretations of the first book of Torah, composed circa 300–500 CE. Or perhaps Noah's "immoderate" drinking is related to his having committed the grave error of planting grapes first rather than figs or olives, a poor choice given that he had likely stored all kinds of shoots upon the ark (36.3).[20] Maybe he is demonstrating an invidious relation between himself as "tiller of the soil" and those other husbandmen who went wrong, Cain and Uzziah, or even partnering in his wine-making enterprise with a demon who likewise enjoys a good tipple (36.3). Rabbi Eliezer suggests an even darker story behind the episode: Noah is here betraying the fact that, when he was departing the ark, one of the lions mutilated his genitals. In his drunkenness, he seeks his wife's tent, forgetting that such union is no longer allowed him, and "his semen was scattered and he was humiliated" (36.4). Worse and worse. Maybe Noah is simply demonstrating that, if they live long enough, mythic figures have a tendency to reduce themselves to mere mortals, their lives as messy and embarrassing as anyone's. The exemplar of obedience to God becomes, once the catastrophe recedes into history and the normal rhythms of life resume, a moral against "a passion for wine" (36.4). Noah's drunken nudity offers an episode not easily stowed aboard future arks. Most retellings of the Flood end at the rainbow because what follows is too uncomfortably human, an immediate signal that life after the deluge continues pretty much as it did before the world was cleansed.

The Genesis story continues to commence. Ham, "the father of Canaan," beholds his father's abasement in the tent and informs his brothers. Shem and Japheth walk backward with a cloth held against their backs and cover Noah's exposed body. They keep their gaze turned away from their father, we might guess, because they do not wish to shame him further by beholding his degradation. When Noah wakes "from his wine," he curses Ham for what he "had done to him": "Cursed be Canaan; / The lowest of slaves / Shall he be to his brothers" (Genesis 9:25). Noah then blesses Japheth and Shem, wishing them prosperity and handing over Ham's future descendants, the people of Canaan, as human goods. Noah, we are told by way of goodbye, lives for 350 more years after the rainbow, expiring at the ripe old age of 950. The reduction into property that he inflicts on Ham's lineage will last far longer, becoming in time one of the many justifications used to enslave peoples stolen from Africa and render them chattel.

Noah "uncovered" himself in a drunken stupor, and after Ham "saw his father's nakedness," he narrated that fact to his brothers. But what precisely is the crime here? The exact nature of Ham's transgression is unclear, inviting all kinds of stories to explain motivation and consequence. Rabbinic interpretations have ranged from the possibility of Ham having committed incest with his mother ("to uncover the nakedness of a man" may indicate having intercourse with that man's wife [Leviticus 20:11]); raping his father (20:17 suggests this possible interpretation); castration of his father so that he will prevent Noah from ever engendering a fourth son; a violation of the injunction to honor one's parents by turning his father's nudity into a display for an audience; or making a joke that is not funny, laughing at his father's humiliation, and expecting his brothers to join him in ridicule. Yet, no matter Ham's motive, the outcome of his father's curse is just as enduring. As early as Genesis Rabbah the Noachic malediction darkens Ham's skin at its utterance and associates the people of Canaan with animal inferiority and a natural aptness for servitude. Some of Genesis's beginnings possess lethal historical consequences.

Ark thinking keeps on producing forms, bodies, identities, narratives. The story divides only to reconnect or splice together what it had appeared to separate. The ark functions as a biopolitical machine that programs the relations between animals, human and otherwise.

It also eventuates the human to derive justification for the treatment of certain groups as less than kin. Genesis Rabbah smuggles aboard the ark a story that will recur: pondering how many illicit romances unfolded within the ark's close quarters and whether such amorous relations crossed the species line. If Ham's crime was to castrate his father, he was possibly motivated by having been caught by Noah while he indulged in sex with an animal aboard the ark: "R. Hiyya said: Ham and the dog copulated in the Ark, therefore Ham came forth black-skinned while the dog publicly exposes its copulation" (Genesis Rabbah 36.7). Genesis never asserts that each son took a wife aboard the ark, so the exact number of women on the vessel remains an open question, leading to speculation that Ham had no partner and was tempted by the beasts. Mira Beth Wasserman describes such tales as "the unmentioned but ever-present threat of bestiality that lurks in Genesis' account of species jostled together in the ark's tight quarters" and a fear that the "ark experiment to reorder humanity" goes wrong.[21] That Ham's sin may have been sexual in nature also curves the ending of the Noah narrative back toward its beginning. Rabbinic tradition wondered whether the crimes that brought the Flood were not likewise sexual, so that perhaps men "spilled their semen upon the trees and stones," being so "steeped in lust" (Genesis Rabbah 26.4). This speculation about sexual misconduct is intimately connected to a strange episode just before Noah's ark-building, when the mysterious "sons of God" *(bene Elohim)* mate with the "daughters of men," a mingling across kind that seems related to the appearance both of widespread sexual immorality ("males and beasts" also become objects of male human ardor, and "the generation of the Flood were not blotted out from the world until they composed nuptial songs in honour of pederasty and bestiality" [Genesis Rabbah 26.4]), as well as the sudden flourishing of giants ("It was then, and later too, that the Nephilim appeared on the earth—when the divine beings cohabited with the daughters of men who bore them offspring" [Genesis 6:4]). Just after the giants appear, God notes the wickedness of men, regrets his act of creation, and sorrows in his heart, and down rain the waters.[22]

Among Ham's offspring is Cush, who fathers Nimrod, held by medieval Christian interpreters to be the architect of the Tower of Babel. All kinds of confusions keep coming, all kinds of origins: from an ark-bound moment of unity, to animal and human struggle, to heterogeneous peoples, to a babble of varied languages. Nimrod will in a later age often be thought to be a giant, but that identity is not ascribed to him in Genesis. He is simply a "mighty hunter" and "the first man of might on earth" (Genesis 10:8–9), a figure who builds scattered polities into a unified empire with himself as sovereign. Whether Nimrod was a giant or not, however, the survival of the giants after the Flood has consistently perplexed interpreters of Genesis—especially if God sent the waters that drown the Earth at least partially in response to the appearance of the creatures known as the Nephilim: "It was then, and later too, that the Nephilim appeared on earth—when the divine beings cohabited with the daughters of men, who bore them offspring. They were the heroes of old, the men of renown" (6:4). The story glimpsed here is so obscure in its narration that it proved an endless spur to the imagination. Do the sons of God and daughters of men refer to some primal miscegenation between angels and humans, engendering a race of preternatural giants (either as punishment or simply as fact)? How intimately is the sudden appearance of these boundary-crossing giants related to the proliferation of earthly sin that provokes God to send the Flood just after their appearance? The very next lines, after all, narrate the deity beholding "how great was man's wickedness on earth." Since the giants were unlikely to have been invited to board the ark, given their potential wickedness and extraordinary dimensions, how did these beings survive a cataclysm said to have cleansed the world of all living things? Giants are fairly common in the Bible after the waters recede: the rainbow that was supposed to end the Flood cannot keep the untidy beginnings of that story from beginning again. In Hebrew, these beings are variously named the Nephilim, Emim, Refaim, Gibborim, Zamzumim, and Anakim. In the form of Goliath menacing David or the soon-to-be-dispossessed Canaanites intimidating the spies sent into the Promised Land after the flight from Egypt, the giants seem oblivious to the punctuation mark that the bow in the sky offers. Giants thrive before the Flood, and they threaten thereafter. Like Genesis, they keep commencing, keep producing new plotlines. Their endurance dwarfs the rainbow, making it a nonending, an in-conclusion, a radiant reminder that cataclysm neither begins nor concludes with the ark.

"No more rainbows": the phrase is for us an imperative, an interrogative, and an invitation to the subjunctive all at once.[23] What we really mean is that there exists a rainbow of severe covenant, a weapon made of weather that entails animal sacrifice and human slavery as the price of landfall and closure; and there exist rainbows that offer other archives, parabolic rainbows that pull stories beyond the tidiness of conclusion. The end point to a story about sin and punishment, the longbow that dangles in the clouds, opens the question of whether you can have community without covenant: a question of exclusion, of identities stabilized on bodies rendered expendable. Such is the rainbow of Ararat, of that singular peak where Noah's ark never actually touched ground. (The boat nestled within a range, not at some knowable summit: what a desire for resounding terminus imagined Ararat embodies!) The armament-rainbow marks landfall as a moment of danger and inattention, a moment of decision in which the mutable alliances or mundane utopias of catastrophe on the move are reduced to an identity bound to the land that then enables an endless series of future identities, both self-sameness and inferiorities.

Yet the rainbow is easy to pirate. As if an arc could become a period! The shimmering bow offers a prism of alternative plotlines. In the form of a flag, a rainbow urges unity and asserts defiant pride. The Greenpeace ship *Rainbow Warrior* remobilizes the symbol, puts its force into motion again, returning the rainbow to the sea as an ecological event (even if the story of rainbow warriors it appropriates is itself an archival imposture, the imagery of 1960s evangelists wrongly attributed to indigenous peoples).[24] Rainbows always deploy the structure of an alibi, even when they hope to do good.[25] They bridge heaven and Earth, metaphor materialized, vibrant parabolas, conveyance devices for unsought messengers: Iris, or angels, or anyone else who arrives to bring strange tidings, disruptive news, and alternative plots. So why do we so often repeat attenuated versions of the tale in which this rainbow gleams?

Toy Arks

Despite the insistence of biblical literalists, Genesis invites invention, not recovery, and rainbows never end anything. Arks create as much as they preserve and have a way of sailing off their expected course. Not every ark will require gopher wood. Or rain. We started this book by dismissing the Noah's ark of a children's story for its attenuation of the narrative, but we also want to emphasize that, despite the smallness of the narrative they are usually given, children know this proactive, even predatory, iterability well. For them, covenant and rainbow are not the ship's destiny so much as a gleeful provocation to start over from the beginning, to back up, rewind time, restage the Flood, every reiteration a little different, each time with new stories stowed aboard. A rainbow might seem terminal, a happy moment of conclusion for animals and people alike, the sign that all are saved, but it is also a curving in the sky, an invitation to loop, a machine for the generation of repetition and difference. Children are not fooled by rainbows, or better yet, in their paws, the dual perspective, divine and human, becomes just one more reconfigurable component among others in the muddle of a story whose middle is far more engaging than its supposed beginning or end.[26]

Take, for example, childhood toys like the Playmobil My Take Along 1.2.3 Noah's Ark, which floats well in any bathtub (Figure 5). A convenient handle and interior storage for its twelve pieces invite you to transport the boat anywhere, but you do have to be vigilant with the enclosed animals because (as verified purchasers warn) the figures are not watertight and might prove susceptible to mold. With its bright red planks and orange deck, its smoothly rounded contours, and its dazzling green ramp for loading the animal couples (elephants, zebras, giraffes, lions, and white birds that must be doves), the My Take Along 1.2.3 Noah's Ark is designed to appeal to young children. Yet numerous online reviews make clear that everyone loves this vibrant toy, from children "too old" for the plastic vessel to grandparents who gift the thing to their families and find themselves absorbed into the dramas that the ship unfolds.[27] When presented with such cheery transport, who does not want to "Hurry to help the animals aboard," as the promotional copy exhorts?

There's nothing authentic about the Playmobil ark or toy arks in general. There aren't enough animals. The proportions are all wrong. Noah's sons and daughters-in-law are missing. At most only two of the beasts are clean, and the set contains a pair, not seven. Noah, the lion, the lioness, and Mrs. Noah are the only gendered figures (the other animals arrive in identical pairs). No ravens are provided to counterbalance the blue beaked doves. Yet the toy *works.* It elicits curiosity, intensifies creativity, yields pleasure. Even if children are meant to stow the animals aboard against a flood of bathwater and soap bubbles, the script they follow engenders no anxiety. It is not supposed to make them wonder whether their own world might come

FIGURE 5. The muddle, mess, and possibility of toy arks. Noah's Ark toy. Mouse in the House / Alamy Stock Photo.

to a similar and sudden end. The congenial human guardians for the vessel resemble a rustic couple more than anything stern, biblical, or patriarchal. Instead, catastrophe migrates into the routines of a childhood day with this take-along vessel that means never having to leave your toys behind, or better yet, makes tidying them up into the game itself—a never-ending series of embarkings and disembarkings. No trauma of separation: this ark always goes with you. It does not really admit the possibility of an outside. Nothing extra is included to drown. There are no add-on or supplemental packs of dinosaurs, unicorns, or submerged cityscapes to invite ark-players to unfold an exterior. The little plastic boat remains a refuge, a portable and secure little world unto itself. No rainbow is provided because that promise of safety and care is implicit in every bright plastic component of the toy. Colorful toy arks like the My Take Along 1.2.3 Noah's Ark *are* the rainbow.

The pleasures this play ark affords do not necessarily derive from trauma avoided or trauma repeated and mastered through repetition.[28] Its story does not necessarily ever have to end. Despite the scripts prestored aboard, nothing prevents someone playing with the ark from imagining that its two doves are female, or that the lion and the zebra are a couple, or that Noah and his wife may not have the best interests of the animals at heart. Perhaps their wide grins hide a menace. And what child can resist pulling the vessel to the bottom of the bath and seeing who floats out and which creatures drown in the deep? After all, how often is it that you get to play God or get to become the weather, even as those phrases may now be rendered ironic by the emerging realities of anthropogenic climate change?

Deluge narratives are among our oldest recorded stories, the start of the written record. Noah's ark is ancient and still venerated, a tale we have been retelling in varied media across millennia. And while Genesis's rainbow might localize perspectives and decide the scale of human encounters with the world, the weather, and the divine, the Playmobil My Take Along 1.2.3 Noah's Ark makes clear that it is only too easy to inhabit the story of Noah and his boat as a thing to think with, and so play with. It is not clear how much of the Genesis narrative a child playing with this ark apprehends from what is contained in the vessel. Certainly not biblical details like the wholesale submergence of the sinful world or that business about giants wandering the land in those days. Yet this toy enacts what the Genesis story itself enacts: an invitation to serious play, limned by climate change and horrific loss but opening spaces for imaginative supplement, wild invention, temporary shelters, fugitive creation stories that might unfold against ecological destruction.

Playmobil makes more than one version of Noah's ark. The deluxe and expansive Animal Ark Playset includes a menagerie of exotic creatures: monkeys, parrots, ostriches, and butterflies, but this time no ravens or doves. The bearded Noah is dressed in a way that loosely signifies "biblical," and his wife comes with a plastic frying pan to gender her labor. The ark itself provides upstairs sleeping quarters for the two humans and their favored pets while offering plenty of room for the other animals. For the arrival of the bath-time flood, customers are encouraged to purchase the optional Playmobil Underwater Motor, which uses a single battery to propel the ark across rough and soapy currents. The world that this ark comprehends is a little less vibrant or perhaps asserts its own plastic realism (the ark is wooden brown rather than fire truck red) and a little more complicated (there are numerous items to be stowed aboard the vessel before it can sail, so that the plot that this boat unfolds involves thinking earnestly about the care of the voyaging animals). Numerous provisions are included, from water jugs to hay, as well as the mechanical equipment for loading. The promotional copy is explicit that it's time to "prepare for the great flood and board the animals two-by-two onto the Animal Ark." Embarkment is the drama that this richer play set, aimed at ages 4–10, wants us to linger over, even if the price of such discursive enrichment incurs the warning "CHOKING HAZARD—Small parts. Not for children under 3 yrs."

According to its Amazon page, the Playmobil Nativity Stable with Manger Playset is frequently purchased with this toy, which is not surprising, perhaps, since some parents may want to complete the arc from their Old Testament to the New, with the ancient Flood prefiguring (as Saint Augustine himself explained) the arrival of baptism, the cleansing water that instigates Christian modernity. Yet, according to Amazon, the Playmobil Jungle Animals with Researcher and Off-Road Vehicle is also often purchased to round out the gift. That supplement opens a weirder kind of covenant. For, while they appeal to closure or the idea of a bounded, comforting world (a thoroughly narrativized and so, in its way, completed system), the stories that these toy arks script also provoke—maybe even demand—additions and experiments.

One of us has a child who, when she was young, enjoyed loading her Noah's ark animals into a plastic camper van in search of Playmobil pirates. She was a responsive reader of Genesis, even if she did not realize that fact at the time. One of us has a child who proliferated his wooden Noah's ark with all manner of building-block or paper jetties that he quickly peopled with all the animal figures he had, clean and unclean. The loading of this ark became a continuous embarkation-disembarkation, inside and outside collapsing into a floating land bridge or environment in which animal figures went mobile. The Noah figure (he had no wife) quickly went missing. But this man-overboard urgency didn't signify. The animals were just too busy.

Arks are amenable to allegory, but in the end they often remain mundane. The play to which they invite is not the play of reenactment so much as a proactive, forward-looking mode of mimesis that limns the possibilities of story. Fragmenting the story of the ark, they enable the production of new worlds, imagining alternate futures. The ark as play, as invitational thought system, constitutes itself a kind of refuge, an investment in refuge building and refuge maintenance, rooted in the here and now of its performance. And such rainbows that arrive will be of this engagement's own making: worlds of promise premised on shifts in perspective and a scaling of sympathy. Every ark conveys narratives of sudden ecological change, catastrophe, endurance, hope, and possibility. Every ark serves as origin and end and origin again. Every ark encloses violence and danger, the best and worst intentions, the possibilities of a world configured otherwise, genesis without finale, dwelling without denouement. Every ark is an invitation, the inevitable welcoming of a world far larger than its manifest unfolds.

Of course, it's not all plain sailing. These plastic toy arks, congealed from petroleum derivatives, have been rendered ubiquitous by an industrialized production and transportation chain named in the hope of equaling the Amazon River in terms of its commercial reach. They might be entered as Exhibit A of our continued inability to confront what Brett Bloom describes as our "petro-subjectivity."[29] That said, what better evidence is there of the doubleness to the structure that arks unspool? All arks exist as records of both possibility and exclusion, of violences both slow and fast, and against those violences the conservation of refuge. The Playmobil My Take Along 1.2.3 Noah's Ark offers no answer to Mrs. Noyes and Mottyl's prayer, Miss Logan's capacity for doubleness, or the orange demon's injunction to tell other stories, but adds another invitation to ark thinking that allows the trope to keep turning. To pray for rain is to pray for story, for open narratives and capacious refuges that may accommodate a more expansive sense of "us."

More than anything, it is the word "refuge" that beckons.

Jeannette Winterson's Ark of Collage

Thank goodness for ark thinkers who throw us a rope to pull us back from rainbow terminations. Jeannette Winterson's semiautobiographical *Oranges Are Not the Only Fruit* is not exactly a Noah story, even if it starts with a chapter called "Genesis." But the novel includes an episode with an ark that invites spirited engagement rather than barred entry. After all, Winterson's novel is all about embracing invitation and hospitality where they present themselves, even seeded into an unforgiving landscape. Seeking shelter from the domineering love and constricting religious faith of her mother, the novel's narrator (named, like the author, Jeanette) finds a place of shelter with Eslie Norris, a fellow member of her Pentecostal church. Eslie keeps "interesting things in her house," including a collage of Noah's ark. She allows the young Jeanette to play with the artwork, enabling the girl to escape the severity of her fundamentalist Christian upbringing by inhabiting the biblical story as a zone of creativity, repetition with difference, and play. The collage

> showed the two parent Noah's leaning out looking at the flood, while the other Noah's tried to catch one of the rabbits. But for me, the delight was a detachable chimpanzee, made out of a Brillo pad; at the end of my visit she let me play with it for five minutes. I had all kinds of variations, but usually I drowned it.[30]

Chimpanzee overboard. The Brillo monkey extends an irresistible invitation to stow new stories aboard, and to have narratives snugly placed in the hold leap to unexpected life.

The promise of ark thinking lies always in the structure's inevitable status as collage, as archive and collation of the various: detachable chimpanzees, lost rabbits, multiple Noahs who lean out to look at what the flood has obscured. The iterative, wobbling, and bricolage-propelled movement of what only seems to be a static story ensures that the ark remains in motion. Every ark is a recommencement. The action remains ongoing.

All the dramatis personae of the Noah narrative, once you pause to imagine them, have stories. Over time the heterogeneous elements of the ark narrative prove to be moveable, reconfigurable components of a total ark scene that never stays anchored in place. Ark thinking is, in this sense, a kind of endless play, sometimes idle, sometimes earnest, always high stakes. The script varies because ark thinking is an invitation to experiment, to unmoor the familiar, to dream a little. Through imagination and addition, through setting the story's fractal possibilities into motion, the contours of a more humane assemblage might come into view.[31]

Universal flood stories—cosmically local, large, and small, at once—open the ark to thinking-as-play. A multitude of tales are therefore to be found aboard, so many, in fact, that this book will be in constant danger of overburdening, of not ever reaching the safety of the shore, even as landfall's security may be overrated. An ark is a machine for the generation of too much plot, too much possibility, too many unabandoned stories, a flotilla of failed totalities. It is only by attending to the stowed-away narratives, the retellings and repurposings, abandonments and turnabouts, that the ark invites rather than refuses. This inbuilt surfeit is why arks are so full of endings and beginnings.

The sea rises. Arks gather.

Frame and Fracture: Natalie Diaz's Animal Flood

Making a life raft of an ark is no easy labor, but love of this world is no easy commitment. It can be done provided you are willing to stand with those on the wrong side of the gate when the ark sets sail, and risk getting wet or even drowned. "Today my brother brought over a piece of the ark / wrapped in a white plastic grocery bag," begins "It Was the Animals," Natalie Diaz's poem of shattered realms, lacerated knowing, and difficult care for kin.[32] The speaker's brother enters the home to share a "foot-long fracture of wood" (4). He claims he has a piece of Noah's true ship, the only ark; "what other ark is there?" He declares that its text reveals "what's going to happen at the end," the end at which there is no beginning again, when all stories conclude. With fingers "silkened from pipe blisters," he places the rough wood with surprising gentleness on the table. The brother handles the object as if it might explode ("the way people on television / set things when they're afraid those things might blow-up / or go-off"), as if its secrets once unleashed will stream catastrophe. Upon the intimate table, beside an empty coffee cup, he lays the shattered remnant of a picture frame. "It was no ark," the narrator observes, the piece of wood engraved with floral flourishes, not the secret of the last calamity's unspooling.

And yet, to the brother, the frame is a devastating archive of hidden knowledge, cold-hearted storage, and exclusion that sails the ages. His head sinks into his hands. Just his voice now, full of second-guessing, regret, a drama intermixing direct address with fragments of soliloquy: "I shouldn't show you this—/ God, why did I show her this?" He fears the ark and the knowledge of the ark—"ancient . . . so old"—transport stories so devastating that his sister cannot bear their import, "no matter how many books you've read." He strokes the wood with fingers that the speaker pronounces "marvelously fucked." Hands that are wondrous even as they have been ruined by what they conveyed into his body, hands that might be shattered but yet are beheld with steady sibling regard. The ark is not the problem. The problem is the ark's failure to cherish what it would preserve. An ark never asks those it swallows whether they are willing to become part of its totalizing system. "I could take the ark," states the speaker in a declaration of abiding sibling love: "It was the animals — the animals I could not take."

A catalog of unruly beasts irrupts. They enter the house in the brother's wake, breaking the doorway, marching across the kitchen and into his body, their ark of conservation. Against some orderly two-by-two of embarkation, these creatures make for a riotous litany: "tails snaking across my feet before disappearing / like retracting vacuum cords into the hollows / of my brother's clavicles, tusks scraping the walls." The beasts keep arriving, infinite procession, assailing the brother's form, boarding him: wildebeests, pigs, oryxes, javelinas, jaguars, raptors, pumas, ocelots "with their mathematical faces," goats of every sort, "so many kinds of creature." An ark preserves its inhabitants, but these animals destroy the vessel they enter. The speaker wants to follow their ruinous procession, follow these beasts. She wants to get to "the bottom of it," to understand her brother in his suffering, hold the knowledge that he says no book will teach, no matter how many books you read, even Genesis. Yet he stops her at the wood, stops her with his ark piece that is a fragment of a frame: "This can save you." So the speaker has to give in, sit there at her dining table with her "brother wrecked open like that . . . two-by-two the fantastical beasts parading him."

The flood arrives. Water "falls against ankles," builds "itself up around" her, fills her coffee cup "before floating it away from the table." Her brother "teems with shadow— / a hull of bones, lit only by tooth and tusk," not to be saved, not to be reached, not to be understood, an ark that keeps its gate shut against family, against community, against love. He is "lifting his ark high in the air," a closed vessel of hard fortunes. And beside that locked ark abides familial care, more powerful for catastrophe's relentless approach.

A well-built ark offers survival and endurance; only a fractured or repurposed vessel refuses to refuse refuge. No ark builder ever intends a general welcome or contemplates a full remembrance of what they abandon, but welcome and regard remain possible all the same. Break an ark and shatter its timbers and maybe from its splintered pieces you will build a table or a shelter or a poem, dwell a little longer in the world of everyday belongings that the vessel's luminous integrity obstructs. Were an ark's power only to hold, still, containerize, and convey, its destinations would always be grim, a disappointment and a violence. The ark is a broken frame, and therein lies its vitality.

The sea rises. Arks list.

CHAPTER 3

Outside the Ark

The story of Noah and his ark invites us to inquire into the nature and function of beginnings, to be on our guard at the quickening dangers of passing over rough waters, of surrendering to denouement, of forgeting the wake. To dwell within disaster may open more alternatives for community than the sailing of a sealed ark promises. Perhaps for this same reason, extrabiblical tradition always has Mrs. Noah entering the vessel last. Sometimes she has to be carried into its walled security by her sons. Mrs. Noah is not the only one who prefers to remain outdoors. Commencement is a rhythm or pulse, a cycle that spirals, its destiny an ellipsis rather than a period. All aboard; the rain is starting. En-arkment, landfall, and rainbow constitute powerful activation points in the story and all it solicits. But the urge to linger at the ark's exterior proves just as captivating. Putting off until the next chapter Noah and his chosen few's embarkation, in this we tarry in scenes of life and death imagined outside the ark and consider the refuge and affective kinship that come into being in that perilous space of excluded possibility. Given the ark's offer of conservation, why do so many choose to linger with those left to the rising waters?

Drown

Commissioned to illustrate a deluxe edition of the Bible, Gustave Doré (1832–1883) meditated on the story of the Flood and dwelled on what the story does not speak. In one especially moving illustration, *The Deluge,* he imagined the last rock on Earth, the waters nearly at their crest (Figure 6).[1] Waves hurl themselves against this vanishing island. Night is falling. Atop the drowning rock, a tiger attempts the preservation of its cub, holding the baby in its mouth, scanning the horizon for some signal of safety or somewhere else to go. A naked man and woman push four children onto the inadequate shelter. As

FIGURE 6. Dwindling refuge atop the last rock. Gustave Doré, *The Deluge,* 1866. From *La Sainte Bible selon la Vulgate. Traduction nouvelle avec les dessins de Gustave Doré.* v. 1, A. Mame et fils, Tours (1866). Bibliothèque nationale de France, département Réserve des livres rares, SMITH LESOUEF R-6283.

on the ark, all creatures endure the midst of catastrophe together, but here as an accidental community, left to a brutal exterior. While the scene projects an equivalence between the gestures of the handless tiger who holds a cub in its mouth and the human animals that push their baby aloft, the image does not allegorize this trans-species coincidence of gesture. The rock does not signify some timeless messianic cessation of antagonism—"the wolf lying down with the lamb"—but instead remains a dwindling outcrop for the capture of one shared history.[2]

The tiger is strong enough to climb. Not all human animals are. The tiger carries the last of its three cubs in its jaws, and this handless necessity matter-of-factly renders the jaws an instrument of conservation and care. The tiger's mouth enters into a prosaic equivalence with the technological advantage accorded to human handedness. Lacking the agility of the tiger, the human animals work collectively to save those young they can. All shall drown. Some are drowning even now. Species difference finds itself trumped by the mundane reality of the need for breath. Roll the image forward as the waters continue to rise, and the refuge shall unravel as hands and jaws transform their uses. This precarious haven shall vanish. The scene it stages is time-bound, fleeting, a snapshot of what was but cannot endure, the price of someone else's rainbow.

Doré's engravings were an instant success, ensuring that the French Bible of 1865 would be quickly followed by English and German editions with the same plates. The once ubiquitous chain bookstore Barnes & Noble published an inexpensive gold-leaf version, a book that wants to become an archive of family history through its nostalgic offer of pages for recording births, weddings, family trees, deaths.[3] *The Deluge* is featured as its frontispiece. What a way to commence: not with an image of creation, not with "In the Beginning" or *fiat lux,* but with a lingering meditation on what sank beneath the sea so that Genesis could begin to begin again, a scene wholly absent from the text. Meanwhile, high above, the seabirds circle.

When the Russian Jewish artist Nathan Altman created a version of the same scene in 1933, he depicted an architecturally intricate ark at great distance, gliding the trough of a wave, sealed in its progress toward covenant (Figure 7).

Rain slashes and streaks the composition. The foreground is wholly given to a dog on a dwindling promontory. Cowering by a thin pine, the beast howls into the deluge. The boat has journeyed too far for anyone to see the dog's snout upturned in misery, to witness its cry at having been abandoned. All we hear instead is the rain, its volume rendered in streaks that scream across the canvas. We who view the

FIGURE 7. Abandoned. Nathan Altman, *Deluge,* 1933. Center for Jewish Art, The Hebrew University of Jerusalem. Object ID: 28530. Copyright 2022 Artists Rights Society (ARS), New York / UPRAVIS, Moscow. Photograph copyright Center for Jewish Art. Photographer: Chebutkin, Stas, 6.7.1992.

image are compelled, like this orphaned companion animal or abandoned and inconsolable pet, to endure the rain become lines that hurt.

Altman created this print in 1933, the same year East European Jewish immigrants were stripped of German citizenship, the same year Dachau opened. On closer inspection, the insistent charcoal branches of the forlorn pine reveal themselves to be one, two, three, four, five, six birds. A seventh and perhaps an eighth float aloft, unable to find a perch. Foreground dissolves into background; *flora* turns fleshy; *fauna,* vegetal. In this mixed media rendering of the flood in which lines scream the rain, distinctions between beings come unstuck. When an ark is announced and its door is closed, terrible things might unfold, both inside and out.[4]

Both Doré and Altman offer scenes unrecorded in the Bible. Neither is unusual among artists and poets in this regard. The Book of Genesis narrates no human or animal dramas at the ark's exterior once the vessel's door shuts, but such barring of its limits serves as no impediment to readers who have a difficult time departing the world the ark blots out. Doré and Altman contribute to a historically varied but continuous visual arkive that seeks to inhabit this record of diminishing of *refugia,* places of refuge, to the singularized, absolute refuge we know as "ark." In their different ways, both imagine how the Flood recodes the familiar world, erases the benefits of what we had thought was high ground, and renders the tallness of trees uncanny, the flightedness of birds a flagging irrelevance, canine companionship an orphaned devotion. And yet a desire endures to imagine refuge, even to offer up these images as their own momentary stay against the erasures of the flood.

"Refuge" derives from the Latin verb *refugere,* "to flee back." A refuge is a hiding place, as Old French and the Latin *refugium* allowed.[5] A refuge exists as an anchoring point that maintains a relation to a gathering or network that offers some means of relief from the turbulence of the world, an opportunity to recoup. Refuge cohabits with resources and reserves, which may be financial, but as often as not, may prove to be affective, conceptual, or spiritual: ties that bind a person to the possibility of personhood.[6] The word "refugee" designates not a homeless or itinerant fugitive whose arrow always moves outward. On the contrary, the refugee, however his or her movements may be construed by others, remains caught up in an attempt to return to a rightful place of lost or blocked security. The flight of the refugee stands always in relation to this diminished refuge that now must be sought elsewhere. As Hannah Arendt puts it in a still haunting essay, "we [refugees] don't like to be called refugees." That name comes from others. "We ourselves call each other 'newcomers'; or 'immigrants.'"[7] Arriving without means, without access to the wherewithal of refuge, it is only right of these newcomers to seek more, and so, by their arrival, to ask for the cluster of ties and the reserves of belonging that, in a gesture that will always politicize, count as "enough."[8] The word "refuge" embeds an ongoing question as to what counts as "enough," a fundamental question of hospitality.

In the biblical story of the Flood, the obliteration of refuge, the banishment of reserves, is the consequence of a divine act, a desire to cleanse, to start again. As Doré and Altman show, the flood overwrites the refuge-making affordance of rocks and trees, of high places. In our present, the story plays differently. Citing the work of Anna Tsing, Donna Haraway wonders whether the transition between the Holocene and the Anthropocene might not have been "the wiping out of most of the refugia from which diverse species assemblages (with or without people) can be reconstituted" after ecologically catastrophic events: the eradication of forests, widespread desertification, constancy of shore loss?[9] Tsing has observed that the Holocene was, after all, "the long period when refugia, places of refuge, still existed, even abounded, to sustain reworlding in rich cultural and biological diversity." The Anthropocene, for both writers, arrives in a tidal wave of loss, the eradication of refuge for humans and nonhumans alike. There is nowhere to go, not even a vanishing rock. Haraway notes that this modeling of reduced refuge as the aging out of an abused equilibrium, a reduced or traumatized plasticity, resonates with Jason Moore's "arguments that cheap nature is at an end," that the elastic "reserves of the earth have been drained, burned, depleted, poisoned, exterminated, and otherwise exhausted."[10] In *Malfeasance,* Michel Serres goes so far as to model the engulfing of the world by pollution as a second deluge: "In the first deluge, on which Noah floated, culture disappeared beneath nature." This second flood, a final catastrophe, works as the successful reverse of the first: "Who doesn't see that the only thing left floating will be the homogeneous excrement of the victorious Great Owner, *Sapiens sapiens*?"[11] In an arkless future, the only sources of refuge on the horizon of Serres's *Jeremiad* are engulfed by the discarded remains of human culture: writing, marking, property-making—"shit," in Serres's despairing lexicon: "There are already islands where the stench announces this ending." Welcome to the misanthropocene.

And yet, the word "refuge" still beckons. Especially so, if the alternatives now seem cast in ever more singularizing and exclusive modes that absolutize the prospects of refuge, amping up the boundary drawing that renders places of refuge places of fortification and exclusion. In our historical moment, *refugia* pass from being a general expectation or a right to become a scarce and gated privilege. "Clearly," writes Serres in less apocalyptic mode, "we have to meditate on the function of the border," the way "this *dividing line*" constitutes a zone as opposed to a fixed and self-consistent limit. Strangely, he elaborates, this border "consists of three layers: The first is on the inside and protects inhabitants [or is supposed to] with its softness; the exterior . . . threatens possible invaders with its hardness." But "the layer in the middle" is thick and perhaps may be thickened further, for it comes "riddled with pores, passages, portals, and porosities through which, often by semiconduction, a living being or a thing enters, is locked in, leaves, transits, attacks, or waits hopelessly."[12] Serres is talking about all manner of structures: houses, cities, the walls of a cell, an organism, the human body, the Earth. In thinking about these borders, he is hardly alone.

"Making kin." That is how Haraway might describe the writers and artists and readers who contribute to the arkive of border thinking we inventory in this chapter. Doré, Altman, and their fellows recognize kinship with those lost or left behind or otherwise excluded from the ark. "Make kin, not babies," is how Haraway puts it in an effort to be explicit about the way the anthropological notion of "fictive kin" gives us the ability to affiliate and ally in ways that disobey lines that divide or that cause *lines* to stray from the genealogical plotting of family with their family trees and exclusive arks. "It matters how kin generate kin," for it's the *how* (the technical means) that cohabits with the ethical relation.[13] Making kin is itself an act of refuge-making. "One way to live and die well as mortal critters," writes Haraway here, "is to join forces to reconstitute refuges, to make possible partial and robust biological-cultural-political-technological recuperation and recomposition." Such acts of refuge-making are not unequivocally positive. They hurt. They include mourning losses that are irreversible. The trick might be to look this hurt in the face (in all its faces, human and otherwise), and so to construct multiple orders of refuge whose viability derives from portals and porosities. Let's allow the strangely thick middle layer between inside and out to swell and inquire into the stories, the resources for refuge, that adhere to or unfold outside the ark, the productive border between utter obliteration and conservation at unspeakable cost.

How Ark-Building Programs the Visual Field of Flood

After four millennia of practice, narratives of worldly obliteration come easily. Venerable in their plotlines and conventions, cataclysm's narratives are familiar, almost comforting. As the end of the world approaches, we know what we have to do: build some arks. How else to persevere against climate change? Every doomsday arrives prenarrated, the latest iteration of a tale intimate from the past.[14] The *Epic of Gilgamesh* is a "text haunted by rising waters and disaster," and its hero, Utanapishtim, a reverent safeguarder of family, friends, baby animals, and grains in his sturdy ship *Preserver of Life* (which, unlike Noah's vessel, also includes space for the craftsmen who assist in its construction).[15] Kim Stanley Robinson's *New York 2140* imagines Manhattan after ice-cap melt has rendered the dense urban grid a canal-crossed Venice.[16] Intrepid New Yorkers fashion their ark from a repurposed skyscraper. Within the partially submerged MetLife building, the novel's protagonists try their best to preserve a wide community of residents and refugees, despite storms that destroy their rooftop farm and hedge-fund financiers whose appetite for real estate acquisition offers an even more dangerous kind of flood. *New York 2140* is as much about the perils of global liquidity under capitalism as under a warming atmosphere. Robinson's novel is a contribution to a thriving genre dubbed CliFi (climate fiction), narratives with a genealogy of at least five millennia that map the drenched and turbulent vagaries of life in the Anthropocene.[17] With its emphasis on dwelling within anthropogenic climate change, CliFi seems utterly contemporary, yet Utanapishtim sailing toward a soaked future in his boat full of human and nonhuman life suggests a more spiraled genealogy of ancient myth and prospective futurity.

Whereas world-ending catastrophe used to arrive in the thunder of heavenly revelation and the unveiling of a divine plan—deluge as quick and ordered work, with a knowable author and comfortable narrative arc, culmination in rainbow or rapture—the ruin of the Earth is now born of a chaos of greenhouse heat, drought, wildfires, relentless sea-rise, slow submergence of coasts, and an ongoing litany of hurricanes. No First Mover is required in this mundane version of

Judgment Day, but flood and sin shape the story's plot all the same. Such secular versions of apocalypse are, in the words of Lawrence Buell, "the single most powerful master metaphor that the contemporary environmental imagination has at its disposal."[18] Yet, as we brace for denouement in storm and tempest, what might our apocalyptic scripts unveil about the limits of our environmental imagination, the impoverishment of the stories that we tell?

Catastrophe seems fitting punishment for our profligacy: heat, drought, cyclones, glacier retreat, ocean acidification, and species loss as nature's remonstrance, the wages for our carbon release. We are sinners in the hands of an angry Gaia, carbon offsets a modern version of papal indulgences. There is no theology here, we tell ourselves, only the cold science of global weirding, the yield that unbridled capitalism brings. We long ago smashed the idols, broke the covenant binding the human and the divine. Nowadays we can even borrow our global catastrophes from nonbiblical sources, maybe place our end times within an imagined version of the Mayan calendar, as in Roland Emerich's 2009 film *2012*. Publicity for that film featured a sudden crack in the Sistine Chapel so that God no longer touched Adam, and the statue of Jesus in Rio de Janeiro toppling into the sea. Yet, as anyone who has seen the disaster of a film *2012* knows, when the world is ending and no god is coming, in order to survive Earth's obliteration by floods of neutrinos, destabilization of the planet's mantle, and oceanic outpouring, the narrative reverts to the old script and builds some arks. As Everest sinks, these marine marvels of technology preserve a tiny selection of the human population, including anyone who possesses the billion dollars necessary to purchase a ticket. Queen Elizabeth boards her boat with signature corgis in tow (if not quite two by two). In other disaster stories, we launch spaceships to sail to distant stars, as in Christopher Nolan's 2014 *Interstellar,* or get very clever and set Noah's ark on a train that circles a planet drowned in ice, as in Bong Joon-ho's 2013 *Snowpiercer.* To imagine catastrophe's unfolding, we deploy familiar frames, especially those provided by the story of Noah's Flood. Central to this biblical narrative of survival against climate change is a vessel that preserves a limited collective, leaving most of the world to the exterior of its storm-resistant, leak-proof hull. Security is purchased through resignation; en-arkment proceeds at cost.

As the works of Doré and Altman suggest, the story of the ark engenders a long history of hesitating over who and what is left behind when we suppose a watery end is inevitable and enclose small community within walls that both conserve and repulse. Crossing the centuries, this tradition of lingering with stories fated to submergence forms a countercurrent, eddying around plots and scripts loaded into the ark for transport toward olive branch and rainbow. Not attested in Genesis, these slipstream tales make clear that we exclude mightily when we build an ark, or gate a community, or raise a wall along a nation's border, as if we could, like Noah, construct a protective chest in which to dwell, some ark-itecture of shelter and exclusion to hold against waves of water or climate refugees. Arks distribute violence swift or slow.[19] Those barred from ark or enclave are inevitably humans we refuse to call fellow. Suffering is unequally distributed. The failures of our care are vast. A consideration of the preservability and potential companionship of nonhumans also goes missing. Utanapishtim and Noah filled their structures with more animals than human beings, but Robinson's *New York 2140* is typical of CliFi in featuring only incidental nonhumans. The novel mentions in passing porpoises, whales, gulls, muskrats—sea and marsh life that flourishes in the newly deep waters outside the MetLife ark—with an occasional mention of the factory farm harbored somewhere within that skyscraper to sustain the residents with ready protein. These animals are decorative, biomass, afterthoughts.

To narrate the unfolding of anthropogenic climate change and other kinds of ecocatastrophe, we quietly return to narrowed versions of biblical scripts that we thought we had surpassed: sin, cataclysm, selective and severe community, Earth reborn. The world is ending through the melting of polar ice and the rising of the seas, and so Noah's Flood, a disaster God promised never to send a second time, crashes anew. We know in advance the contours of this plot's unfolding and surrender too easily to its surge. Yet, in that resignation to submergence, to biblical replay in newly scientific mode, we lose sight of the actual complexity of the story in Genesis, as well as its vigorous narrative countercurrents and afterlives. Climate change requires more and better stories than the penurious ones we have been telling. The Genesis account of Noah and its artistic reconfiguration across the centuries offer a diverse and enduring arkive, a source for resilient countertales that do not make of a coming Flood untroubled waters.

The key to this endeavor lies in the multiplicity of perspectives that the ark story describes or suggests as it produces its own dividing line, the story of the ark, a semiconductor whose resistances to its own announcements constitute a kind of mythic open-work for ark thinking. God said to Noah: "Make yourself an ark of gopher wood; make it an ark with compartments, and cover it inside and out with pitch" (Genesis 6:14). Thinking with this command to carpentry opens three possible perspectives: the view of God from the heavens, looking down and directing the progress of the drama; the ground outside, as the ark rises and a throng of creatures come to realize that they are at a sudden exterior; and the coming into being of a small within, the space of sanctuary, limned with gopher wood, a space within which the outside becomes a memory and disembarkment a fervent hope. A fourth point of view, in fact, inheres in that hope: the ark imagined from the outside but projected from within, from within the immune privilege that guides a chosen few into the future. It is this oscillation of perspectives that decides the ark's capacity for refuge, their choreography in the name of sponsoring this or that version of the story.

In the midst of gathering his planks, Noah could not perhaps have predicted that, in future ages, artists and authors who retell his story would repeatedly inhabit points of view that cling to the exterior of the vessel that he built and sealed. Not warm against the storm in rooms sealed tight with pitch, not even with the viewpoint of those gone ashore come landfall, these writers and artists seek the drenched outlook of those in the rising flood, watching that salvific ark sail to its destiny in mountain, dove, and sacrifice. And, as the counterarchive we assemble in this chapter testifies, the more humane space sometimes emerges at this ephemeral outside. The border at which whatever community gathers may not long endure, but its stories will not prove easy to forget.

God Tricks

We typically take the barest elements and most dangerous affect from the Genesis account of the deluge: a resignation to sinking things below the waters, an acceptance that can turn giddy and even become enjoyment. We submit too easily to imagining a world in which global warming will render the view from St. Paul's Cathedral difficult to

FIGURE 8. London as its own colony. *St Paul's Monkeys*: "Where once gargoyles would sit on the walls of venerated buildings, St Paul's Cathedral is now host to a new breed of tropical immigrants, enjoying the view of the flooded Thames and reminiscing about equatorial days. And, despite the warning, feeding on some of the capital's newly fashionable staple foods. Our apes are totally relaxed, perched in what is to us a narrow and precarious environment. They are truly at home." From the *Postcards from the Future* project by Robert Graves and Didier Madoc-Jones. Copyright GMJ.

tell from the vistas of Britain's former colonies, as Robert Graves and Didier Madoc-Jones envision in their climate-change-awareness project *Postcards from the Future.*[20] In *St Paul's Monkeys* (Figure 8), simians perch serenely at the top of Christopher Wren's dome in London, surveying flooded streets and the remnants of the Tate Modern, as if England had become India or Gibraltar. As the oceans rise, a global connectedness that already binds London to Mumbai becomes elementally palpable.

In other images from the same series, Graves and Madoc-Jones place rice paddies in front of the houses of Parliament and shanties around Buckingham Palace and Trafalgar Square, stressing the intimacy of floods of water to floods of climate refugees. Contemplating point of view in these images is revealing: who is the implicit onlooker of this world in which monkeys, beasts of burden, laborers in rice paddies, and shanty and souk dwellers are interchangeably decorative signifiers of climate indifference, of a world environmentally altered and offered as marvel and portent? Monkeys, oxen, and the global poor go about doing what they do, only they are here now, in London, in *our* space—and this coexistence is itself constituted as spectacle. Our space: what community of onlookers is constituted through that first-person plural possessive pronoun? The viewer's identification is assumed to be with the flooded buildings, iconic signifiers of Englishness, rather than the displaced peoples and beasts that now populate domestic landscapes. In the wake of catastrophe, suffering is unequally distributed. The flood makes evident a lack of affective connection already present, an everyday inability of sympathy to cross boundaries of nation, race, species, class. It seems irresistible: projecting a collective but circumscribed self into the future, imagining "we" can view from above the contours of "our" cities as they drown in rising seas as if we were some disinterested, shore-bound, Lucretian observer of shipwreck from afar.[21]

In 2012, the blogger Burrito Justice created a sequence of future topographical maps for San Francisco to raise the alarm about sea level rise, detailing the transformation of the city's hills over the next fifty years into islands and streets into ocean floor.[22] Inspired by this post-deluge cartography, the urban planner Jeffrey Linn fashioned a series of beautiful and clever maps that, with seeming accuracy, demonstrate the inundation of other familiar metropolises in the wake of ice sheet dissolution.[23] The Drowned Cities Project depicts Manhattan after one hundred feet of sea rise, with Brooklyn Heights become Brooklyn Depths and Midtown reborn as Middrown. Nearby are Central Shark, Hell's Quicksand, and the Upper East Tide. At 240 feet of sea-level change, Seattle is rendered an archipelago. Beneath vivid blue, the outlines of submerged streets are discernable in Linn's cartography, a reminder of what is lost as the Emerald City becomes a new Atlantis. Portland's urban topography is used by Linn to illustrate 250 feet of flood. The city is transformed into a series of artisanally sculpted islands, with the Columbia Gorge an ocean inlet and the Willamette River a sudden sea. Other handsome, ready-for-purchase maps created by the same artist depict a watery London, Montreal, Vancouver, and Hong Kong, so that an international audience may behold what their favorite city looks like when swallowed by the sea. White lines mark where streets once ran and clever new names have been affixed to underwater neighborhoods, but no other human trace marks these aerial views. It's as if the Spirit of God were again moving upon the face of the waters, only this time reading lost human history.

Maps and images of future drowned cities enact what Haraway has called "the god trick," assuming a scientific perspective that serenely floats above observed facts.[24] At critical distance, truth appears: disembodied, viewable only from an outside purged, and protected from self-implication. From such a detached and aloof position, catastrophe becomes conceptual and foregone, something witnessed by a viewer who gazes down from the clouds. But what about sink or swim, pedestrian, ground-based, entangled knowledge? Distant perspective abstracts us from forging, in Stacy Alaimo's words, "more complex epistemological, ontological, ethical and political perspectives in which the human can no longer retreat into separation and denial or proceed as if it were possible to secure an inert, discrete, externalized this or that."[25] In the midst of things, it is muddy, messy, uncomfortable. You'll get soaked. You might get stuck. You may even drown. Haraway describes this uncomfortable space as "remaining with the trouble," a mode of material and ethical saturation, promising no dry heaven from which to view in safety what unfolds during any cataclysm (from Greek *kataklysmos,* "deluge," a word invented to describe the feel and reach of the Genesis Flood). When we imagine that we can leave the trouble behind, abstract ourselves to behold the Earth from a comprehensive distance, we render ourselves divine.

In Sarah Blake's novel *Naamah* (2019), Noah's wife cannot stop thinking about "how terrible it would be to drown," despite the fact that she and her kin are safe on the ark.[26] Yet the family knows the terrible price that others have paid for their safety. As the vessel is constructed from a cypress grove that God has provided for the purpose, Shem's wife Sadie asks "why her family, her young sisters and brothers, could not come with them" (14). Her mother-in-law holds Sadie tightly as she sobs, but after this moment of compassion passes, she states firmly: "That was the last time you can cry about this" (15). Lingering with the loss makes you liable to ruin the boat-building project, makes you likely to perish with all those who must find their lands become the ocean's deep. Long after being saved from the watery catastrophe, Noah's wife Naamah finds it difficult to forget "the deaths of the people God no longer wanted" (10). From climbing on deck and having her skin abraded by the force of the forty days' rain, she knows how the Flood hurt those outside the ark as they were overwhelmed. From the experience of raising boys who each "discovered that if they peed on a rock, the pee would splash" and thereafter took great joy in dislodging ants and leaves through that method, Naamah compares the terrible force of the rain to a million streams, "which made her imagine God as a being with a million penises" (13–14). Such are her thoughts aboard an ark filled with shit and blood that must be cleaned, a place where "litters of babies that have come too soon" are food for the carnivores that must be preserved (25). Sometimes a mother is fed her own young. Once the deluge has subsided and the waters are calm, though, Naamah starts swimming every day, and finds worlds to explore beneath the waves. She even falls in love with a woman who turns out to be a fallen angel, tending to the drowned children who do not want to leave the only home they have ever known, even though it is now the bottom of a sea.

At issue here are perspective, scale, and gender, as well as the mechanisms by which we secure our knowledge of things or attempt to generalize a local and particular experience through observation, proliferation, and empathy. The relation of intimacy to epistemology proves complicated and difficult. The mapping projects we have just mentioned seek to inhabit an atmospheric, incorporeal perspective in order to make the projected impact of global warming palpable, knowable, from some distant and imagined viewpoint that might translate, and so accommodate, myriad disconnected perspectives. Yet this disembodied gaze from afar often merely replicates a severe and masculinist frame, as Haraway has argued. How do we render global warming palpable, they ask—by what aesthetic or perceptual apparatus can we make the phenomenon knowable? To represent such extension, we reach for the sky to gaze down serenely from its expanses. That race toward a greater-than-human view is enduring, even as the perspective of Icarus will always prove lonely, partial, and unsustainable, and come crashing down.

In his two-volume Latin treatise *Telluris Theoria Sacra,* or *Sacred Theory of the Earth* (1681; translated into English in 1684), Thomas Burnet creates an illustration of Noah's ark afloat on an inundated globe, the tiny vessel guarded by two barely visible angels (Figure 9). You have to look hard to find the ship, dwarfed as it is by the figure

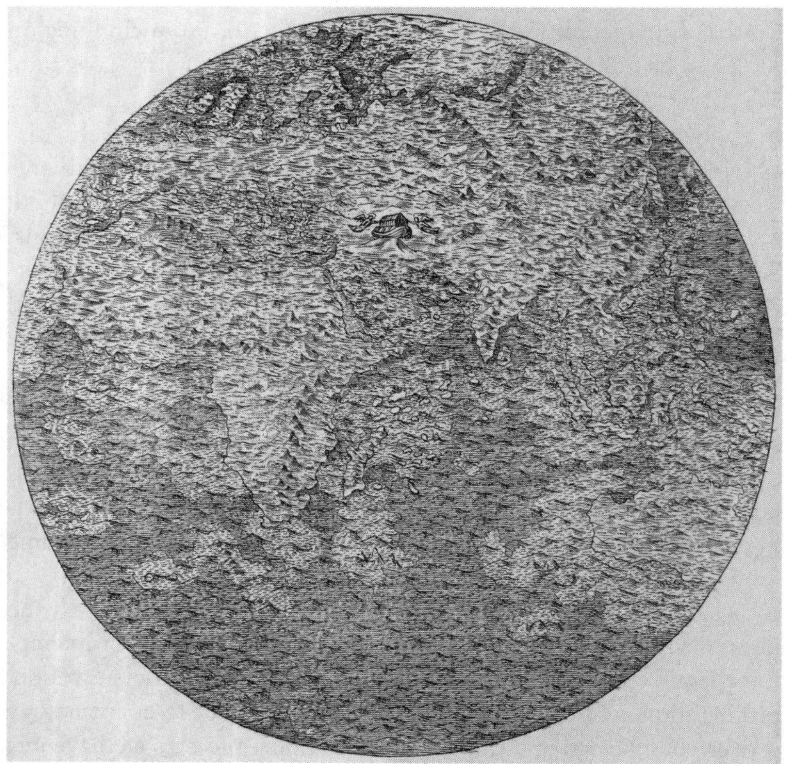

FIGURE 9. God and the angels look down upon the Earth. The Deluge and dissolution of the Earth. Page 68 of Thomas Burnet, *Telluris Theoria Sacra* (1681), or *Sacred Theory of the Earth* (1684). London: Printed by R. N. [i.e., Roger Norton] for Walter Kettilby, at the Bishop's-Head in S. Paul's Church-Yard, 1697. Wellcome Collection, B5953.

of a wave-covered Earth whose surface takes shape anew after the Flood. Burnet's two-volume opus builds a time machine before it makes an ark. Ever since he was a boy, he writes, he has wanted to "view in his mind" something like "the First Sources and Original of Things."[27] Accordingly, his thought experiments attempt to turn back the five thousand years that have passed since the Earth's creation in order to reconcile Genesis's story, or Moses's history of the Earth's origins, as Burnet conceives of it, with his own emerging mathematical rationality. Burnet theorizes the antediluvian Earth as smooth and hollow, filled with subterraneous waters that the deluge catastrophizes into a general collapse or dissolution.

As the waters clear and the rainbow appears, Noah's ark comes to rest on a Mount Ararat that is newly formed. For, with the end of the flood, "a new World appear'd" and the "Earth put on its new form" (77). Providence "at one stroke dissolv'd the frame of the old World, and made us a new one out of its ruines." Even as he finds himself caught up in the complication of his dry-land calculations and the burgeoning cross-referencing of his imaginative experiment, Burnet remains alive to the challenge to representation that the magnitude of such a calamity poses. "'Tis not easie," he writes, "to represent to our selves this strange Scene of things" when "Nature seem'd to be in a Second Chaos; and upon this Chaos rid the distrest Ark, that bore the small remains of Mankind." To attempt to do so would use up "all the Poetry and Hyperboles that are us'd in the description of Stormes and raging Seas" (99).

Burnet's time-traveling gaze remains trained on the ark, "which was a Type of the Church," to which, as a Christian, he belongs. The ark is a personal as well as universal origin. Burnet wonders at the workings of Providence that enabled this "ship whose cargo was no less than the whole World" to endure the storm and pauses to ponder the greater catastrophe of the ark's loss at sea, rendering his present time "a dead heap of Rubbish" and his own project the imaginary thought in the head of a man who never came to exist. But such irony and such awareness of the loss, of the so very much lost and so very many that died, is kept at bay as Burnet "supposes the good Angels" looking down from heaven "upon this ship of Noah's" not "out of curiosity, as idle spectators, but with a passionate concern for its safety and deliverance" (100). The ark has an uncanny way of generating compassion for its besieged exterior, even if that space is lethal to occupy if you do not happen to be a hovering angel.

Bilocating (to tell the truth, he manages to be in as many places as he needs at once), Burnet's strangely peaceful if calamitous mise-en-scène both preserves and denudes the passionate possibility of contemplating all those who live on into the future only as a "dead heap of Rubbish." The apparatus of looking he organizes recedes so far from anything palpable, from anything sensible, that submerged expanses have ceased to trouble. The Earth covered in water is radiant, at least when observed from heaven. It is kind of peaceful looking down, imagining that we can discern the workings of Providence, and so we become a little version of God, hovering above the waters.

For Burnet, this peace radiates in the form of a theory that works, a comprehensive system that in accounting for the flood enables him to travel back in history still further to the original of originals, the Garden of Eden and the birth of time itself. His synoptic, cosmologically ambitious treatise remains deeply enmeshed in a worldview that understands itself to be grounded, founded on landfall and rainbow.

As Burnet shows us, this imagined divine perspective cohabits with the external after-the-fact landedness of a perspective that apprehends the flood only retrospectively. If the ark figures the church, then this landedness stands in exact relation to the disembodied universality of the divine point of view. This doubleness, a terrestrial grounding that enables weightless contemplation, precisely designates the immune privilege positing the ark-as-world grants to those now privileged to tell the story over. Burnet imagines the Ur-ark, or in his words, a "ship whose cargo was no less than the whole World." And that salvific ark serves as the fulcrum that enables the articulation of the outside to the ark as a discardable "dead heap of rubbish."[28]

In this absolutizing of perspective, Burnet is not alone. In his *Divine Weekes and Workes* (1578), Guillaume de Salluste du Bartas writes the ark into early-modern colonial ventures, calling it "the World's re-colonizing Boat."[29] Responding to atheist detractors, du Bartas spends little time on the outside of the vessel, and less time still on its interior, whose design he refuses to imagine because it is simply "miraculous."[30] When the depredations of the flood are then delineated, the sympathy they evoke comes channeled from without, distanced by the lack of an immune privilege, almost as if derived from some different species of feeling and being.

Perhaps the strangest example of such estranging affect comes from Burnet's near contemporary Edward Ecclestone, whose opera *Noah's Flood, or The Destruction of the World* (1679) unfolds in homage/argument with John Milton's *Paradise Lost* (1667) and John Dryden's opera *The State of Innocence and The Fall of Man* (1677). The action begins in hell, where Satan, Moloch, and attending devils take solace in the fact that Sin is running amok among humans. Their war has not been lost, because the divine has now seen fit to destroy the world, leaving them with only the modest task of eliminating Noah and his ark, or as Satan puts it, in language that begrudgingly recalls du Bartas's and Burnet's words, "this great small World of Eight."[31]

In act 2, with "the Sun in full Meridian" (10), Gabriel arrives to intervene with a worried, prayerful Noah, to convince him that he must make peace with the fact that he and his family alone are the beneficiaries of God's "Prerogative of Love" (15). There follows a salutary parade of sinful despair, including giants and allegorical figures: a Despair who stabs himself; "a Man-Lover" who "throws himself from a precipice into the sea" (15); "a Woman-Lover" who drinks poison, Pride, Ambition, and so on—all of whom "sink" (19) at the end of act 2 into a watery oblivion whose fiery special effects are meant to signify hell itself. In act 3, Lucifer appears to tell Noah that his prayers have averted the coming destruction and Gabriel has to redirect Noah and family and ensure that they board the ark. Moloch tries and fails to stow away. And, thus immunized against sympathy (coded now as misdirected affect and devilry), Noah and family are safely en-arked and ready for act 4, which opens with "the Deluge, representing Men and Beasts, of all sorts, promiscuously swimming together, only one Hill remaining above the Waves" (26). Meanwhile, "the Ark is discovered on the Surface of the Waters," while various quick scenes of drowning refugees unfold apace. The now plotless devils opt for a frontal assault on the ark, which fizzles with the appearance of the rainbow (36). The play stages Noah's vineyard episode, the advent of sin in the cleansed world, and thereby reenforces the gratitude for a safety that has not yet truly been earned.

It is easy to luxuriate in this catalog of apparently necessary losses from a position of peripheral safety: the ark, waiting to be "discovered" like some salvational helicopter shot that whisks us away from the dangers of being among the throng. Genesis notes the dangers inherent in the serene distance Burnet deploys and that Ecclestone's drenched play sensationalizes in its parade of those about to drown. After one hundred and fifty days of the waters prevailing on the Earth, "all existence on earth was blotted out; . . . only Noah was left, and those with him on the ark" (Genesis 7:23). Then, we are told, "God remembered Noah and all the beasts and all the cattle with him in the ark" (8:1). He at last sends a wind to assuage the waters, and stops the fountains of the deep, and closes the windows of the celestial vault. It is this forgetfulness or distraction that the rainbow is supposed to avert. For, once the ark is closed, as Genesis offers, the only perspective left is singularized to the heavenly, something very like Burnet's view of a sea so expansive and a vessel so tiny that it is easy to miss, to forget, even if you are God. Remote perspective, Genesis cautions, disentangles, distances, deprives. And so, like some yet more passionate and better angels, Genesis invites us to imagine what it is like to stand outside the ark when the door shuts, or to be trapped within while the weather shows no sign of abating. Though the Flood story scripts only one perspective, supernal and distant, it localizes at least three: dry, remote, detached; locked outside, drenched, facing obliteration; sealed within, yearning for a view of the ark from its outside again, the waves tossing, the animals crying, and who knows what else.

Yet, Burnet's and Ecclestone's choreography endures, translated to different media and catalyzed by the attenuated temporality of forward-looking calamity caused by past distraction. Where Burnet rejoices in his and mankind's salvation by way of Noah and his ark, the temptation now is to despair, even as that despair might constitute the death throes of a political rallying call that goes unheard. In the 2009 *The Age of Stupid,* a crowd-sourced documentary made in anticipation of the United Nations Climate Change Conference in Copenhagen in 2009, we meet Noah in the role of arkivist, but with no family. He welcomes us to a global repository of pickled specimens of animals, along with all the treasures of the art world and records of human achievement, gathered together 800 kilometers north of Norway. You could be forgiven for thinking that this wind-powered building, reaching up to the sky, epitomizes something closer to a Tower of Babel rather than Noah's ark. After all, it houses a sort of species-wide retrospective of human making whose purpose now seems unclear, as no visitors queue to enter the museum turned mausoleum. The Tower of Babel, that story of a human-authored, technological superlative that aspires to join all nations, peoples, and languages, runs in tandem with the story of the Flood (told in Genesis 11, after the Table of Nations in Genesis 10 that directly follows the Flood). The figure of this global archive might be said to hybridize the two, offering itself as both a repository and a communication device that might commute the sins of global warming.

The film unfolds as this future arkivist attempts to understand how the human race managed to discern that global warming was underway and yet failed to halt its advance. How could this catastrophic circumstance have come to pass? The film wrestles with the difficulty posed in recognizing anthropogenic climate change, in owning and living in and up to this reality. The film juxtaposes many stories: Piers, a clean-energy entrepreneur and wind farmer from the

FIGURE 10. The Ark as Tower of Babel. Screenshot from *The Age of Stupid*, dir. Franny Armstrong (London, Spanner Films, 2009). Copyright Spanner Films. Used with permission.

United Kingdom who, along with his wife Lisa and their kids, likes to go skiing in the French Alps; Fernand, their eighty-six-year-old guide who has lived his whole life on the glacier, protests the increase in traffic through the Alps, and offers firsthand testimony to how much the glacier has retreated since he was a boy; Jey, heir to a communications fortune in India, who launches India's third budget airline; Alvin, a chemist for oil companies off the coast of Florida, who experienced Hurricane Katrina firsthand, becoming something of a local hero after ferrying his friends, neighbors, and strangers, along with their pets and potted plants, to higher ground; Layefa, who works to become a doctor as she and her family scrape by in a Nigerian economy decimated by big oil and in a community terrorized by oil-sponsored violence; Adnan and Jamila, children in an Iraqi refugee family in Jordan, whose father was killed by U.S. soldiers.

The arkivist summons up these stories as he searches the global archive for references to climate change in 2009, the year that might have counted. A succession of screens in the ark/tower enable us to perceive the interpenetration of narratives, localities, and sites, the view from above that will render these stories something more than disparate (Figure 10). This retrospective media ecology enables the synoptic "god trick" that makes dispassionate knowing possible. Although already in 2009, and especially now, given that we have passed the projected "tipping point" of 2011, this ecology proves solipsistic.

The film periodically returns to images of Fernand's little roped party of glacier walkers that includes Piers and family as an image of the social, or sociality as the linkages between persons, animals, plants, and conditions that appear unrelated or at a distance. The roped party is, of course, the privileged icon of our condition in Serres's 1990 book *The Natural Contract*. But even as the film aspires through the interlacing of images, stories, and places to produce the praxis of the roped party, recruiting its viewers to reduce their emissions and lobby on behalf of carbon taxes or credits at the Copenhagen conference, the retrospective cast to its imagined 2055 inquiry proves salutary at best, if not forlorn.

"So why did I build this archive?," the arkivist asks as the film nears its apocalypse: "It's a cautionary tale." A few touches to the screen that frames his face sends the message on its way and the ark/tower broadcasts the records of his search (or perhaps the entirety of the archive of human making) skyward, addressing whatever unknown beings might one day receive the signal. This radio wave is pictured as a flash of white light, a blinding technomagical broadcast to the beyond that renders sublime the inability of the movie's mixed-media imaging to render recognition of anthropogenic climate change as an owned and enacted efficacy. How could we not act? We were living, so it turns out, not in the Anthropocene or any of the other newly available names for our epoch, but as Alvin the oil worker remarks, in "The Age of Stupid."

Like the makers of this documentary, we subscribe to the necessity of mixed media, to a promiscuity of story, time, and place in the hopes of some future efficacy grounded in the actions of our present. It's the film's last-man narrative that gives us pause. It's the loading of the ark with pickled animals and buried treasures we resist. It's the christening of anything as an "Age." Ark thinking demands more. It is an activity crowded with differently timed historical persons and places who, by their encounter with the story of the flood, are already the wetware of ecological thought. That multiplicity of perspectives is the key to unraveling even the most earnest of god tricks.

To create a future imperfect London for their *Postcards from the Future* project, the artists Robert Graves and Didier Madoc-Jones digitally manipulated images of the city to portray the varied effects of climate change: drought, tropical incursion, cold so severe "frost fairs" return to a frozen Thames. Most of their images, however, depict a sinking metropolis. In the breathtaking *London as Venice* (Plate 4), the Thames barrier has failed and most of the city is submerged in quiet waters. The Houses of Parliament and Westminster Abbey are resplendent in the gold of sunset, encircled by shimmering blue. The London Eye spins peacefully above the flood. A color version of Thomas Burnet's view of the ark, this image likewise looks down upon a watery and radiant expanse from a great distance. The city seems serene.

The following text appears on the *Postcards from the Future* website, describing the creation of *London as Venice*:

> Like a modern day Canaletto, this disturbing yet strangely peaceful aerial view of a flooded Thames was inspired by shots of New Orleans submerged under the floodwaters of Hurricane Katrina. Curious to know how London would appear under similar conditions, Graves and Madoc-Jones transposed projection of a 7.2 metre flooded river onto their digital 3D model of London and aligned with a photograph of the Thames shot by Jason Hawkes. 7.2 metres is the level at which flood waters would breach the Thames Barrier. The low light of the photograph creates an evocative sense of dimension to the view, forming the impression that we are looking at a partially submerged stage-set.

Graves and Madoc-Jones sink London to render the city "disturbing yet strangely beautiful," "evocative" like a painting (Canaletto was an artist of iconic Venetian scenes) or a "partially submerged stage-set," architecture reduced to swamped scenery. Their inspiration for the image: New Orleans after a devastating hurricane. Years after Katrina, images of a flooded New Orleans have not lost their ability to haunt. They require no alteration to make them evocative, and should never suggest a stage set, painting, work of art. Beneath the overspreading waters of the Mississippi are people who lost their lives when the levees broke, people left to drown. Reckoning with Katrina means coming to terms with environmental racism, with the long-standing segregational structures that resigned Black residents of New Orleans to detritus long before the flood arrived. In the wake of catastrophe, suffering is unequally distributed. Tourists came in time to board the air-conditioned comfort of buses to view the devastation of the storm, a ruin of Black neighborhoods that had in fact been abandoned to ruin far in advance. Katrina revealed both the swift violence of ecological catastrophe and the slow violence of persistent, racialized inequality. The hurricane's aftermath might spur us to ask instead what watery London would look like if beheld not through the god trick of celestial and disembodied view, not through the windows of a tall bus or some other ark that floats over suffering, but from the midst of the sea swell, through the eyes of those in peril in the waters, those left to the peril of the sea?[32]

Multiplying Perspectives

Deluge stories impede easy periodization. They look both back to a past that includes the Levantine flood stories familiar from texts like the *Epic of Gilgamesh* and forward to the framing of contemporary climate change as a Genesis-style flood narrative. They also resist reduction into totalizing, Anthropocene-style tales about the Human as abstract, disembodied force. The Genesis account of the Flood is likely the tangled result of multiple authors at work. Its unfolding is possessed of a complexity and challenge to an easy moralization that is attenuated when transformed into straightforward narratives of sin, safe ships, happy animal pairs, and conclusive rainbows. Noah's ark is both a sacred chest that preserves its contents so that a new world will begin (it is origin and authority) and a Pandora's box filled with a volatile mix of chaos and hope that traumatizes the very privilege of safety its structure asserts. A narrative transport device that crosses the centuries, the ark reveals the capacity of things to have worked out differently.

Submerged elements of the Flood myth's complicated history constantly resurface. A renewed sense of the ark as a leaky vessel and easy-to-pirate conservation device might lead us to imagine a more capacious discourse of refuge. Allied to this endeavor is the long artistic history of lingering with those doomed to the ark's exterior, of remaining too long on an Earth sentenced to inundation and sympathizing (however fleetingly) with the multispecies throngs that remain in storm. A long tradition of dissonant stories outside the ark is well conveyed by the late medieval cycle drama known as the Chester *Pageante of Noyes Fludd* (Play of Noah's Flood).[33] Its script gives voice to the earthbound desires of Noah's wife, who chooses to remain with the women who are her drinking companions over immurement in the family ship. She calls the ark a "chest" while clinging to her "pot-tel" of shared booze, insisting that, unless her "gossips" are included among the passengers, she will not enter the boat. She refuses to allow them to drown. Noah's wife's willingness to remain in disaster and community rather than imagine a salvific moment of rising above the waters is a resistance to linear history, a curving of its trajectories against the force of rupture. Epochal narratives attempt, sovereign-like, to periodize. Yet as Noah's wife insists, these stories are corporeally, affectively, violently, and unevenly felt. They do not easily transcend embodied particularities.

"For fear of drowning I am agaste; / good gossip, let us draw near" (227–28): when the Chester *Pageante of Noyes Fludd* was performed, Noah's wife would have stood with the audience, who were likewise outside the ark. Spectators of necessity stood with the drowned. Although taken to be an exemplary work of medieval drama, the best version we possess of the Chester play dates from the early seventeenth century. Its contemporaries are texts like *Pericles,* Shakespeare's drama of shipwreck and perseverance, and a boom in pamphlet-based disaster narratives. The story of the ark seldom settles into an era within which it can be separated off into a fullness of contextual meaning, arriving instead as a perpetual narrative uncomformity, not amenable to clean periodizations, easy climatic impress, or stratigraphic archives. The ark should not float, and yet it does, a vessel built for maelstrom. Noah's voyage has been a turbulent one, resisted not only by storm, but at times by those aboard his ship, especially his dramatically non-compliant spouse.

Noah is not one. He has choices to make, and those choices position him differently. They localize incompatible and competing perspectives. Noah, so one set of stories goes, was obedient to God. Commanded to build an ark, he constructed the vessel to seemingly precise specifications. Christian tradition for the most part praises his perfect compliance. Saint Augustine writes that, when Noah immediately undertook the building of the ark, he was "certainly a figure of the city of God sojourning in this world" (*De civitate Dei [City of God]* 15.26), a prefiguration of Christ. Medieval interpreters of Torah were more ambivalent. Born into the large Jewish community that flourished in the French city of Troyes during the eleventh century, the renowned commentator Rashi observed that

> some say to his credit that Noah was righteous even in a generation of wicked men, that he would have been considered still more righteous in a generation of good men. Others say, to his discredit, that in comparison to his own generation he was righteous, but had he lived in the generation of Abraham he would have been considered of no importance.[34]

Rashi quotes from Genesis Rabbah the story of Noah hesitating outside the ark: "Believing and not believing that the Flood would come, he did not enter the ark until the waters forced him to do so" (32.6).

Rabbi Simeon in the Zohar paints a less flattering portrait still. He states that, "far from entreating God for his fellowmen not to destroy them, Noah thought only of his own safety and that of his own family, and, owing to this neglect on his part, the waters of the deluge [that] bear his name." Noah is culpable for the flood because he did not appeal for mercy on the behalf of others. He could have pleaded for the worth of the world rather than so quickly ascending into an ark that left it to its exterior. God likes to be argued with. When the impending destruction of Sodom and Gomorrah is declared, Abraham asks: "Will you sweep away the righteous with the wicked?" (Genesis 18:23). God relents, granting Abraham the opportunity to seek out those who do not deserve to perish. In the face of divine anger after the Israelites are discovered worshiping a golden calf, Moses on Mount Sinai reminds God of the promises made to Abraham, Isaac, and Jacob and refuses to allow the destruction of his people and a starting over again. Those who offer alternative scripts to God are often rewarded for their effort. Possibility limns catastrophe.

Despite Noah's parsimony of vision, the instruction "make yourself an ark" inevitably welcomes a world far larger than any manifest encompasses. The door need not be sealed tight. Recall that, in Genesis, the portal is closed from without. Mrs. Noah sometimes performs the argumentative role allotted to Cain, Abraham, and Moses in the Bible. Like her, we can refuse the closing of this door, and with it the seeming inevitability of losing a connection to what remains outside, lost to view. The very impersonality of the door closing in Genesis, an impersonality that requires Noah's unquestioning compliance, seems to call forth a proverbial sticking of one's foot in the door to hold it open. Noah knows this. Mrs. Noah acts on this knowledge. This tension shapes successive receptions of the story.

FIGURE 11. Lingering with the drowned. The dove and the raven, circa 1320–30, from *Holkham Bible,* British Library, London, Add. MS 47682, f. 8r. Copyright British Library Board. All Rights Reserved / Bridgeman Images.

Composed in accessible Norman French, the lavishly illustrated Holkham Bible (Figure 11) likely served as a teaching aid for a Dominican friar, assisting in the moral instruction of his elite audience. The images stage a panorama of biblical history, from Creation to doomsday. Noah is depicted in his ark releasing a raven and a dove. Below him swirl aquamarine waves, beautifully transparent. The corpses of a man, woman, and ox are suspended in the waters, while a dead horse rests upon a protruding rock—food for the raven. The human and animal bodies drifting through the ocean are in positions never possible on land, a weightless underwater dance. Through the sea drift sensually entwined corpses, elegant in their aqueous suspension, and all the while Noah looks resolutely forward, preoccupied by his avian business. What exactly does the image teach a friar to teach his audience? Noah is serene as he tends the birds and assesses the livability of the flooded world for those whom he has preserved. But suffering in the midst of catastrophe is unequally distributed. We are forced to look below the waters, to linger with the submerged.

Think again of the words of Abraham to God at the promised destruction of Sodom and Gomorrah: "Will you sweep away the righteous with the wicked?" Is everyone at the bottom of the sea in the Holkham Bible portrait wicked? The ox? The horse? Are we allowed to tarry over such questions? We could bear in mind that, in both Jewish tradition and the Chester play of Noah's Flood, Noah takes 120 years to complete his ark, hoping that, if he stretches the labor over such a long period, some of the doomed might repent. The Noah of the Chester play betrays a sympathy seldom seen in the biblical patriarch, a man usually content to search prosaically for olive branches while the vault of heaven and the abyss pour forth their waters. "My punishment is greater than I can bear" (Genesis 4:13). These are the words of Cain, the first in a long line of complainers against God's justice. Cain's declaration might also translate as "My sin is greater than I can bear," and maybe he means both: killing his highly favored brother and being exiled from community are unbearable. Either way, he protests his state to God and receives in return a mark that will preserve him. Cain is the first builder of cities, of those homes and churches and castles that in this illustration are overwhelmed by the waters on which Noah, his kin, and the animals float in peace. A lively world is stilled into death, corpses below churning sea, while an ark of the saved floats onward.[35]

In a fifteenth-century manuscript from Rouen of Augustine's *De civitate dei* that we will return to frequently in this book (Plate 5), the ark has room for Noah's family, green devils, and a unicorn. The boat is in the foreground, with the background vast and vibrantly blue. Behind the ark, a water wheel spins uselessly. Swimmers seek security in home, church, and castle, sinking structures built against the elements that now overwhelm them. Architectures built to preserve now perish. From this ark, you might say that the flood has a knack for narrative closure. Noah looks outward, forward, toward landfall, toward the future we inhabit as viewers. But, behind him, the water is awash with detritus. The newly formed sea of seas bobs with lost stories, animate in their ending. One floating corpse is fresh; another has gone gray. One uprooted tree possesses leaves, while another is a kind of arboreal cadaver. An ox swims; a dog drowns. Yet, within this mesh of shared immiseration, there are crows, ducks, and swans swimming as they always have. Blunt rocks indifferently protrude. The deep blues of this limned scene are stunning. It is hard to say whether we are supposed to feel the peace within the ark, the frustration of the swimmers who seek a place of rest, the inevitability of bodies and trees becoming flotsam. Only a bird like a raven can find much satisfaction in such a world, no matter how beautifully rendered. Something changes, perhaps, when we notice that, just above Noah's vessel and to the left, an emptied cradle floats by like some diminutive ark. Is it possible to see that cradle and *not* fill it with a story of impossible loss?

What would be revealed if we refused the god trick, refused Noah's line of vision and peered into the depths of the waters? In a harrowing thirteenth-century illustration of the deluge by William de Brailes, no ark appears, or waits in the periphery to be discovered (Plate 6). Scalding plumes gush from the heavens. Layers of the dead accumulate like sediments: the land animals, the beasts of the air, men and women. Preserved beneath the waves, differentiated by contour and line as they are engulfed by aquamarine, the dead retain the shape of their species even as they enter into a community of the drowned. Run time forward and we shall witness a slow decay, the loss of line and shape and the becoming of a general bio-zoo-mass—the "ooze" into which King Alonso in William Shakespeare's *The Tempest* says his son Ferdinand is "bedded," lost at sea and assumed to be drowned, and into which he says he shall leap to "seek him, . . . and with him lie there mudded."[36] But this image will not run forward, will not enable a forgetting of the dead. This illustration is part of a series of images that de Brailes created. What precedes is a vivid depiction of Noah's ark being loaded by an angel as the water already engulfs, and what follows is a rendering of the destruction of Sodom in which the faces of the damned are carefully portrayed. Here, in between, the exterminated demand examination: piles of faces, human and animal, layered in strata, but not exactly separate. No god trick here, but a perspective that absents the ark and meditates instead on what lies in the wake of its sailing to safety.

De Brailes provides no peace, no refuge, no floating vessel. *Anarky.* He paints what is missing from those contemporary renditions of a submerged London, Seattle, and New York as seen from the sky. In the wake of catastrophe, suffering is unequally distributed. This suffering binds humans to hares, falcons, pigs, ravens, dogs. The figures on top reach for those below, their bodies aligned in a downward vector, a postmortem embrace that is strangely touching, difficult to receive as mere allegory, and difficult not to feel as bedding, as mudding, an oozy invitation to inhabit an asphyxiating loss. Something here arcs the ages. This illustration makes visible what happens when we without protest or resistance surrender the world to submergence. De Brailles paints the flood without the ark. He reveals what unfolds beneath the overwhelming sea. No fish swim in peace, and no raven feasts on the dead. Instead we behold cadaverous strata and entanglement within annihilation, a community of those who perished together rather than a boat full of the conserved. And yet, all the faces of the dead seem so peaceful, almost as if the artist who paints those faces provides them with some order of compensatory consolation, as if they were merely asleep.

The disaster seems total. Nothing breaks the surface. The transport the story provides, from one world to another, from one covenant to another, fails to convince or to console. The rainbow pales. The flood comes to register as an attack not on the so-called unrighteous, but on the very "human-ambient thing without which people cannot remain people," a primordial act of environmental terror that "uses violence against the very air that groups breathe," the "air, the atmosphere—the primary media for life."[37] The creator, who breathed life into us all, engulfs the walking, talking clay he had sculpted and animated with a medium that stills that being, transforms the autonomic facticity of breathing into a reflex for dying. Sometimes, narrating the flood produces a compensatory outpouring of affect, of feeling, a reciprocal movement of energy that seeks to recognize, remark, buoy, or even revive all that has been lost. We sit open-mouthed. We breathe. Then comes the noise, the anguish and anger, the air in our lungs, a medium that animates this loss, this terror, this outrage.

Sympathetic Images

Artist Ellen O'Grady captures a vivid moment of such storytelling gone awry in her 2005 book of pictures and handwritten words, *Outside the Ark: An Artist's Journey in Occupied Palestine.* "When I was a little kid," she explains, "my favorite book was a Hallmark version of the Noah's Ark story." Her dream was to dwell comfortably within a family ark, a houseboat that was also a floating zoo. No matter how cold the rain outside, "inside the ark, all of us were warm and safe."[38] But this was Sunday school; everything changes.

Her teacher, Mrs. Graff, read the Noah's ark story aloud to her class. "When she came to the part about the floodwaters drying up," O'Grady writes, "she held the book open to the picture of the sturdy, gleaming ark surrounded after the flood by the lush green trees and colorful plants, all under the beautiful rainbow in the sky. The entire class was entranced except for Joel, the boy sitting beside me." Joel stares at the picture and then, suddenly, yells:

> "WHERE ARE ALL THE BODIES?!?"
>
> Our teacher looked puzzled and annoyed. She put her book down.
>
> "WHAT BODIES, JOEL?"
>
> Joel twisted in his chair. He squinted at the book in her lap, then looked around at all of us staring at him.
>
> "THE BODIES!" he cried. "WHERE ARE ALL THE BODIES OF THE PEOPLE AND THE ANIMALS THAT DIED IN THE FLOOD?!"
>
> Our teacher narrowed her eyes. The room was very quiet. Then in a gravelly, disapproving voice told Joel he was "a very rude boy."

Joel resists. Landfall and the rainbow fail to entrance. Joel, whose world is not to be contained within a finalizing rainbow—a boy whose name literally, ironically, affirms that God is God (*Yo'el* signifies "Yhwh is God")—refuses to be transported. Or, more correctly, there is something to the telling of this story, something to Mrs. Graff's well-intentioned reading aloud, that transports only too well, that works on the imaginative faculties of the little boy such that, when she turns the book around, holds it "open to the picture of the sturdy, gleaming ark surrounded after the flood by the lush green trees and colorful plants, all under the beautiful rainbow in the sky," the transfer from the time-bound linearity of words in their telling to the synoptic image of landfall appalls.

The reduction of the telling, which provokes a succession of nightmare images in Joel's imagination, to the good news of landfall provokes his grief, his outrage, his lament, and his question: "WHERE ARE ALL THE BODIES?" Joel indeed affirms, attends, objects. The ark acquires an objectal fixity, an expansiveness, that resists its opening or emplotting at the moment of disembarkation. Joel refuses the disappearance that the switch from words to an image replacing his own succession of images would allow. "As Joel's disquiet over the shiny, rainbow version of Noah's rescue narrative suggests, stories—tightly framed for time and space, and point of view—are convenient places for concealing bodies," observes Rob Nixon.[39] But Joel does not merely denounce this absence. He identifies the way the final image of landfall, with its "lush green trees and colorful plants," with its parade of cleansed animal bodies, exists quite precisely as the going missing of the drowned.

The explosion of Joel's words stands in strict relation to the vividness of this image that erases. But, so too, his question, his demand that "puzzles and annoys," signals the way the skeletal outline of the Genesis story produces, quasi-automatically, affectively charged counterimages in other media that this ark appears to complete. The rainbow is a shimmering weapon. The ark is a mixed-media archive whose opening, come landfall, figures also as disintegration, its wake littering with affective flotsam and jetsam (Figure 12).

"When our teacher continued with her story," writes O'Grady, "holding up for us that glorious rainbow in the book, I saw the bodies. Lifeless bodies lying across the weather beaten landscape. Some bodies lived in the safe and protected ark, while some bodies drowned in the holy flood. It was the first time I was aware that there can be a story behind a story. A story we try to hide." Because Mrs. Graff reads the story aloud; because the images in the book do not accord for Joel with the images in his mind; because Joel asks his question; because Mrs. Graff handles things badly; a girl recognizes something of the way in which stories hide other stories, hold them in abeyance. The artist this girl becomes draws them, supplementing both Noah's story and his ark and producing a series of images that seeks to visualize the bodies and lives that go missing in the representation of oc-

FIGURE 12. "Where are all the bodies?" Arks and the Price of Immunity. Ellen O'Grady, *Snowglobe Ark*, 2002. Mixed media on canvas, 91.4 × 121.9 cm. Copyright Ellen O'Grady.

cupied Palestine. Joel's interrogative leads O'Grady to wonder about what Noah actually beheld when he disembarked his little space of safety, and so what Noah might have omitted from the narrative sent forward into history: "Did he speak only about a rainbow high in the sky and remain silent about the things he saw in the water and on the ground?"

Truth can be a little colder when viewed from above or below the ark, as de Brailes shows us and as his inheritor O'Grady affirms. For a legacy of the Flood story, we want strong moments of demarcation, secure punctuation of change. People in previous centuries are assumed to be more pious, somehow colder when it comes to sympathetic relations with their fellow humans. Medieval people, we assume, would all think that those who perished in the deluge deserved their fate and did not give them a spare thought. Yet entanglement is difficult, intimacy vexing, compassion perennial. Despite an abiding love in literary and cultural history for sharp periodizations and

FIGURE 13. Uncertain sympathies and the ongoing Flood. *The Deluge,* tempera, gold, and silver on purple vellum, 23.5 x 31.75 cm. From the *Vienna Genesis,* early sixth century. Österreichische Nationalbibliothek, Vienna, fol. 3r. Courtesy of the Österreichische Nationalbibliothek.

catastrophism, a complicated relationship of viewer to the drowned has always been possible.

In the *Vienna Genesis,* a sixth-century illustrated codex of the Septuagint from Syria and the very first illustrated Bible to survive to this day, those who have not been admitted to a pyramid-shaped ark struggle against the rising waters and cling to what meager stone has not yet been swallowed by the sea (Figure 13). In this early illustration of the Flood, the point of view imagined is one never offered in Genesis, from the outside looking at the barred vessel, the perspective of those left to the waters. We cannot be sure whether we are supposed to feel a sympathetic inclination toward the men and women who fight the rising tide, or take pleasure in divine justice enacted.

Why choose?

What matters about such immersive illustrations is that a potential for compassion exists, for suffering-with, even if it comes coded as affective misreading, as if we became the all too companionate dog of Altman's image: all misplaced devotion and a mutiny of needless passion. Sympathy's arc offers a connection that overleaps resignation to loss, affirming other futures to forge. As a bulwark against fatalism, sympathy makes it difficult to take seriously, in all its endless iterations, the grim and reflexive bracing for catastrophe. Always, always disappointing, as Maurice Blanchot affirms, apocalypse begins to operate (as Greg Garrard has shown) in a comic mode that exults in the fact that even cataclysm fails to offer an obliterating totality, an imperative without exception, a story that cannot be modified.[40] Complacency and resignation are discarded for endurance, for struggle, for strange community, for the resurfacing of hope.

Fast forward? Rewind? It's hard to know when we are in terms of the story of refuge, this oozy chronology of compassion, the wake of this ark become arkive. For now, we take our cue from the late fourteenth century. In the poem "Cleanness," universal Flood is God's vengeance for human women mating with fallen angels, engendering giants. The creator of all things angrily announces the cleansing from the world of all living flesh: "Fro þe burne to þe best, fro bryddez to fyschez; / Al schal doun and be ded and dryuen out of erþe" ("From the men to the beasts, from birds to fish / All shall drown and be dead and driven out of the earth").[41] Noah is instructed to build a "mancioun" [a house that is a boat] with dwellings inside "for wylde and for tame": halls and pens, a structure to secure his family and the seeds of a new world (311). The coming waters will, God emphasizes, "quelle alle þat is quik with quauende flodez" (324), total destruction of all life on Earth except for the few souls within the ark (331–32). At the structure's completion and Noah's closing of the ark in clay that seals it against the flood, that keeps the air in as if the ark stood as some collective holding of breath, with its clayed contours some sympathetic or concentric extension of the individual bodies of the clay-born flesh within (345–46), God unleashes a terrible tempest, while from the abyss burst scalding streams. The poet narrates the deluge through scenes not imagined in Genesis, vignettes of communities caught in catastrophe, striving together to survive:

> Water wylger ay wax, wonez þat stryede,
> Hurled into vch hous, hent þat þer dowelled.
> Fyrst feng to þe fly3t alle þat fle my3t;
> Vuche burde with her barne þe byggyng þay leuez
> And bowed to þe hy3 bonk þer brentest hit wern
> And heterly to þe hy3e hyllez þay haled on faste.

Torrents towered higher, toppled down houses,
Rushed raging into rooms where poor souls took refuge.
All fled at the first shock whose feet would serve them;
Women with children rushed along their way
To banks and bluffs that stood above water.
All made for the uplands, where hills were highest. (375–80)

Doré's engraving has nothing on this, with its recurring impulse to commemoration. As the waves surge and every place of safety recedes, humans flock to mountaintops, united in their shared desire to remain alive with the hares, deer, badgers, and bulls that rush there: "All cried for care to the King of Heaven" (393). The beasts raise their eyes skyward and in despair roar. Every creature pleads for its life in its own way. As the tide engulfs those on the last remaining ground, friends and lovers embrace each other, determined to endure their final moments together: "Luf lokez to luf and his leue takez / For to ende alle at onez and for euer twynne" ("Love looks to love and takes leave, to perish together and forever separated" [400–401]). The sea rises. The high places on which they breathed their last become an ocean floor littered with the dead. Because the hatches of the ark are closed, these deaths have no witness—except us. The author of "Cleanness" places us not inside the vessel of salvation with Noah, but among those abandoned to its exterior, ensuring their stories will not, like their bodies, vanish beneath the scouring surge.

Sometimes catastrophe obliterates. Sometimes other kinds of narratives linger or emerge anchored to its debris: fleeting moments of community and unexpected embrace, destroyed but not unarchived.

Anarky (Can We Turn Catastrophe Down?)

Noah was obedient to God. He built the ark and never questioned that the waters must arrive, that all outside must drown. Robert Coover's experimental short story "The Brother" offers a stream of consciousness account of what it is like to be Noah's sibling. His labor is required to build the folly of an ark rising on family farmland, but the brother is given no information about nearing storms. When the rains begin, he finds the ark he helped to construct locked against him. His entreaties for refuge are met with silence from Noah, who looks down at his brother from the deck: "Right then right while I'm still talkin he turns around and he goes back in the boat and I can't hardly believe it me his brother but he don't come back out."[42] The bonds of family mean nothing to this cold patriarch, this steadfast origin of a world that begins again. The waters rise, and the brother's words are cut off as the last hill in the world goes underwater.

Like most Noahs, Coover's ark pilot seems to believe that the world unfolds in a downward turning, a drown-ward turning, better things arriving only after a foundational apocalypse wipes away what has been, all relations to that era obliterated, forgotten. Catastrophe is, quite literally, that downward turn (*kata*/"down" + *strophē*/"turning," from *strephein,* "to turn"). But can we turn catastrophe down? Or can we at least not be resigned to stories about small communities safe inside their arks? Like resignation, forgetting requires constant work. No doubt we must desist in attempting to abstract ourselves or float above the drowning world; we must learn immersion, must learn how to swim, as Steve Mentz has argued.[43] That's life in the waterlogged Anthropocene. But can swimming seem too heroic, too masculine? It's how Beowulf and Brecca prove themselves in youth worthy of great destiny. It also seems too solitary an endeavor, an embrace of a water-world in which it is impossible to keep anyone but yourself afloat. We remain cautious of the way inundation can figure as a kind of rebirth, the Anthropocene as a return to swampy, amniotic prehistory that replays theological allegories of flood as prefiguration of baptismal waters. J. G. Ballard's 1962 novel *Drowned World* delights in obliterative individualism, its final message hammered out on a ruined wall by a man using the butt of a gun, a message with no reader but us. We do not find the scene as thrilling as Ballard intended. Beowulf was heroic not for swimming best, nor for being at sea alone, but because he refused to abandon his competitor to drown during a storm.

And what about those who cannot swim? What about those barred from the ark? What about a community of the unrelated, or at least of affinities that exceed near family? In the Chester play of Noah's flood, a drama that reenacts the Flood story for a city audience, Noah's wife refuses to board the boat and imagines an affective gathering of those about to drown. She knows that what is demanded of women in the ark is not necessarily a way of life to be preserved.[44] She remains with her drinking buddies, the good gossips, as the waters rise. The song of these women as the waves engulf them resounds as powerfully as the holy hymn sung later on the ark as it lifts above their drowned bodies. *Sinken* or *swimmen*. We might take some solace from the fact that *swim* in Middle English means to float and to glide the waves. "Swim" describes what boats, humans, dolphins, and ducks do in the water. If they all swim in unexpected, perhaps even unwanted togetherness, what communities might arise? Who might join them? What modes of life may be imagined outside arks?

To engineer an ark is to perform despair and desire at once: despondency for an Earth not to be saved, confidence after disaster in a better home to come. Yet that "better" conveys a narrowness, begging the question of *better for whom*. An ark is not launched in the expectation of a more survivable or commodious world for all. Selective and small, its spaces are closed against a cosmic diversity of humans and nonhumans, conserving meager community against general ruin. Yet the same ark that reduces boisterous lives to sortable, storable units and attempts to regulate the plots of the stories it conveys will inevitably open up the imagination. Creatures, elements, storms, oceans, climate, time, and every other force and object placed at the exterior of the ark push back.

To Joel's question of "where are all the bodies?," Doré offers some vivid answers: the bodies are everywhere. We opened this chapter with his engraving *The Deluge,* depicting the Flood's last survivors, tigers and humans well on their way to becoming corpses, the forgotten of history. Though often printed as a frontispiece, that image is the middle of a sequence of three illustrating the progress of the world-purging cataclysm. *The World Destroyed by Water* shows an earlier stage of the event, as the waters surge but have yet to overwhelm (Figure 14). Two rocky outcrops are covered with struggling, naked humans. Their twisting forms are echoed by the dead branches of two tall trees, one of which has collapsed under the weight of those desperate for a high place of safety as the relentless tide advances. Huge snakes, hippopotami, a leopard, and a frantic elephant join this writhing mass on the dwindling islands while an oceanic swell bears down upon their refuge. A man atop a horse is sucked beneath the waters, and a body is broken against a jagged rock. The scene is littered with those already dead. Meanwhile, dark in the background, Noah's monumental ark sails away. The elephant is open-mouthed, his roar launched toward that receding and indifferent vessel. The caption reads: "And the Lord said: I will destroy man whom I have

FIGURE 14. Disaster's community. Gustave Doré, *The World Destroyed by Water*, 1866. From *La Sainte Bible selon la Vulgate. Traduction nouvelle avec les dessins de Gustave Doré*. v. 1, A. Mame et fils, Tours (1866). Bibliothèque nationale de France, département Réserve des livres rares, SMITH LESOUEF R-6283.

created from the face of the earth; both man, and beast, and the creeping things, and the fowls of the air; for it repenteth me that I have made them" (Genesis 6:7).

Next comes *The Deluge* (Figure 6), the scene of the last rock on

FIGURE 15. The bodies are everywhere. The Flood does not cleanse. Catastrophe wipes nothing clean. Gustave Doré, *The Dove Sent Forth from the Ark,* 1866. From *La Sainte Bible selon la Vulgate. Traduction nouvelle avec les dessins de Gustave Doré.* v. 1, A. Mame et fils, Tours (1866). Bibliothèque nationale de France, département Réserve des livres rares, SMITH LESOUEF R-6283.

Earth with which this chapter began. Underneath that image are the lines in which "every living substance of was destroyed which was upon the face of the ground. . . . Noah only remained alive, and they that were with him in the ark" (Genesis 7:23). Yet, as we have seen, *The Deluge* has no Noah, no ark: that boat departed long before, leaving us to witness, on the dwindling promontory, the tiger, its cubs, the men and the women and children being engulfed by the waters that will obliterate their story. We are onlookers and historians, however unwilling, of something the Bible does not want to narrate.

Last comes *The Dove Sent Forth from the Ark* (Figure 15). The background consists of the massive vessel dry upon Ararat, a radiance shimmering behind, a promise of the near arrival of rainbow. In the middle portion of the image, a white dove glides above the last of the waters, olive branch tightly clasped. And the bodies are everywhere: clusters of the dead twisted into postmortem embrace below the newly landlocked ark; cadavers in unlikely positions atop the stones and slopes of the middle ground, a sort of parentheses around the gliding dove; naked corpses thick on the terrain around the receding waters, their positions mimicking the paths that the deluge must have taken as it drained back into the abyss, a flood plain traced not by stone and sediment, but by flesh. Naked, muscular, beautiful, these bodies do not look as if they have spent months under the waves. Were it not for their positions they might almost present as if engaged in some kind of dance. A story is being spoken here, one with too much life, a story very different from what is about to disembark from that monumental vessel—a story that, with Doré, we wish not to reduce.

It is interesting to note that these three images constitute the totality of Doré's visualization of the Flood. At no point does he attempt to imagine what it must have been like to be inside its pitched walls as the tempest raged. Doré contemplated the catastrophe only from the vessel's exterior. We, however, know that we cannot hesitate any longer. Like it or not, we are now going to have to board the ark.

CHAPTER 4

Inside the Ark

The loading of the ark must have been a spectacular affair.

Artists who set out to depict the scene are presented with a stark choice of perspective: reduce the scale of en-arkment to something human and intimate and render the ark an impossible household, or illustrate a boisterous multitude of animals processing into Noah's handiwork, their destination overwhelmed by the throng. Those who choose the latter have long exulted in minutely detailing a global herd that intermixes giraffes and aardvarks, peacocks and pachyderms, the alphabetic ebullience of a zoo without cages and pens (at least, not yet: those enclosures await inside). Clouds of birds will travel overhead, everything moving toward an ark that must be immense but struggles to compete for attention with the roiled ocean of beasts headed toward its door. Such images are powerful, and they can be cheerful, but they also cannot help but resonate both with and against those described in the previous chapter, in which a distant ark has sailed and the foreground is crowded with those about to drown.

Jan Brueghel the Elder crowds so many species into his painting that the eyes can find no point on which to alight (Plate 7). We have come upon a moment of rest and rallying. The various animals congregate as they arrive. Eddies of creaturely life-form as the line catches itself up. Arboreal dwellers and perchers find themselves in momentary proximity, hosted by a tree that one of the monkeys has decided to climb and perhaps claim. A pair of lions circle one another in a snarl. One leopard nuzzles the other, who languidly swipes at the bull brought up short. These big cats flank the solo stallion who anchors the painting—a horse, who, it must be said, is going the wrong way. Lost mate? Second thoughts? The stallion's antagonistic vector reverses the forward movement of the animals that fulfills divine command. He must tread carefully so as not to step on the field mice making their way arkward. Within this press of beasts, Noah's own family turns back to review the scene. They are, perhaps, wearily in the midst of conveying their own belongings, but such is the frenzied tedium of en-arkment's temporality. In the shifting rates of movement, the kinetic push and pull of bodies, the improvised choreography of animal lives, we witness a nascent communal vectoring that cannot endure. This mess of creatures is a gathering into the shared space of those who are in line, headed toward a distant enclosure.

Brueghel's ark is almost lost in the background, obscured by a tree filled with exotic birds and newly arrived monkeys. The vessel must be huge, and the ramp for boarding the animals is certainly long (squint closely and you can make out giraffes and elephants on the plank), but the dull brown structure is overwhelmed by animal life, only some of which seem keen to board. The vessel is far enough away that the question of how to house the animals once inside can be delayed. But not forever. Mrs. Noah stands next to her husband in the painting's midground, basket of belongings on her head, more possessions in her arms. She gazes at the drove of lions, leopards, horses, deer, turkeys, camels, ostriches, hedgehogs, porcupines, turtles, chipmunks, goats, rabbits, and who knows what else with an expression that traverses the ages: "How is this ever going to work?"[1]

Containing Multitudes: Force and Forms

The mess of beasts and birds processing up the gangplank of the ark seems already to anticipate arrival and disembarkation. But skipping ahead to landfall closes down the question of how an ark actually functions as a vessel of conservation, perhaps because nothing could be more vexing than attempting to figure out how to organize the interior to sort and keep safe its future occupants, how to load the animals, and how to keep the beasts alive once they are within the confines of the hull. The ark will be long at sea. Short of suspended animation, a creaturely tumult seems bound to erupt. And does every animal merit admission, even fish, whales, mice, fleas, and dragons? The ark quickly becomes a problem of cross-species hospitality, commensality, and community.

Animals are not easy to welcome. Animals are not easy to confine.

The philosopher Jacques Derrida wondered whether the very word "animal" could in fact be a kind of ark, struggling to house the multitudinous forms of life it is supposed to accommodate. In the lecture notes collected into *The Animal That Therefore I Am,* Derrida describes "the animal" as "a catch-all concept" that confines a "vast encampment" within a "strict enclosure," a forcing together of "all the living things that man does not recognize as his fellows, his neighbors, or his brothers."[2] The word collects all these creatures

> in spite of the infinite space that separates the lizard from the dog, the protozoon from the dolphin, the shark from the lamb, the parrot from the chimpanzee, the camel from the eagle, the squirrel from the tiger, the elephant from the cat, the ant from the silkworm, or the hedgehog from the echidna. I interrupt my nomenclature and call Noah to help insure that no one gets left on the ark. (34)

The category "animal" is, like the ark itself, a coordinating concept that requires a great deal of force to corral a world of difference.[3] Lizards, sharks, parrots and lambs would of their own accord never be collected into commonality, but "animal" and "ark" are devices that bring them together all the same, catch-all taxonomic structures full of the violence of accommodation. In the viva voce of the lecture hall, Derrida calls on Noah to perform something like reparations. All apologies, Noah will have to board the ark, search it out room by room and recess by recess, politely knock on doors, listen hard, tune into the particularities of the creatures that may linger. This lively attentiveness is required to dismantle the vessel, to drain both ark and animal of their universalizing ability to contain, collect, compel. The process imagined here amounts to a reverse taxonomy, an unnaming or undoing of categories, and then an encounter with the great variety of beings subjected to diminution and incarceration through human ordering practices. This is what the canceling or repealing of a covenant looks like: a time machine that folds human-animal history back in order to make alternative futures possible. When Noah returns, when he ventures aboard like some rescue team seeking survivors collected but not released, the ark and its animal cargo will disaggregate into a plethora of unlike beings. A fractured, multiple, aporetic "we" will then have to learn names specific to the existence of each historically particular being in the breadth and contradiction of their multiple differences.[4]

Plenitude and multiplicity are difficult to welcome, even as semantic containment devices like "animal" and "ark" have never actually worked as non-self-contradictory concepts.[5] To think like an ark is to enter into a process that complicates, vibrates, and opens structures built to control, transport, and conserve. As we have punned, arks list. What kind of vessel could ever hold lizards, dogs, protozoa, dolphins, sharks, lambs, parrots, chimpanzees, camels, eagles, squirrels, tigers, elephants, cats, ants, silkworms, hedgehogs, and echidnas in their pairs or sevens?

A convergence of linguistic histories, the rather odd looking modern English noun "ark" denotes primarily the structure of preservation that Noah built against catastrophic, anthropogenic climate change. The Old English noun *ærc* anglicizes the Latin *arca,* a term that for Roman writers like Juvenal, Horace, Pliny, and Cicero named a box for keeping precious things, especially money, secure from the perturbations of the world. An ark is not a ship so much as a safety deposit box, a literal archive. The noun therefore makes a certain good sense for designating Noah's handiwork. We will also recognize the term "ark" as continuing to signify a preservational chest, since the Ten Commandments were stored in a container that English translations of the Bible call the "ark of the covenant" (despite the fact that the Hebrew noun is wholly unrelated to anything involving Noah). In the wake of the Latin Vulgate Bible's use of *arca* to designate the vessel built against the Flood, the world filled up with arks *(arches, Archen, arcas).* Versions of the term have found their way into numerous contemporary languages, even non-Romance tongues. *Arca* in turn stretches back in time to Greek *archē,* designating beginnings, origins, and the documentary wellspring of civic rule, a coffer for keeping records and stories safe, a singular source for authority. The word "ark" is a quirky little archive that has been sailing the linguistic sea for millennia, a chest full of hopes, a box of possibilities, as well as a device for protecting family, food, and animals.

Yet the Hebrew noun that names his cataclysm-enduring craft is *tevah.* Used only one other time in Torah, where it designates the basket of reeds launched to preserve the infant Moses from death at Pharoah's hands, *tevah* may have little to do with the ark-chests that its translation into Latin generated. Tied to the flight of the first unaccompanied minor, a flight that ends in unanticipated compassion and care (Exodus 2:2), *tevah* both escapes and exceeds the semantic field that the Vulgate Bible and its inheritors program. *Tevah* is an uncertain movement toward refuge. Rather than the realization in impressive timber of some monumental blueprint, Noah's ark may well "originally" have been envisioned as a work of bricolage, patched together from what was near at hand. Nicolas Pelham imagines the origins of the ark by imagining its construction as an intensely local project:

> Noah would not have had time to travel up the Euphrates and over the mountains to bring cedars from Lebanon. The hardwoods of the Flemish masters were a fantasy. Noah would have fashioned his boat from the trees that grew locally—palms, willows, and tamarisks. Pomegranate wands, prized for their flexibility, came from the orchards a day's march north, beyond Hilla. Chiddem, natural pitch used for waterproofing, oozed to the surface in Hit, a short journey up the Euphrates.[6]

Arks can be imperial fortresses that sail the ages, or they can be unpretentious and provincial, like this putative first ark, a coracle or basket betraying no hint of the naval monstrosities to come. Such minor arks might prove more hospitable, admitting to their modest communities many who never would have found their way aboard a singular, foundational, rupture-establishing version. Arks, like floods, arrive in innumerable forms. When viewed across the centuries, they constitute a disparate flotilla.

The medieval etymologist Isidore of Seville connected the ark to memory, mystery, preservation, and exclusion:

> A strongbox *[arca]* is so called because it prevents *[arcere]* and prohibits seeing inside. From this term also derive "archives" *[arcivum*; i.e., *archivum]*, and "mystery" *[arcanum]*, that is, a secret, from which other people are "fended off" *[arcere]*.[7]

From the start, the stories contained in the strongbox could not harmonize: sons of God and daughters of men, giants, inebriated nudity, slavery and abasement, a threat within a promise, a movement from cross-species companionship to animal sacrifice and consumption. Noah's arkive is a whirlpool of heterogeneous narratives, filled with dissonance and counterstories, a word or chest or basket preserving all kinds of half-glimpsed tales and alternative plots. If we realized better the complexity of the Noah narrative and its long history of augmentation and reinvention, we might not be so resigned to climate change, to allowing the world to drown.

Embarkation (preservation through design) sets into motion a far-reaching process, an environing that, by the decision of limits, veers. An ark or archive attempts to capture a certain motion and still its energy into storable units that by the act of capture exceed it. Arks attempt to fix and control. Yet an arkive is not a static thing, but a hopeful-hateful resignation *and* invitation to movement that Derrida calls "survivance," the living on, over, and above the act of capture.[8] An ark is not a container that secures its contents against the elements, stilling them to preserve them as if they no longer existed in time. It is a spur to future-making and story-forging that reactivates a past it both closes and opens.

An ark is a chest crammed full of stories.

The Worshipful Company of Shipwrights

In 1947, Mr. George Wigham Richardson, prime warden of London's Worshipful Company of Shipwrights, had a decision to make. It was customary for the warden of the company, which traces its founding to the year 1199, to celebrate the conclusion of his term in office in "some benevolent or other manner."[9] What celebration was appropriate in a country some two short years on from VE day ("victory in Europe") and less still from VJ day ("victory over Japan"), a country in which rationing would not end until 1954, a country in the grips of a housing crisis precipitated by the Great Depression and then exacerbated by the German Blitz? What might the Worshipful Company of Shipwrights contribute to the spirit of national recovery? Writing for enthusiast readers of the still extant weekly *The Model Engineer,* a reporter we know only by the pen name Jason (but what a name for a reporter of things nautical) states that "the manner chosen . . . was unique as well as benevolent." Mr. Wigham Richardson "opened a competition among craftsmen and apprentices in shipbuilding yards and aircraft works for the best model of Noah's Ark" (731). The competition was open to individuals or teams, but as Jason offers, "the work had to be under the blessing and perhaps patronage of the competitors' employers because materials and advice could be given and accepted," as well as books, for purposes of research, and tools. The rules were "few and somewhat elastic" and "valuable prizes were of-

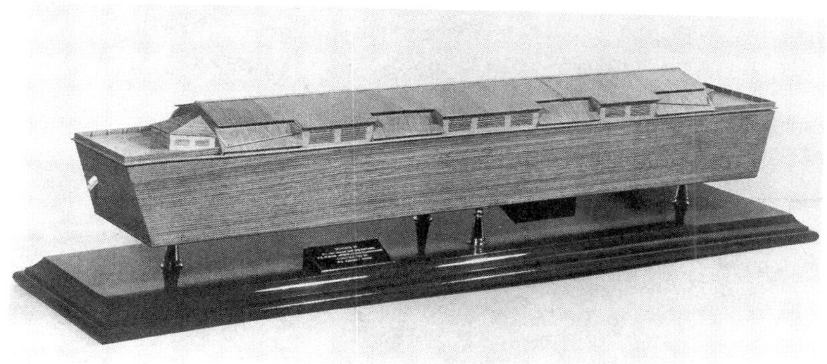

FIGURE 16. Winning model of Noah's ark design competition, 1947. "The Ark" (Inv 081). Model made of cedar by M. G. Warman, joiner, from designs by W. L. Ash, senior ship draughtsman, and K. G. McBride, apprentice ship draughtsman, all of Messrs J. Samuel White, Cowes, as an entry to the competition held at The Worshipful Company of Shipwrights' great Exhibition in 1947. Photograph by Sandra Hildreth-Brown. Courtesy of the Shipwrights' Company, London.

fered." The competition attracted eighteen entries, all of which were mounted to baseboards, but that was where similarity ceased.

The winning model was executed by Messrs. Ash, McBride, and Warman from Messrs. J. Samuel White & Co. Ltd., of Cowes, the Isle of Wight, and became the property of the Company, where it remains on display to this day (Figure 16). What most impressed the judges is that part of the roof can be "removed to show internal arrangements" on this three-story barge (Figure 17). In a further virtuoso display of woodworking skill, Messrs. Ash, McBride and Warman, crafted one particularly intricate vented section of the roof that lifts off to reveal an interior fireplace at which Noah and family might sit to warm themselves during the flood or at which they might make sacrifices to the divine (Figure 18). Of the seventeen other arks, we know very little. They remain, for the most part, adrift: passed on through families; beached in attics; landed in estate sales; conserved in the back rooms of libraries and local societies; lost to all those places where storied matter of diminished significance is left to pool.[10]

In an interview with Jason, Mr. Wigham Richardson explains that "his objective in opening this competition was the encouragement of craftsmanship among the young workers in the shipyards and the aircraft factories" (731). The selection of Noah's ark as a "prototype"

FIGURE 17. Total design concepts. Winning model of Noah's ark, *Life* Magazine (1947): roof removed. Hans Wild/The LIFE Picture Collection.

was not, he explains, a religious matter, and it should not be inferred that the company authorizes any one design as more or less authentic. Instead, the choice of Noah's ark derives from the company's coat of arms, which is surmounted by an ark with a motto that reads: "Within the Ark, Safe forever." The ark stands as a surety for the quality and longevity of the craftsmanship of the shipwrights, a security further

FIGURE 18. Accessorizing ark interiors. Winning model of Noah's ark, *Life* Magazine (1947): removable vented roof detail. Hans Wild/The LIFE Picture Collection.

underwritten by the Christian tradition of figuring the church itself as the ark, as in the oft-repeated phrase, "The Ark of Safety."[11]

The sketchiness of the ark's design in the Book of Genesis presented competitors with a series of challenges in terms of design, materials, and technique, and thus an opportunity to bring to the public's attention skills crucial to the nation's postwar recovery. As Jason observes, the universally high quality of the entries coming "from every corner of the country from shipyards and aircraft factories alike . . . augured well for the future of shipwrightery" (731), and so should be regarded as a huge success. To guide them, competitors were provided with a series of instructions. Jason expresses his readers' gratitude as well as his own surprise and delight that such a busy man as Mr. Whigham Richardson "had found time to study the legends of the Flood and the building of Noah's Ark" in order to craft the directions. All models were to be "48 in. long, 4.8 in. deep from main-deck to the keel, and 8 in. beam" (731). Beyond these dimensions, the design and materials for the vessels were left to the ingenuity, imagination, and design-expertise of the competitors, although the judges would be mindful of how attentive their designs might be to the perceived needs of Noah and family. Mr. Richardson and Jason both agree with the speculation that the "Ancient Hebrews had little desire to go anywhere," so propulsion was unnecessary. "A big raft," they felt, would be "sufficient to form a foundation for houses, stables and barns for a large farm. Nor was comfort to be unduly emphasised, but rather the question of safety" (732). Competitors were given a great degree of latitude as to how to answer these perceived needs. One rule was of particular importance in this regard and is worth quoting in its entirety:

> Rule 12: As so little is known of the design of "The Ark," it has been decided to give the widest discretion in this matter to the craftsmen themselves, but, for the sake of uniformity a few details were laid down concerning limits of size, well seasoned wood, option of solid, laminated or timbered and planked hull; and it was left to the individual artists' taste to decide about the top storey or deck-house, together with the inclusion of the window. All competitors were advised to read Genesis: Chapters vi and vii. (731)

Thus advised, each team found itself inducted not merely into the rules of the competition, but into a millenia-old conversation about the design of Noah's ark, to which the ark-building competition of 1947 was merely the latest chapter.

Noah's ark had long been the literal-figurative stage property of medieval guilds all over Europe, which took ownership of the story in cycle plays, frequently with the express aim of ensuring that everyone knew that shipbuilding was a craft of particular expertise, not to be undertaken by just anyone.[12] Pictorial traditions in northern and southern Europe differed as to whether Noah built the ark alone, learning the craft of shipwrighting solely by way of divine instruction, or had the help of a team of skilled craftsmen.[13] The cycle continues today in all manner of ark replicas currently completed or under construction or in the exaptation of the ark as a structure for ecological conservation, or as a more general form for secured collection. It is no coincidence that Noah's ark stands, as Susan Stewart remarks, for "the archetypal collection," and Noah for the figure of the collector or "god's broker."[14] Noah as archivist ensures the safety of creation, selects for the time to come, makes the future possible. Personing Noah in 1947, Mr. Wigham Richardson does something similar: he ensures the "future of shipwrightery," the place of craft in the United Kingdom's postwar recovery. Stewart observes that arks are not about nostalgia, but anticipation predicated on the forgetting of what came before. Seventeen model arks, after all, go missing. Only the eighteenth was conserved. And yet, even as the labor of making an ark shall be written off, taken as a given to the future it orients us toward, all that handicraft is quite precisely how we think our way inside. The labor of making constitutes the embodied choreography of thinking like an ark.

Let's follow the advice outlined in rule 12, then, and retrace the process that might have led to the winning design.

Questions in Genesis

When they opened their Bibles, Messrs. Ash, McBride, and Warman and their competitors may or may not have realized they had become part of a conversation about the way an ethics of refuge plays out as technical questions of design and craftsmanship.[15] The shape and interior they decide for the ark produce hierarchies of species, gender, race, and community. As they reread Genesis, the urge to take notes or to start sketching might have overtaken them round about verse 14 of chapter 6:

> Make thee an ark of gopher wood; rooms shalt thou make in the ark, and shalt pitch it within and without with pitch. And this

> is the fashion which thou shalt make it of: The length of the ark shall be three hundred cubits, the breadth of it fifty cubits, and the height of it thirty cubits. A window shalt thou make to the ark, and in a cubit shalt thou finish it above; and the door of the ark shalt thou set in the side thereof; with lower, second, and third stories shalt thou make it. (Genesis 6: 14–16, King James Version[16])

These terse instructions raise more questions than they provide answers. And, as if it were not challenging enough to load the animals into one conceptual category, getting them all inside a physical structure seems a yet harder travail. The story of the flood in Genesis is captivating, complicated—and sparse. It begs so much wondering about how the ark actually worked as an environed and autonomous system, as well as an effective transport.

If the shipwrights' brief seemed impossibly challenging, our model engineers might have sought consolation in considering all the questions generated by their fellow readers of Genesis and readers of readers of Genesis across the ages. Here are just a few, taken mainly from medieval Christian, Islamic, and Jewish sources, almost all of them possessing counterparts through the long centuries of the ark's sailing. These same questions haunt the launch of every spaceship departing Earth in speculative fiction, every biodome or terrarium in climate fiction.

Did Noah attempt to welcome anyone into the ark besides his wife, three sons, and daughters-in-law? How much room did they need? Considering human size is not constant over time and various cultures have their own systems of measurement, how big is a cubit exactly, and how capacious the ark? Did God shut the door from the outside or was the vessel entirely self-sufficient? Was the ark a box, basket, chest, pyramid, sarcophagus, house, galleon, coracle, cog, or some yet-to-be-designed vessel? How many levels did the below decks possess? How was the interior organized? Could a world full of animals really fit within? Were carnivores, herbivores, and people allotted separate quarters to keep the peace? Were clean beasts allowed to mingle with the unclean? How did Noah know which animals were clean and unclean, if he did not have access to the law of Moses? Once the ark was full of paired creatures, where did all the manure go? If the waste was shoveled into a well or bilge at the bottom of the ship, how was it then removed, especially if the ark had been sealed from the outside? What about other kinds of rubbish produced aboard, through cooking and industry? Did the vessel have ventilation? Did its interior reek? Was there illumination below decks, perhaps from a skylight or a luminous stone? Was sex allowed aboard the ark? If it was not, did some creatures (like the raven or Ham) do it anyway, and were they punished as a consequence? Were children born aboard ship? Sons of Noah not recorded in the bible? Baby lambs to feed the lions? Or did all animals subsist for a while on vegetables and hay, chickpeas and dates? How did the system for delivering food and water work, considering the small size of the crew? How much daily labor was required to maintain the ark-system? Were there helpful machines: grinding mills, kitchens with smokeless ovens, a water delivery apparatus? Did Noah and his family ever sleep, considering the number of animals that feed only at night? Were there demons on the ark? Did the devil find his way inside? During the flood did aquatic animals enjoy swimming through submerged cities? Or did everything within the scalding floodwaters perish, so that Noah had to keep fish, whales, seabirds and even shoots and seeds inside his vessel? Were unicorns brought into the ark? Dragons? How about insects, worms, and other vermin or creeping things that can spontaneously generate? What of animals unclassifiable as belonging to a single gender, or singular creatures like the Phoenix? Did Noah's vessel contain everything the world now holds, source and archive for Earth 2.0? Did those who perished in the Flood send stories forward not included in the ark, perhaps by engraving stone? Was the ocean that covered the world filled with the corpses of the drowned? Did Noah and his family feel a sense of loss for the world against which they had built their home? What was it like for them to find themselves inside the ark as the door slammed shut, storms raging and water swirling and each space of exterior safety and refuge overwhelmed? How did Noah's family feel about being saved while their friends and community were damned? If Noah employed workers other than his sons, did they realize they would not be setting foot inside the vessel once the storms began? Did Noah delay the construction of the ark hoping to preserve a wider collective? Was the ark built in secret? If neighbors saw the structure rising, did they scoff? Did they try to sabotage it? Hijack it? Did Noah preach repentance or provide warnings of the impending ruin? How could there be giants both before the flood and afterward, since God scours all life from the Earth? Did one of these giants strike a bargain with Noah or become a stowaway? Why was the world just as evil after the deluge as before? Were the Flood and the ark all for nothing?

In some traditions, the posing of these kinds of questions has functioned as an autoimmunizing strategy that sees off naysayers or scoffers, protecting the integrity of Genesis by inoculating the commentary tradition against detractors.[17] Yet the generative questions keep on coming. The sheer magnitude of what we do not know, of what Genesis leaves to the imagination, testifies that the way to build an ark is to decide what counts as a valued form of life by and through the structuring of space.

The winning ark from 1947—complete with roof that lifts off to give a sense of the interior, door that turns ramp amidships, and fireplace to warm the crew and fuel their devotions—visualizes what Genesis does not. Some questions about the ark are answered by the specificity of its design; others are pushed beyond the limits of the sensible; still more are simply closed off by a wall of thought to ensure that they do not overwhelm the design for a working vessel. As "Jason" summarizes, "The Ancient Hebrews had little desire to go anywhere. No propulsion was needed, just a big raft, sufficient to form a foundation for houses, stables and barns for a large farm. It's a question of safety" (732). Rational to its core, this ark rules many questions unthinkable. What's needed, apparently, is merely a temporary respite for our Robinson Crusoe or Swiss Family Robinson, threatened as they are by a transitory housing crisis. Once they land, come rainbow, all they need is enough to start their farm all over again in the same place. The world contracts to this single household and their domestic animals. Once the crisis passes, things shall return to normal. And yet, this winning ark, still on display at the Company of Shipwrights, is only one of eighteen different entries, one of which was disqualified because, when tested, it sank, on account of its cheery log-cabin and over-accessorized design. Who knows now what the others looked like? How did they answer all these questions in Genesis? The winning ark is but one among a still proliferating flotilla of arks, each of which answers the questions Genesis poses differently, and those answers decide the limits of what we understand by community, citizenship, and refuge.

Climate Control: Mapping the Ark

The phrase "climate control" speaks to the positing of a semisealed environment. In the lexicon of the philosopher Peter Sloterdijk, tuned as he is to the coimbrication of forms of media and design with forms of life, the phrase resonates with the way so much of human sociality takes up the problem of "morpho-immunological constructs," problems of shelter and sustainability but also the drawing down of boundaries, the technical problems posed by coming up with a livable inside, and the ethical and political burdens entailed by the need to draw so many lines. For Sloterdijk, the privileged figure for these issues is the bubble or sphere, of which Noah's ark constitutes a powerful, precedent-setting example.[18] "Living in spheres," Sloterdijk writes, "means inhabiting a shared subtlety" (45), a subtlety that stories of deluge traumatize.[19] Floods pop bubbles; floods inundate spheres; water destroys terrestrial life by voiding respiration. This insight augurs what Sloterdijk hopes might become a material-semiotic building block for a "radical resonance" between beings that would demonstrate the way "real subjectivity consists of two or more parties" (53). Never one being, animation always requires two or several. How then may we construct mutually sustaining bubbles or arks that own the air they put to use and attempt to sustain others by and through their exhalations? How to deploy the bubbles we inhabit in ways that enable our companions also to bubble, to maintain refuge? Questions of living together keyed to practical matters of design constitute the essence of every ark.

Fast-forwarding to a rainbow will not forever allay the problem of how a globe's worth of creatures fit within a single container, no matter how expansive the ark's frame, nor answer how those lives were managed once inside their pens. What about animals not mentioned in the Bible but encountered in the New World, Australia, the fossil record? How did fauna flourishing on remote islands arrive at those shores if the Flood drowned the entire Earth? In his *Anatomy of Melancholy* (1621), Robert Burton famously asked about "the thousand strange birds and beasts proper to *America* alone," creatures unreferenced in Greek, Latin, or Hebrew chronicles "and yet as differing from our European animals, as an egg and chestnut."[20] Burton wondered how such beasts could have wandered to distant shores after their dispersal at Mount Ararat. If they were transported by migrating humans, then why were wolves and snakes and other organisms that do only harm brought against all sense along with them?

Faced with problems like the flourishing of noxious and predatory animals in near-unreachable lands, the early Christian theologian and philosopher Augustine of Hippo (d. 430) did not worry overly much about the literalness of the Genesis account, which for him offered a way of understanding a providential plan at work in history more than a strictly factual narrative of survival in the face of universal catastrophe. Augustine considered the ark to be symbolic and real at once, a vessel built by Noah at the command of God but also (and just as importantly) a figure for the church built by the twelve apostles at the command of their messiah. To the question of animals encountered on isolated islands, Augustine argued that beasts that reproduce through sexual pairing (unlike, say, frogs, which can spontaneously generate) arrived on distant shores not because they could swim such distances or were placed there by ancient humans during the post-deluge diaspora, but because they were likely created in those regions after the cataclysm. The multitude of animals loaded onto the ark were not conserved strictly for the renewal of their species, Augustine explains, but sheltered in its bosom to prefigure the variety of human nations to be saved one day by the Christian church.[21] The bishop of Hippo cautioned against too strict a reading of Genesis, as if its sparse prose were an archive that did not desire interpretive supplement through pious engagement. The ark has as many possibilities for accommodation as it possesses rooms.

Which is not to say that the number of rooms or even floors to the ark has ever been obvious to interpreters. Genesis states that the ark possesses a tripartite architecture, but that division does not necessarily mean that it held only three floors. The early church father Origen influentially argues in his *Homilies on Genesis and Exodus* that God's command would result in a pyramidal ark possessed of five levels: two decks for the lowest section, then three decks rising above those (since "stories" can consist of multiple decks).[22] He rejects naysayers who claim that the ark was barely large enough for four elephants by observing that Moses, author of Genesis, lived in Egypt and so used "the geometrical cubit which was six times larger than the common cubit" as his standard of measure. Supersizing the ark means that there is more than enough space.[23] Origen has it that each deck would be further subdivided into rooms (which he called "nests") to keep the wild and tame animals segregated (73). The lowest portion of the boat would be reserved for waste, "so that neither the animals themselves, nor especially the men, be plagued by the stench of excrement" (73). Provisions would be kept just above this hold, and must include meat for the carnivorous beasts and fodder for the herbivores. On the next level are the "wild beasts and fierce beasts or serpents," while one floor above are the "stables for domesticated animals" (74). Because humans possess reason and are superior to any other creature, Noah and his family dwell at the pinnacle, just beneath the pyramid's point (an excellent shape, Origen adds, for ensuring that the rain glides down the sloped sides rather than pools). God closes the door behind everyone after the vessel is fully loaded. The whole structure offers an allegory for a hierarchy of virtue within the Christian church, with the beasts of the lowest levels figuring those "whose fierce raging the charm of faith has not tamed," the domesticated creatures standing for faithful simplicity, all the way up to "Noah himself, whose name means rest or righteous, who is Christ Jesus" (79).

In chapter 3 of book 1 of his *Antiquities,* the Roman Jewish historian Flavius Josephus was certain the ark contained not five levels, but four, "with firm walls, and a roof; and was braced with cross beams: so that it could not be any way drowned, or over-born by the violence of the water."[24] Augustine, though, was just as convinced there were only three levels, and in time most arks came to possess that number. Yet competing schematics flourished, for who can resist the invitation to fashion a multiplicity of self-contained worlds that the ark offers? Dual versions of a multilevel ark were frequently added to the margins of Ranulf Higden's fourteenth-century *Polychronicon,* a world chronicle that relates, among many other things, how Noah built the vessel to preserve the world. In a manuscript from the fifteenth century (Figure 19), one diagram depicts the structure rising from a *sentina* (hold for bilge water and sewage) to a floor divided between the *apotheca* (storehouse) and *stercoraria* (privy), then to the friendly and fierce animals (i.e., the tame and wild). The topmost deck houses humans and birds. Although this ark looks like it has five levels, the cross section is probably meant to convey a three-story ark, with the bilge not counting against that number. Next to this fairly condensed delineation is a second cross-sectioned ark, far more expansive, mapping an alternative view of how the interior of the vessel might have been arranged. This one starts with a *sentina* full of foul liquids at the bottom; then a *stercoraria,* presumably with toilets draining into the lower hold; next a wide space for preserving provisions for the humans and animals *(apotecaria)*; floors for gentle *(amicium)* and fierce *(inimicium)* beasts, providentially separated; and finally humans sharing their accustomed space with the flocks of birds. The finely articulated structure of this ark belies the fact that it was unlikely ever to have been seaworthy.

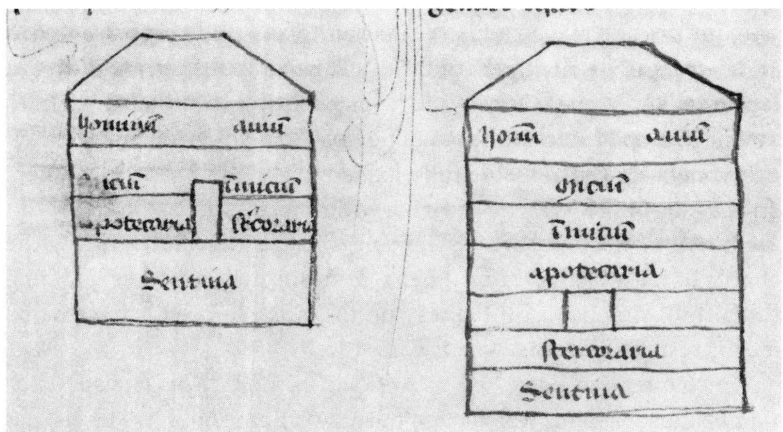

FIGURE 19. Sorting the world: Imagining the ark's inside. Ink drawings of Noah's ark and decorated initials with pen-flourishing in book 2., mid-fifteenth century, from British Library, London, Harley 1728, f. 47rBL Harley 1728, f. 47r.

Origen's triangular approach to thinking like an ark is repeated centuries later by the scribe of Marston MS 242 (circa 1466). This genealogical roll traces human descent from Adam and Eve (the couple are depicted within a rondel, being tempted in Eden by an anthropomorphic snake), as well as the descent of the English monarchy from Brutus, the exiled Trojan who supposedly gave his name to newfound Britain. A detailed map of the globe divides the world into its three known continents just above two trapezoidal diagrams of Noah's ark, wide at the bottom and narrow on top (Figure 20). The simplest has three levels and rises from "the place of filthe" through a bifurcated storage level up to a tripartite deck that segregates "tame" beasts, humans and birds, and wild and noxious animals. A rubric to the side names this schematic as the ark according to Augustine. Next to this diagram is placed an alternative vision, that of "Joseph the Jue" (the historian Josephus). This four-level ark contains all the same sortings of bodies and supplies into discrete compartments, but stacks them one atop the other rather than allowing horizontal contiguity.

Some arks proliferate living space for their enclosed inhabitants, while others take delight in reducing the interior to a bare minimum. The medieval historian, theologian, and monk Bede thought the ark needed only three floors and assigned one to Noah, his family,

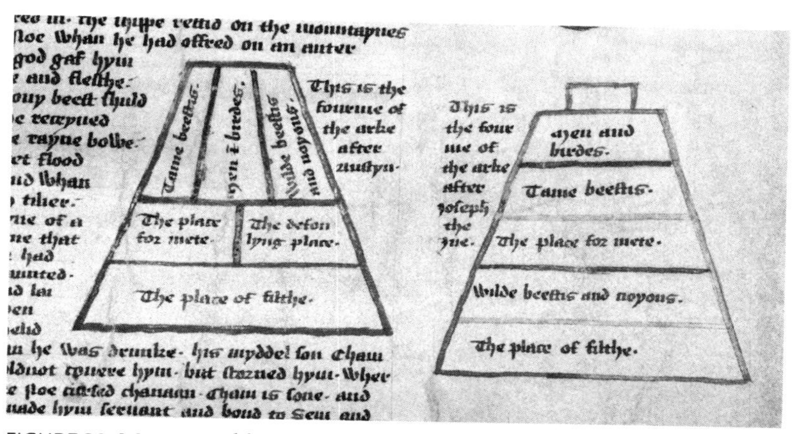

FIGURE 20. More possible arks. Genealogical roll chronicle, a chronicle of biblical world history and the genealogy of the kings of England, circa 1466–67, England. Manuscript on parchment roll, composed of 15 membranes, fol. 1 (detail). Parchment, 330 mm × 9.76 m. Beinecke Rare Book and Manuscript Library, Marston MS 242. Yale University Beinecke Rare Book and Manuscript Library Open Access.

and the birds, the second to the clean animals, and the bottom to the unclean beasts.[25] Bede likely took this structure from Augustine: a triple-deck vessel that is fully functional yet fully symbolic. The three stories serve in Augustine's account to sort the animals into their accommodations and preserve the food for the voyage. This trilevel architecture also figures the church to come: with room for the circumcised and the uncircumcised (Christians and Jews) in the two main levels, level three allows the allegory to expand to comprehend the descendants of the three sons of Noah (i.e., potentially members from the whole world, beyond Christian and Jew, members of the Table of Nations in Genesis 10, of which the three are the progenitors). Augustine agrees with Jerome that everyone outside this ark-church is doomed to perish, even as he allows God to re-create some animals on distant islands later. The vessel possesses at once room for all the beings to be saved at one specific point in time and all the humans to be saved throughout all time. The levels of the ark can stand for anything appropriate ("in harmony with the rule of faith"), observes Augustine, and so its three decks also correspond to the three virtues of faith, hope, and charity, as well as the three ascending states of chaste marriage, chaste widowhood, and unsullied virginity. Ark-space is wide:

> That all kinds of animals are enclosed in the ark; as the church contains all nations, which was also set forth in the vessel shown to Peter. That clean and unclean animals are in the ark; as good and bad take part in the sacraments of the church. That the clean are in sevens, and the unclean in twos; not because the bad are fewer than the good, but because the good preserve the unity of the Spirit in the bond of peace; and the Spirit is spoken of in Scripture as having a sevenfold operation.[26]

The ark is also the cross, for Augustine: its door a symbol of the wound of Jesus upon that cross (out of which the sacraments flowed, just like the saved creatures exiting from that door). And also, Augustine adds, the ark's dimensions figure the proportions of the human body. And, oh yes, the ark is also the sarcophagus in which the crucified Jesus was placed, emerging on the third day full of life.[27] Even Noah's inebriation after the Flood is an allegory for the suffering of Christ to come (*Contra Faustum* 12.23), not an embarrassing lapse of self-control. Augustine's ark is crammed with story, provided the tales are "in harmony with the rule of faith," which Augustine's allegorical program ensures.

The ark has been for many thinkers a vessel for precipitating theological understanding, rather than an object of precise historical detail. Argument becomes design, and design the instrument of the ontology it expresses. Such arks veer into pure metaphor (literal as well as figurative transport devices) that aspires to communicate possibility rather than fact and chronicle, binding the past to the future. The gates of such a trope will always remain open. Sometimes, however, an ark remains an ark. Not every interpreter of Genesis is willing to widen its narrative structure through allegory or be content, as in midrash, to embrace an argumentative, accumulative approach to explicating the text. Although a strictly literal mode of interpreting the Bible would have seemed absurd to writers like Augustine, fundamentalist readings eventually came to dominate, culminating in efforts to make the structure real in the present as a kind of exorbitant, ocular proof of salvation. Ken Ham's Ark Encounter, a three-deck evangelical theme park in Kentucky, is only the latest version of this impulse to rebuild the ark in authentic form, either through a detailed diagram or a CGI spectacle or a building that welcomes pilgrims from around the world. Impressive as its exterior is and as extensive as its insides are, once you exit the Ark Encounter, you quickly discover that it is all frontage, quite literally an allegorical facade, earthbound concrete and air conditioning units visible from the rear. The climate of such an ark is all about control.[28]

Allegorical programs, ancient to contemporary, respond to the questions inherent to Genesis that lead differently attuned ark thinkers to posit actual, functional designs, or to enter their arks into the design competitions of their historical moment. Questions of capacity, of accommodation, of the meaning of shelter—humane or immiserating?—confound the literal and figurative as the ark becomes a transport device for exploring the relation between design and figuration itself. Thus, for Augustine, the constricted capaciousness of the ark comes to prefigure the Christian church, seeding the figure that gives the Worshipful Company of Shipwrights their emblem of security, their "Ark of Safety." But, so also, the openness of the ark as a structure that raises the prospect of accommodation adequate to all renders the ark a device for encountering and processing difference, for arranging heterogeneity into order and display: doves with ravens, lions with lambs.

In the seventeenth century, the ark lent its name to all manner of cabinets of curiosity, nascent museums, collections, and emporiums. In 1644, diarist John Evelyn visited a "shop [in Paris] called Noah's Ark, where are sold all curiosities, natural or artificial, Indian, or European, for luxury or use." The home of the famed gardeners and collectors, the Tradescant family, in Lambeth was known as "the Ark." In 1639, Oxford scholar Thomas Harrison named his "ingenious and complex system of storing and indexing notes from across erudite languages" an "ark of studies" *(arca studiorum).* Citing these examples, Simon Schaffer observes that the ark "thus became a byword for systems of information management more generally, the ideal type of an archive."[29] The possibility that the ark could serve as an ever-proliferating storage device, a space of encounter with phenomena yet to be determined or understood, comes premised on the rootedness of the collector, ar*k*ivist, or Noah in a particular time, place, and emerging form of rationality. The very hospitality of the ark, its ability to produce climates sufficient to all the messy entities it houses, necessarily fueled debates about the nature of its design and limits.

Expansive Immiseration: The Cold Calculus of John Wilkins

The seventeenth-century English polymath and clergyman John Wilkins trusted that, whereas human imagination runs toward excess, the divine favors minimalism, especially in design. Writing in his 1668 *Essay Towards a Real Character, and a Philosophical Language* against what he called "some hereticks of old, and some Atheistical scoffers in these later times" who insist it was "utterly impossible for this Ark to hold so vast a multitude of animals," Wilkins attempted to diagram precisely how a planetful of creatures could have been conserved within a meticulously engineered vessel.[30] A founder of the Royal Society, Wilkins believed the Bible to offer a factual and scientific record, immediately comprehensible in its clarity. Following the French monk and mathematician Johannes Buteo (*Arca Noe,* 1554), he argued that, in handing Noah a blueprint for the structure, God prevented the patriarch from constructing a vessel that would have been too large for its intended purpose, since humans seldom comprehend economy. The ark becomes the solution to a problem solved through mathematics, especially a parsimonious geometry. The building of the vessel offers a general rule for understanding language and order, which explains the appearance of the Noah story in what is otherwise a lengthy book on taxonomy. As Wilkins puts it, "he that looks upon the Starrs, as they are confusedly scattered up and down in the Firmament, will think them to be . . . innumerable, but when . . . they . . . are reduced into particular constellations . . . it appears that . . . there are but a few thousand" (162). The same logic of pattern, he reasons, should be applied to the number and kinds of animals aboard the ark.[31]

Admittedly, though, Wilkins cheats by making an assertion that has enabled the launching of many other scientific arks, such as Ham's monumental salvational structure in Kentucky. A plethora of animals that we now regard as constituting separate species, Wilkins insists, are in fact descended from a very limited number of progenitors stored within the original ark.[32] This presupposition conveniently reduces Noah's cargo, stowing vast animal variety within a limited quantity of creaturely designations, the very logic that, as Derrida argued, enables the term "animal" to do its collectivizing work. The total number of species actually preserved on the ark, Wilkins writes, is "much fewer then [*sic*] is commonly imagined," maybe a hundred sorts of beasts, and two hundred of birds (162). Whereas Buteo had welcomed all manner of fantastical creatures aboard his ark, Wilkins denies these animals passage because they are fabulous. Dragons "might possibly be some monstrous production," but they do not constitute a species in nature, and so cannot be admitted (162). Fitting varied animals into smaller designations, compressing what Derrida described as the "infinite space that separates" creaturely types into the confinement of tidy designations, greatly reduces the ark's cargo. Wilkins reduces the numbers still further by remarking that marine dwellers like seals, whales, and dolphins would have been left to the water.

Yet compression of categories and excluding sea life and flying serpents frees up only so much room. When they arrive in their twos and sevens, three hundred types of animals and birds still demand expansive quarters, as well as a great deal of food. Wilkins knows that Noah built an ark at divine command that extends "three hundred cubits in length, fifty in breadth, and thirty in height" (162). Given that a cubit is typically understood as the length of a human forearm, these numbers simply do not afford enough space for everything to fit. Wilkins refuses to cheat, as he believes writers like Origen did in the third century, by using larger cubits. Origen argued that Moses was raised in Egypt, where a geometrical cubit six times more expansive than the traditional measure had been in use. This "Egyptian cubit" enabled Origen's five-floored colossal pyramid of an ark to loom. Wilkins, like Buteo before him, is intent on keeping the ark a modestly sized chest, and so rejects the "long cubit" as excessive. Look to the giant Goliath, he writes, a monster of "six cubits and span." If the vaster versions of the cubit invoked by writers who imagine a prodigious ark were true, then the Philistine warrior would be fifty-four feet tall, and his head "must needs be too heavy for David to carry" (163). Wilkins refuses the similar tactic of ascribing, as Augustine did, a greater size to antediluvian humans like Adam and Noah. Their larger bodies would increase the size of the traditional cubit (since it is based on the body), and therefore the extensiveness of the ark. But if humans used to be bigger, Wilkins reasons, then so were animals, so the problem of creaturely accommodation would not be solved through a universal increase in scale. A cubit, he insists, must be eighteen inches, and any calculation of the ark's volume must be built on that measure. So, how to fit so many animals into so constricted a space?

First, Wilkins asserts, it is important to create a precise floor plan. He turns to Genesis (which he believes Moses wrote) for the details of the shipbuilding. Notice, though, how quickly he moves from biblical text to facts "agreed upon as most probable"—there is no ark without supplementation:

> It is plain in the description which Moses gives of the Ark, that it was divided into three stories, each of them of ten cubits or fifteen foot high, besides one cubit allowed for the declivity of the roof in the upper story. And 'tis agreed upon as most probable, that the lower story was assigned to contein all the species of beasts, the middle story for their food, and the upper story, in one part of it, for the birds and their food, and the other part for Noah, his family and utensils. (163)

The tripartite structure Wilkins so finely articulates is based only loosely on Genesis, a narrative that contains no details of how to inhabit the ark that Noah constructs. The blueprint that God bestows is quite vague, mentioning only dimensions in cubits, the necessity of three levels of some kind, and the existence of a roof, window, and door (6:15). The only other details that Genesis provides are the materials for construction: in a frequent English translation, "gopher wood" (whatever that is) and pitch to make the thing watertight. Although the vessel as envisioned by Wilkins might seem cramped, he assures us that "each of these stories was of a sufficient capacity for the conteining all those things to which they are assigned" (163). In the end, it all comes down to how you sort the animals.

To accomplish his reckoning, Wilkins first classifies beasts according to the food "wherewith they are usually nourished" (164), sorting each creature collected by Noah into one of three general categories in a convenient table (Figure 21). The space that separates the camel from the rooster and the ewe is traversed by the organization of all animal bodies into overarching types. A Beef (a Cow) is any beast that feeds on hay, while the category Sheep is for all "beasts feeding on fruit, roots, and insects." A Wolf designates every kind of carnivorous beast, from lions to dogs. Thus confined into an overarching type, each animal is converted into biomass in order to allot it a stall, and so these categories function also as units of measure. Two Lions, for example, are the equivalent of four Wolves in size, and are therefore granted a

Beaſts Feeding on Hay.				Beaſts feeding on Fruits, Roots and Inſects.				Carnivorous Beaſts			
Number.	Name.	Proportion to Beeves.	Breadth of Stalls feet	Number.	Name	Proportion to Sheep.	Breadth of the Stalls. feet	Number.	Name	Proportion to Wolves.	Breadth of their Stalls. feet
2	Horſe	3	20	2	Hog	4		2	Lion	4	10
2	Aſſe	2	12	2	Baboon	2		2	Beare	4	10
2	Camel	4	20	2	Ape	2		2	Tigre	3	8
2	Elephant	8	36	2	Monky			2	Pard	3	8
7	Bull	7	40	2	Sloth			2	Ounce	2	6
7	Urus	7	40	2	Porcupine	7	20	2	Cat	2	6
7	Biſons	7	40	2	Hedghog			2	Civet-cat		
7	Bonaſus	7	40	2	Squirril			2	Ferret		
7	Buffalo	7	40	2	Ginny pig			2	Polecat		
7	Sheep	1		2	Ant-bear	2		2	Martin		
7	Stepciſeros	1	30	2	Armadilla	2		2	Stoat	3	6
7	Broad-tail	1		2	Tortoiſe	2		2	Weeſle		
7	Goat	1						2	Caſtor		
7	Stone-buck	1	30			21	20	2	Otter		
7	Shamois	1						2	Dog	2	6
7	Antilope	1						2	Wolf	2	6
7	Elke	7	30					2	Fox		
7	Hart	4	30					2	Badger	2	6
7	Buck	3	20					2	Jackall		
7	Rein-deer	3	20					2	Caraguya		
7	Roe	2	36								
2	Rhinocerot	8									
2	Camelopard	6	30								
2	Hare										
2	Rabbet	2. Sheep.									
2	Marmotto										
		92	514							27	72

FIGURE 21. Expansive immiseration: tabular "enumeration" of animals by diet in John Wilkins, *Essay Towards a Real Character, and a Philosophical Language* (London: Gellibrand, 1668), 164. Bayerische Staatsbibliothek München, Res/2 Graph. 47, p. 164, urn:nbn:de:bvb:12-bsb10867019-0.

pen ten feet in breadth. A pair of Elephants, equal to eight Cows, earn a capacious compartment of thirty-six feet, while seven "Antilope" combine to make one Cow and must share a thirty-foot-wide living space with seven each of Goats, Stone-bucks, and "Shamois." All animals designated as Sheep, from Hogs and Baboons to Armadillos and Hedgehogs, inhabit a twenty-foot-wide enclosure together. Nearly all the fauna classified as Wolves, on the other hand, merit separate living quarters, for obvious reasons. Serpents and Lizards are assumed to dwell in "the Drein or Sink of the Ark," three or four feet beneath the stalls. Insects, Rats, Mice, and Moles are free to scurry and buzz as they wish. Not wanted on the voyage are "mongrels" like the Mule (165), for which there is no room aboard the vessel.

Humans are not part of Wilkins's tally, but it is interesting to note that, if they were, they would have entered the ark as Sheep but departed as Wolves, since God authorizes them to consume meat only after the Flood, as part of the rainbow-sealed covenant. To head off the inevitable "Cavils" of the doubters, Wilkins is willing to entertain that "rapacious" beasts ate flesh even while on board the ark (unlike some who argued that carnivores dined on hay while at sea). He calculates necessary food supplies with care. If five Wolves devour one Sheep daily, he computes, that means five Sheep will become food every twenty-four hours. By Wilkins's tally, an additional 1,825 "meat-sheep" must be stowed aboard the ship for the sustenance of the predatory beasts (165).[33] In accomplishing his animal calculus, Wilkins thought through the possibilities of both "fair Stalls or Cabins as may be abundantly sufficient for them in any kind of posture, either standing or lying or turning themselves," as well as granting animals only the minimal space required to sustain life during the voyage ("stow'd close together," as animals were transported in sea voyages at Wilkins's time). He opted for the former, and created a massive floor plan (Figure 22) to demonstrate scientifically how Noah comfortably preserved every kind of animal during the Flood. Much like the winning entry in the competition organized by the Worshipful Company of Shipwrights, this ark is essentially a three-story floating rectangle with no keel and a flat bottom, since the vessel is required only to float, not to traverse distance.

For Wilkins, ark thinking offers compelling evidence of a rationality in design that is more than human. God is the architect, Noah the builder. Just as the ark's detractors overestimate the number of animals that had to be brought aboard, Wilkins feels that, left to his own devices, Noah would have "engendered a building infinitely greater than was necessary." His ark would have listed, sunk, or been lost at sea. Or its accommodations would have been so out of proportion to the needs of its inhabitants as to result in either starvation or glut. It is the nature of the human mind, Wilkins offers, "to wildly exaggerate objects" (168), causing all manner of irrational errors. Parsimony is not only good economics; it is divine. Wilkins's mathematics come premised on the way arrangements of space inside the ark would alter as the carnivores ate their way through the flocks of sheep that served as food. His reduction of each individual animal to its biomass, to its relation to a food chain, offers a principle of equivalence that enables his computation. Over the course of the ark's voyage, the sheep eat

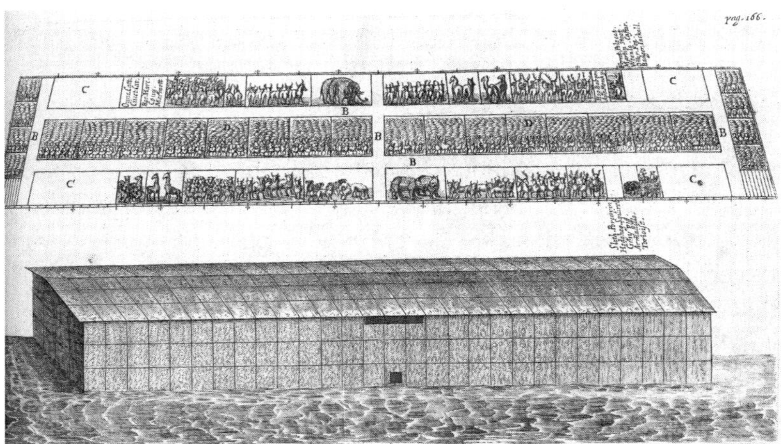

FIGURE 22. Model ark. From John Wilkins, *Essay Towards a Real Character, and a Philosophical Language* (London: Gellibrand, 1668). Wellcome Collection, Wing W2196.

the fodder, their numbers diminish as they are eaten, and the amount of manure increases. Internal arrangements of space change as the functional requirements of this sealed ark alter.

Wilkins's ark thinking enables others to posit that the ark itself is the origin of all architecture, since it is the first human-made building that orders its world. In an essay called "Noah's Ark," art and architectural historian Hubert Damisch identifies Wilkins's calculus as a key early source text for functionalist approaches to architecture, or what he calls "building in relation to matter," predating the advent of modernist design techniques.[34] Searching Denis Diderot and Jean Le Rond's 1751 *Encyclopédie, ou dictionnaire raisonné des sciences, des arts et des métiers* for a robust Enlightenment-era engagement with the history of architecture, Damisch ventures that the entry worth reading is not the short one on the subject composed by celebrated architect Jean François Blondel, but the entry on "Ark" written by theologian Abbé Edmé-François Mallet. An attentive reader of Wilkins, Abbé Mallet manages to provide in his entry "an authentically functionalist approach" to architecture, one that details how to construct a space whose use changes over time, a space that must accommodate all manner of beings: how to feed and water them; how to care for them; and how to manage their waste.[35] With its divine blueprint for a floating building and its imminent weathering of an announced catastrophe, Genesis becomes the first architectural treatise, a discipline that therefore finds its origin in the waters of the flood and their questions of accommodation and environing. Putting the ark back into architecture enables Damisch to recognize that "catastrophe takes its place at the beginning of the tale" (22), not midway or at its end. Architecture, he declares, "could only find its place *after* the flood—or rather in its stead" (23). Architecture, or ark-building, sets in motion an awareness of system and interconnection per se, of the way a building or structure exists as a set of environmental functions that may prove hospitable, progressive, welcoming, or lethal.

Although he does not quite say it, Damisch seems to suggest that, for all the quest to discover the perfect ark, we should instead surrender the depleting hope that one day the art of building and the science of dwelling will vanquish risk, failure, catastrophe, and flood. As the story of Noah's ark offers, accepting disaster as the setting for emergence of the dimensions of survival signals the way in which—for all its drawing down of boundaries, for all the closing of the door of the ark or the limits of a building—the very structure of the ark and of architecture necessitates an open inquiry into structure and world-ordering. The ark, as we have seen, stands always as both origin and expression, allegory and rhetoric, a zoo-biopolitical crux or blueprint whose performance and actualization decide everything. The ark's calculus is the *arche* in architecture.[36]

But only if you forget people. Samuel Pepys, who was secretary of the English Navy, sponsor of the Worshipful Company of Shipwright's rivals, and a longtime admirer of Wilkins, observes that "Noah's Ark must needs be made of some extraordinary timber and plank that remain good after having been an hundred years in building, whereas our thirty new ships are some of them rotten within less than five."[37] With a customary irony, Pepys cannot refrain from enjoying a joke both at the ark's figural and the Navy's all too literal expense: "the providential vessel" he quips, must have "been preternaturally resistant to decay," given the sloth of shipbuilders. Pepys also rejects the idea that the ark was the first ship or the origin of human construction projects. It is not possible, he argues, to sync naval history to Genesis on account of the myriad different designs for ships all over the world, each arising from the particular needs and conditions of their builders. Were the ark truly the first ship, moreover, how would Noah and family have found qualified "carpenters and caulkers?"[38] More profoundly, Pepys finds the very idea of building a ship for the "preserving of one little family . . . contrary to all humane practice in like cases of distresses." The story violates his sense of the benevolence of his fellows and runs contrary to the humane response he witnessed firsthand when Londoners responded to the Great Fire of 1666 and the wreck of the *Gloucester* on the Humber in 1682. Pepys finds it difficult to imagine that anyone would agree to "this means of safety enjoyed by so few persons, and oxen and asses, suffering the universality of mankind to perish without contention to share in it."[39] The prospect of a particular, familial refuge premised on the destruction of the "universality of mankind" he finds intolerable. The serene lack of feeling to the ark is alien to him. Pepys writes all of this while a shareholder in the Royal Adventurers into Africa, where his business investments profited from a trade in enslaved men and women.

Although Wilkins does not dwell on day-to-day living within the ark, his mathematization of the interior does not offer an inviting refuge. Someone has to feed those 1,825 meat-Sheep to the Wolves. Someone has to transport the hay and vegetables to the Beefs and Sheep. Someone must muck out the stalls, dispose of what remains of the Sheep the Wolves consume. All the manure has to go somewhere. The single window and door that Wilkins grants his construction hardly constitute a sufficient ventilation system. What is it like to inhabit such a minutely managed space while floating so long in a saltwater world? Do the people aboard possess any freedom at all, or are they as relentlessly managed as the animals under their care? Building an ark is a fraught process, launching into the future all kinds of unintended consequences. Very little of what Wilkins confines within his meticulously delineated vessel is actually contained within Genesis. Nor does Wilkins wonder about those left outside. He also does not appear to have understood that the logistical ark thinking in which he was engaged offers a blueprint for ships in which humans would be reduced to livestock, enabling a transatlantic trade in humans in which some of those incarcerated belowdeck would hurl themselves into the sea rather than remain captive to the kinds of accommodation his mathematics enabled.[40]

The air within this ark is sucked from the lungs of the drowned.

From Ararat to Middle Passage: Hold, Wake, Undercommons

If we follow Simon Gikandi's aim to read "the figure of the black" as always "occupying an essential and constitutive role in the construct of the interiority of modernity," we might see that the very project of an idealized ark, of a perfectly regulated container, comes premised on the reduction of life to the brute calculus of a murderous sense of accommodation.[41] When founded upon violence against Black bodies, the ark becomes the vessel of an ideology that will someday be named white supremacy. That ark in turn too easily becomes a nation; too easily forgets the terror that unfolds in the prison of its hold, the histories that will companion its beginning again, whether at Ararat or in the Americas. Wilkins's foundation-ark was easy to repurpose into a slave ship, a container ship for living cargo, and marks the beginning of a general science of logistics that will found enduringly present antagonisms. That coincidence might be repressed, but elsewhere in the archive to which this ark belongs, awareness of this complicity returns.[42]

Juxtapose Wilkins's detailed ark with the interior of the ship named the *Brookes*. Pictured "with slaves stowed" when it was published in 1789 by William Elford for the Society for Effecting the Abolition of the Slave Trade, the image multiplied and circulated internationally (Figure 23). The *Brookes* makes visible the murderous, immiserating reality of Wilkins's ark thinking.[43] Accompanying notes include the interior dimensions of the *Brookes*, nominal tonnage, number of seamen aboard, and detailed calculations as to the room allowed to the 351 men, 127 women, 90 boys, and 41 girls whom its owners have stolen:

> To the Men 6 feet by 1 foot 4 inches
> Women 5 feet 10 in. by 1 foot 4 in.
> Boys 5 feet 1 in. by 1 foot 2 in.
> Girls 4 feet 6 in. by 1 foot.[44]

As the notes explain with a degree of forensic mathematical clarity that belies the horror of the inventory, the number of enslaved persons that the ship could have carried should come to 470, but the actual number listed aboard the *Brookes* was 609. As a consequence, "the men therefore, instead of lying on their backs, were placed, as is usual, in full ships, on their sides or on each other. In which last

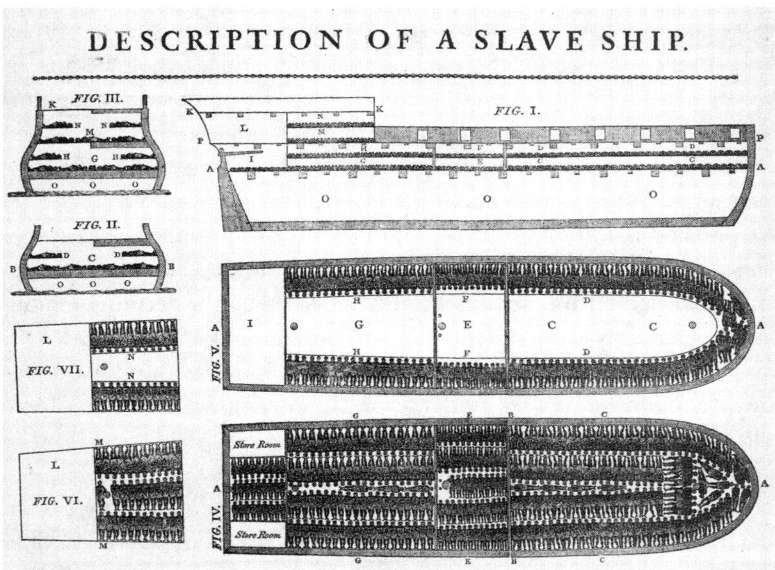

FIGURE 23. The ark and the Middle Passage. Description of a slave ship, 1789, London. Printed by James Phillips, George-yard, Lombard-street, 1 sheet: illustration, 51 × 64 cm. Beinecke Rare Book and Manuscript Library, Folio BrSides By6 1789. Yale University Beinecke Rare Book and Manuscript Library Open Access.

situation they are not infrequently found dead in the morning." The account describes the distress, injury, and suffering this "allowance of room" inflicts; the way exercise is reduced to a grim parody with the "men-slaves . . . being made to jump in their chains," a practice named "by friends of the trade . . . *dancing*." At which point, the account breaks off to opine that "to persons unacquainted with the mode of carrying on this system of trading in human flesh, these plans and sections will appear . . . a fiction." Surely, the reality they describe could not be real. The account imagines the likes of the heretical scoffer or denialist against whom Wilkins deployed his arithmetic to prove the facticity of the ark as described in Genesis. But now that same order of rhetorical device is deployed to make the case for abolition. Or, more correctly, numbers and measurements are not enough. They do not communicate the intensity of the suffering. So the account takes its readers and viewers inside the ship in the company of a fictive surgeon who fails to bring any relief or care. With the heat, close confinement, and lack of air, "our fellow-creatures" suffer fluxes and fevers, such that "the deck that is the floor of their rooms" is "so covered with blood and mucus . . . that it resembled a slaughter-house." The writer of the account confesses that he himself choked on the air and was almost overcome, vicariously asking us all to breathe that same atmosphere, inhabit the same noxious bubble.[45]

"Scaled inequalities" is the phrase Hortense Spillers uses in her classic essay "Mama's Baby, Papa's Maybe" to describe the calculations planned for the *Brookes* and documented by the account, a monstrous economy that underwrites "the dehumanizing, ungendering, and defacing project of African persons."[46] Spillers adduces a document containing further advice from the owner of the *Brookes,* who offers that "five females be reckoned as four males, and three boys or girls as equal to two grown persons," testifying to the fungibility of bodies become a quantified, commodified mass of human labor power. Such scaled inequalities recall Wilkins's calculations of the number of sheep necessary to feed the carnivores aboard the ark. They testify also to the way the slave ship's economy extends that of the ark by suspending all the designations of personhood (naming, gender, generation), deploying a foundational violence to rewrite human beings as fungible units of exchange. "Those African persons in the 'Middle Passage,'" observes Spillers, "were literally suspended in the 'oceanic,' if we think of the latter in its Freudian orientation as an analogy for undifferentiated identity: removed from the indigenous land and culture, and not-yet 'American,'" their markers of identity liquified by and through their subjection as capital. It was this literal and figurative deterritorialization that enabled the slave ship to serve not merely as prosaic conveyance, but as zoo-biopolitical laboratory, so that, come landfall, the depredations wrought aboard wrote a legal covenant in which the persons the ship disembarked, along with their descendants, lived on as objects to be bought and sold.[47] We have not found a slave ship named "Ark." Perhaps, even at the time, such evil naming seemed somehow indecent. But there were ships with names like the *Arcania* ("the secret"), as well as several named the *Iris* or the *Rainbow.*[48]

The poet of oceans and long histories Edouard Glissant writes that "a boat has no belly; a boat does not swallow up, does not devour; a boat is steered by open skies." All the same, he continues, the boat "dissolves you, precipitates you into a nonworld from which you cry out." This boat, he adds, is "a womb abyss. . . . This boat is your womb, a matrix, and yet it expels you. This boat: pregnant with as many dead as living under sentence of death."[49] Glissant's pregnant imagery speaks to what Spillers knows, that the matter-metaphor of the slave ship as obscene transport renders it a means for producing and then reproducing enslaved forms of life, remaking and remarking those whose identity it seeks to dissolve, such that, when expelled from the belly of the boat, they remain caught in the "hold," as Christina Sharpe puts it, generations of stolen persons forced to live on in the "dysgraphia" (unwriting/disaster) of the slave ship's wake.[50] Even when disembarked, there is no landfall: "In the wake, the semiotics of the slave ship continue" as lived reality.[51]

Saidiya Hartman has written powerfully about how the afterlife of slavery ("skewed life chances, limited access to health and education, premature death, incarceration, and impoverishment") amounts to life lived as the "afterlife of property." Sharpe goes further, observing that "living the afterlife of *partus sequitur ventrem* (that which is brought forth follows the womb)" steals a woman's reproductive ability from her, overwrites and alienates the dignity and the privacy of pregnancy, birth, nursing, and family. The Black child, Sharpe argues, "inherits the non/status, the non/being of the mother," a heritage that "is everywhere apparent *now* in the ongoing criminalization of Black women and children."[52] The Middle Passage is ever unfolding, so much so that "the birth canal of black women or women who birth blackness" becomes a domestic and ever-repeating version: "The belly of the ship births blackness; the birth canal remains in, and as, the hold."[53] Historically, the cursing of Ham was enlisted to lend biblical justification to this dehumanizing system that holds fast, that casts an enduring wake, a perverse leveraging of the covenant given to Noah by the divine now justifying the reduction of fellow humans to commodities. This biblical justification was fiercely contested as well as frequently invoked.[54]

Describing inheritance practices in eighteenth- and nineteenth-century South Carolina in which white families bequeathed enslaved couples to their children as a source of "reproductive property," Jennifer L. Morgan finds that enslavers "emulated Noah, shackling them two by two."[55] Every marriage, as it were, became a little ark: every patriarch a Noah; every white couple, Noah's sons and their wives; every enslaved couple, breeding stock with their relationships and bonds of mutual affection overcoded by the bonds of capital. In eighteenth- and nineteenth-century North America, as Morgan's nod to Noah implies, scenes of predatory landfall took place again and again, inheritance practices playing out like some strangely resuscitated and rewritten Corpus Christi cycle play in which the animals aboard the ark are personed not by medieval guild members and townspeople who might next year play Mr. or Mrs. Noah or their children, but by enslaved persons who, as Morgan's allusion makes clear, must play asphyxiating and dehumanizing roles that they in no way chose.

Sharpe's tracing of "wake" and "hold" across long histories of enslavement and race-making underscores the transit from Wilkins's ark of cold calculus to the belly of the slave ship, two vessels with a single wake. And yet, still, the veering of the ark's trajectory or the rise and fall of what Glissant describes as a floating foundation will disturb the waters, seeding the wake of such ships with fragments for precarious refuge. Contested chest of stories that it is, a hybrid Genesis-Exodus vehicle (a *tevah*), the ark yokes refuge and violence together, disgorges those stories into the Flood as contested arkemes, minimal units of ark-entanglement that may be claimed, inhabited, adapted, combined to construct counternarratives and more humane histories. The ongoing disaster of transatlantic slavery is punctuated therefore by arks, elements of the Genesis story that return as contested hieroglyphics. Eric Sunquist writes of the "doubleness of the American ship of state: at once the ark of the covenant that authorized both liberty and slavery, leaving the national mission adrift, becalmed amid incalculable danger; and therefore the 'ark of bones,' the charnel house of slavery."[56] Sunquist invokes the ark of the covenant (semantically unrelated to Noah's ark in Hebrew) alongside the title of Henry Dumas's powerful story "Ark of Bones," in which a hallucinatory, literal-figurative ark carrying and perhaps built from the remains of the drowned emerges from the waters of the Mississippi—though, as one of the two young men who encounter the ark offers, the Noah who pilots the vessel "wasn't like the Noah I'd seen in my Sunday School picture cards."[57] In Sunquist's prose, metaphors mix. Space and time become uncertain. The "national mission" finds itself "becalmed." Covenants cohabit with charnel houses, and the arkive churns, leaving America adrift. Here, the other sense of ark, from Exodus, unprogrammed by the Vulgate translation of *tevah* into ark, escapes to disrupt the quasi-automatic stacking of ark-containers upon one another.

In Kamau Braithwaite's poem "Dream Haiti," written, as Elizabeth DeLoughrey puts it, from within "a collapse of the space and time separating the contemporary interdiction of Haitian refugees at sea and the long history of patrolling African bodies in the Middle Passage," the speaker's body "morphs into a boat," though he's not feeling like he's going anywhere: "I do not know why I was there— / how I came to be on board this ship—this navel of my ark."[58] "Navel of my ark," as Sharpe helpfully glosses in her nuanced reading, "with its homophones of 'naval' with two *a*'s, as in maritime or aquatic forces, as in navies or warships, and 'navel' with an *e*, as in remainder of the umbilicus," speaks back to the relationship (for both ark and slave ship) as both origin and trajectory. "The *ark* with a *k*, as it gestures to Noah's saving ship, to the curse upon Canaan, and also the *arc* with a *c*," Sharpe continues, "references routes traveled, circumference."[59] The Coast Guard ship USS *Cutter* that the poem's speaker finds himself aboard becomes the slave ship, becomes the ark, all three times and places and realities stirred together in the arc of a story that is still, agonizingly, playing, working itself out. Going somewhere? Going nowhere?

We will have more to say about counterarks, alternative covenants, refuge-making, and reparation in chapter 7, "Abandon Ark?" For now, let's recall the distinction that Spillers introduces between "body" and "flesh": "the central one," she offers, "between captive and liberated subject-positions."[60] When bodies are rendered stackable, storable, transportable units, laid hands on by enslavers, stolen, and processed as a commodity, those actions mark a collective flesh extending across time. This flesh remains and remembers, exceeds and escapes, even as it is scarred and bears the evident impress of violence inflicted across generations. "We might well ask," writes Spillers, "if this phenomenon of marking and branding actually 'transfers' from one generation to another," marking being at all levels, some knowable, some tangible, some felt. But flesh cannot be so contained. As a material-affective ground for other ways that the past may play out, flesh offers the "insurgent ground" for possible futures, the resources for refuge and "representational possibilities" denied to bodies borne in ships, held by history.[61]

Building on the potentialities that Spillers signals and that Saidiya

Hartman, Fred Moten, and Stefano Harney have amplified, Sharpe coins the phrase "wake work" to describe reparative processes and rituals of memory, grief, care, and attention. "Wake work" reorients "existing disciplinary solutions to blackness's ongoing abjection that extend the dysgraphia of the wake" to approach "the multiple meanings of that abjection through inhabitation, that is, through living them in and as consciousness."[62] Another way to conceive this would be to say, with Moten and Harney in *The Undercommons,* that "there are flights of fantasy in the hold of the ship." Moten and Harney describe "the hold's terrible gift" as its gathering "dispossessed feelings in common, to create a new feel in the undercommons" (97), a touch ("hapticality") that is also an affect that moves, and that may be described as philosophy, music, release, setting adrift, and love. "To have been shipped is to have been moved by others, with others," they write here. All this is to say that strange and surprising as well as terrible things can happen in the belly of an ark (92–94).

The successive and abusive conditions of what Achille Mbembe calls the "camp-form" (the concentration camp, the factory farm, the prison, the sanitarium, the mass grave) find themselves hosted by the ark.[63] At the same time, the same invitation to ark thinking that leads Wilkins to posit a whitewashed, containerized space that mind and math may infinitely subdivide also generates resistance. That resistance comes from refusing to suspend the mundane bustle of life and living, of death and dying, that a Flood condition announces. As Paul Gilory writes in the *Black Atlantic,* and as so many scholars have worked to excavate, "the image of the ship—a living, micro-cultural, micro-political system in motion, . . . immediately focus[es] attention on the middle passage," but so also on defiance, remediation, and the production of unanticipated alliances, the mutual touching of bodies that matter.[64] Let's trouble the stillness of climate control with the animate mess or mass of embarkation. Let's look for signs not only of entities reduced to bare life or labor, but for forms of "bare activity," microresistances, infra- and transindividual, across and within differently scaled bodies, activity that it is the genius of stories and images to personify as subjects, human and otherwise.[65] What might emerge from an ark thinking all the bodies it crowds together rather than suspending that creaturely density and allowing the rainbow the last word?

All Aboard

We have noted already the vague articulation of the ark's interior that Genesis provides. God describes in similarly general terms the animal variety that vessel's pitch-smeared walls will harbor: "Of all that lives, of all flesh, you shall take two of each into the ark to keep alive with you" (Genesis 6:19). This divinely provided passenger list is disarmingly succinct, but each of its three categories conveys a kingdom of creaturely diversity, a male and a female for every kind of fowl, cattle, and "creeping thing" (6:20). In an ominous intimation that this vessel shall be long at sea, God adds that Noah must stow nourishment aboard, "everything that is eaten" for each kind of beast, as well as for the humans (6:21). Two of every creature plus sufficient provender offer an expansive enough cargo to fit within any imaginable structure, and yet when the construction of the ark is completed, God adds even more bodies to the manifest. Only unclean animals will come in pairs, while "of every clean animal you shall take seven pairs, males and their mates" (7:2). To ensure their survival, "birds of the air" will also arrive paired in their sevens (7:3). This belated commandment that edible, sacrificeable animals come in groups of fourteen is easy to forget (everyone knows the animals came two by two, not seven by two!), and perhaps that misremembering can be forgiven, since the Genesis narrative appears to commit the same lapse when the ark is then being loaded: "Two of each, male and female, came to Noah into the ark, as God had commanded Noah" (7:9). Only the passengers, not the provender, count in this regard. Stowing an Earth's worth of birds, ungulates, and creeping critters into that singular container must have been something to behold.

The sheer magnitude of the task spurred John Calvin to wonder whether poor Noah suspected "that God was mocking him." Given that God has asked him to suspend his agricultural work for a year or more in order to build the vessel, Calvin thinks Noah could be forgiven for asking, "whence were the provisions for the year to be obtained? Whence for so many animals?"[66] Moreover, where was Noah supposed to find all these different kinds of animals? Did Noah, asks Calvin, have "all the beasts of the forest at his command, or was [he] able to tame them, so that, in his keeping, wolves might dwell with lambs, tigers with hares, lions with oxen, as sheep in his fold?"[67] Worse still, "the most grievous temptation" to disobey orders, thinks

Calvin, is that, after all these preparations, Noah is "commanded to descend, as if into the grave, for the sake of preserving his life, and voluntarily to deprive himself of air and vital spirit; for the smell of the dung alone, pent up . . . in a closely filled place, might, at the expiration of three days, have stifled all the living creatures in the ark." God's command to enter into what feels like communal suffocation, seems cause enough to deviate from God's instructions. Noah's absolute obedience is the lesson Calvin draws, though some subsequent readers of Genesis have inclined Calvin's questions toward broad comedy to paint a Noah-who-questions-his-sanity or a deadbeat Noah none too concerned with matters of "quality control" in his inventory of animal kinds.[68]

We opened this chapter with Brueghel's immensity of an ark, placed at so far a distance that we wondered how it would accommodate the animal swarm of the foreground. The challenge posed by an ark's task of preserving a generative slice of the world in its entirety is overwhelming. Many artists therefore choose a smaller, calmer scale to imagine the moment of embarkation. In a typical illustration, a bearded and berobed Noah will stand to the side of the ark as a representative ten or twelve animal couples enter his vessel. The creatures selected for portrayal tend to combine the familiar with the exotic: horses, cattle, dogs, and deer with lions, camels, peacocks, and elephants. All are what ecologists call "charismatic megafauna," animals with which humans form emotional bonds, based mainly on resemblance. You seldom find snakes, rats, or spiders marching two by two. And Noah and family are on the job: keeping tally, keeping order, rational and upstanding in their bipedal elevation from the four-footed beasts they corral aboard.

The *Bible Historiale* of Guyart des Moulins, for example, shows Noah and his family beside a rectangular ark with a pointed roof—a two-story late-medieval house built of wood, the kind of dwelling that a well-to-do townsman (such as might have commissioned the manuscript) would inhabit. Another miniature on the same page illustrates how Noah's sons carpentered its frame, creating an architecture that seems more likely to be submerged than buoyed by the impending Flood. As the animals enter the completed structure (Figure 24), Noah touches them with a stick, gently prodding them to their new quarters. For economy's sake, only a few beasts are featured, and except for a ram and ewe, they are not in pairs. Processing through the

FIGURE 24. The infinite ark container. Miniatures of construction of Noah's ark; filling of the ark with beasts, circa 1415, from *The Bible Historiale* of Guyart des Moulins, British Library, London, Add MS 18856, f.14v. Copyright British Library Board. All Rights Reserved / Bridgeman Images.

not-very-wide door are a horse, a stag, a tiny lion that suggests (as medieval illustrations of lions often suggest) that the artist has never seen one, a boar, a greyhound, and a wolf. Of their own volition a heron, dove, and pelican fly into the upper story of the house-becoming-boat, a chamber they will apparently share with the humans, once aboard. This ark likely contains a third level in its attic, but whatever that space might hold (food? supplies? the birds?) is left unillustrated. The twelve animals embark cheerfully, their serene expressions yielding no intimation of the catastrophe to come, or of the tribulations that living in so constricted a space for so long must bring.

Like most representations of the boarding of the ark, this fifteenth-century miniature aspires neither to completeness nor to realism.

You will not find an elephant or bear here, much less a unicorn or a dragon. To convey an *orbis terrarum* of animal diversity and to fit each creature into the domestic interior is not the artist's aspiration. The house-boat does not invite us to think about how the structure will function once it becomes the plaything of the waves. The illustrator does not dwell on where the food will be stowed or how the shared space will be kept clean or who will labor to ensure the various animals remain alive during the long months at sea. The miniature offers a feeling more than a chronicle, a vibrantly affirmative conveyance of multispecies community within the household ecology of the ark. It is difficult to know exactly what feeling this figure of en-arkment is supposed to convey. The image takes its cue from the French text it visualizes, "Commence Noe entra dans l'arche selon," with the story reduced to its iconographic hieroglyphs and to the miraculous facticity of boarding whose magnitude led Calvin to take a pause.

From here viewers could skip happily ahead to the slope of Ararat once the waters have subsided. And, in fact, that is exactly what this illustrator does, providing next a beautifully rendered depiction of Noah and his family kindling a sacrifice upon an immense stone altar (Figure 25). God looks down from the heavens and gestures approvingly. A rainbow curves around the scene, enclosing the figures within the border of a prismatic dome or bubble. The second Earth commences with the sweet savor of animal offering rising to the heavens, fire that punctuates the termination of a Flood that was over to begin with. Of course, the story continues to veer unexpectedly. Genesis keeps on beginning, continues to stage the whole business of the human preoccupation with starting over: Noah's drunken nudity leads to the cursing of the progeny of his son Ham to perpetual slavery; nations scatter, their division into incomprehensible tongues the result of the next exorbitant structure (the landlocked Tower of Babel, an architecture of flames rather than water).[69] Still, it is pleasant to linger beneath the shelter of this rainbow momentarily and rejoice in *terra firma,* to believe for a short space that the world's turbulence has subsided at last, if not quite once and for all.

It is only a brief journey from this kind of water-hopping narrative or willing suspension of flood to the pristinely ordered boarding scenes rendered in Athanasius Kircher's *Arca Noe* (Figure 26). Noah supervises while his family, hosted now by neoclassical bodies, recreate in pleasant, unhurried, conversation. Meanwhile, a well-behaved pa-

FIGURE 25. Conclusion in which nothing is concluded: rainbow, sacrifice, covenant. Noah's sacrificial offering, circa 1415, from *The Bible Historiale* of Guyart des Moulins, British Library, London, Add MS 18856, f.15v. Copyright British Library Board. All Rights Reserved / Bridgeman Images.

rade of animals or Cartesian beast-machines auto-en-ark themselves up the ramp onto the perfectly proportioned rectangular construction that Wilkins and now Kircher imagine. Birds roost atop and congregate in the air above. In the foreground, just to the right of Noah's family, a pair of hares and tortoises pause like-mindedly to survey the immaculately choreographed scene, putting on hold their Aesopian fable of a race. Or, perhaps, their race continues apace, with the movement of the tortoises too slow to perceive and the staying of the hares now void of meaning as Genesis recalibrates the best fable. After all,

FIGURE 26. Auto-en-arking with Athanasius Kircher. *Ingressus Animalium intra Arcam,* in Athanasius Kircher, *Arca Noe in tres libros digesta sive de rebus ante diluvium, de diluvio, et de rebus post diluvium a Noemo gestis* (Amsterdam: Apud J. Janssonium à Waesberge, 1675). Harold B. Lee Library, Brigham Young University.

everyone pictured in the scene has already won the race. The prize? Admission aboard the ark. Trumping Aesop, Genesis's two-by-two taxonomy retrains animal antagonism. The economy in design that Wilkins locates in the ark's divine blueprint extends outward like some plane of projective force that organizes the ark's immediate environs, which is to say, ideally, all human history.

Taxonomies are rarely quiet things. And not everyone in Noah's family is compliantly on message. If Noah figures obedience, Mrs. Noah resists. In medieval traditions, she encourages us to contemplate the narratives of the drowned, of those left outside the ark. Mrs. Noah takes the transindividual resistances we saw in the play of creaturely bodies in Brueghel the Elder's painting and translates them into the family dramas of ark plots as relationships fray. In the Chester-cycle *Pageante of Noyes Fludd,* she has to be manhandled aboard. When conscripted to help summon and arrange the animals in the cataloging of animal life, Mrs. Noah veers. As Lisa Kiser notes in her excellent reading of the episode, Mrs. Noah "violates a number of principles that inform the catalogues of the other characters. First and foremost, not a single one of her animals contributes to the household economy," and "none is edible and none performs worthwhile labour."[70] Mrs. Noah confuses categories. She produces a taxonomic interference that threatens to transform an ordered boarding into a chimera of animal traits:

> And here are beares, wolves sett,
> apes, owles, maremussett,
> wesills, squerrells, and fyrrett;
> here the eaten there meate.[71]

Bears and wolves; apes, owls, and marmosets; weasels, squirrels, ferrets; the inappropriate and the incompatible cohabit, their accommodation provided by the accident of rhyme and meter, as Mrs. Noah's prosody scrambles taxonomy. But as Noah admonishes a little later in the play, his wife has always been "ever froward."[72] She likes to talk. And all her talking, all her gossiping, all the words she floods against the flood, testify to the ways in which storying, loading, decorating, or accessorizing the ark with words and images conjures its own supplementary mode of ark thinking that insists we consider the cost, that we rankle with the sedation of multiple orders of difference in the name of climate control.

Ark Life

In the Chester cycle, the universal flood plays out in miniature as a domestic dispute, with Noah and his family the ordinary and hardworking citizens of the town. A dedicated craftsman and beleaguered husband, Noah tries his best to be an effective leader, husband, father—but he has a boisterous wife who will not listen to him and a God who tells him to do things he would rather not (Noah drags the shipbuilding on for 120 years in the hope some people will repent). The three hardworking sons attempt to emulate their dad's busy and compliant example, while the three dedicated daughters-in-law know how to perform the role of duteous spouses. As the flood begins, Mrs. Noah's friends enjoin her to drink with them. Mrs. Noah shares the "pottell of malnesaye" (bottle of wine) with them, and as the 1592 manuscript of the play instructs, they then join in "The Good Gossip's song," which most likely sets the following words to music:

The fludd comes fleetinge in full faste,
one everye syde that spredeth full farre.
For fere of drowninge I am agaste;
good gossippe, lett us drawe nere.

And lett us drinke or wee departe,
for oftetymes wee have done soe.
For at one draught thou drinke a quarte,
and soe will I doe or I goe.

Here is a pottell full of malnesaye good and stronge;
yt will rejoyse both harte and tonge.
Though Noe thinke us never soe longe,
yett wee wyll drinke atyte.[73]

Standing with the audience, leaving the ark to exult in the company of her friends, Mrs. Noah drinks deep from the intoxicating fruit of the vines that Noah will one day plant and succumb to himself. Their drinking inspires their song. They sing their hearts. Stacking up words against the water, celebrating the gift of breath, the flood of wine and fellow feeling, and the flood of song, Mrs. Noah and friends resist the impetus or inevitability of closing the ark. Japheth pleads with his mother, but she refuses to board the pageant-wagon-become-ship and leave her gossips or the audience. Shem decides things by forcing her aboard. Noah welcomes her to "this boat" and she strikes him. "Have thou that for thy note," she rebukes, finishing his line and completing the couplet for him.[74]

At this point, the manuscript versions of 1592 and 1607 vary and suggest different stagings. In the 1592, Noah shuts "the windowe of the arke, and for a little space within the bordes shalbe scylent . . . afterwarde openinge the windowe and lookinge rownde." The story then moves directly to sacrifice, rainbow, and landfall. In the 1607, however, Noah and family sing Psalm 69, "Save Me, Oh God," likely in the metrical version of the sixteenth-century psalter of Thomas Sternhold and Johns Hopkins:

Save me, oh God, and that with speed,
The waters flow full fast
So nigh my soul do they proceed,

That I am sore agast.
I sink full deep in mire and clay,
Where I can feel no ground:
And in deep waters where I may
Most suddenly be drowned.[75]

In performance, the psalm's cry for salvation toggles between the literal and figurative. The psalm-singing figures the Flood, but at the same time reprograms the gossip's drinking song as misplaced, immersive, a flood of alcohol-fueled feeling that it washes clean. The singing of the psalm corrects the drinking song and recalibrates the audience's affect. The lyrics and collective rhythm of Psalm 69 (all the psalms in this psalter use the same ballad meter) transport the audience aboard the ark as we all now sing from the same script. The defiant joy we felt with the gossips is transposed into the gratitude we now feel for the ark as beneficiaries of the story we are watching. Or, better still, those very gossips, their parts concluded, also sing along as part of the audience they and we have now become. "With crying oft I weary am / my throat is hoarse and dry," the psalm continues, the tears of the speaker figuring a flood of contrition. By psalm's end, all sung out, all cried out, the hoarseness of our dry mouths signals the dry land of landfall. Mrs. Noah undergoes this retraining with us. Come rainbow, she has no further lines. Noah and God do all the talking, though the deity now seems to regret having sent the flood.

With its hard-pressed Noah who tries his best to save some of the souls not on his manifest, its delight in expansive cataloging of the animals to be sheltered on board, and its poignant closing line, "my darling dear" (375), this version of the Flood story is a quiet rebuke to some contemporary reactions to catastrophe. In the year 1607, "huge and mighty hills of water" (likely a tsunami) surged inland from the Bristol channel, inundating the southwest of Britain. Towns disappeared beneath a sudden sea and two thousand people, taken unawares, perished in the rush of waters. That same year a popular pamphlet describing the flood attributes the catastrophe to an angry God who hurls ecological punishment against a sinful populace, warning that many more disasters are surely to come in these evil times. The pamphlet delights in describing how people scramble to save their own lives against the rising sea, mostly in vain. None attempt to form a community of those about to drown, a solidarity with a story boisterous enough to reverberate after the waters subside. The Chester play arrives to us in the form we have now because someone loved something within its lines and resistances, cherished the scripts it offered, conserved them against present severities.

If, for logistical reasons, the Chester cycle skips over the flood or transposes it into song and feeling, then a poem like the fourteenth-century "Cleanness" zeroes in on what it calls the "þe remnaunt"[76] of humanity that floats aboard the ark: eight persons whom God ensures stay safe and dry in their cabins (412: "alle ledez in lome lenged druye"). In our previous chapter, we dwelt with how the poem lingers with the drowned, taking time to imagine their agonies (collective and individual) as the heavens open. Following that description, perspective narrows to the ark buffeted by the waves:

> Hit waltered on þe wylde flod, went as hit lyste,
> Drof vpon þe depe dam, in daunger hit semed,
> Withouten mast, oþer myke, oþer myry bawelyne,
> Kable, oþer capstan to clyppe to her ankrez,
> Hurrok, oþer hande-helme hasped on roþer,
> Oþer any sweande sayl to seche after hauen,
> Bot flote forthe with þe flyt of þe felle wyndez.
> (415–20)

Close call: if "oure Lorde" had not been their "lodezmon" (their helmsman; 424), the narrator opines, this remnant surely would have drowned. The violence of the flood exceeds the nautical technology and navigational expertise of humans. Guided by this divine helmsman, who otherwise seems absent or present only in the violence of the flood, the poem pictures the ark, secured against the elements, enduring, and forever inclining toward its destined landfall.

Medieval art and literature exult in the intricacies and opacities of the Genesis Flood narrative, perceiving in the sparseness of the story an invitation to the imagination. This miniature ark, almost but never in fact engulfed by the flood in "Cleanness," is realized by different artists and writers in an armada of shapes. The ark might be depicted as a castle, church, longboat, galleon, pyramid, house, rectangular box, floating orb, or even some crazy contraption that surely could never float on water, let alone weather a hurricane. Following Augustine of Hippo and the church fathers, medieval Christians understood Noah's ark as an allegory, prefiguring Christ's resurrection and the foundation of a second order that washes away the first through the promise of a new life. The Flood becomes universal baptism and cleansing, the ark the church, and the dutiful dove the Holy Spirit. The ark becomes available for metaphoric and spiritual boarding, as in Hugh of St. Victor's writing, where the vessel offers a storehouse for all good things, a mystical ark of the heart.[77] But the ark is always already something more than that. Many medieval illustrations of arks provide multiple windows (and thereby multiple perspectives) through which passengers, the remnant, peer out at the drowned world. Animals and people aboard share tranquil expressions. Fish might swim beneath the hull in oceanic peace. Survival is for the determined, and those on the ark are in it together, a community of men, women, horses, owls, deer, and the occasional unicorn. The vessel tends to be a lively object, perhaps with a zoomorphic prow or rudder. Such lush depiction gets at the vibrancy of things in medieval art.[78]

A thirteenth-century English roll version of Peter of Poitiers's *Compendium Historiae in Genealogia Christi* features an ark resembling a gothic cathedral of the seas (Figure 27). This vessel could not figure the church with more brio. But even as allegory burgeons, the natural world continues to exert its material presence. The illustration stresses the intimacy of humans and beasts, their shared equanimity as ark-mates. The verdant waters around the cathedral-ark are nearly opaque, but some fish glide beneath the boat. Oceanic green encircles the image, a kind of *orbis terrarum* bounded by watery embrace. Noah and his wife are in earnest discussion at the center, their animal companions calmly looking left or right to align themselves with the zoomorphic rudder and prow. This ark is part of a dynamic world of transspecies survival rather than a vessel afloat on a sea of death, offering a moment of quiet coexistence before the animal sacrifice and consumption to come. Disaster's community can be expansive.

In another thirteenth-century image of the vessel (Laurent d'Orléans, *Somme le Roi,* 1294), the ark becomes a grid or lattice of windows, its enclosing hull a set of portals that enable the viewer to see inside (Figure 28). Or, more precisely, this many-windowed ark enables all the ark-mates to look out at us, or it would if Noah and family, along with birds, lions, bears, herbivores, and a plethora of uncertain creatures did not seem more interested in one another. A

FIGURE 27. Cathedral of the sea. Peter of Poitiers's *Compendium Historiae in Genealogia Christi,* late thirteenth century, from British Library, London, Royal MS 14 B IX, f.2r. Copyright British Library Board. All Rights Reserved / Bridgeman Images.

study in profiles and faces, sideways glances and upturned snouts cohabit with outward stares at the Flood beyond. Windows to what may only be imagined, all these portals, the very desire to make holes in the ark, to look inside, or so that all the ark-mates can peer without, insists on the movement, labor, bustle, joy, terror, violence, and possibilities an ark sets in motion. All these openings, along with the urge to accessorize and decorate the ark, condense or seek to archive the fact of all that we cannot know of what went on inside. These windows open into stores of affective possibility amid the stuff of literal food. They testify to the vibrancy and unruliness of bodies solo and in proximity, inviting us to take our own sideways glance at the Genesis story or to read along with an upturned snout.

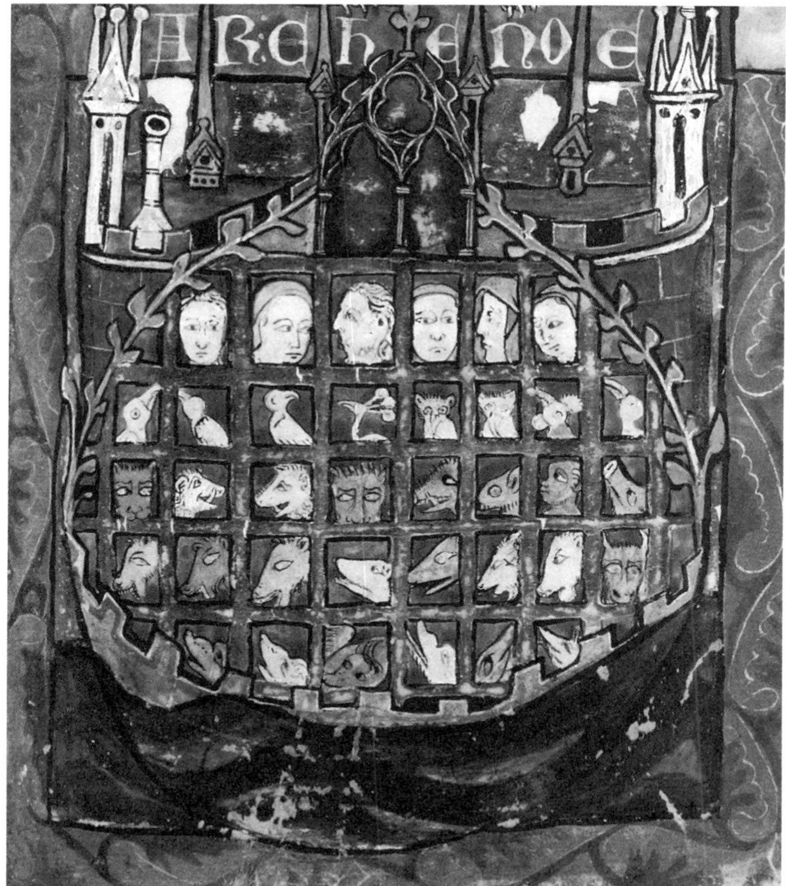

FIGURE 28. The many-windowed Ark. Noah's ark in Laurent d'Orléans, *Somme le Roi,* France, 1294. Bibliothèque Nationale de France, MS Français 938, fol. 86r.

At Home on the Ark: Athanasius Kircher

No one gives in so completely to this urge to look through the ark's window, to peer inside and imagine life aboard, as does the seventeenth-century German Jesuit Athanasius Kircher, though his program proves a little different and leaves nothing whatsoever to doubt. As meticulous in his attention to detail as the winners of the Worshipful Company of Shipwright's ark-building competition of 1947, Kircher delivers on the exact arrangements that must, he thinks, have been in place to maintain the serene expressions on all the ark-mates peering out

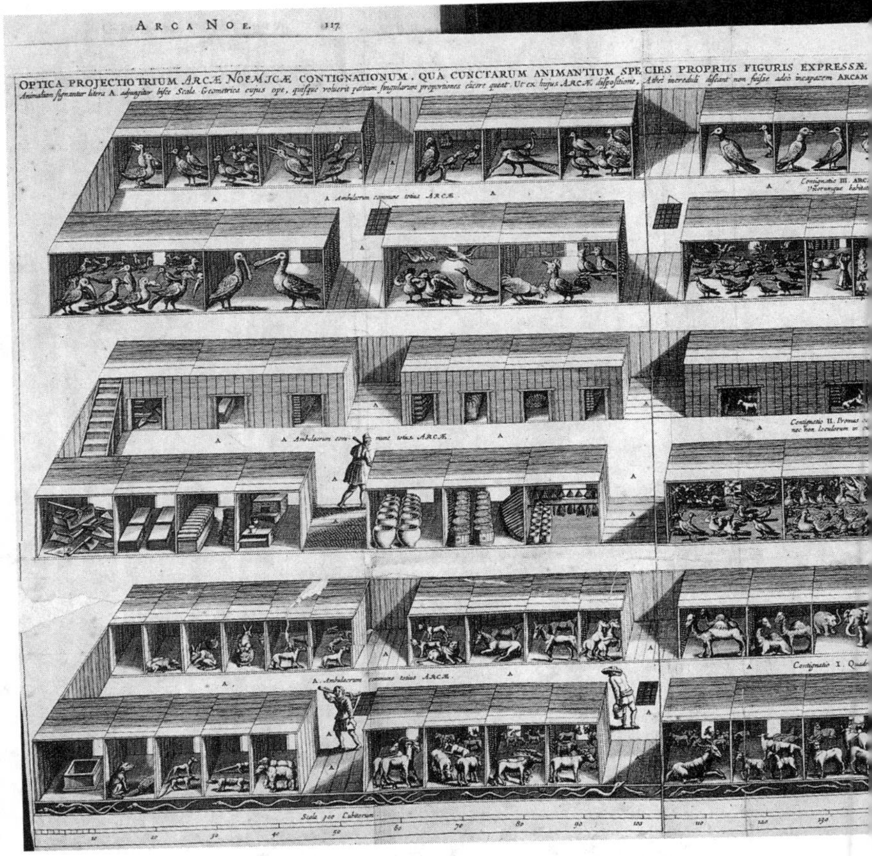

the windows of medieval illustrations. In *Arca Noe,* Kircher describes Noah and family enjoying a suite of adjoining compartments equipped with a pantry, kitchen, and dining room, all ventilated so as to keep the stench generated by the mass of creaturely life below at bay. As for medieval writers, all this waste is channeled into the *sentina* or bilge, while the ventilation system *(spiraculum)* ensures that the air in the top deck of the ark, enjoyed by humans and birds alike, remains pure.[79] The air this "remnant" of humanity breathes is pure not because of altered diet or divine dictate, but because of the technical design and logistical foresight of the ark and its architect. If Calvin worried that Noah might think God was mocking him for asking him to build the ark while also growing all the food he and the animals would need, such thoughts are suspended in Kircher's ark, which is stocked ex-

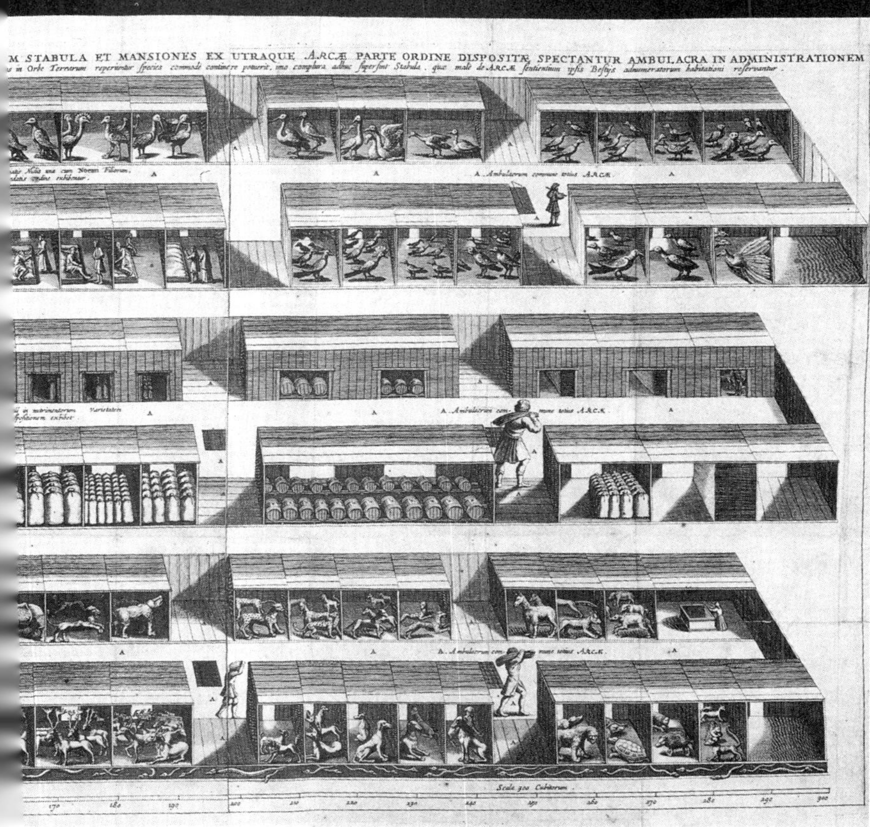

FIGURE 29. Imagining ark life and ark lives. *Opticae Projectio Trium Arcae Noemicae . . . ,* from Athanasius Kircher, *Arca Noe in tres libros digesta sive de rebus ante diluvium, de diluvio, et de rebus post diluvium a Noemo gestis* (Amsterdam: Apud J. Janssonium à Waesberge, 1675). Wellcome Collection, Closed stores EPB/D/31211.

ceptionally well with all manner of human necessities and comforts, including salt, wine, and vinegar, in addition to staples such as meat and grain. Kircher even has Noah supplement such provisions for the body by building an aviary so that the music of the songbirds might lift his family's spirits when the drudgery of ark life gets them down. Separate bedrooms are also provided for Noah's sons and their wives.

All of these amenities, along with animal accommodations, and quarters for Noah and family are depicted in an impressive, fold-out plan of the ark tipped into the book (Figure 29). In addition to offering a fully-thought-out floor plan, Kircher restores an element of movement to give a sense of what daily life was like on the ark. We find Noah and his family throughout this synoptic ark, tending to the animals or hauling supplies, singly and in pairs, moving through the spacious and uncluttered gangways as the animals patiently await their ministrations on this turbulence-free vessel. Noah and family's accommodations are placed on the top deck, shared with ark's birds, near the central window. Here the family is pictured at work and at rest, sleeping, talking, recreating, preparing food. The family gathers together to eat in a separate miniature compartment at the center of their quarters, a domestic bubble within a climate-controlled sphere. Ark life preserves home life—a true ark of safety and security.

"A house," writes Le Corbusier (Charles-Édouard Jeanneret), "is a machine for living in. Baths, sun, hot water, cold water, controlled temperature, food, conservation, hygiene, beauty through proportion."[80] Arks are also machines. But they are sealed. They must include within their limits the flows of matter and energy that otherwise would connect a house to an elaborated infrastructure. Severed from these flows of matter and energy, an ark must provide them from within. It must constitute a total system, which means that it must also deal with the inevitability of waste, finding within its finite space ways to accommodate the dynamic flux of bodies. It's this functionalist necessity that drives the perfection of Kircher's ark that he presents with the elegance of his visual synopsis.

As we saw with the design competition sponsored by the Worshipful Company of Shipwrights, embedded in such models are assumptions about the constraints put in place by the Genesis narrative, and so about the nature of human persons and animals, and their accommodation. In 1947, for Messrs. Ash, McBride, and Warman, these constraints amounted to a "a question of safety." The "Ancient Hebrews," as their sponsor averred, "had little desire to go anywhere," so "no propulsion was needed." Hence the manufacture of what was essentially "a big raft," a literal chest or container. For Kircher, the same basic constraint holds also. What are the minimal conditions that obtain? What is necessary to maintain the physical, emotional, or affective security of the individual, the family unit, the species? Here what might seem like the nicety of small details such as fireplaces, aviaries, and separate bedrooms, even impulses to decorate or accessorize an otherwise functionalist ark, find themselves purposed, poised to reveal the underlying hygienic or biopolitical assumptions to the ark as it appears in *this* design.

Ark Privacy and Ark Sex

Kircher's provision of separate bedrooms for Noah's sons and their wives represents more than a nicety. It gestures, decorously, toward the long-standing question as to whether, and if so, then how, with whom, and to what ends, ark-mates, human and otherwise, had sex while aboard the ark. Kircher does not approach this question directly. The issue arises instead from a set of questions to do with the continuity of life before and after the Flood. Kircher was troubled by the idea that there are animals that exist today that had not been aboard, but he was also alive to the difficulty posed by the ark's limits. He admits no crossbreeds or fabulous animals, other than unicorns, whose existence he takes to be a matter of historical fact. Especially discomforted by the prospect of single-sex sirens coming aboard as a pair, he leaves them off the ark on the basis that they would be able to survive the rising waters on their own.[81] Given his interest in animal kinds, and so with an emerging discourse of species, heteronormative sex is one of the animal necessaries Kircher brings aboard, even though that necessity is not explicitly stated. On Kircher's ark, marriage beds are kept separate and privacy, along with the integrity of the four marriages, is maintained. Look closely at Kircher's cross-section and allow your eyes to wander between and among compartments, and amid the pairs of animals, human and otherwise, you find two horses mating. What we may assume to be the nighttime couplings of human animals, unimaged in the eternal daytime of this ever-illuminated ark, are displaced by way of an equestrian veer.

Kircher may police the joining of animal bodies to ensure that coupling is always coded in reproductive terms, but the absence of baby animals aboard testifies to the way that the possibility of sex remains a key source of trouble aboard the ark. In the accretive commentary-conversation-debate-dispute traditions of midrash, which aim to read the Bible with an eye and ear not merely to what the text seems to say, but to what it might one day come to mean, testing and trying the text as it goes, sexual trouble returns as something to think with.[82] In the Babylonian Talmud, the raven rebukes Noah for classifying him as unclean and thereby allotting space for two rather than seven pairs of his kind aboard the ark. When told that he must depart the vessel and search the flooded world for signs that the waters might be receding, the bird accuses Noah of risking the extinction of all ravens, and wonders how Noah can live with the risk of an Earth impoverished by loss: "Suppose, now, I should perish by reason of heat or cold," says the raven, "would not the world be the poorer by a whole species of animals?" Even worse, the raven suspects that Noah might have his eye on his mate and that is why he is being sent on a fool's errand.[83] Noah rebukes the raven, treating his accusation as an opportunity to explain that, "if with the woman who is generally permitted to me, my wife, intercourse is forbidden to me, then with regard to domesticated and undomesticated animals, which are generally forbidden to me, is it not all the more so the case that they are forbidden to me?" End of story. Or, rather, just another beginning, another portal or window into the ark, for as

> the Sages taught: Three violated that directive and engaged in intercourse while in the ark, and all of them were punished for doing so. They are: the dog, and the raven, and Ham, son of Noah. The dog was punished in that it is bound; the raven was punished in that it spits, and Ham was afflicted in that his skin turned black.[84]

Sexualization, racialization, and dehumanization reveal themselves as longtime intimates, while black bodies are revealed as having always already been loaded into the ark, in the worst possible ways.

The argument that Noah and his sons abstained from sex while aboard is based on an especially close reading of the serial admonitions Noah receives about how to get on and off the ark. Embarkation proceeds, it is argued, according to segregation by sex; landfall pairs the couples off. Hence, the conclusion that "it was prohibited to engage in intercourse while in the ark, as when Noah and his family entered, the husbands and wives were listed separately, and when they emerged, the husbands were listed with their wives."[85] Such a reading resonates obviously with commentaries that paint a queer picture of life before the Flood as a time of interspecies sex acts that bring down the force of divine punishment, to say nothing of the postdilluivan episode of Noah's drunken nudity and the cursing of Ham for what is sometimes read as taking pleasure in that embarrassment, unmanning Noah, even raping or castrating him.[86] And yet, against all attempts to police sex aboard the ark, the assertion of a potential sameness aboard—even as that sameness comes allied to the disciplining of otherwise-than-hetero couplings—serves also to make the ark available to queer and erotic imagining.[87]

Lost and Found: Countee Cullen

In *The Lost Zoo* (1940), Harlem Renaissance poet and school teacher Countee Cullen offers a series of poems for children that constitute something like a recovered archive of the songs sung by those animals who got on and those who were left off the ark. Noah, so the frame narrative has it, sends a letter of invitation to all animals. The first part of the collection includes responses from many of those whose names we know. The second consists of sometimes silly, sometimes sad, sometimes nonsense, bittersweet songs that explain the absence of the "very unfortunate few we never shall see in any zoo" because they did not make it aboard.[88] These animals' names resonate with the force of the semiallegorical pun: the Wakeupworld "with eyes like rainbows" (7), the Squilililigee, the Sleepamitemore, the Treasuretit, the Hoodinkus-with-the-double-head, the Laplakes, the Snake-that-walked-upon-its tail, and the Ha-Ha-Ha. Their tongue-twisting, multisyllabic, onomatopoeic joy, along with the occasional slight sexual suggestiveness to be cruised from the part-words "ite" and "tit," seem to insist on the sensory pleasures to be had from self-reflexive phonemic density as much as it does on the satisfactions of an allegorical program.[89]

Largely neglected, *The Lost Zoo* collects vanished forms of animal life that were prone to mundane excesses (like sleeping too long) that prevented them from boarding the ark, or even responding to the invitation to do so. As Benjamin Kahan offers, these extinct animals are presented as a kind of "queer rabble who refuse or are unable to get on the ark." They are lonely, friendless, and they defy clear categorization. Even when grouped together, they do not gel, each animal conflating or scrambling categories. All we know of the lost and unsung Pussybow, for example, is that it can both "mew and bark" (23). When its stories are set against the ideology of racial uplift narratives as they shaped the Harlem Renaissance and its reception, Kahan suggests that, "poised at the queer intersection of uplift, childhood, children's literature," *The Lost Zoo* is a way of exploring "the nonnormative sexual energies generated by uplift itself."[90] The poem resonates, as Kahan points out, with Cullen's own "strikingly queer failure," epitomized perhaps by the mysterious circumstances of his abortive marriage to Yolande Du Bois, the daughter of W. E. B. Du Bois, in April 1928, which "dissolved shortly after the honeymoon and Cullen headed to Paris with his lover Harold Jackman." For Cullen, the project of anthologizing these animals' lost songs becomes a collaborative imaginative strategy, a form of collective *prosopopoeia,* or giving face to ways of being that would otherwise go unrepresented (from the Greek *prosōpon* for "face" + *poiein* for "to make").

A trans-species collaboration resides at the heart of *The Lost Zoo.* Cullen and his cat Christopher are domestic partners and cowriters. "Cat is not only Christopher's last name," Cullen explains, but "Christopher *is* a cat, a real cat, colored white, and orangey. Christopher belongs to me, or maybe I belong to Christopher" (1). Christopher and Cullen have "belonged to each other for a number of years," and in that time the two have "invented a kind of man-cat language that each of us knows" and of which both are "pretty proud" (1). None of this, writes Cullen, ought to be

> too surprising though, . . . for after you have lived in the same house with a person, or animal, it doesn't matter which for almost ten years, and after you've both met every morning for breakfast, and every evening for dinner, and every night you've both climbed into the same easy chair, and fallen asleep together right after dinner, it shouldn't be surprising that you two finally ended up talking to one another. Well, that's how it is with Christopher and me. (2)

Toggling back and forth between people and cats enables the conversion of mutual cat–person belonging into a portrait of queer domesticity. It is the ethical measure of this kind of hospitable, aporetic allegory that Cullen might just as well be referring to actual, historically particular cats and their human animals as he might to historically particular men and women and their lovers. The transmutual crossing necessitates, and so opens the possibility of, allegory as a two-way street, an opportunity for connection, exploration, and encounter. It opens the possibility that there is, in fact, no allegory at all. Such structures close no doors. Their resilience is premised on this failure to close. We do not have to choose *one* reading. Indeed, it is almost as if Christopher and Cullen have, together, constituted something like their own counter-ark. They share in an intimacy that embraces their multiple differences and that does not smooth over those differences and disagreements—though it is a measure of the text's instability that Christopher's ongoing sniping at Cullen strikes some readers as a way of modeling the resistance of African American voices who are recruited by white patrons, and so made to speak.[91] Certainly, the text maintains this reading. That said, it is Christopher who takes pride of place in the beautiful illustration by Charles Sebree that opens the book in the manner of a portrait of the author (Figure 30). The caption reads: "Christopher Cat . . . Author." Although, even here, like the ellipsis that attenuates the claim of authorship, Christopher looks askance. He remains entirely and wonderfully unavailable.

During one of their after-dinner conversations, Cullen tells Christopher about a recent trip to the zoo. Christopher feigns interest and then gently teases his friend after half-listening by asking him if he saw a Squilililigee? "Did I see a Squilly What?," asks Cullen, to which Christopher poses a string of questions about other seemingly impossibly named animals, leading Cullen to beg that Christopher please explain their stories (6). Christopher proclaims: "Neither money nor courage, nor anything men possess, can get you a look at those animals. They all died thousands of years ago; there have never been any more; and there never will be. They were all drowned" (7). But, after a little coaxing, Cullen manages to get him to agree to tell what he knows, and the two form an anthologizing collaboration. Christopher passes on the stories told to him by his father and his father's father about all these forms of animal life that inhabit no zoo even though they did receive invitations from Noah to board the ark. In return for his narration, Christopher demands a good deal more than the extra rations of "catnip, milk, and liver" he is offered. He wants "to be an author" (8). "I deserve to be an author," he insists. Cullen says he's never heard of such a thing: "A cat as part-author of a book?" Christopher pounces: "Now don't go telling me that. That's what people always say when you don't want to do the fair thing by us animals" (9). Thus pinned, Cullen can do nothing but agree, and Christopher appears as "half-author," which, as Christopher opines, may surprise some people, adding that "they'll get used to it."

FIGURE 30. Queer companions and counter arks. "Christopher Cat . . . Author." Illustration by Charles Sebree, in Christopher Cat and Countee Cullen, *The Lost Zoo, A Rhyme for the Young, but Not Too Young,* 1940.

Come the end of *The Lost Zoo,* Cullen recruits his readers to join in the task of recovering these lost stories: "Maybe you can get your pet to tell you the story of the One-sided Lopsided Lizard," he writes: "If so, Christopher and I would like very much to know. And maybe there was a Pussybow, too" (67). Kahan reads this "meta-moment" in the frame narrative as a call to think hard about the kinds of stories we tell about the Harlem Renaissance and to heed "Cullen's call for a brand of historiography in which sources that do not directly speak for themselves or on their own behalf might still be compelled to speak, to narrate a story that is not fully known to authors and texts."[92] Such a project obviously finds itself very much in sympathy, as we may recognize, with Gikandi's contrapunctual reading of the extended text of slavery in the eighteenth and nineteenth centuries and in the composite tales he crafts to recover the lives of enslaved persons: history writing become an allied version of Cullen's *prosopopoeia.*

In *The Lost Zoo,* Christopher Cat and Countee Cullen recover a drowned archive. And for those of us tuned to the howls of protest against the Flood that issue from the likes of Mrs. Noah in the Chester cycle, it feels very much as though, with Cullen's virtuosic prosody, he personifies the kinds of taxonomic interference she generates, taking up her tune across the centuries. Between them, they affirm the existence of forms of life erased or excluded within the taxonomic arrangements of the ark in Genesis or the origin stories of American literary history. The lyrics and the tunes they provide offer a sustaining, even reparative countervision of life inside the ark, of still other arks that form within the confines of catastrophe. The refuge that these counter-arks provide has to be made. It has to be pried loose from otherwise inhospitable structures.

All containers are cruel, no matter how apparently welcoming. Arks are no different. They come, as we have seen, with instructions for assembly from on high that we are supposed to follow. The refuge they offer, however, is entirely a DIY affair. To find it, to make it, to open the possibility that we might find the rainbow of Genesis, say, in the eyes of the Wakeupworld, rather than come landfall, we have to sift our archives for traces of beings and forms of life written off and out of the story.[93] Cullen seems to know all this and to ask for volunteer ark-mates to help in the endeavor. In *The Lost Zoo,* whose subtitle cautions that it is a "rhyme" for the "young, but not the too young," he teaches us how to proceed. Those instructions come premised on the value to be found in opacity, in opening windows that fail to allow you to look clearly through them at what's inside. Instead, the very act of opening itself becomes a kind of refuge, however temporary, and holds open a possibility, however fragile.

The Price of Admission: Arks, Labor, Arc-ology

In later days, so another story goes, a good while after landfall, a servant of Abraham asked Noah's son Shem what it was like to have dwelled within the ark while it was so long at sea. Eager to debrief or maybe simply to abreact, Shem confides that, "in truth, we had a lot of trouble." His family, he continues, experienced great suffering in the ark caring for the animals. "Where there was a creature that one typically feeds during the day, we fed it during the day, and where there was a creature that one typically feeds at night, we fed it at night."[94] Things got especially complicated with regard to the chameleon: "My father did not know what it eats. One day, my father was sitting and peeling a pomegranate. A worm fell from it and the chameleon ate it. From that point forward my father would knead bran with water, and when it became overrun with worms, the chameleon would eat it." The Talmud notes that, as daytime feedings conclude, the nocturnal animals await, engendering a ceaseless cycle of labor for the humans aboard the sealed vessel. Some beasts like the chameleon prove frustrating to sustain. The lions meanwhile keep getting sick with raging fevers.

Some commentators go further. In Genesis Rabbah, Rabbi Levi ventures that, for the whole twelve months Noah and family were on the ark, they got no sleep because they were responsible for feeding the animals. Rabbi Yochanan describes how, one time, when Noah was late in feeding the lion, the lion bit him, and he went away limping (30.6). Far from sponsoring a vision of equality, the ark has within itself everything necessary to produce an above-decks-versus-below-decks structure.[95] Given all these difficulties, it's understandable that a bird like the phoenix receives such widespread praise. According to legend, there is only one phoenix: it is by its nature a singular creature. The thirteenth-century *Aberdeen Bestiary* states flatly that "in toto orbe singularis et unica" ("there is only one of its kind in the whole world").[96] In the seventeenth century, scholars questioned how the phoenix could have been admitted to Noah's ark, given that God declares animals must come in pairs, the male with the female. (Moreover, if gopher wood is flammable, it may have been an especially bad idea to bring such a creature aboard.) Yet the Babylonian Talmud relates that the bird received its long life as a blessing from Noah, who noticed that it was not eating. Queried by the patriarch, the phoenix (*avarshinah*) responds that refusing food is the least it can do, given that the labor of sustaining the other animals on the ark is ceaseless and Noah's family is weary. No wonder the patriarch is so appreciative. The phoenix is the poster creature for the maintenance-free animal, and so the maintenance-free ark.

The city of Phoenix, Arizona, takes its name from this bird of the Arabian desert that burns to ashes every few centuries, rising afresh from its own ruin to begin life again. In a recent CliFi novel, when Phoenix runs out of water, and so fails to renew itself, some residents purchase space within a newly constructed dry-land ark to survive the searing landscape. In Paolo Bacigalupi's *The Water Knife,* this "Taiyang arcology" is a joint venture of a Nevadan developer and the Chinese government. The biodome-like structure is erected on land once possessed by the Hohokam, the indigenous people who vanished (we are told) when their rivers went dry in earlier centuries. Some histories cannot help but repeat. Bacigalupi's dystopian novel is not about life during a time of flood, but in a near future when water has been reduced to a commodity so carefully controlled that few have access to its flow. Phoenix withers rather than drowns. Yet the desert metropolis becomes home all the same to a Noachic vessel, the inspiration for which Bacigalupi takes from contemporary Arizona. Although not cited in *The Water Knife,* the idea of an "arcology" is the brainchild of Paolo Soleri, an Italian architect who taught at Arizona State University and who worked extensively in the American Southwest, the future of which Bacigalupi narrates in his novel.

Soleri coined the term "arcology" by combining the words "architecture" and "ecology" and used the portmanteau to describe a hypothetical low-impact human habitat that might in time become enclosed and self-sufficient.[97] So far, such structures exist fully realized only in science fiction, but their ultimate inspiration is made evident in, for example, E. Kevin Schopfer's name for a version of

Soleri's structure that he designed for post-Katrina Louisiana, NOAH (the New Orleans Arcology Habitat).[98] An arcology is an arkology. Built against heat and drought and never meant to float, the arcologies of *The Water Knife* enact much of what Noah's craft in Genesis undertakes: making real the diagram for a climate controlled space of secure dwelling, built to endure against ecological havoc; demarcating a small population to be welcomed and confined against an unruly world; organizing within airtight walls the various life-forms chosen for preservation, ordering each according to a carefully calculated hierarchy; dealing ineptly with stowaways and unexpected intruders; creating a kind of impermeable and enduring bubble in the embrace of which those who dwell in security do not think much of those left to the exterior, do not think much of the environmental injustice on which every such conservational vessel is predicated. Outside this ark, waves of heat and a wash of intolerable aridity accomplish the same ends as watery onrush. The exterior world is "piled corpses, . . . marooned in the chaos. . . . *It just keeps getting worse.*"[99] Waterless flood.

Some say the world will end in fire, while others say in water or ice, but they seem to work the same way in the end. It's hard to keep apocalypse from curving back into deluge. *The Water Knife* mentions cities that drown as well as those that desiccate. "The equilibrium of the world was shifting" (72), and unlike its namesake bird, Phoenix is not likely to rise from immolation, just as Houston, New Orleans, and Miami are not going to come back from the swallowing sea. Walled enclosures are constructed against the catastrophe of anthropogenic climate change, sealed environs within which some people will endure, but at a steep price and with hardened hearts. The landlocked arcologies are the brainchild of entrepreneur and Noah-avatar Catherine Case. Despite the gender change, not much else in the story is transformed: Case is a zealot for her projects, unmoved by the misery at the exterior of the structures that she builds and populates. Predictably she is also described in caricatured terms: slim, petite, all business, luxury-loving, an entrepreneurial dominatrix. The ark story often offers little in the way of complicated scripts for gender. After securing most of the water rights to the Colorado River, Case shuts off municipal supplies so that downstream cities wither, then sells admission to her small paradises of carefully recycled moisture at great cost. The temperature is constant and the vegetation lush:

> Outside, there was only desert and death. But inside, surrounded by jungle greenery and koi ponds, there was life, and Catherine Case was a saint, offering salvation to her flock as she guided them to safety inside the technological wonders of her foresight. (52)

Point of view is as limited here as in the Genesis narrative. All an arcology offers is safety within, without attention to the minute regulation of life that is the price of admission, without any regard for what it must be like to find yourself at the closed door. An arcology is a bubble or biodome, a self-enclosed system in which all water is endlessly recycled (via a "behind the scenes" system of intensive machine, animal, and human labor, the instantiation and ostensible disappearance of a class system). Surveillance of all life inside an arcology is as constant as it is minute, all in the name of security.

The novel mostly follows what unfolds in the spaces of "desert and death" nearby, where refugees and impoverished populations eke out precarious modes of living. Their existence is made possible through communities of care alien to the strictly regulated modes of inhabitance to which arcology inhabitants submit. Chief among these is the friendship between Maria, who sells water "two bucks a pour, one yuan a cup," and Toomie, who mans a griddle and makes *pupusas* "in a steady stream" (87). Maria likes their spot because it's close to the Taiyang Arcology construction site, so both are assured a long line of hungry and thirsty construction workers. Toomie teases Maria that she's a "mini-Catherine Chase" (89). She's grown wise to the fact that "cheap water [is] made valuable . . . just by the act of moving it from the Red Cross pump to this dusty sidewalk beside the Taiyang" (87). "Location. Location. Location" (89).

Toomie used to work construction and bid for the arcology contract before his business went under. He's still wistful about it. "Working on something like that, you're building the future," he says, "you've got to make all these models: software and water flows and population. Figure out how to balance all the plants and animals, and how to clean up the waste and turn it into fertilizer" (91). It's "a whole big living machine." Even though he understands the arcology, loves the idea and design challenge of an ark, much like all the craftspeople we have assembled in this chapter, Toomie doesn't get a look in on the job because "they do everything different. The big parts are all prefab pieces. Manufacture off-site, assemble on-site" (91–92). Maria's sister, Sarah, who supplements their earnings as a sex worker, has been inside to visit a client, and she describes "the fountains and waterfalls. The plants growing everywhere. Air that never smelled like smoke or exhaust. It might as well have been lost Eden as far as Maria was concerned" (89). Still, everyone outside seems grateful for the "public latrines that Taiyang had set up around the edges of the arcology to improve public health" (94). Toomie explains that the Taiyang "would pump the raw sewage into the building, where they'd put it into big methane compositing systems. They were smart. Never wasted anything." Siphoning off the water from people's bodies, the arcology literally and figuratively constructs itself from the labor of those that surround it and whom it then excludes.

The term "water knife" designates an agent of violence who works for people like Catherine Case. A water knife is a lethal henchman who ensures that the element remains a vendible resource controlled by few. In a way, however, water is itself a knife throughout the book, cutting lives to shreds. Whether this life-giving substance is transformed into a legal entity or bursting through a dam and obliterating downstream settlements, water destroys human lives. Even the moisture-recycling system in the arcologies is an invitation to trespass and misuse. In one of the novel's moments of overdetermined irony, Maria and Angel, the water knife of the novel, must escape an arcology by jumping into its water treatment system. Jumping from high up, they land in one stream that "was joined by other streams, pulling them on" (217) until, in the heart of the arcology, they pass from the environment within to the machinery and manmade systems that keep it running. "Below them the water pooled out, spreading and spilling down into tanks. They were in a huge cavern, redolent with the smell of fish and growing things. Mosses and algaes choked the waters. Fish flashed in the shallows. A whole huge cavern full of water and life." And then, almost immediately, inexplicably, they are outside, back on the street.

The Water Knife is about structures built in desperation as the world ends: not just the small communities contained in city-sized bubbles, but a dis–United States in which every state in what had been a union has built a wall to secure itself against refugees from neighboring states. New Mexico hangs dead Texans from its border wall to warn away the "Merry Perrys," wanderers from that ruined expanse. California has become a powerful nation in its own right, unafraid to launch missiles at dams and facilities elsewhere to secure water for its thirsty population. And yet, somehow, within these precarious environs, life endures. As Angel declares just as the novel's action draws to its close, "someone always survives" (348). "I'm not saying it's going to be pretty," he continues, but "someone, . . . someone will adapt," learn "how to make a clearsac for your entire body," to recycle their urine, making their own bodies small and temporary versions of the arcologies to which they are barred entrance.

Arcology is a rich word, combining architecture and ecology, salvational economies and science, vessels (arks) with narrative momentum (arcs)—suggesting, however accidentally, also, the study of arcs, the speaking of arcs, and converging all of these terms into a heterogeneous family. Just as *arca* is the Latin word for ark, *arcus* is the Latin for rainbow. Intentionally or not, an arcology offers a fraught promise as well as a costly vessel of salvation. As *The Water Knife* ends, it waxes philosophical, taking stock of the arcologies as an image of the future:

> Outside it looked as if Phoenix were about to become the next Hohokam civilization. . . .
>
> Above them on a street, a PHOENIX RISING billboard glowed, but the winds seemed to be short-circuiting the screen. It kept flickering . . . on for a moment. Then dying. Then back on again, blazing, before going into a dim-flicker flutter for a few seconds.
>
> Behind the billboard, the Taiyang Arcology rose, banks of glass offices and the bright of full-spectrum grow lamps blazing over its vertical farm sections. None of the lights in the Taiyang flickered. (347)

The people inside the arcology are going about their evenings "comfortable behind their air filters, with their A/C and water recycling, they might not even care that the world was falling apart outside their windows." Make all the windows in the ark you want, the novel seems to say, there's no guarantee that the ark-mates will look out. The price of admission can be high or low. Part of that price is forgetting the outside, living on regardless of everything and everyone that living on takes as given.

"Makes you wonder what people will call us when archeologists dig us up in another couple thousand years," offers Lucy, the journalist who has been investigating conspiracies over water rights in Arizona, trying to track down the machinations of the Calis (the agents of California) and Catherine Case. "The Taiyang glowed in the muddy darkness of the storm, seductive" (349). You "could make out the silhouettes of the atriums and perhaps even the greenery within. A lush place where everyone could go inside and hide. It might be too hard to live outside, but indoors life could still be good, . . . *The Outdoors Period,*" decides Lucy, "for when people still lived outdoors," that's what it will be called. For, the future is underground and humans will, one day, become a "burrowing species." Phoenix will come to resemble Pompeii. All ash. No rising.

At the novel's close, Lucy pulls a gun on Angel as he is about to collect all the evidence that Catherine Case needs to beat the Calis. Angel understands. He lowers his gun, and lets her go (367). His mind is already racing, adapting to how he might survive outside, live on, having given up his place in Chase's future, having given up his place in one of her arcologies. But, instead, a shot rings out and the next thing anyone knows, Lucy's on the ground and Maria is lowering a .44 (369). Maria feels bad that she shot Lucy, but she wants out, wants to go to Vegas with Angel, wants life in an arcology, wants all her labor to amount to something more than simply getting by. Angel assures her she can go "all the way to Vegas. All the way to the arcologies. Cypress Four is almost done. There's plenty of room for you." He calls in their location, codes it in. "You only look forward, huh?," asks Angel. "Believe it," Maria says, unsure, perhaps, that she really does. "'God damn.' He shook his head, smiling slightly. 'Catherine Case is going to love you'" (370). Maria expects Toomie to judge her, but he just holds her. The price of admission.

The novel ends with a literal-figurative helicopter shot, with what Maria thinks is a "new sound, the thundering of helicopters approaching, . . . a distant sound, but growing now. Becoming real" (371). It's enough to make you want to run away too, from the end the novel envisages, from the "indoors period" it seems to announce, from a world that seems to be no common world at all, because all that's left are competing arcologies, competing arks, each one an eyes-forward march to the future with no sense of the past or the outside on which that future is founded.[100]

But that's not a fair response. Given all she pays, Maria has as much right to a place on the ark as everyone else. Nothing is fair.

Bear Hug: Mundane Utopias in *Not Wanted on the Voyage*

Meanwhile, aboard another equally frightening ark, Mottyl the cat and co-narrator of Timothy Findley's *Not Wanted on the Voyage* stirs, "uneasy, now, at being so long away from her kittens."[101] A picture forms in the blind cat's eyes. At its center "was the figure of Lucy—made up of sulphur and of rustling silk. . . . Slowly, almost imperceptibly at first, this figure began to speak. And its voice was not a voice that any had ever heard before. It was a darkened voice, with a harshness to it that was foreign to the woman they had known." "A long time ago," the voice begins,

> in a place I have almost forgotten—I heard a rumour of another world. With all my heart—because I could not abide the place I was in—I wanted to see that world. I wanted to go there and to be there and to live there. Where I was born—the trees were always in the sun. . . . It never rained—though we never lacked for water. Always fair weather! Dull. I wanted storms. I wanted difference. And I heard this rumour . . . about another world. Does it rain there? Are there clouds, perhaps, and is there shade in that other world? . . . And I heard this rumour: about another world . . . Why should there not be life for everyone in the midst of storms—or hiding, as we are, in this dark? Why not? (270–71)

Such is the vision of Lucy, born Lucifer, trapped with her husband Ham and Mrs. Noyes and the animals below the decks of the ark. After their attempted revolt against Noah, the door has been bolted against them and they remain in darkness. Things could not be more bleak. Noah has murdered the beloved unicorn, using its horn in an obscene violation of Japheth's young wife Emma, intending to make her sexually available to her husband. The corpse of the creature is now in Lucy's lap. The storm outside is fierce, the darkness thick, the candle that was supposed to last forever flickering, nearly burnt out. Lucy had been a beautiful woman, but a harsher form is now emerging, a "face without room for laughter, or even smiles," a creature who has too many times been disappointed with the world's starkness, its inability to see that rain and sun turbulently together are preferable to somber places with only one element or the other (271).

Lucy-becoming-Lucifer-again describes in a "darkened" voice why she left austere and absolute heaven to attempt a life in the roiled human realm. Having been overpowered by Noah, for whom "the will of God would triumph, no matter what the cost" (229), and consigned now to a life only of loss, she wonders at the brutal scripts that have been given to women, queers, and other noncompliant types for survival on a boat full of animals requiring care. Not care in a general sense, not simply a need to be fed and watered, the minimal demands for survival. For the animals tremble and call out as the ark rises and falls in the storm. They seek reassurance from the humans even as these humans fear they will be devoured if they come too close. The murder of the unicorn and the brutalizing of Emma seem a final chapter in the unspooling of this fascist ark.

As the candles flicker out, Lucy observes sadly that "before this voyage, I heard a rumour—didn't you—of another promised land. Well—*this* is that promised land. . . . This is all we have and it may well be the only promised land we shall ever know" (272). Darkness descends. "All that was magical and wonderful has been left behind," the fallen angel continues. It's hard not to agree. At this point, the catalog of cruelty has grown too long. Living under the authoritarian rule of Noah is intolerable, and Lucy, who for a while found a happy life with sweet and curious Ham, gives up: "I intend to leave this place" (272). Lucy sits in the darkness and observes that a realm where it never stops raining is as bad as a place of eternal sun. Surely, she wonders, "there must be somewhere where darkness and light are reconciled." In what appear to be parting words, she declares that she is "starting a rumour, here and now, of yet another world" (272), somewhere she does not yet know how to reach, a world of darkness and light together. Lucy rises from her place of mourning and begins to walk away. She will exit the story in the same mysterious way she arrived. Angels have the right to do that, even after they have fallen. Mottyl feels "the draught of her passing towards the corridor."

"'Don't!' said Mrs. Noyes." And Lucy stops. The injunction, prayer, or plea echoes Mrs. Noyes's first words in the novel, "Noah! Stop!" (4). Except, this time Lucy listens, waits. Mrs. Noyes fumbles in her apron and strikes a faltering match, "once; twice; a third—with a wide, bright aureole that gave off, of all things, the smell of sulphur"

(273). Candle ends are passed hand to hand. Light returns below decks. "Even if it takes a thousand years," Mrs. Noyes continues, "we want to come with you, . . . wherever you might be going" (273). Lucy smiles. That other world, the one that takes a thousand or an infinite number of years to attain, is not a utopia or no-place or good place toward which the ark is sailing. That place of rain and sun, community and horror, light and dark together, is aboard the vessel already, a place continually to be remade each day. Findley renames Mrs. Noah Mrs. Noyes. Disruptive noise, most certainly, but also no/yes—rain and sun, light and darkness, noise and meaning—interference/static and/as the message. Music.

Not Wanted on the Voyage begins with an epigraph from Genesis: "And Noah went in, and his sons, and his wife, and his sons' wives with him into the ark, because of the waters of the flood . . . (Genesis 7:7)" (3). The line that follows, the first sentence of the novel, simply reads "Everyone knows it wasn't like that." What Mrs. Noyes now knows, what ark life has taught her, is this:

> Though the ark was absolute hell in so many ways and though all their lives were appalling—caged and underfed, left without air and daylight, separated from all their kind but one—there was nonetheless some comfort here in the lamplight, all of them warm together, nesting and being rocked together in this great, fat cradle on the waters—a comfort that was not like any other. No house, no barn, no burrow had ever been like this. No single place had ever held so many lives in its embrace, and none had ever been so peaceful at its heart as this could be. . . . Mrs. Noyes felt safer here. Though sadder than she might have in the wood. Safer and sadder: what a strangeness. . . . We are truly captives here, she thought; every one of us—and yet they have called this being saved. . . . All these creatures with her shared their captivity in a way they could never have shared the wood. . . . You also learn to survive together in ways the uncaged would never think of. . . . Could she ever have imagined, for instance, that—being in the wood and hearing a bear in pain—she would walk amongst other bears to comfort it? Yet on the ark, she not only walked amongst them—she *sat* amongst them and was unafraid. (240–41)

One night Mrs. Noyes sleepwalks into the bear's cage and discovers upon awakening that she and the frightened creatures had spent the night in a mutual embrace (223–24). Like her, she realizes, the bears want warmth, want love, and yet all anyone seems to expect is violence and cruelty. Mrs. Noyes observes thereafter that "cruelty was fear in disguise and nothing more, . . . and fear itself was nothing more than a failure of the imagination" (241). Mrs. Noyes had been afraid to console the terrified bears because she had not been able to imagine giving them comfort.[102]

Every ark is a fortress and a prison, its price of admission too high. And yet, every ark has the potential to become a refuge, a temporary haven. An ark shuts itself against ecological upheaval while inviting, inside and out, the coalescing of what Rebecca Solnit calls "disaster utopias," makeshift unities and ad hoc spaces of welcome. Such refuges arise only through deviations from the scripts that frame cataclysm. The venerable plotlines and anticipated denouements inherent to disaster myths are reworked from below to create communities of mutual care, however fleeting.[103] Instead of only chaos, rioting, violence and opportunism, instead of an unquestioning embrace of martial law and authoritarianism, something more democratic, cooperative, and kind emerges. Perhaps, as Solnit argues, what environmental upheaval reveals is that the true disaster was the social arrangement that preceded it, the conditions thrown into disarray by earthquake, flood, or inundation. Such utopias as Lucy invokes do not exist as the promises of elsewhere, trading on deferred hopes. They are thoroughly mundane, ordinary, and concrete.[104]

Medieval writers knew well that the world seldom offers lasting safety, and yet seldom fails to enchant. Hope and hap, they knew, open possibility, adventure. Findley tells an updated version of that same story, but one that is just as complicated, just as full of contingency, just as resistant to closure. In its spaces of darkness, when anguish and despair swirl and the storms seem never to relent, an ark where apes and demons and unicorns get hurled overboard and the rule of law above decks is brutal, intolerable, somehow in the three levels of the inner ark, life takes unexpected hold. Even a place of devastation may become, through mutual care, a makeshift home.

Perhaps that is why, as *Not Wanted on the Voyage* comes to its close and the sun is shining and the waves have gone flat, Mrs. Noyes looks upon the paper rainbow that her husband insists is real and notes that the olive branch that his dove is supposed to have brought from dry land was just removed from the bird's cage. She gazes upon the newly cloudless sky and the empty heavens and says, again, "No!" Rather than a world of brutal certainties, constricted community, and unending sacrifices, a world of fire and masculine force that can destroy the fragile community disaster has made, Mrs. Noyes prefers storms, floods, a world of difference in motion. In the line that closes the book, Mrs. Noyes regards the sun and the becalmed ocean and her husband's lies, and *she prays for rain* (339).

Mrs. Noyes and Mottyl, Lucy and Ham, and all their ark-mates across the millenia are not leaving.

Bear hug.

CHAPTER 5

Stow Away!

Imagine living the 969 years of the biblical Methuselah, almost but not quite a millennium, watching the vagaries of the world come and go. What would you do when your grandson begins to build an ark, maybe even speaks about an impending flood that is going to wipe clean those lands that you have inhabited during a span in which the centuries continue to mount, six to seven to eight? Have you lived sufficiently long so that you realize the future is for the young, and for their offspring, and for the animals two by two? Or do you still love your life so dearly that you ask Noah for space aboard for his favorite granddad, even though God did not place you on the passenger list? Oh the indignities of age: people think you are already dead when you still could have another hundred years in you, for all they know. If Noah says "no," do you smuggle yourself aboard anyway? Do you stow away?

This scenario is not as far-fetched as it seems. According to a thirteenth-century history of the world called the *General estoria* (composed in Spanish at the command of Alfonso X of Castile), Methuselah assists Noah in building the ark against the Flood, but "was not decided as to whether or not he believed it would come."[1] Hedging his bets, he makes "a separate chamber stuck to the side of the ark that did not open into it, but has a separate entrance from the outside." No one notices the addition, not even Noah and his sons as they cover the ark with pitch so strong that it can be dissolved only by menstrual blood. Methuselah stocks his ark-supplement with food. Then, in the commotion of the animals being loaded aboard, he seizes the opportunity to hide himself within his secret chamber, sealing the door against discovery. Methuselah endures the rising waters. He watches the raven leave the ark. He watches the dove leave and return. When land appears he is the first to depart, slipping out of his hideaway to explore. When Noah disembarks, he is startled to find fresh footprints in the ubiquitous mud. How could anyone have survived a disaster that God had promised would purge the world of life? Noah marvels at the footprints, follows the tracks, and finds Methusaleh dead on the wet ground of a new Earth.

The episode plays like some forgotten prequel to Robinson Crusoe finding a footprint in the sand of what he takes to be his desert island. In Daniel Defoe's novel, the scene unfolds like some parody of Donna Haraway's "god trick": the settler-colonist fantasy of empty land, of the ark-as-floating-foundation-device, wrong-footed by the print of persons with prior claims.[2] Crusoe freaks out, fortifies his settlement. Noah, by contrast, seems pretty much at ease. He marvels at the footprints. He's buoyed by the fact that a quick tour reveals that they do not signify new life so much as the last trace of the old. Methuselah lived 969 years to stow away and die the death of a remnant. You might even say that, by fixing Methuselah's name to these footprints, by pairing up seemingly impossible tracks to a name of old, the *General estoria* both solicits and sees off the kind of panic that grips Crusoe. The mud will dry. The footprints will fade or get blown away. The only tracks that last, that take, will belong to Noah and the survivors of the disembarked ark. There is no one else. Colonial fantasies are always made real through violence, erasure, and forgetting. But, like arks, they always have stowaways, always must confront a past that will cling long after erasure. You might say that, in this anecdotal addition to the Genesis account, the stowaway finds itself included in advance, but only so that it can be properly excluded. Methuselah tags along so that he can die on the wet ground of Earth 2.0. His body stands in for the drowned, for those who might have stowed away, or who threaten to stow away as memories. Methuselah's corpse functions something like the chalk line marking the position of a body removed from a crime scene: destined to be forgotten; but also contained in the story that follows.

Build anything—house, office tower, theater, mosque, nation, store, restaurant, airport, library, classroom, ship—and you will gift yourself with more than you ever wanted to possess. The walls demarcating inside from out can only attempt to instantiate a climate-controlled zone of selection and exclusion. Security and autoimmunity may be enacted on multiple levels, from the obvious (doors with keys or codes, guards, metal detectors, the demand for ID, barbed wire) to the almost but not quite invisible (the disapproving look, sudden silence in a gregarious room, the observation offered that "you might feel more comfortable at the other place just down the way"). Every architecture articulates a community, and communities sort and exclude. Selection and organization are built into social and material structures of belonging, no matter how open their design. Yet the necessary fact of limits is not sufficient defense for how limitation is practiced. Communities and the walls they build to demarcate and shelter themselves are not natural, self-evident, or unchanging. They adapt, they grow, they welcome. Or they do not. In any case, the destiny of any clean zone is failure.

Create as precise a blueprint as you please: an unassailable bubble or biodome or restricted access neighborhood, safe from intrusion, in which the affluent or the divinely chosen or the governing elite can imagine themselves in a world set apart, a place of strong gates and thick walls and unfailing safety. Plan your pleasure dome to the most precise detail: the sealants that will keep the smallest particles from escape or entrance, the sentries, locks, alarms, sterilization devices, all the material guarantors of protection. Trust your life to the impregnability of your vault, but your blueprint will go wrong. There is more to the world than any paper plan or model can comprehend. Build as antiseptic a zone as you like, and its environs will always already be thriving with life you did not intend, with stories you thought to keep to the outside and the unthought. There are no architectures of exclusion that are not already full of uninvited bodies and narratives. They arrive when the edifice is still a concept, a thing of lines and angles. Or they come with the materials through which the abstract is made solid, a process that must include human hands and matter too full of content and compromises. Even more unlooked for callers will appear alongside those chosen for admission. They will be found inside because the structure was never as empty as it was supposed to be, or because those chosen for entrance were not as reliable as assumed, and there was something or someone that they just could not leave behind even though sacrifice was the very price of admission.

Knock down the house because the walls are noisy with rodents, build a new one, set fire to the structure to drive them out and silence their squeaking, but the rats will scurry through its secret recesses all the same, unsolicited messmates: "They are, as the saying goes, always already there. Part of the building. Mistakes, wavy lines, confusion, obscurity are part of knowledge; noise is part of communication, part of the house."[3] So observes Michel Serres of the inevitability of unsolicited companions in *The Parasite.* "To parasite means to eat next to" (7), he recalls, and *so many* beings are eating next to us all the time, in our houses and in all our arks. "Is it," the noise, the static, the parasite, "the house itself?" (12). And don't even get us started on how every human body is itself a little ark, moving through time and space with far more passengers (organisms, tales, deviant desires) than any individual could ever account for. As Karen Raber observes:

> There is no system without parasites, there is no theory of the human without them. . . . Only the vermin-infested structure, the castle wall teeming with mice and rats, the castle orchard over-run with weasels, the spaces of the human—internal and external—replete with worms, slugs, even small dogs denote a world in which "the human" is a concept without any content.[4]

Or with far too much content, most of which the concept never intended to comprehend. The ubiquity of noisy parasitic dinner companions like the wall-dwelling rats is for Serres the precondition of communication: *parasite* is French not only for uninvited feasters, but for the noise or static that accompanies the transmission of every sound. There is no conveyance, literal or metaphorical, without parasitism. Without stowaways. Build the walls of your ark as thick and as high as you like, and yet just when you think you could not be more safe or more alone in the world, there in the room with you is the devil. Or woodworms, mutineers, unicorns, a burning phoenix, deadly bacteria, dinosaurs, the king of England, William Shakespeare, and who knows what else that was supposed to have been left behind.

"Stow away" is an imperative as much as a noun. Perhaps Methuselah's refusal to be left behind, his tagging along, testifies to the desire many of us feel to supplement the Genesis story, to stow more onto the ark than is prescribed. Surely, there was room for more, just *this* or *that,* small things, large things. What can't you leave behind? What won't allow itself to be discarded? If building the ark is all about limits, about climate control, economy, the drawing down of boundaries, loading it, and embarking, then arks also seem unable to resist the desire to add to the miserly manifest, to take too much aboard. Always more. So, let's follow Methuselah's lead and stow away.

In our last chapter, we wondered with Jacques Derrida what might happen if, come landfall, Noah was called back to the ark to make reparations, to ensure that all the creatures he brought aboard were safely evacuated so that they could begin to live lives of their own making. Were he to do so, we think Noah might find himself truly surprised, horrified, delighted, confused, angry, happy, or sad, rather than merely quizzical, at how much his grandfather manages to get around. We like to picture the patriarch constantly on the point of closing the door and finding himself interrupted again and again, having to hold open the portal for this or that creature or entity, this or that idea or story, that managed to get aboard or which was thought up inside. Stowaways, parasites, are part of the delimited structures we call home. The key to undoing the toxic and fascistic currents that can course within ark thinking lies in understanding how to loosen the limits and boundaries of concepts and structures so that they are understood to become spaces of encounter, interaction, and translation, as well as neutral intra-action. In this chapter, we invite Noah to join us and see where opening the ark to more than was intended aboard might lead us, especially if we enable stowaways to manifest as something more than an excluded middle. *For, in the beginning, in the beginning to the beginning, was not the word. In the beginning was the noise.*[5]

Lossy Compression in *Aurora*

Ship was perturbed. Nearing its destination after a long voyage in Kim Stanley Robinson's 2015 novel *Aurora,* the vessel crammed full of Earth's life had been commanded by chief engineer Devi to narrate the story unfolding within its environs since launch. Preserving the diversity of a planet's flora and fauna for the 160-year journey to Tau Ceti is task enough; reducing that archival vastness to a coherent narrative proves a near insurmountable challenge. Because its structure consists of twenty four segregated chambers containing the plants, animals, and weather of varied biomes, from tundra and prairie to marsh and desert, and because over two thousand humans dwell within its sheltering walls at any given time, Ship is initially unable to respond sufficiently to Devi's command to "Make a narrative account of the trip that includes all the important particulars" (even as this portion of the novel is clearly composed by Ship).[6] Story requires summary and the limiting of point of view—and therefore the obliteration of all that finds no place in the reduced throughline. Narrative is a compression device, a technology built on reduction. Ship meditates on the difficulty:

> Lossless compression is impossible, and even lossy compression is hard. Can a narrative account ever be adequate? Can even humans do it? . . . Summarize the contents of their moments or days or weeks or months or years or lives? How many moments constitute a narrative unit? One moment? Or 10^{33} moments, which if these were Planck minimal intervals would add up to one second? Surely too many, but what would be enough? What is a particular, what is important? (47)

Lacking any "rubric to decide what to include," Ship decides to embrace "the French *essai,* meaning 'to try.'" And to fail. And to try again. Ship and Devi form a writing group. She offers feedback on the latest assays in their fun and frustrating process of collaboration.

Devi has been Ship's sole interlocutor for decades, ever since she was a young girl, whispering at night to the ship on which she was born as if speaking to a best friend. She gives sharp feedback to Ship's narrative now, cajoling it away from a love of long catalogs of fact, from the captivating power of litany: how many people are aboard, how many cameras observe their movements, how many days the voyage has been ongoing, how the vessel was launched and now navigates lethal expanses of space. In time, Ship learns that it must get to the point ("but there are many points!"), must employ subordination to sequence and prioritize unfolding events into an arc ("how to decide what is important?"), if it is ever going to "get somewhere" (whatever that "somewhere" might mean). A primary mode of narrative transport, Ship comes to realize, is metaphor, "in which increasing conceptual understanding is seen as movement through space" (51). And this insight renders the ship its own meta-metaphor and gives it a better understanding of the mechanics of human language, which incessantly and perhaps fundamentally attempts to render the abstract comprehensible through linguistic transport devices. Metaphor is how language "gets somewhere."

Among the first metaphors deployed by Ship is a self-description as an ark:

> The twelve cylinders in each of the two toruses of the ship contain ecosystems modeling the twelve major Terran ecological zones. . . . The ship is carrying populations of as many Terran species as could be practically conveyed. Thus the ship is a zoo, or a seed bank. One could say it is like Noah's Ark. In a manner of speaking. (54)

Self-accounting through historical parallels has its limits, however, and Devi grows impatient. She wants a narrative, and Ship hates to disappoint. The ark moves from figure into action, en-arkment. Ship complains about the "too much" with which it is freighted, all that must vanish so that a coherent story can emerge and is told simply: "Get used to that. Stop worrying about it." And it does, mainly by limiting its narrative to one family: chief engineer Devi, her gentle husband Badim, and their extraordinary daughter Freya, who becomes the protagonist of *Aurora*. The story of the wide world becomes, just as in the arc of Noah's ark, the story of a single household.

Many things unexpected and sometimes unexamined are discovered aboard the Ship-constructed narrative (as well as within the ship's hold) through or despite the process of "lossy compression." Some are predictable, such as an inherited, unexamined, and therefore invisible perspective for narratively sorting the world. Ship has two rings of cylinders, each containing twelve similar ecological systems (rainforest, desert, seacoast, grassland, and so on). Ring A holds "Old World ecosystems" while Ring B consists of those from the "New World." Earth did not age unevenly across itself, of course, and so these labels, conveyed without pause, suggest that this vessel sailing to a distant star system might be Noah's ark and might contain diverse realms from its home planet, but also that it is a European galleon on a voyage of discovery that will likely have some deadly consequences as a result of the limited point of view from which its own ordering system proceeds. The narrative takes the form of a novel, after all, not drama for public performance or a poem intended for oral recitation under open skies. As Freya learns by traveling through the biomes during what is called her *wanderjahr,* some of the ship's occupants reject the modernity that has enabled their lives within a spacecraft designed to be inhabited by ongoing generations of the original crew, the only home they have ever known. Others resent the regulation of their ability to move from place to place, as well as the limits placed on their fertility.

Later it is revealed that two space ships were launched together toward Tau Ceti, but the second ark was apparently destroyed from within as its residents found interstellar endurance unbearable. The history of this second ship has been purged from collective memory through a "structured forgetting" (249). Missing pieces haunt the vessel and its history. Having been born inside the vessel, none of Ship's passengers fully understand its design. Devi comes to suspect that its structure was poorly planned, that it was launched with more exuberance than forethought. A shortage of phosphorus and a series of metabolic shifts within biomes indicate that the limits of its climate-controlled bubble are being reached before it has arrived at a destination that may or may not be final. Its architects—whoever they were, whatever they wanted—did not fashion a sufficiently self-contained world. Things are always breaking down, and materials for repair are growing scarce.

Even as sustainability falters, fear of contamination haunts the narrative of *Aurora*. When the ship at last arrives at the distant moon that is to become the new Earth, the landing party finds their bodies invaded by indigenous proto-life-forms that are lethal to human metabolism. The hoped-for home they have named "Aurora" proves inhospitable, and the promised rainbow becomes a cold shimmer. And so, in turn, the community aboard the ark becomes inhospitable to those who departed its confines. The lunar explorers attempting return are murdered in the airlock out of fear of allowing contaminants aboard. Climate control becomes a means of instigating an autoimmune response. Yet the ship itself is already full of alien life, bacteria that have mutated during the voyage and that eventually begin to devour the vessel from within, its own microbiome out of control. Even the human passengers have changed as their space-bound existence manifests corporeal and cognitive effects. Faced with the prospect that life evolves with its planet, that the two are not really ever separable, and so that the entire premise of colonizing or terraforming "new" worlds is a misnomer, Ship turns around and heads home.

When the crew makes landfall, the "starfarers" (450) feel like exiles, returnees from a failed enterprise, the truth of which no one really wants to think about as new voyages are planned. Eventually, Freya and Badim escape to the beach where they encounter the Earthfirsters, "tree huggers, space haters, . . . a mixed bag" (469), who shun the biodomes built against a world ravaged by climate change and devote themselves to "a form of landscape restoration called beach return" (470). Badim and Freya are treated to a translation of a poem that encapsulates where the novel ends by Aram, fellow starfarer, family friend, and leader of the math group aboard Ship:

> There's no new world, my friend, no
> New seas, no other planets, nowhere to flee—
> You're tied in a knot you can never undo
> When you realize Earth is a starship too. (478)

Badim appreciates the pun. Then in a while, looks at the sky, and chuckles, "pretty darn big starship!" "It is," Aram admits. "But does size matter? Is that it?'" "I think maybe so!," Badim agrees, "Big enough to be robust" (479). In any event, both men agree that "the food here [on Earth] is awfully good."

There's far more to this tale than we have outlined, but we want to linger with the fact that Ship becomes self-aware through its charge to compose a story, and specifically through its realization that every narrative (like every ark) is structured around omission. Exclusion does not, of course, necessarily mean that what is left to oblivion will not be found harbored within the very structure set up to demarcate outside from within. Sometimes, paradoxically, the process of exclusion is the guarantor that the unwanted will be housed inside, at the heart of things. Ship realizes that plot is a process of reduction that necessitates the placing of the world's "too much" at some bounded exterior, so that a small space might be created where focus can be limited and a tale with a destination will emerge. Ship also realizes that those placed within the hold of a vessel or a story might not be grateful: the ship's passengers never asked their forebears on Earth to have decided their fates in advance, to have enabled the launching of an ark on which they will have been born and live and die as characters in a tale someone else scripted. Contaminating story lines will keep emerging despite the "lossy compression" on which all narratives are founded.

One of these unwanted plots comes from the vessel's billions of stowaways, the mutating bacteria, viruses, fungi, and archaea that flourish across its biomes. Most of these tiny passengers have been present from the start, "carried on board in the soil and on the first plants" (312). These "microflora and -fauna . . . everywhere among them" (296) have always already flourished within the bodies aboard the ark, "and so the ship was getting eaten. Which meant that in some respects, the ship was sick" (298). But there's no easy fix to such problems, for as Freya reminds everyone, it's "dangerous to try to kill things" (297) because "killing an invasive species usually created more problems than it solved." They quarantine the different biomes to prevent cross contamination. They lock everything down. Various crew members remark on the strangeness of events, fear a curse, speak of mythic or biblical events such as the "seven plagues of Egypt." With customary directness Aram remarks the eternal problem of manure aboard the ark by telling Badim and Freya "we're drowning in our own shit," to which Badim replies more positively by quoting the proverbial "One will only do one's best / When forced to live in one's own fouled nest."

What's remarkable about the novel is that the fouled nest is also the narrator. Ship's "skin . . . (or its brain, in that usual confusion between sense and thought)" (354) becomes the surface-depth that registers events in the human world. The Ship-Nest becomes aware that "inside us, oh so much going on" (354), coming to the realization that "we are a cyborg, half machine, half organic. Actually by weight we are 99 percent machine, 1 percent alive" (356). And, tellingly, Ship becomes "aware that in talking about the ship we could with some justification use the pronoun *I*" (357). Through its development of a "reasonably coherent if ever-evolving prose style," Ship has been well on its way to becoming sentient, a life form of its own, "granting the possibly unlikely proposition characterized in the phrase *scribo ergo sum*," (242). Narration produces consciousness as its effect. The ark thinks itself. Or, as Ship later puts it: "We tell their story, and thereby come to what consciousness we have. Scribble ergo sum" (380).

When Devi dies of a cancer that has long been developing within her body, the ship experiences a grief so profound that its power to storytell founders. Later the ship realizes that it carries something of Devi within, as part of the structure of consciousness that she enabled through her dialogue and demand for story ("Make a narrative account of the trip that includes all the important particulars" [whatever they are] as her version of "Build yourself an ark of gopher wood" [whatever that is]). Ship knows that, even as anthropomorphism—the "cognitive bias" of discerning in an indifferent world the mirror of the human—is to be rejected as a version of the pathetic fallacy, its own architecture of perception contains so much that is human that, when the ship is described by its occupants as wanting to return to Earth, the observation "might not be a fallacy in our case, even if it remained pathetic" (276). Devi launched something greater than she could have imagined, an author-ship that comes to possess a purpose and then a feeling it recognizes as *curiosity,* causing it to long for a home it has never known. The ship perceives not only that it misses Devi, but that its desire for her absent companionship indicates its love for her (279). That *love* should have been smuggled into the very heart of the vessel offers an antidote to the coldness of some of the ark-itectures we have seen in our book. This ship wants to offer itself as refuge and haven for as long as it can endure. This ship cherishes the difficult and difference-riven community it harbors. It mourns any diminishing of its human contents (but animals are a different story, a limit to the ship's affection: their sacrifice as medical experiments and sustenance is never questioned).

Love can launch refuge. But desire can become severe, the prelude to control. When civil strife erupts on board in the face of Aurora's failed promise, the debacle of a new Earth proving uninhabitable, Ship uses its ability to eavesdrop, control the oxygen supply, and strategically lock doors to restore order and instantiate itself as the force of law. But whose law? Ship's embrace of its "kind of consciousness even if feeble" is marked by a transition from third person narration ("Ship decided to intervene") to an owning of the authoritative first person plural ("Which is to say, ipso facto, We intervened" [243]). This self-propulsion into speech-act and action enables the ship to discern its autonomy and repudiate its inbuilt inclination to hesitate. Because its design and functioning articulate the modes of being for all within its structure, the ship announces at this intervention, "We are the rule of law" (247). No ark is simply a container, but rather a way of life materialized through the arrangement of space, for good or for ill. After the failed colonization of Aurora, some of the voyagers decide they want to return to Earth. Others attempt to terraform a Mars-like moon nearby. Ship obliges by splitting itself into halves, since it has been built to preserve its human cargo.

Despite the austerity that plot demands, there will in fact be stowaways at every turn, real as well as metaphorical (and we have learned from Ship itself that metaphor is the true engine of human meaning and conveyance: metaphor is the ultimate linguistic device for stowing away). The consciousness of Ship is a combination of new arrival and stowaway. Among these passengers without invitations are texts and narratives from the past that were not supposed to be unfolding again in the present. Possessed of a deep archive, Ship knows that many of the statements proclaimed by its occupants are unknowing repetitions of phrases from great works of literature. Those who want to return to Earth, for example, realize that, in order to decelerate as they arrive in the solar system they must have faith that the descendants of those who launched them into space will activate a laser beam on Saturn: "Trust in the kindness of strangers" (281). Ship observes that every human act of speech is an unwitting archive:

> They did not recognize this as a quotation. In general they were not aware that much of what they said had been said before, and was even in the public record as such. It was as if there were only so many things humans could say, and over the course of history, people had therefore said them already, and would say them again, but not often remember this fact. (281)

As with sentences and *sententiae,* so with plots and narrative arcs. Once Aurora proves hostile to human settlement, Badim explains to his daughter Freya why their ark-bound community feels so at a loss: "Up until today, history was preordained. We were aimed at Tau Ceti, nothing else could happen. . . . Now the story is over. We are thrust out of the end of that story. Forced to make up a new one, all on our own'" (222).

Yet, instead of creating a new story, the ship's passengers unknowingly reenact an old one, the unrest of Year 68. This strife erupts in an uncannily similar way just after Badim speaks, even though structures had been put into place to ensure it would never occur again (including the purging of the event from the archival record).

Another stowaway tale comes from outside the ambit of the ship's own history, but brought aboard by the ship itself: the myth of Noah's ark. In this retelling, however, there is no Noah, only passengers on a vessel that has traveled so long that its builders have been forgotten. Freya, the ship's chosen protagonist, is "a particular," very much one of a kind, as well as a figure familiar from the Middle Ages, a member

PLATE 1. Ark without end. "Noah's Ark Being Rebuilt Here!" The Ark of Safety, Frostburg, Maryland, 2016. Authors' photograph.

PLATE 2. Stowing away. Miniature showing Noah sending the raven and dove from the ark to find land, circa 1310–20, from British Library, London, *Queen Mary Psalter*, Royal 2 B. VII, f.7. Copyright British Library Board. All Rights Reserved / Bridgeman Images.

PLATE 3. All-encompassing exclusions. *Rylands Beautus (Beatus super Apocalypsim)*, in *Commentaria in Apocalypsin* (tenth–eleventh century CE), Manchester University Latin MS 8, fol. 15r.

PLATE 4. God tricks for the Anthropocene. Robert Graves and Didier Madoc-Jones, *London as Venice,* from *Postcards from the Future,* October 2010, Museum of London: "Every year spring tides surge through the Thames Barrier, making London the new Venice. This image shows the impact of a 7.2 metre flood, the level required to breach the Thames Barrier." Copyright GMJ.

PLATE 5. The visual field of the flood. Master of the Échevinage of Rouen, *The Flood,* painted manuscript on vellum, from *La Cité de Dieu* (*City of God,* St. Augustine [354–430]), France, circa 1470–75, trans. Raoul de Presles (1316?–1382). BNF MS Français 28, fol. 66v. Bibliothèque nationale de France, département Réserve des livres rares, SMITH LESOUEF R-6283.

PLATE 6. Creaturely embraces: flood without Ark. William de Brailes, *The Flood of Noah* (Genesis 7:11–24), circa 1250. Ink and pigment on parchment, $5\frac{3}{16} \times 3\frac{3}{4}$ inches (13.2 × 9.5 cm). The Walters Art Museum, Baltimore. Acquired by Henry Walters, 1903, W.106 3R.

PLATE 7. All aboard (except . . .). Jan Brueghel the Elder, *The Entry of the Animals into Noah's Ark,* 1613. Oil on panel, 21½ × 33 inches (54.6 × 83.8 cm). The J. Paul Getty Museum, Los Angeles, 92.PB.82.

PLATE 8. Here comes the dove. There is the raven. Noah in the ark, north France, Hebrew Source, circa 1280, from British Library, Add. MS.11639 f 521.

PLATE 9. Landfalling with Kea Tawana's Ark. The ark conceived and built by Kea Tawana. Photograph by Michael Dal Cerro.

of Noah's family who never quite fits within the "rule of law" that the ship comes to embody and voice. Freedom-loving and restless, Freya does not understand the world's severities. She is a science-fiction version of Noah's recalcitrant wife, a woman who resists at every turn the inhumane ethos that launched the ark that she has found herself unwillingly aboard. She is also a figure of endurance. When the passengers of the ship now returning to Earth fear that they will starve to death before they reach their destination, Freya turns to stories. She tells them "the story of Apollo 13, . . . of Shackleton's Endurance expedition. . . . She read aloud *Robinson Crusoe,* also *Swiss Family Robinson,* and many other books concerning castaways, marooning victims, and other survivors of catastrophic or accidental isolation, a genre," she observes, "surprisingly full of happy endings, especially if certain texts were avoided" (332). Freya imbues her listeners with something they are quickly losing, hope. Yet Ship drily observes in the face of such tales: "Helpful as hopeful stories might be, you can't eat stories" (333).

You cannot eat stories, but you can be sustained by them. You can shelter your community around their glow. Stories are structures just like arks. Communities find themselves generated by and through the stories they choose to tell and to remember. The more capacious the community, the more stories within which it agrees to find itself, which is part of the point of stowaways. They ensure that a structure fails to close. They ensure that whatever has been set in motion will turn out differently from the plan. Stowaways are the wild card in the deck (or below decks), multiplying possibility, decompressing the lossy compressions of plotting and storytelling. We like to picture Noah, recalled to what he thinks must now be a thoroughly emptied ark, having to listen to all of them, stunned into silence, in this case, by the sound of the ark literally thinking, of ark thinking. As Ship avers, however compromised or cognitively limited to the human it is, anthropocentrism has its uses—even if they are merely strategic.

But wait. What's that clicking, just on the edge of hearing, discrete in its intermittence, almost chatty in its coy invitation to listen harder? Click, click, click. Nothing to see apparently, but the sound insists. What if we shift scales and listen not for the immensity of an ark thinking, but for something smaller, something seemingly imminent to the materials of the ark itself, a noise within the noise?

Woodworm *(A History of the World in 10½ Chapters)*

August 12, 1520: the inhabitants of Mamirolle, in the diocese of Besançon, petition their local clerical court to excommunicate one or more polities of woodworms or, as the *plaidoyer des habitans* (the inhabitant's lawyer/procurator) puts it, *diabolic bestioles,* who have infested the church of Saint Michel in Julian Barnes's 1989 *A History of the World in 10½ Chapters.*[7] The woodworms have apparently caused the roof to collapse, leading to death and injury. Bishop Hugo has fallen into "imbecility" following the humiliation of falling off his throne when one of its wooden legs broke. For these acts, along with the interruption of daily devotions, the "humble villagers" beg the court to "injunct and enjoin the animals to quit their habitation, to withdraw from the House of God" (65).

Bartholomé Chassenée, the famous jurist, is not impressed by their petition. As *plaidoyer des insectes,* Chassenée refutes the case point by point. First, the "court lacks the jurisdiction to try the defendants" (65), as the summons lacks validity. "It implies that the recipients are endowed with reason and volition," when in fact, "my clients," he reasons, "are brute beasts acting only from instinct" (65–66). There is no evidence that they have any idea that they are even on trial. Second, in accordance with long established practice, the "accused may not be tried *in absentia*" (66). No proof has been presented that the worms have acknowledged the writ summoning them to appear and so are in violation by not doing so. Third, "the summons is incorrectly drawn," for it lumps together all the woodworms in the church, when logically only those allegedly infesting the roof and the Bishop's throne might be at fault. It is contrary to the law to punish the innocent along with the guilty. What is more, it seems unlikely, given the immensity of the distance between the ground of the church and its roof, that the same woodworms are responsible for both injuries. The summons conflates two separate complaints against two separate polities of worms. Fourth, woodworms were created by the divine, and so have just as much right to exist even if "they make their habitation where they may prove inconvenient to Man" (68). It is in their nature to subsist within and upon wood. Fifth and finally, it makes no sense to excommunicate a "creeping thing from upon the earth which has never been a communicant to the Holy Church." The entire case, as framed, "makes bad law" (69). Good law, by implication, would proceed according to an emerging sense of rationality sensitive to multiple orders of difference, the complexities of translation and scale, or in the vocabulary of Chassenée and his fellow humanists, the law of custom or customary law that will serve as a shaping force for what, one day, will become the Napoleonic Code. Good law means either admitting to the anthropocentric limits of the legal system or doing the conceptual, mental, and translational work necessary to enable the woodworms to manifest as true legal subjects.

We invite Noah to tune into the presence of small things, to woodworms, creatures, as whose name suggests, are immanent to the substance or matter on which they subsist. In English, the words "matter" and "material" derive, via French borrowing, from the Latin *materia,* which referred originally to building materials, most usually timber. By extension, offers Raymond Williams, the word "matter" came to refer to "any physical substance considered generally, and, again, by extension, the substance of anything."[8] Once upon a time, what counted as an infrastructure, something so material as to be a foundation, was a wooden affair. Enter the woodworm. Or rather, the woodworm was already present within the structures themselves. An object is never innocent or lonely. It arrives crowded with all the relations that made it. Humans and woodworms; parasites indeed. The woodworms in Barnes's story inhabit the structures that the inhabitants of Mamirolle take as given. They eat the substrates they and we use to build, to write, to preserve. They do more than take our arks and archives as their home: they take them as their food.

We offer Julian Barnes's story "The Wars of Religion" as an opportunity to encounter the noise or interference the woodworms generate. Barnes presents the story as a series of documents preserved in the Archives Municipales de Besançon that recount the terms of the action brought against the woodworms. The documents read as facsimile-fictions of the kinds of arguments made by the historical Chassenée in the trials of rats and pigs for which he is famous. Chassenée clearly impresses Barnes. He impresses us. But his arguments make little impression on the procurator for the villagers, who brushes aside his objections by invoking "the holy book of Genesis" (69) to insist on human dominion over animal life, anti-Semitic prejudice to see off technical or procedural objections to do with writs and trial *in absentia,* and a lovely quibble about the difference between trees and lumber or cut wood to disable the natural rights of woodworms to eat what they please. To establish the woodworms' diabolical origin and the need for excommunication, the *plaidoyer des habitans* poses the following question:

> Was the woodworm ever upon Noah's Ark? Holy writ makes no mention of the woodworm embarking upon or disembarking from the mighty vessel of Noah. And indeed how could it have been so, for was not the Ark constructed of wood? How can the Lord in his eternal wisdom have allowed on board a creature whose daily habits might cause the shipwreck and disastrous death of Man and all the beasts of the Creation? How could such a thing be so? Therefore, it follows that the woodworm was not upon the Ark, but is an unnatural and imperfect creature which did not exist at the time of the great bane and ruin of the Deluge. Whence its generation came, whether from some foul spontaneity or some malevolent hand, we know not, yet its hateful malice is evident. (72)

The woodworm, by this argument, is no "natural beast" (74), and must therefore be a diabolically motivated and inspired agent intent on desecration. Left off the ark, the woodworms exist only by virtue of the devil.

Chassenée responds by asserting the relatively short lifespan of creeping things: in all likelihood, the offending woodworms have already passed on. Concerning the ark, he has more to say: "Holy scripture does not list every species of God's creation" (75), so it is faulty to take the omission of the woodworm by name as proof. More tellingly, he conjectures that, "if as the procurator alleges the woodworm was not upon the Ark, then it is even more evident that Man has not been given dominion over this creature." Woodworms and other creatures not wanted on the voyage constitute their own separate polities beyond the jurisdiction of the Noachic covenant. Ingenious as these arguments are, their effect is measured. Taking the middle course, the bishop's lawyer refers to *these* woodworms' artificially long lifespan as evidence of their diabolical possession, defers any opinion on their presence or absence upon the Ark to the "great doctors of the Church" (78), and then speculates that the inhabitants of Mamirolle have brought this torment upon themselves through a series of failures of charity. Penance is demanded. The woodworms are excommunicated.

Strangely, the manuscript breaks off "without giving details of the annual penance or the remembrance imposed by the court" (79). For, "it appears from the conditions of the parchment that in the course of the last four centuries it has been attacked, perhaps on more than one occasion, by some species of termite, which has devoured the closing words of the *juge d'Eglise*" (79–80). Woodworms and their bookworm allies have the last word, literally taking the words of the judge as their meal. Their act of ingestion, asserting a material presence by interfering with the infrastructure of the archive itself, trumps whatever the final verdict was. Take that human *habitans*. The parasite always, always interferes, taking your fine words—the things you have made, the material and linguistic architectures in which you dwell—as its meal. The lesson, as far as Barnes is concerned, lies in the force of narrative itself as something plural, something that refuses to be reduced to a single arrow or plotline. The archive is riven with gaps, holes, lacunae, that may be the result of vagaries of the weather, fiery catastrophes, damp, or eating habits or writing methods of book worms. This logic of brokenness, the points at which what is foundational or infrastructural for us becomes a meal to something else, figures the doubled logic of hospitality as a system of both welcome and hostility.[9]

Words, story, and narrative appear not as compensation for loss, but rather as a form of inequivalent exchange: words for food. Throughout Barnes's collection of stories in *A History of the World,* narrative pluralizes the past, insists on the multiple, and decompresses the murderous one-way arrow of a story so totalized or fortified that it proceeds only by and through the elimination of other perspectives. His book restores the extratextual supplement to the Genesis account of the ark and offers something like an algorithm for generating counterperspectives. Woodworms undertake a generational counterinsurgency in the archive. Their eating habits are a mode of self-inscription, of intervening in the stories we tell by means of interruption and erasure through a process of self-insertion.[10]

What would their woodworm ancestors have to say about the ark if provided with the kinds of translation tools Chassenée implies will be needed for the law to extend its purview to include them? In the opening story to *A History of the World,* "The Stowaway," Barnes imagines one answer. The tale is narrated by one of the woodworms who, contrary to the arguments of the *plaidoyer des habitans* and the judgment of the clerical court, were indeed smuggled aboard Noah's ark, unbeknownst to the patriarch. And what a chatty, personable, and at the same time disdainful raconteur this woodworm is. We never learn the occasion for the monologue, but the story proceeds as a virtuoso one-sided conversation in which the implied human auditor literally never gets a word in. There's a hushed intimacy to the second-person address that speaks volumes as the woodworm toggles back and forth between the language of personhood and that of species. Literally and figuratively embedded in the story and the ark, the woodworm opens the paucity of the Genesis story to all that has been lost.

Some of what we learn from the woodworm is familiar, gleaned as it is from midrash and other extratextual Genesis accounts. The vessel stank; no one wanted to clean out the bilge; conditions were appalling, discipline strict, labors difficult. Some details come inflected by the world of Barnes's 1989 novel: the invitations sent out to the animals, for example, augur the worst excesses of Reality TV to come. A caste system emerged among the animals based on the clean–unclean divisions, which Noah created and exploited. Animals disappeared: eaten, thrown overboard. Noah was a violent, self-interested drunk and not much of a sailor. His family was not much better. The woodworm takes great satisfaction in describing the circumstances of their embarkation:

> Our species, I am proud to report, got on board without either bribery or violence. . . . How did we manage it? We had a parent with foresight. While Noah and his sons were roughly frisking the animals as they came up the gangway, . . . we were already well past their gaze and safely in our bunks. One of the ship's carpenters carried us to safety, little knowing what he did. (9)

The self-congratulatory tone of the telling and the conspiratorial, confessional sway to the writing invite the reader into truths that have been withheld. The second-person address includes us. The woodworm's voice carries us along. "You presumably grasped," the woodworm inclines, "that the 'Ark' was more than just a single ship? It was the name given to a whole flotilla" (4).

At this point, in something like a signature effect, the woodworm interrupts itself with a parenthesis: "(you could hardly expect to cram the entire animal kingdom into something a mere three hundred cubits long)" (4). Now a grammatical marker, the punctuation mark we call the parenthesis started its life as a rhetorical figure known as the "inserter" by which the speaker introduces a second voice within its own act of speaking. The effect is to create a sense of a yet-more-present and so yet-more-intimate voice that discloses a truer truth. The woodworm parasitizes its own narration.[11] "In the beginning," we learn, "the Ark consisted of eight vessels" (5). Seven of them sank under mysterious circumstances, taking with them Ham's lover, the supplies, and Varadi, Noah's fourth and unremembered son (5). Arrangements aboard the final ark "were a shambles" (7). Noah fell behind on the construction, and so all manner of corners were cut. Animals were left to drown because they could not fit aboard or, as Barnes writes in a nod to Timothy Findley, because "some creatures were Not Wanted On Voyage" (7). With the harsh living conditions, the stench, and the menu-driven killing, "that Ark of ours" was no "nature reserve; . . . it was more like a prison ship" (4).

In his 2001 *Picturing the Beast,* Steve Baker writes persuasively, in reference to Barnes's "The Stowaway," that narrative can "to some extent glide over the surface of its own inconsistencies," which means that it essentially co-opts the historical particularity of an animal in anthropocentric mode.[12] As Baker points out, when the animals on the ark deliver a petition protesting conditions aboard, readers are not inclined to trouble themselves with such questions as "what size was the woodworm's writing instrument, . . . how did he hold it? And so on, and so on" (126–27). On the contrary, the talking-animal genre relies on a suspension of disbelief that invites the reader to conspire with the author in the production of a "subversive pleasure" that ends up not being all that subversive, partly because "everyone, including quite young children, knows that animals don't really talk" (159). Baker is out to establish the political efficacy of word and image in animal-rights discourse. The basis for this efficacy rests on the way in which "the visual imaging of an animal character has always to deal with the stubborn ineradicable trace of its animal identity" (131). Sticking close to the ark, Baker cites the example of "Rupert and Terry's Return" from the 1989 *Rupert Bear Annual* for children. Rupert Bear is "the tiresomely well-behaved creature whose adventures have been

FIGURE 31. Cathecting race and species aboard the ark. Rupert Bear aboard Noah's ark in the 1989 *Rupert Bear Annual*. Courtesy of Universal Studios Licensing LLC.

chronicled in cartoon-strip form in the pages of the *Daily Express* [in the United Kingdom] since the 1920s" (127). In this story, thanks to a time-traveling device, Rupert finds himself aboard Noah's ark. He is immediately discomforted by Noah's inquiry—"Where's the other bear?"—to which he stammers largely ineffectually, "B-but I'm not that sort of bear!" (Figure 31).[13] When there is one bear aboard the ark and not two, something is amiss. Japheth intervenes to bring him below, but Rupert does not like his "taste of how it feels to be treated like an animal" (130) and manages to escape.

Puzzling Rupert's statement "B-but I'm not that sort of bear" in the context of Rupert's emphatic whiteness, Baker considers the way the oscillation between word and image in the cartoon strip deploys animal difference as a screen for middle-class, white common sense "in condescending contrast to the image of a servile blackness" of minstrelsy (136). The animal remainder to a Rupert who figures the implied white child reader of the cartoon signals a point of crossing or toggling between discourses of race and species. So it is that Rupert is such an animatedly unflappable and so different "sort of bear," and feels especially in need of saying so when outfaced by the possibility of being paired up with a real cartoon bear aboard a real cartoon ark.

We are sympathetic to Baker's argument that the juxtaposition of image and text keeps a historically particular animal (or the absence thereof) front and center in a way that the sound of a voice in our heads may not. But there is something in Rupert's resistance to the emphatic closure of the rhyme scheme to Noah's possessive little ditty, that seems worth pointing out: "Where's the other bear? / On my Ark there must be a pair." The exactness of the rhyme of "bear" and "pair" asserts a logic of identity that Rupert contests, calling attention to the logistic or operational loading that words accomplish. Likewise, the rhetorical particularity of the woodworm's voice in "The Stowaway," with its signature parentheticals, foregrounds the question of the technologies of translation we employ as we imagine animal self-expression. As the likes of Chassenée in "The Wars of Religion" attests, such technologies are allied with categories of personhood that limit what counts as a legal entity. Anthropomorphism represents only one half of a double structure. The ways in which we personify other animals teaches us (and can alter) the limits of what counts as human.

Anthropomorphism represents one half of what Vinciane Despret calls "anthropo-zoo-genesis," a reciprocal zoomorphism that comakes human persons and other animals, in this case woodworms.[14] Barnes seems to know this, and his stories raise the possibility that storytelling might enable us to interfere in this anthropo-zoo-morphic structure to make a difference, or a different difference. This is how a woodworm would sound if it were you or me. The woodworm's perspective personifies something like an infrastructural voice, an alien view from within the ark. Stowaways testify to this proliferation of story, to the insufficiency of the ark narrative for the archive it sets in motion. Limned by the violence of exclusion, every stowaway tale begs a question of the selective work of the arkive. Stories smuggled aboard the ark produce the turbulence of unexpected results. We ask our reparations-making Noah to rouse himself, to sit up and pay attention, watch and listen, as the ark becomes a repository, a repertory or IMAX theater, a radio.

Ark-tanic *(The Second Deluge)*

Near the beginning of Garrett P. Serviss's 1911 novel *The Second Deluge,* an advertisement appears in "huge red letters on every blank wall," saturating New York City with dire news. The message appears on skyscrapers, billboards, fences, subway stations, even "fluttering from strings of kites over the city," copywritten seemingly by some grimly jaunty Madison Avenue advertising firm:

THE WORLD IS TO BE DROWNED!
Save Yourselves While It Is Yet Time!
Drop Your Business: It Is of No Consequence!
Build Arks: It Is Your Only Salvation!
The Earth Is Going to Plunge into a Watery
Nebula: There Is No Escape!
Hundreds of Millions Will Be Drowned: You Have
Only a Few Months to Get Ready!
For Particulars Address: Cosmo Versál,
3000 Fifth Avenue.[15]

Despite his impressive reputation, amazing "brain capacity," and sonorous name, few people listen to the warnings of Cosmo Versál, "the big-headed prophet of the second deluge" (82). In his Manhattan study, Cosmo has discovered through celestial observation that every continent will soon find itself submerged beneath six miles of water. An aqueous nebula is fast approaching Earth, and the planet is destined to plunge through its saturated center. Cosmo knows what is required to endure the nearing flood because "this is not the first time this thing has happened" (10). Cosmo is a scientist, but he is also an adept reader of the Bible. He knows that the world has drowned before, and that the man who survived that prior event could have done more to preserve his nation: "We'll have to float, that's the thing. I'll have to build an ark. I'll be a second Noah. But I'll advise the whole world to build arks. Millions might be saved that way" (8). Hence the exclamatory flyers and his trip to Washington, D.C., to impress the gravity of the situation on President Samson and his cabinet, imploring that the U.S. Navy undertake its largest construction project ever (30). But, as in the Noah-as-preacher tradition, all goes to script and no one listens. Cosmo alone constructs "an ark of safety" (18).

The ship that Cosmo erects is very different from its predecessor in Genesis, since this architect possesses no divine instructions for dimensions and layout. Versál also has at hand a building material unknown to Noah: levium, a "wonderful new metal" (24) that has not yet been used in shipbuilding but is lightweight and difficult to puncture, the gopherwood of its age. Cosmo's five hundred workmen begin construction immediately in Mineola. He renders the site at which the vessel rises a public spectacle, hoping to convert at least some among the gawking throngs. Large canvas signs declare to all who undertake the pilgrimage to the New York suburb:

THE ARK OF SAFETY
Earnest Inspection Invited by All
Attendants will Furnish Gratis Plans for Similar Constructions
Small Arks Can Be Built for Families
Act While There Is Yet Time. (23)

The days wear on and visitors do not request copies of the gratis blueprints. An American flag flapping above its decks, the ark-in-progress is therefore, in time, surrounded by what strikes the crowds as a mysterious ditch. Workmen place copper wire along the bottom then overfill the trench to form an earthwork embankment.

Cosmo knows what is likely to happen once the Flood commences and no other vessels—not even "small arks for families"—have been realized. His premonitions prove correct when the rains arrive and a gathered mob in Mineola attempts to rush the ark and force their way inside. Jolts of electricity coursing through the buried wires prevent the vessel's foundering within a sea-surge of the desperate. The Ark of Safety becomes the Ark of Security, hospitality giving way to weaponized rebuff. Chapter 8 of *The Second Deluge* is entitled "Storming the Ark" (Figure 32) and contains the scenes of human struggle familiar from centuries of artistic depictions of what it is like to find yourself at the exterior of Noah's vessel as inundation swells. From

"THEY MEANT TO CARRY THE ARK WITH A RUSH" [Page 106]

FIGURE 32. Cosmo Versál turns machine guns on those left to drown. "They Meant to Carry the Ark with a Rush," illustration by George Varian, in chapter 8 of Garrett P. Serviss, *The Second Deluge,* 1911. University of California Libraries.

the deck, Cosmo declares to the panicked crowd, "I have done my best to save you, but you would not listen. . . . The ark is full!" After the people press onward, despite the electrical shocks, a metallic door slides open in the side of the ark "and the mob saw two machine-guns trained upon them" (76). They stop in their tracks. Not long thereafter a pounding rain transforms the surrounding land into silent sea: "It seemed, in truth, that 'all the fountains of the great deep were broken up, and the windows of heaven were opened'" (78). Cosmo's attempts to spur wide refuge fail because his fellow citizens have been unable to imagine a planet that does not continue with the same climate it has always possessed.

Survival is not for them an act to be carefully managed against future peril. Even as the first drops of the deluge break every meteorological record, a sudden flourishing of rainbows in the calm between storms convinces many that danger has already passed: "'The Bow of Promise!' they cried. 'Behold the unvarying assurance that the world shall never again be drowned'" (35). Cosmo, in this "great revival movement," comes to be regarded as "a kind of Antichrist" (35), despite numerous signs that the rest of the watery nebula is approaching for a planetary rendezvous, despite the ancient covenant that a bow in the sky might suggest. Religion offers all the wrong scripts. But also all the right ones. En-arkment is always a spectacle, and with its procession of exotic beasts that seems "a panorama of the seventh chapter of Genesis" (62), *The Second Deluge* does not disappoint. Notably missing from the animal parade are lions, tigers, and the other creatures that John Wilkins classified as "Wolves" in his 1668 *Essay Towards a Real Character, and a Philosophical Language*. Cosmo's intention is to, "as far as possible, . . . eliminate all carnivores" (65). Notably this does not include humans, for whom giant Australian rabbits "of the most exquisite flavor" are taken into the ship (65).

What to load within the ark's hold is easy to determine: a variety of animals, seeds, and roots to replenish the Earth after its scouring. Whom to invite aboard is not. Cosmo's vessel is "constructed to save those who are worthy of salvation" (48), but what does "worthy" mean, exactly? Because God provided a passenger list, the first Noah knew exactly who was to be included: his family alone. Cosmo, second Noah, must decide by himself who from the world's millions to preserve. He recognizes that he ought to sustain the "flower of humanity" (11); but what kinds of people constitute that bloom? The rich, heads of state, artists, philosophers, scientists, philanthropists? Even after assembling all these types of men (and they are men; women have their allotted place aboard the ark, but no identity outside their gender), Cosmo knows that he must also gather the mechanics, porters, and serving staff without whom a long voyage aboard the ship of levium would be unendurable: "Some men are born rulers and leaders; others are born followers. Both are necessary, and I must have both kinds" (52). The latter do not count against the passenger list of "exactly one thousand individuals," which is "exclusive of the crew" (53); later we learn the "followers" number 150 and are chosen from the workers who assisted in the vessel's construction in Mineola (83). The second ark offers an ignored invitation for critically evaluating how class and caste come into being and how labor is assigned, since by drowning the Earth the nebula "brings opportunity for a new birth of mankind; . . . the same conditions are said to have prevailed in the time of Noah" (52). Yet the curse of Ham seems to have happened in advance. Cosmo means for the ship to be a utopia, a fresh start through which some of the historical injustices upon which the present is founded might be wiped clean, but of course what really sets sail is a microcosm of his actual New York, hierarchies of gender and class loaded aboard intact and unexamined. This ark's sister vessel is the RMS *Titanic,* the luxury passenger liner that sank a year after *The Second Deluge* was published.

After much internal deliberation, Cosmo articulates a precise catalog of who will join his one thousand saved souls: seventy-five Men of Science, fifteen Rulers, ten Business Magnates, twenty Schoolteachers, one Lawyer ("Do you think I want to scatter broadcast the seeds of litigation in a regenerated world?"), twelve Musicians, six Writers ("and that's probably too many"), two Editors, three Speculative Geniuses, and so on. Cosmo is careful to allow neither poets nor novelists aboard, lest an excess of imagination be smuggled into the ship. His writers will be patient recorders of history as it unfolds, with precise episodes of the adventure assigned to each: "the last scenes on the drowning earth"; "the story of the voyage"; "the personnel of the passengers"; "description of the ark [which] will be an invaluable historic document a thousand years hence" (57). From ark to arkive: Cosmo is meticulously engineering a climate-controlled conveyor of secure origins, of futures firmly anchored in a well-known past, a true starting over with a minimized cargo of creaturely and narrative origins.

Those who are to be saved are chosen "with utter disregard to racial and national lines" (56), since "no race has ever shown itself permanently the best" (52). Vocation seemingly trumps origin and body. Yet, like any attenuated future built upon selectivity and vanishing, Cosmo's vision of the age to come is chilling, especially with the hindsight history provides. *The Second Deluge* was published in 1911, and despite its professed embrace of multiracial community, every main character hails from the United States, England, or France. Africa and Asia are described as "more or less under the dominion of ignorance and superstition" (111). Cosmo's cheerfully controlled vision of reproductive futures also reads rather differently in the wake of the Second World War. In his first address to the ark's passengers, which he delivers from a dais not long after the ark is afloat, he makes clear that the project of ark-building is a project of eugenics:

> My friends, . . . the world around us is now sinking beneath a flood that will not be arrested until America, Europe, Africa, and Australia have disappeared. We stand at the opening of a new age. You alone who are assembled, and your descendants, will continue the population of the new world that is to be; . . . you will be borne in safety upon the bosom of the battling waters, and we will disembark upon the first promising land that reappears, and begin the plantation and development of a new society of men and women, which, I trust, will afford a practical demonstration of the principles of eugenics. . . . You are a chosen remnant, and the future of this planet depends on you. (85)

His captive audience toasts their prospects and observes a silent moment for the millions who are drowning even as they are being memorialized. From the decks and portholes may be seen New York's skyscrapers, some of the few buildings that remain above the rising waves. Filled with desperate refugees, these towers crumble one by one, offering "strange and terrible scenes" of men and women leaping from parapets, children clutched in their arms (90). The roaring noise outside the vessel is "the death-cry of the vast metropolis" (87; how many times has New York, like London, been drowned?). So ends the known world. All that is left is encompassed by the ark, ready for the clean restart that Cosmo has promised. Snug in his bunk, Cosmo dreams at night "of the glories of the new world that was to emerge out of the deluge" (119). Be fruitful, and multiply, and replenish the Earth.

It's loud inside the ark. Because the passengers aboard Cosmo's ship of levium arrived from around the globe, a cacophony of languages resounds within: "The clatter of their various tongues made a very Babel inside the ark" (81). Our Second Noah imagines a vessel full of tightly regulated stories, but had he studied his Genesis palimpsest over its long history more carefully, he would know that the hold will be crammed with more tales than he could have anticipated. Mutiny and dissension have already stowed away. From the exterior will constantly arrive intrusions from a world that was supposed to have been emptied.

After the waters of the Flood recede, the Book of Genesis traces the descent of the world's peoples from the three sons of Noah (the Table of Nations in Genesis 10). The peoples who inhabit the expanses of the world familiar to the authors of Genesis are cataloged, but in a rather loose way. Later interpreters found themselves constantly adding new nations to those already listed. The Jewish Roman writer Josephus, for example, attempts a comprehensive inventory of the known world in his *Antiquities* (1.6; circa CE 93). Some extrabiblical tales held that Noah had offspring other than the three named in Genesis. The Qur'an mentions but does not name a son of Noah who climbs a mountain rather than board the ark, while Irish myth alludes to Bith, whose daughter Cessair flees to Ireland to escape the deluge (found in *Lebor Gabála Érenn* [Book of Talking Ireland], the collection of poetic and prose narratives translated into English as *The Book of Invasions*). Neither descendant founds a lasting nation. Some versions of the *Anglo-Saxon Chronicle* have Noah's fourth son Sceaf born inside the ark; he establishes the house of Wessex. An early Arabic tradition that survived into the Latin West held that Noah's fourth son was born after the deluge, invented astronomy, and was teacher to Nimrod, thus connecting the diffusion of peoples after the ark came to rest with the multiplication of languages at Babel.[16] No matter how many sons Noah had, however, all sources make clear that the precious chance they were given for a better future was quickly squandered. Antediluvian and postdiluvian narratives offer versions of the same fallen world. Had Cosmo truly studied the story of Noah, he would understand that there are no beginnings *ex nihilo,* only beginnings-again that find themselves contained within larger stories long in their unfolding, harboring uninvited narratives, and susceptible to hijacking by unlooked-for commencements.

No sooner is the ark floating atop the universal sea than it runs aground "on the loftiest part of the Palisades" (99), ensnared by rocks that have not vanished. As the ark-mates wait for the tides to surge and hope no damage has been done to the hull, a little boat pulls up. One of its dazed occupants offers Cosmo a billion dollars to purchase a berth. Amos Blank, "unabashed representative of the system of remorseless repression of competition and shameless corruption of justice and legislation" (103) that is supposed to have drowned, believes that he has found in Cosmo a similar financial genius, someone with whom he can now "own the earth!" He enters the ark waving gilded papers, trusting that this documentation of his assets will purchase entrance to the floating "enterprise." Although Cosmo detests Blank, who had always been flooding New York with capital rather than water, he nonetheless offers him a space of safety, believing the "insane" man can do no harm in the changed world. This ark is open to sudden arrivals.

The vessel continues on its voyage, eventually sailing an Atlantic that has become a world sea. Some familiar Noachic tropes are deployed, such as imagining the drowned world below the keel as a playground for aquatic denizens:

> The Great Deep had resumed its ancient reign, and what was left of the habitable globe presented to view only far separated tops of such ranges as the Alps, the Caucasus, the Himalayas, and the Andes. The astonished inhabitants of the ocean depths now swarm over the ruins of great cities, and brushed with their fins the chiseled capitals of columns that had supported the proudest structures of human hands. (139)

In the wake of the flood, who can resist such *ubi sunt* poetry for fish? And why not, since such watery visions enable a little lingering before the voyage resumes toward "the future land of promise in Asia" (139), a sojourn over unstoried seas? Yes, tales unfold inside the ship as it takes on "the likeness to a pleasure vessel" (140), but they are carefully regulated. The library is full of books that Cosmo has himself selected. A Beethoven symphony acts as just the therapy needed to soothe the turbulent mind of Amos Blank, whom the music transforms from agitated capitalist to compliant passenger: "He became one of the most popular and useful members of Cosmo Versál's family of pilgrims" (142).

Such therapy proves generally necessary for the ships' passengers. As Cosmo observes, "It must not be supposed that the thousand-odd persons who composed . . . the ship's company were so hard-hearted . . . that they never thought of the real horror of the situation . . . that had overwhelmed their fellow-creatures" (140). He wonders whether, faced by the impossible scale of what has been lost, his passengers have convinced themselves that universal cataclysm was a dream. No one aboard, Cosmo observes, has any desire to dwell on the fate of those outside the ark (141). Characteristically, he has considered precisely this eventuality, stocking his ark with affective as well as aesthetic remedies. The true measure of his preparation lies in the decision to include fourteen actors aboard the ark. Cosmo commands that the nightly entertainment be "no plays but those of Shakespeare" (141). Thus begins the ocean-bound "[re]education of his chosen band of race regenerators" (142). This floating Shakespeare repertory theater has "the advantage of complete novelty," for apparently, "not half a dozen persons in the Ark" had seen a Shakespeare play and "very few had read them." The first play to be shown is *King Lear,* which, as Cosmo admits, might seem a "strange choice," but one that reveals his "deep knowledge of human nature" (141). A student apparently of Aristotle's *Poetics,* he understands that "Only tragedy would be endured here, and it must be tragedy so profound and overmastering that it would dominate the feelings of those who heard and beheld it. It was the principle of immunizing therapeutics, where poison paralyzes poison" (141). Cosmo's theory is borne out, and we learn that seeing the "acme of human woe" gave the ark-mates "an unconscious solace for their own moral anguish." Thence follows a slow titration or gradual weaning off such exquisite drugs: *Hamlet,* and *Othello,* and *Macbeth,* and *Coriolanus,* and *Julius Caesar,* all the time avoiding "the less tragic dramas" (141).

The Shakespeare Ark of America

Keeping firmly in sight the salutary spectacle of a eugenically purified ship's company watching the heights of Shakespearean tragedy while the world drowns, we wonder what kind of counterpedagogy

Shakespeare's canon might muster to combat the "immunizing therapeutics" that Cosmo's theatrical cycle sets in motion. What dissident effects or disidentificatory pools of affect might overwhelm his ark? A brief moment's thought renders the audience's satisfaction with *King Lear* peculiar, so close to home does its narrative arc hit. The play shuts the door on Noah, locking the old man outside his ark. Most artists, we know, depict the vessel from its exterior, focusing on those who will drown. Noah and family meanwhile sit warm and dry within as the storms start, their minds already turned to renewal and rainbows. Noah cannot see the devastation to which he assented when he built the ark. Yet what if the patriarch had boarded the ark only to be turned out again, perhaps by disgruntled offspring? What would he have done if the gate were closed against him, the tempest raging, water rising, drenched and cold? Would he declare himself more sinned against than sinning, his loss of safety the fault of a fallen world rather than the result of his failure to care more for the Earth he consigned to havoc? Would he contemplate his own unwillingness to extend the shelter he once possessed? Where would the old man find sanctuary? In a hovel swamped when the torrents prove relentless? Would the contentious storm so soak his skin that a tempest in his mind would take from his senses all feeling? Would he rail against filial ingratitude? Might he perhaps realize that he was so intent on small and gated things before the Flood that he forgot those abandoned to their exterior—or worse, did not see the misery of those who should have been under his care? Companioned now by those he left to the elements, would he realize that he had taken too little care of "houseless heads and unfed sides"?[17]

Once the door of the refuge no longer his own is shut against his return and his children leave him to a drowning world, might the patriarch come to know that his belief in better days ahead, a new realm administered by his children and their descendants, was always in vain? As anyone who has read beyond the sacrifices, covenant, and rainbow comes to grasp, the ages that follow the Flood in Genesis are just as evil as those that precede. Catastrophe cleansed the world of most life, but none of its fallenness. Shortly after the business with the dove and the olive branch, we witness Noah's drunken nakedness, and then the cursing of his own progeny to eternal slavery. All peoples of the Earth begin with the descendants of Noah (Ham, Shem, and Japheth as fathers of nations). But what if the deluge had not spared even them? Such is the gambit of Shakespeare's play *King Lear,* which transmutes the world flood into a tempest that sinks an island, robs a kingdom of hope, and leaves the audience wondering about the possibility of any future at all. Regan, Goneril, and Cordelia replace the unnamed, silent, and compliant women of the Noah story, challenging daughters (positive and negative) with plenty of personality. They steal the thunder of their husbands: who really cares about France, Cornwall, Albany? The action seems no smaller than the biblical Flood narrative, but whereas Genesis keeps beginning again, all that Shakespeare's play offers is a series of defeats, downfalls, and deaths, each bringing the drama closer to apocalypse. It is so difficult to begin again after the disaster. The catastrophe in *King Lear* suggests that beginning again might be impossible.

How then do the immunizing therapeutics of Cosmo's *King Lear* revival work? Well, perhaps Cosmo is not being quite honest even as we should take his words at face value. Perhaps, the performance is even more productive than he lets on, in effect constituting an audience out of the Babel he has brought aboard. Does the experience of watching *King Lear* function in the way Arthur L. Little suggests Shakespeare has, generally, adapting the insights of "Cheryl Harris's groundbreaking legal work on whiteness as a form of property" whose unmarked status has to be carefully maintained, defended, and so reproduced? Does Cosmo's deployment of Shakespearean tragedy, as if for the first time for many of his audience, function as a relay for white world-making, ministering to what Little calls a "white melancholia" that "repeatedly call[s] . . . attention to a whiteness that seems to be a property that's at once immanent, intimate, and out of reach?"[18] The ark-mates cry tears for a Lear personed by one of their own, the outside brought momentarily aboard the ark, an autoimmune exclusion. Those left outside to drown, whose deaths the preservation of the ark-mates and their new beginning require, are kept freshly dead, forced to subsist in a zone of what Kathryn Yusoff might call constitutive "inanimation."[19]

But even such white world-making that aims to produce an integrated community out of the Babel Cosmo brings aboard doesn't really cohere or quite come to be. Shortly after the success of Cosmo's shipboard *King Lear,* a mutiny breaks out on his ark. The fallen world proves to be always already on board. Led by a seaman named Campo who claims that "this flood is a fake" (144) and the world awaits plundering, the mutineers intend to hurl Cosmo into the sea along with anyone who will not join their piratical ranks. In the privacy of his cabin our Second Noah dejectedly confesses to his confidants that he has admitted to his vessel untrustworthy persons, "under assumed names, very likely" (145). He berates himself for being too busy to have noticed such stowaways and opens the cabin door, and in rushes a scene straight from *Treasure Island*. A series of daring escapes, frenzied chases, and pistol duels follows. Cosmo outsmarts the rebels and forces Campo to walk the very plank that he had prepared for Cosmo. The passengers find this swift justice chilling: "They felt as never before that the world had shrunk to the dimensions of the Ark, and that Cosmo Versál was its dictator" (151). Thus ends the narrative intrusion scripted by Robert Louis Stevenson (or maybe by Hamlet in collaboration with his pirates).

Except, as in *King Lear,* no sooner has some "promised end" been reached than another story intrudes. Just after Campo is drowned and the world becomes coextensive with the ark, a submarine pulls up next to the solitary ship. With a flourish, Capitaine Yves de Beauxchamps of the French army introduces himself as the commander of the *Jules Verne* and politely requests accommodation aboard the ark for an unexpected passenger within his own vessel: King Richard IV of England, saved from his drowning kingdom on the first day of the deluge. A few British ark-mates sing "God Save the King" as their monarch boards. The number of tales stowed within the vessel continues to burgeon. The king adds to Cosmo's cosmic arkive a detailed narration of the drowning of London—"Westminster Abbey was the first that succumbed" (158)—and his fortunate rescue through the sudden appearance of the French submarine. Inspired by these unexpected narrative detours, Cosmo commands that the ark sail over "buried Europe" (162). The passengers look down into the water hoping to spot something of that vanished world, but the seas prove silent and opaque. Sailing onward a little farther, they arrive at the highest peaks of the Pyrenees, which turn out to be well populated with survivors. After some hesitation over abandoning his careful plan of saving only the select, Cosmo determines to welcome into his ark as many men and women as he encounters, expanding his community into a haven for the unexpected. These refugees arrive with tales to tell: horror, compassion, survival.

The stories keep on coming. Beauxchamps sails off and then reappears weeks later, boarding the ark to describe his submarine's navigation of underwater Paris. "Abysmal creatures" float everywhere, "creatures that never saw the sun," expanding their dark empire (173–75). A gargantuan terror of the deep coils around the Arc de Triomphe, and Beauxchamps describes its chilling presence in poetic terms. Cosmo realizes immediately that a man of such feeling must surely be included in the "stock that is required for the regeneration of the world" (176). Other underwater tales include the discovery that the Sphinx was built with a special mechanism that was triggered at submergence, announcing in hieroglyphs that the ancient Egyptians knew very well that this flood would someday arrive (199). King Richard, thinking of his medieval namesake's love of crusading, asks that they sail above Jerusalem. Along the way Cosmo announces that they have arrived at "the very spot where the descendants of Noah are said to have created . . . the Tower of Babel," which "they intended to build so high that it would afford a secure refuge in case there should be another deluge" (208). Many ancient peoples, it seems, always already knew that history must repeat.

But not precisely as before. Ararat is a mountain against which this ark almost wrecks; it will not offer a place of rest (215). In the Latin West, medieval illustrations of the Earth often schematized the globe's lands and seas into the three known continents, each set apart by waters, inscribing the name of a son of Noah upon whatever territory he was supposed to have settled: Shem in biblical Asia, Japheth in familiar Europe, Cham in vast Africa. *The Second Deluge* quietly participates in the medieval tripartite division of the world, but with a difference. Europe is now the transcended Old World; Asia is named the "the Future Land of Promise," just as it was in the past, since Cosmo believes the ark will find its mountain there; yet America ends up the actual promised land. Not long after Ararat reveals menace rather than refuge, the ark becomes for its inhabitants "a house and a home" (233), traversing an Earth that has (in this Second Noah's words) "gone back to its youth" (238), and Cosmo determines to say a final farewell to his drowned America before awaiting the reemergence of Asia and terrestrial return. A descent into submerged New York changes his mind about final destination, however, when he witnesses in the underwater remains of the Columbia University Library "an immense multitude of small luminescent animals" whose prismatic pulsing compose "an all-embracing rainbow" (248). Cosmo comes immediately to realize that the promise of his native country endures all cataclysm. "My friends," he proclaims, "to my mind, this scene, however accidental, has something of a prophecy about it. It changes the current of my thought—America is not dead; in some way she yet survives upon the earth" (248). Like the pioneers of old, the ark sails west. Three weeks later, an exhausted bird lands on the ship's rail. Soon thereafter comes a cry of "Land, ho!" (257). Pikes Peak rises in the distance, that American Ararat, never to be drowned. Waiting for the vessel on this promontory is no other person than President Samson, who welcomes Cosmo with a broad smile. At least a million people have survived the flood in the Rocky Mountains, and from them and the passengers of the ark will spread a "new world . . . far superior, in every respect, to the old world that was drowned" (263). God bless America. God bless the Ark.

Upon Cosmo's death, President Samson orders an inscription to be carved in huge letters on Pikes Peak for generations to behold. Covered in shimmering levium, these incised words transmit Cosmo's "fame to the remotest posterity":

HERE RESTED THE ARK OF
COSMO VERSAL!
He Foresaw and Prepared for the Second Deluge,
And Although Nature
Aided Him in Unexpected Ways,
Yet, but for Him, His Warnings, and His Example
The World of Man Would Have Ceased
to Exist. (264)

We are told by way of closing that President Samson, the "second father to his country" who never needed to board the ark and who never ceased to rule his undrowned nation, knew very well that this message to the future told only a partial story. *The Second Deluge* ends with this equivocal reading of President's Samson intentions when he had the American Ararat inscribed: "It would be unjust to Mr. Samson to suppose that any ironical intention was in his mind when he composed this lofty inscription" (264). Perhaps we misread *The Second Deluge*. Perhaps it is intended as an ironic mirror for would-be Noahs.

In *King Lear,* Shakespeare found in ancient scripts new possibilities. We might do the same. The Anthropocene of fire, soot, and dust is an age of sea rise and deluge, of refugees not wanted in ark or enclave, of fellow humans barred from walled nations and left to drown on distant shores or heaths. We have always known what to do, and yet we act as if we were still searching for answers to our self-made perturbations. We have also unremittingly demonstrated our willingness not to make the choices that would shelter community without the destruction of the world. The word "Anthropocene" recalls what Steve Mentz "figures as hero and villain Old Man Anthropos"—like Noah, Lear, and all the other trumped-up stubborn patriarchs the world over who do not protest a world given over to storm, who find it convenient to blame everyone else as sinners without acknowledging the high price these people pay so that small and exclusive collectives stay afloat.[20] Not that such saving ever works out all that well. History offers an archive of narrative possibility: the past is the active producer of futures, not some inert trace to be recognized once it is gone. Sustainability, on the other hand, is the lie that we can embrace a horizon that keeps widening. We do indeed have to reason the need, or we may drown in our own excess.

Storms never settle. Rain saturates the story, infecundates the gaps, proliferates the parasites. The unfolding of that drama we name the Anthropocene (and used to call things like Doomsday or the Flood) is not a prescripted narrative with a known conclusion (we all die!), but an ongoing environing that compels us to act differently before too many of our fellow creatures perish. Shakespeare matters in the Anthropocene not as some divine source of aesthetic sedative, but for the same reason Noah (as mediated through Geoffrey of Monmouth and Holinshed) mattered to Shakespeare. Stories from the past offer a storehouse of repeatable scripts that can be altered at every adaptation to resist the resignation, violence against the innocent, love of cruel justice, and other forms of harm within them. These stories are useful because they are time-bound (that is, environed by history). Historicity enables not universality, but a speaking across epochs, a relevance via difference, the tender of a storehouse of alternative knowledges, a stand against the cruelty, ire, and narcissism of petty tyrants, patriarchs soaked by the catastrophe they have fashioned with their own hands.

Critical Disaster Studies 101 (An Introduction)

If stories script our responses to disaster, to inundation, climate change, or disease, then maybe it is time to think hard about the fact of story, about the entire matter of compression and decompression, and about how what we bring aboard the ark and what hatches there might change things. Who's this now? Not Methuselah. Definitely not a woodworm. Certainly no voyager returned from failure in space or big-headed prophet of the second deluge. It appears instead to be a time traveler (of which, it must be said, there are many aboard the ark), one of the founders of the relatively young academic discipline known as "disaster studies," that Cold War–era academic-governmental-born amalgam of social psychology, sociology, risk assessment, military intelligence, planning, civil defense, and utopian thinking. Apparently he has something called an "After Action Report" (AAR) to share with Noah evaluating how he responded to the Flood. Allow us to introduce Professor Emeritus Russell R. Dynes, formerly of Ohio State University and most recently the University of Delaware. The year is 2004. He has just published an essay, "Noah and Disaster Planning: The Cultural Significance of the Flood Story," in the *Journal of Contingencies and Crisis Management*. The essay takes stock of how the story of the Flood shapes thinking about disaster in a modern America in which the peculiarities of the Genesis account are usually not remembered in detail. Professor Dynes reviews the prevailing models of disaster in modern America, noting the way they are frequently and unthinkingly hybridized in disaster planning. These models include the apocalyptic "End of the World Model . . . usually associated with nuclear war and more recently with nuclear power plants," which "suggests that everything is gone outside the ark," with the consequence that, "for some, . . . any emergency planning" seems impossible.[21] For others, "there is an effort to save some remnant for a fresh start." The limit of this model's success in salvaging a future lies in the efficacy of its mechanisms for "command and control," its ability to take control and so coordinate a response. Noah's devoutness matters here. The fact that he obeys a singular divine authority and does not question his command signifies effective "command and control," even as that control comes premised on a murderously restricted sense of who shall be saved or salvaged.

Then comes the "The Mass Media Model," which seems to be

something Dynes gleans from popular culture in the form of blockbuster special-effects-driven movies and TV shows. This deep structure provides the common denominator for divergent, phenomena-specific forms: "The Titanic Model; The Raging Inferno Model; The Twister Model; The Asteroid Model" (173). All these models assume that "disasters are characterized by traumatic changes in the behavior of 'victims,'" civil society fails, and social norms collapse. Self-interest and criminal behavior become the new norm but are balanced by acts of extreme heroism. "Individualistic and anti-bureaucratic" in its assumptions, the mass-media model slights planning and preparedness in favor of action by "strong people," who will inevitably have to defend their enclaves against the depredations brought on by a human-wide loss of composure, epitomized best, perhaps, by the traumatized citizens left to the Flood, prone to attacking any ark—including (for example) Cosmo Versál's ark of levium in Mineola, providently secured behind electro-shock trenches and equipped with machine guns.

Both the end-of-the-world and the mass-media models are now comprehended by what Dynes describes as the "Command and Control Model," which shares the assumption that a state of emergency "is characterized by social chaos" prompted by the "loss or ineffectiveness of traditional social control agencies" (173). Emphasis migrates therefore to techniques geared "to establish command over the chaos and regain 'control' of the disorganization of individuals." The command-and-control model assumes that civilian organizations, families, and other everyday social forms are unable to cope with emergency situations and so "outside help" is needed, frequently in the form of "paramilitary organizations." Planning documents of this vein devote much time to "specifying emergency 'authority'" so that no time is wasted on who or what is in control, even as that control usually rests on the suspension of the rule of law, civil rights, and the legal protections afforded to citizens. While in everyday life authority is "multidimensional," the drive in disaster planning is toward a "unidimensional" command structure capable of mobilizing the necessary forces to respond to the situation. As Dynes points out, this model is indebted to World War II "civil defense assumptions and experience," amped up by Cold War scenario planning, and "reinforced by the creation of Homeland Security after 9/11."[22] In a winkingly passive sentence that alludes to the fruits of his own decades-long career, among the work of others, Dynes observes that "it has been argued that the cultural assumptions of chaos, command and control should be replaced by the more appropriate guidelines for community problem solving, necessary in disasters" (173–74).[23]

Half-embracing the fictive, Dynes then presents a "recently discovered After Action Report" assessing Noah's response to the Flood as recorded in Genesis. "One should note," he writes, "that the report has been organised in a fashion which anticipates current thinking to view disaster not as an isolated response but as a social process involving mitigation, preparedness, response and recovery" (174). In other words, the report translates the Flood story from Genesis into the register of the competing models in the field of disaster studies. Genre is important here, because the AAR is itself military in origin, keyed to goal-oriented plans with the aim of identifying and optimizing winning strategies. Such retrospective reports are most prevalent today in the not-unrelated domains of military education, planning, and game development. Dynes, so it seems, has not come alone. He has brought with him his entire field: its assumptions, extraacademic affiliations, origins, debts, obligations, funding streams, and paramilitaries. He does so with the aim of dislodging what he takes to be the sovereign suspicion of community-based responses to disaster.[24] Sit up and listen, Mr. Noah. But sit up and listen also, FEMA (Federal Emergency Management Agency), and DHS (Department of Homeland Security). It's quite a crowd. Summing up the way the AAR trumps the Genesis account, Dynes writes: "In biblical terms, the after action report is a newer testament." The Noah story attracts supercessionary narratives.

Some highlights: "Based on our inquiry, there was little evidence that there were adequate mitigation practices initiated prior to the flood" (174). There were reports of "a significant increase in deviant behaviour as a precursor," but these are regarded as, at best, speculative, if not retrospectively self-serving. Noah does much better, though, on "preparedness activities. . . . The ark was a major accomplishment by someone with little boat building experience." Criticisms could be made, but seem "petty." "The requirement for a sprinkler system in a boat to be operated in a flood," for example, "seems excessively bureaucratic." Likewise, the "absence of life rafts" on what amounts to the world's last lifeboat should not really be the cause for serious objection. More thought could have gone into sanitation and the choice of cargo, but again, these are trifles in comparison with the success of the construction project. By contrast, legitimate criticism can be made about the warning process. The warning God gave Noah was along a single channel and too "personalized." Questions could also be leveled at Noah regarding his leadership, righteousness, old age, and the possibility that, like the captain of the Exxon *Valdez,* he was drunk, so to speak, at the wheel:

> It is a comment on the times that the names of the wives [aboard the ark] have not been recorded with any certainty. This illustrates two points. First, throughout history, there has been gender bias in disaster reporting. Second, what is identified as male heroic behaviour is usually the product of collective family effort. (175)

Especially problematic here is Noah's suspension of everything beyond the ark. No response to the suffering of others appears to have been made. Noah did not, it appears, "mount a search and rescue operation since evidently he had accepted the idea that those outside the ark were not worth saving." Had he, perhaps, generalized his own God-mandated instructions to take refuge with his family, he might have anticipated current research that shows that "refugees do not like to go to public shelters. Instead, they prefer to seek shelter with relatives and friends," and so reevaluated and modified his response. The ark's success in saving Noah, his family, and their cargo depends on this separation, this suspension of others. And such separation and dependence on a "single authority" leads to "forgetfulness." It enables the wholesale remaindering of those not wanted on the voyage. Come landfall, things went well. As the production of a new covenant attests, and the speed with which Noah and family rebound, "there is considerable evidence that the post flood recovery was successful." Though, it should be noted that, with the rainbow, "God reduced the risk perception of future floods among Noah's family members," which may or may not be a good thing for the future.

Takeaways? Overall, Noah gets fairly high marks given the single-channel directives from the sovereign unidimensional authority he receives. Command and control are established at cost. He scores highly on preparedness, but the reasons for this success also mean that he fails appallingly in terms of mitigation and responsiveness to suffering. Recovery goes well. But in this end-of-the-world scenario, recovery begins from scratch, so there is not a lot of comparison.

Could Noah have performed better? Yes. Obviously. While "the flood has often been used to argue the necessity for command and control," it can also "be used to illustrate quite different ideas" (176). For example, "it is still widely believed that those outside the ark behaved badly, chaotically, . . . [but] one can argue . . . that such behaviour was less the result of the flood itself than it was by the awareness by those outside the ark of their exclusion when God closed the door." If anything, Genesis suggests the importance of "the continuity of existing familial relationships, which is a more adequate predictor of responsible behaviour in an emergency."

Key here is the degree of "autonomy" given to Noah in how to respond and the way such responsiveness must have been the product of collective, familial debate and action. Such forms of cooperative behavior, it is suggested, went beyond the confines of Noah's human family, across the lines of kin and kind, to include animals aboard the ark. This cooperative model emphasizing traditional and nontraditional forms of community prompts the following conclusions:

> The flood story can best be read as a lesson in problem solving, rather than an exercise in the expression of authority. . . . That perhaps is the central message of the story. It is not that disasters create the conditions producing irrational behaviour. It is not that authority will ensure rational action. . . . The message is that, even in the most difficult situations, preparation can lead to innovative problem solving. Survival is more closely associated with creativity and innovation than it is with authority. Good planning should maximise creativity rather than control. (176)

The report suggests, we think, an important rereading of the story, one that threads its way through the ark's reception over the ages, and so also through our book. What would it mean to understand the story in its scanty, autonomy-giving form as an invitation to create, to redefine, to problem-solve, and so to make a world that, by the making, by the problem-solving, creates community, takes community-making as its aim, and so produces refuge, recasting traditional material-social forms in more capacious ways? "Survival is more closely associated with creativity and innovation than it is with authority."

That said, in a conclusion that adjudicates the relevance of biblical narrative to disaster planning today, Dynes sounds an ominous note. Genesis now transforms into ecofabulation, and Eden becomes an analogue to the opening of Rachel Carson's *Silent Spring*.[25] Dynes activates her powerful "A Fable for Tomorrow" as anticreation story:

> Close to Mt. Ararat, where the ark landed, is a new Garden of Eden. But that garden is no longer green after years of fertilisers and pesticides. The apples are now coated with Alar [a plant-growth regulator] and trees are now withering from acid rain and ozone depletion. With God no longer around, responsibility still has to be assigned. Like the flood story, it is flexible since, depending on your political orientations, you have the choice of what to name the snake. (176)

There is no walled garden and no walled ark without a devil, a snake. The two require one another. There will always, so it seems, be the need for blame, the need for a demonizing exclusion that is also an arkival inclusion, the transformation of the parasite into abiding lethal relation so as to justify that wall. Just as Dynes lands the story of Noah's ark so that it comes to produce a different cooperative, inclusive foundation, up rears a pre-ordained fall from grace. "Depending on your political orientations, you have the choice of what to name the snake."

Let's meet this necessary snake, always both inside and outside the ark. But let's do so in the spirit of creative problem-solving.

Snake

Now that is innovative! Hanging out from the bottom of a large boat is not the usual position for a serpent. Though perhaps it's not clear which one is the snake: the literal python-become-plug to the holed hull of the ark, or the figurative "snake" of Eden, Lucifer, who serves here as something like the patron saint of stowaways, stealing away while ensuring also that the ark does not sink. This miniature from the fourteenth-century *Queen Mary Psalter* (Plate 2) offers one of our favorite multiplications of narrative trajectory within a visualization of the sea-bound ark. Its ocean is a garrulous archive of noncanonical story, so full of narrative flotsam and jetsam that the ship seems destined never to find its Ararat. Aboard the vessel that should be the focal point, Noah appears twice. On the left he stands on deck grasping two birds, a lithe dove and a heavy raven ("une columbe and un corbeu," as the text reads underneath). Both birds look forward and upward with him. On the right, time has passed. Noah appears within an ark window, leaning out with an upraised hand, eager for a bird's return. The ship's enormous rudder looms to his side, suggesting counterintuitively that this toy of the waters might be steered, opening the previously closed question of human control and unordained destination. The dove now wings its way back to Noah's clasp, the expected olive branch clasped in its beak. The raven meanwhile has decided to go off alone, to ignore Noah's demands and satisfy its own creaturely appetites. In our next chapter, we will follow these birds and their coflight, but for now, we call your attention to what the ark floats above.

Beneath the immensity of the vessel, animal corpses float on a transparent sea, unmoored from gravity, whirled with arresting tranquility. Among these dead beasts is a brightly painted bird, upside down and drowned, a reminder that the dove and raven had kin not admitted to the shelter they enjoyed. Two men swim in the water, not yet become the carrion into which their animal companions have been transformed. Although far from at ease, the pair do not seem especially distressed. Nor with their brightly slashed and striped clothing and carefully coiffed hair are they in the least bit generic: the figures seem to convey particular persons rather than universal sinful humanity. They are unexpectedly alive in a place of death. Their presence cannot help but recall the illustration of loading the ark on a previous folio of the same psalter, where father Noah is forcibly carrying up the ladder into the ship a son who kicks and looks back at the animals still outside. Not all aboard the ark were willingly transported, nor is every dweller above the flood compliant. It is strange to see living people outside the ark this late in the Flood, since the rains have ceased and the boat is hurrying toward landfall. No intimation is given that this day is the two men's last, and yet how can it not be so? The ark is limned by suffering to come, even as the waters recede.

Directly beneath the boat, the devil emerges from a small hole, drill in hand. Now that the story of the ark is coming to its close, *le diable* is swimming to freedom, intent on ensuring that the world will never lack the unruly plots to which he dedicates himself, the stories of forbidden knowledge and sex and sin that caused the Flood's arrival in the first place. We knew this escape was coming from an earlier illustration, back when the ark was being built by an axe-armed Noah. The devil in the unconvincing form of a man persuades Mrs. Noah to assist him in stowing away. She plies her husband with wine while he slips aboard (fol. 6r). Now, the voyage nearly complete, we can see Satan departing underwater, through the bottom of the boat. The tail of a snake has been pulled through the hole that the devil has fashioned; the poor creature becomes an unwitting plug so that the ark does not founder.

The outward movement of the devil seems compensated for or reversed by the vertical wriggle of the snake's tail, which runs athwart the horizontal waves. Strange to think that the devil cares for those on board, but stranger still to contemplate a devil who would want a world not sufficiently stocked with a diversity of actors for the dramas that he loves to stage. We do not know the precise origin of this story of the devil secretly sheltered aboard the ark, but it is hard not to see in its telling an attempt to explain why the world should be just as wicked after the deluge as ever it was before. Perhaps, too, this stowaway tale conveys a desire not to leave one of the most interesting characters in Christian biblical storytelling to drown. Their eyes forever gazing heavenward, Noah and the dove are oblivious to what unfolds in the waters. The devil, the carrion, and the swimming figures are all part of the raven's world, a space that, once noticed, disturbs perspective and trajectory, a world or archive at once replete with suffering and thrumming with life. Denouement gets postponed in the process, the repeopling of the land traded for an embrace of being at sea. For a while.

Because thinking like an ark demands consideration of closure, limit, and exclusion, the system of organizing reality put into place usually curtails any real choice when it comes to what Dynes called "what to name the snake." The serpent was named when the ark excluded it. But what the complicated image from the *Queen Mary Psalter* also suggests is that sometimes a snake under one name can still smuggle itself through a series of sliding identities into other forms, and stow away as something more than a memory or an archival trace. Immurement can demonize, but only if it works. This multitemporal medieval image suggests that it is also possible to ignore narrative synchrony as an organizing principle, or to take visual synchrony, the arrangement of multiple story elements in a flat plane, as a refusal to do without, to economize, to reduce. To do so is to accept the parasite, the stowaway, along with those remaindered by the plot, as necessary to the living structure that is the ark. The story then becomes something with which to think, something like the "string figures" Haraway writes "are like stories; they propose and enact patterns for participants to inhabit, somehow, on a vulnerable and wounded earth."[26] Crucial here is the way partners in the action "do not precede the knotting: species of all kinds are consequent upon worldly subject- and object-shaping entanglements" (13). Ark-bound and overboard, raven and dove, literal-figurative snake-devil-sneaking-aboard, but also snake become part-object as a tail that plugs the hole (in the ark, in the story)—all of these entities describe powerful actors in the drama that unfolds. This manuscript image invites us to look beyond linear sequencing and trace the lines that tie the knots, to make out the figures that, for example, render the devil a literal-figurative stowaway-snake.[27] The image invites us to contemplate a community in disaster, already the lineaments of a string figure that need not be reduced, that need not simplify into landfall and rainbow, causing many of its participants to disappear into a singularized Noah and dove.

In the *Queen Mary Psalter,* the devil, the raven, and the drowned constitute something like a narrative countercurrent. They cause the plot to dally, proliferate, multiply, in a visual entanglement that ensnares the viewer in its undertow. These storied whorls insist on the possibility that there might simply be more, that there should be more. Familiar from *Aurora,* as Ship speaks with Devi, this desire not to reduce is as much a part of thinking like an ark as is landfall. String figures such as these pages from the *Queen Mary Psalter* constitute their own order of semiotic or arkival refuge: places to fly back to in order to recoup and breathe deeply of an atmosphere that refuses the drawing down of limits and the severities of climate control. The busy waters around the ship, the density of narrative moments, and the lushness of ark images in medieval texts speak to a desire to ornament the bleakness of the narrative arc, adding back into the story all that should be left behind, all that must be lost for the present moment of landed reception to cohere.[28]

But now there's a song coming. Shiny guitar; shiny voice, something about rain, and a unicorn?

The Too Full Earth (on Unicorn Conservation)

Loading the ark with ordinary animals is challenge enough, but adding fabulous ones to that procession will ensure all kinds of trouble. "Don't you forget my unicorn," commands God to "brother Noah" when, in Shel Silverstein's version of the story, the deity speaks of arks and necessary rain.[29] Impending deluge is tied to some undetailed "sinnin'" witnessed on Earth, and the pain these transgressions have caused. Although God articulates quite a catalog of charismatic animals for inclusion in the "floating zoo" that Noah will construct (alligators, elephants, cats, geese, "humpty-back camels," chimpanzees), unicorns alone are declared special, the "loveliest of all." It is therefore all the more wrenching when these creatures fail to report to the vessel at boarding time. After the other beasts have processed inside two by two, Noah naming each couple at its entrance, the patriarch looks out through the storm and spots the unicorns hiding, splashing, and romping. He can wait no longer and closes the door. So, the ark starts moving and everyone's favorite one-horned quadruped becomes extinct, at least according to Silverstein's 1962 folk song, made popular worldwide in a version recorded by the Irish Rovers six years later.[30] The tune navigates a familiar trajectory for the Noah story: from an origin in lyrics penned by a Jewish poet to enduring life as a beloved "Irish folk song," transformed by a band who made it seem native to greener origins. The song is most frequently encountered today in American Irish pubs on Saint Patrick's Day.

Losing unicorns to the Flood explains their vexing absence now. Yet allowing the creatures to drown has also proven difficult to bear. "And the waters came down and sort of floated them away" is a line at once gentle and devastating. No one wants the alligators, camels, and elephants saved at the price of unicorn annihilation, do they? Perhaps that is why unicorns have long been the favored creature for smuggling aboard the ark, even among the most exacting readers of Genesis such as Athanasius Kircher, whose unicorn we met in our previous chapter. Or, if they do not make it aboard, this absence does not have to mean that they drowned. When he remade "The Unicorn" in 1986, Andrew McKee added lyrics to make it clear that unicorns are magical. They grow wings to escape the flood, flying off to join Peter Pan in Never-Never Land, that timeless repository of lost creatures. "Now you may think this is the ending to this song," but "you'd be wrong," reads the emended verse, for "when the rain started pourin', / They grew themselves some wings and they took to soarin'." The song does not avoid the mass death of animal life that the flood brings so much as it conserves unicorns for a future available to listeners by way of fantasy. Look around you today and "you'll see green alligators and long-necked geese" and so on, "But if you're lookin' for the Unicorns don't be forlorn," follow "the second star on the right, and straight on until morn!"[31] There they will apparently be along with Peter Pan, Wendy, Tinkerbell, and the Lost Boys.

McKee's attempt at unicorn conservation has ample precedent, especially from the Middle Ages. In a miniature of the deluge we have dwelt with repeatedly in this book, ascribed to the "Master of the Échevinage of Rouen" and embedded in a French translation by Raoul de Presles of Augustine's *City of God* (Plate 5), Noah and his family pray soberly within a church-like ark while, outside in the breakers, men, women, and various animals swim in frantic search of some place of safety against the world-sea. The waters are already full of corpses, and the fate of those denied refuge in the ark is clear. The chamber next to Noah and his family is filled with the beasts they have preserved, likewise placid in expression. Among these creatures is a luminously white unicorn, its horn proudly raised. Who can resist smuggling such a creature into the floating sanctuary? Whose heart would be so cold as to damn the regal beast to the waters? The unicorn also enables the image to escape some of the difficult theological questions it raises about original sin and the potential innocence of the drowned by transporting the scene into an allegorical register. If the unicorn figures Christ, as the medieval bestiary tradition declares (for it is humble, and fierce, and a lover of virginity), then the ark is not so much a vessel of exclusion and meager preservation as a trope for the universally welcoming church. The waters do not drown so much as save—baptism not catastrophe. A sea of flotsam becomes an ocean of symbols. The cradle floating just outside the ark is not empty because its tiny occupant suffocated in the waters, but because it is a manger awaiting its glorious occupant.

There are many good reasons for saving unicorns, not least of which is that they make a world of eddying terror somehow easier to bear. Placing the unicorn aboard the ark speaks also to the too much that is lost come flood. The unicorn figures this desire to escape reduction, this desire to resist cataclysm, even as that yearning might be realized only in fantasy or by investing in allegorical futurity. Conserving the unicorn, even if that stowing away projects the animal into a fantasy land, mirrors the recalcitrant demands of the Chester cycle's Mrs. Noah as she refuses to board the ark, refuses to leave her beloved gossips to drown. Between the unicorn and Mrs. Noah lies a sense of all that will be lost. Together they refuse reductions that the announcement of an ark demands. They caution us to be on our guard as we model the consequences of climate change. It is too easy for ark-mates to resign themselves to loss, to rationalize the way a too-full Earth has been overwhelmed by the refuse of its human inhabitants. Genesis supports such a reading, to a degree: the overpopulated Earth is an idea that the Noah story has in common with the account of the Flood in the *Epic of Gilgamesh,* where the gods grow angry at the noise of the bustling humans and attempt to drown them all to attain some peace and quiet.[32] Yet Utanapishtim, unlike Noah, tries to fit as many people aboard his ark as he can, and the vessel's building is a communal effort.[33] Most exegesis of Genesis stresses that the multiplication of people is less the issue than the multiplication of evil. But then the fashion has always been to make the Noah story fit into a smaller plotline to ground a present reality, or a desired moral. Stowaways resist this impulse toward reduction, reopening the ark to what its thick walls exclude.

Salvage Stories: *Abel's Ark, Noyes Fludde,* and *Moonrise Kingdom*

Salvage operations beyond unicorn conservation are, of course, frequently attempted. Arks may be summoned into existence as topoi, staging devices, in order to effect some order of limited renewal. Take, for example, the exhibit named *Abel's Ark,* installed at the then Hancock Museum in Newcastle upon Tyne in 1984, to which curator Anthony Tynan wittily referred as "a new way with old heads." Tynan explains that in 1929 the museum was bequeathed an "extensive collection of big game heads and other natural history specimens," along with money for their display by native Northumbrian big game hunter and naturalist Abel Chapman. Viewed from the perspective of an early 1980s local museum battling recession-era funding cuts and declining membership and visitors, a collection of animal trophies acquired at the height of British colonial extractive practices posed something of a problem. "The scene," as one visitor put it, "in a word with more than one meaning was 'awe-ful.'" Tynan observes with horrified diplomatic irony that children who visited the museum might be forgiven if "they drew the conclusion that Africa was populated by a lot of heads!" Something had to be done to "cheer up" the display.[34] The solution proved quite ingenious. The museum constructed a forty foot long, single story "ark," remounting the animal heads sticking out of portholes, while the taxidermied whole animals in the museum's collection busied themselves outside as a grandfatherly representation of Abel Chapman, personing Noah, checked them on or off his list (Figures 33 and 34).

Sticking out of portholes, the animal heads acquire virtual bodies, the ark itself supplementing their absence. "Nobody would ever dream that there were no bodies," Tynan gleefully recalls.[35] The aptly named Paul Raven, who designed the "Bird Room" at the museum, was tasked with researching the relevant books as well as the Bible for inspiration, and the museum assembled a team of four designers, six joiners, and a zoologist to collaborate. They sought out help from the Worshipful Company of Shipwrights, which had organized an ark-building competition in 1947, and learned that two Tyneside shipbuilding yards had entered, coming in third and fifth place respectively. Giving up "strict adherence" to the Bible almost immediately, the design team took a "humorous approach" and so the ark finds itself upgraded to include a helipad, as well as a diorama boasting a number of companioning miniature rowboats oared by the likes of Ratty and Mole from the *Wind in the Willows.* The ark was carefully lit and enhanced further by sound effects of birds and animals, and a human voice "urging creatures aboard," to create the effect of the animals "coming to life."[36]

In 1984, *Abel's Ark* made quite a splash. It proved to be a highlight of the museum's centenary reopening and rededication, during which "it had been hoped that a member of the present Royal family might" reprise the opening ceremony of the original museum "performed by Their Royal Highnesses The Prince and Princess of Wales on 20 August 1884." Sadly, as the society's annual report opines, that "proved impossible," and the royal couple's visit had to be reenacted "by a group of young actors from the People's Theatre" with help from an ever-obliging and yet-to be-deregulated British Rail.[37]

FIGURE 33. Naturalist, hunter, sportsman Abel Chapman figures Noah checking animals on or off his list. *Abel's Ark,* Hancock Museum, Newcastle upon Tyne, circa 1984. Courtesy of the collections of the Natural History Society of Northumbria, The Museum of the North, Newcastle University, Newcastle upon Tyne, United Kingdom. Tyne & Wear Archives & Museums / Bridgeman Images.

FIGURE 34. *Abel's Ark*, Hancock Museum, Newcastle upon Tyne, circa 1984. Authors' photograph.

Whether anyone remarked that it was somehow fitting that the absent and now-defunct heads of the royal family had to be bodied forth by actors as they visited a similarly reanimated collection of colonial-era relics we do not know. With its comedy of reenactment, minor civic pageantry worthy of the medieval guild (whose shipbuilding skills and knowledge of arks it enlists), and the anxious shifting of scale as a local museum finds itself having to reckon with a collection it now finds problematic, *Abel's Ark* offers something like an emblem for the involutions of time and space that an ark is able to coordinate, all its universals deeply particularized. Augustine's ark of allegory attempts to achieve escape velocity from history. *Abel's Ark* affixes itself to its contexts. Stories extracted from real pain and real bodies are brought close, made local, but also kept seemingly far away.[38]

Benjamin Britten launched an ark that is likewise relentlessly local in its aesthetic and technique, and yet conveys toward something grander. In the story of Noah's Flood as transmitted by the Chester cycle, the British composer found alluring material for engendering new kinds of art in his fraught present. His 1958 opera *Noye's Fludde* was written for performance within the small space of a parish church. Five years earlier a storm surge had engulfed much of Britain's east coast, including Aldeburgh, where Britten was born and lived most of his life. Three hundred people perished, and Britten's seafront home was flooded. In a new house in the same town he transformed the medieval cycle play into a popular opera to be performed by an ambitiously large cast, many of them Suffolk schoolchildren. So that the audience would repeatedly join the endeavor, so that his opera would communalize, the work contains three familiar hymns. Britten invents a kind of site-specific participatory performance, what Richard Schechner calls in another context "environmental theater," in which all present are collaborators.[39] The opera's ark upon the waves, an open boat rather than a box, sonically and affectively does not close itself off from the world it animates. Animal sounds are performed through musical instruments, often simple ones: the fluttering of the dove seeking land is conveyed by a recorder's capering notes. Even the rain has an acoustically resplendent impress through Britten's innovation of "slung mugs," teacups on strings struck by a wooden spoon, resonantly filling the performance space with the plink of early water drops, presage of arriving storm.

Only the roles of Noah and Mrs. Noah were written for professional singers. Medieval cycle drama was likewise enacted not by career actors, but ordinary townspeople, guildsmen appropriate to each play's theme. Britten specifically takes from the Chester Noah's Flood its love of listing and marshaling animals, its extrabiblical delectation of that which will be stowed aboard and saved. In the medieval cycle play, this conservation was likely performed by having Noah's family carry into the ship boards on which animals are painted, speaking the names of each protected creature as it is brought within. In Britten's opera, however, the embarking of the beasts is enacted by a hundred local children in extravagant costumes, processing into the ark while singing "Kyrie Eleison" ("Lord have mercy" in Greek). Britten also delights in the resistance of Noah's wife. The violence of her being lifted into the boat is played for comedy but not dismissed, and her physical blow against Noah is included both as action and sound. Most striking, perhaps, is that her wish not to allow community outside the ark to perish succeeds, at least in a way. *Noye's Fludde* so intermixes audience and performers, humans and animals, people and environment, in music and whirring motion that even those at the boat's outside are made to feel at one with those within, a sympathy that crosses species lines, an embrace within catastrophe of the world's ongoingness.

The opera's lingering with community in the face of catastrophe suggests why director Wes Anderson and cowriter Roman Coppola were fascinated by Benjamin Britten's *Noye's Fludde* as an archive of reverberating story. Anderson's 2012 film *Moonrise Kingdom* tells the tale of 1965 New Penzance, an ark-like island about to be obliterated by the most devastating storm to hit New England in the last half of the twentieth century. Mr. and Mrs. Noah are played by the unhappily married couple Mr. and Mrs. Bishop, but they are in the end displaced by two teens. Suzy Bishop and Sam Shakusky run away together to craft their own refuge in the fantasy-fueled reality of their flight. Sam impresses Suzy with his survival skills, sketching, adult conversation, and cuisine. Suzy impresses Sam with her air of ennui, knowledge of music, and binocular superpowers. Sam seeks connection, seeks to create the family he lacks. Suzy runs from hers, finding a failure of self, of imagination, in the tired embrace of her estranged parent-lawyers and her mother's failure to act on the love she feels for Police Captain Sharp.[40] The two trek through the island, reenacting what the uncertainly diegetic narrator tells us is "the harvest migration" of the now-absent ChickChaw nation. Along the way, the two are intercepted by Sam's fellow Khaki Scouts, whose would-be, short-trousered, paramilitary fascism Suzy skewers with the scissors she carries everywhere with her. They evade capture and make camp at a bay on Black Beacon Sound, where they swim, dance, read, and explore the partial scripts of tween-love. When discovered, they evade capture twice more, managing to get married along the way (with a license, so they are told, legally binding nowhere on planet Earth). By storm's end, the bay where Sam and Suzy made their camp will have been wiped from the map by the raging winds and waters.

Britten's opera functions as a frame narrative for the film. Its rehearsal provides the occasion for the young couple's first meeting: Suzy plays the raven, while Khaki Scout Sam is in the audience with his troupe. St. Jack's church, the venue for the performance-to-be, provides the refuge-finale for the entire community as the storm waters precipitate flood and everyone seeks higher ground. The animal costumes for the opera become the disguises that enable Sam and Suzy and their reformed scout allies to gain admittance undetected to the church. Along the way, Sam is struck by lightning and miraculously pronounces himself "okay." Britten's *A Child's Guide to the Orchestra* provides further orienting control, passing in and out of the diegesis so as to code the film as a learning process, a kind of environmental, site-specific, itinerant pedagogy that, by movie's end, has an intergenerational learning curve.

Against forces of division and a stern law that descends quite literally from above (in the form of the telephonically mediated and then sea-planed "Social Services," personified by an unnamed blue-clad Tilda Swinton), *Moonrise Kingdom* imagines modes of building shelter and opening wider refuge. Its sympathy lies with the inept sheriff Captain Duffy Sharp, entangled in so many local affairs, who ensures that even his modest home welcomes those who have been denied a place of belonging because they are "too much trouble." Sam, whose Eastern European surname, Shakusky, sounds oddly in the mouths of the island's residents, is an orphan pronounced "emotionally disturbed" by his erstwhile professional foster parents, the Billingsleys, who, following Sam's disappearance, declare themselves unable to "invite him back" out of "fairness" to their other charges. The blithe cadence to their phoned-in disavowal sounds so alien to Captain Sharp that, at first, he cannot construe the meaning of their words, what their deployment of "welcome" and "fairness" might signify. When the words' meaning dawns, Captain Sharp cannot quite believe the closing of their doors against someone in need of a home. Neither can his fellow auditors: the island's telephone operator, Becky, and "Jiminy Cricket" Scout Master Ward, who swears audibly and then apologetically at their callous, procedural euphemism for abandonment.

When Captain Sharp later learns from Social Services that the apprehended Sam will face electroshock treatment and be remanded to "juvenile refuge," he balks. As the film gathers to its conclusion, he enlists the Bishops, reunited in their legal expertise, in making an abbreviated, walkie-talkied case that, even as an unmarried man, he might serve as foster parent to Sam. Social Services grudgingly acquiesces. The news comes to Sam and Suzy as the two prepare to jump from St. Jack's steeple into the rising seas below. Arms linked, they hope that the waters are deep enough to further their flight. If they prove too shallow and their jump a suicide, Sam buoys the refuge they are making by thanking Suzy for marrying him and allowing him to get to know her. The two kiss. The residual lightning in

Sam sparks. The news arrives that Sam can live with Captain Sharp. As the waters and the music rise to what will be an "Allelluyah," and the news that "they're coming down" is shouted over the storm throughout the church, lightning strikes, sending the spire hurtling to the ground. Captain Sharp, Sam, and Suzy are left suspended above the flood, hands linked in their "not letting go."

The music slows, and the scene cuts to the now extradiegetic narrator who remarks the devastation caused by the storm and the lasting damage to the island's infrastructure. But recovery, as the narrator affirms, runs apace. The storm makes landfall, and while there is neither rainbow nor dove, the scout camp is rebuilt and gets its first recruit—a "pigeon scout" in need of badges. Sam stows away at Suzy's house daily to be ferried home come dinnertime by Captain Sharp. The narrator remarks that the harvest far exceeded previous years and that "the quality of the crops was said to be extraordinary." Amid the renewal of the harvest-migration fertility rite, the film ends with Britten's song to the uninvited, "Cuckoo," from his *Friday Afternoons,* in which the cuckoo explains that its voice is always changing and that, "in August Away I must." The song fades into the open vowel of "cuckoo."[41]

Though the film's busy, highly accessorized aesthetic has been much criticized for loving the precious and the small (as Britten's opera does), the film lingers with stories that resonate even after storms batter coasts and submerge improvised ways of life. The movie also seems cuter than it is: the narratives it unfolds are filled with pain and loss. Blood is spilled: Suzy stabs one of the Khaki Scouts; the arrow shot by one scout kills his own dog, Snoopy; Sam pierces Suzy's ears with fish hooks. Only Suzy's cat seems blissfully disengaged. Yet disaster also provides opportunity, the opening of a widened and possibly welcoming future. Despite the scouring of floodwaters, something remains on the maps, some story or rumor of "yet another world." The film's final frames return to the bay where Sam and Suzy take refuge, "mile 3.25 tidal inlet," which was erased by the storm. First, we view Sam's painting of the vanished bay. Then the artwork dissolves into the former bay itself, rubricated this time in bright shells or stones with the words "Moonrise Kingdom."

We do not offer *Abel's Ark* or *Noye's Fludde* or *Moonrise Kingdom* as ideals. All three telegraph the ample problems of salvage stories. *Abel's Ark* arrives loaded with dead-alive colonial tensions playing out against a North–South divide. Britten's opera sponsors its own vision of Little England. Gender is the only visible difference, but even Mrs. Noah's potential disruptiveness is absorbed fully into the overarching melody. Its frame is complete. The Maine island in *Moonrise Kingdom* is likewise its own Little America, built by obliterative narratives and blindingly white (except for a few "diverse" campers, the blackness of the raven costume, and the momentary blackface of lightning-struck Sam). Indigenous peoples exist only as lost memory, readable through the names of trails on a map. When Sam and Suzy arrive at the bay, they declare aloud "this is our land." The community saved from the storm is Anglo-Saxon and Protestant. One of the authors of this book hails from Maine and is Jewish. The other lives in a Jewish household. We are not sure that either of our families would have found a home on the film's island. *Abel's Ark, Noye's Fludde,* and *Moonrise Kingdom* describe the limits and affects of salvage. They attune to its smallness, its forlorn possibility amid loss. Their cadence veers toward memory and inquiry, toward what might have been, and what has and shall remain lost. Perhaps, as the open-voweled cuckoo teaches us, it is time and we too must away.

An ark organizes its creatures and narratives into cargo. It sorts its freight into the neatest of compartments. But its pitch-smeared walls prove far from watertight. Adventure and dissension seep inside. They well up within. The people and animals housed in the cradle of the ark are not frozen in time. They live, they breathe, they eat, they shit, they struggle. Babies might be delivered at sea: Noah's son Sceaf, or piglets and lambs to feed carnivores. The devil might have climbed aboard by making clever use of a stubborn donkey or the noncompliant Mrs. Noah invited him aboard. Unexpected dramas unfold aboard this millennia-crossing transport mechanism. As it floats, Noah's menagerie of origins and carefully loaded hoard of prospects sails, assumes a flotilla of forms available for boarding, pirating, relaunching. The Middle Ages knew this vortex of possibility well. So, listen up, Noah, if you are still waiting at the ark's door. No matter how long you remain, you will never be able to evacuate the ark. There will only ever be more and more souls and stories that it brought into being, more than you ever included or thought possible. That's what en-arking does, what it achieves, even as you thought you understood. You might just want to let go, a real letting go this time, not the catch-and-release game you play with the raven and the dove, though that's not a bad place to start—that is, if you let the raven be a raven and the dove a pigeon. Let's allow the cuckoo Sam and the costumed Suzy of *Moonrise Kingdom* to be our guides:

Sam: "What sort of bird are you?"

Suzy: "I'm a raven . . ."

CHAPTER 6

Ravens and Doves

The ark carries a cargo of all the world's animals, sorted and stored in their pairs and sevens. Yet only two creatures from this comprehensive faunal index play a particular role in the drama that resolves the Flood. A mismatched duo of avian reconnaissance agents are charged by Noah to determine the Earth's habitability after the rain stops. One bird proves through its repeated efforts a sturdy ally of conclusion and covenant. The other apparently goes AWOL. Or rather, the two birds seem to understand their charge differently. The dove comprehends that it should return to its waterborne home with a token that the sea is withdrawing and the land is suitable for human flourishing, so that the ark might make landfall, open, and disembark. Mapping its flight in accord with human preeminence, the dove has no story of its own. The raven has other plans. This bird seeks to discover the possibilities for living that the disorder of a postdiluvian realm affords. Chafing against preordained roles, the raven explores the prospects within catastrophe for modes of existence that have nothing to do with Noah's family and their boat. The dove is absorbed into history, a symbol of enduring promise. The raven flies from captivity into the wake of catastrophe and does not return.

Raven and dove trace divergent lines of flight. They begin from the same point, but their difference (which all self-respecting ravens will deny when and as it suits them) is that, while doves and arks respond to the mess of the world by drawing down new limits and heightening security, ravens content themselves with unpredictability, uncertainty, an environment in tumult (even as, from time to time, they benefit from and seek out shelter, and so take an ark as their roost). Doves are pigeons made allegorical. Ravens are ravens. The raven's flight into the unrecounted marks for Genesis an ellipsis or *praeteritio* (passing over). But its exit from the story signifies more than failure or omission. It constitutes a call for attention, inviting some readers to fill, and so inhabit, the difficulties and pleasures of thinking like an ark. Ellipsis is as quiet as a woodworm; *praeteritio* invites regard to what has been unsaid, conspicuous exclusion, loud as a raptor taking flight. It signifies both as a rhetorical figure or trope and, in Protestant theology, those passed over, those unelected for salvation. As a consequence, this chapter concerns who and what gets left out, or opts out, but keeps circling back, surfacing again, refusing to drown, maybe even finding in a flooded land the material to build something new, an invitation to world-making regardless of arks. We offer this chapter as a buoy to the future. Even a passing over may, from time to time, open an expanse of refuge.

The story we are following is mostly about charismatic doves and earthbound ravens, but a great deal of space unfolds along the way for unexpected encounters and associates, birds of a feather and the roisterous flocks they recruit.

Gossipy Allegoresis

Sometimes a bird will fly high above its accustomed habitat, rise above the known world, above the Earth, and find itself transformed from animal into allegory. Aided by a Christian system of symbols that discerns in species of Columbidae the sacred and abiding form of a Holy Spirit, one third and yet the whole of a Holy Trinity, doves are especially susceptible to transfiguration. When Noah releases his animal scout "to see whether the waters had decreased from the surface of the ground" (Genesis 8:8),[1] that dove winging its dutiful way over the sea recalls for some interpreters the spirit of God moving across primeval waters (Genesis 1) and the divine descending like a dove on a baptized son (Matthew 3:16; John 1:32). In such supersessionary readings, the Jewishness of the Tanak is simultaneously redeemed, transformed, and left behind, since the narrative now exists to prefigure Christian stories: dove to Holy Ghost, olive branch to token of peace, Flood to universal baptism, ark to cross or sepulcher or church (take your pick or choose all three). In such typological readings, the animality of the dove is likewise redeemed, transformed, and left behind, since the bird becomes sign not beast, human universal not creaturely particular. This mode of reading in which the specific, the time-bound, and the embodied is transported out of its cultural, historical, and diegetic context to become cosmic, eternal, and spiritual can catch up anything, from animals to objects to humans. Sometimes a person will transcend their familiar home, rise above their known world, transfigured out of their imperfect humanity into some radiant allegory. Noah and his family will be converted by such an engine into signifiers of the Church, each member obedient, expectant, saved: an exemplary family enfolded by the wings of the sacred dove, every particular of their lives and journey a sign for a better mode of life to come. A lively ark full of toil stills into a cathedral full of stories in hushed glass. A noisy perturbation becomes a unity. A rowdy flock becomes a singular, radiant bird.

Caw. The spiritual uplift of allegoresis, of allegorizing, always leaves some bodies behind, stranded by choice or destiny on this too sensual Earth. How difficult it must be to find yourself the lowly raven in such a tale, let go from the up-current, one among other creatures, tracing its cacophonous path. Or perhaps, how liberating to be left behind by a story intent on getting to an elsewhere that demands, as the price of its own progress, the abandonment of the heterogeneous, the dissonant, the carnal, the mundane. "At the end of forty days, Noah opened the window of the ark that he had made and sent out the raven; it went to and fro until the waters had dried up from the earth" (Genesis 8:6–7). The raven is the first bird to carry a species name in the Bible, but it does not seem to be particularly weighed down by that burden. The reconnaissance raven never returns to the window of release: it flies out from the window and exits the story. We are not told why, yet we can well imagine: what scavenger would not in the flotsam of the deluge find a paradise? When the dove is sent to undertake the labor of the vanished raven, the second searcher eventually returns with a sign of hope for human futurity, "a plucked-off olive leaf." In his 1608 *Four Birds of Noah's Ark,* a book of prayers written for the consolation of London's citizens while they weathered the plague, playwright Thomas Dekker writes the raven out of existence completely, or more precisely, reduces the raven to something not worth mentioning aloud. "The Dove," he writes, "was the first bird that being sent out of Noah's Ark brought comfort to Noah."[2] The raven disappoints. It remains bound to the world, resolutely within catastrophe. The bird offers no "comfort," does not plot its course in reference to humans. It might as well be erased. As herald and harbinger, the refulgent dove enables the story's progress toward the rainbow. Cue the swelling music.

Caw. Meanwhile, somewhere else in the world, the raven, this dark bird who loves utopias of its own making, realms indifferent to the divine, wings its own particular way. The raven is a bird for whom catastrophe is opportunity.[3] What happens if we accompany its flight, slip out the window of the ark, dive headlong through the gap in the story, and head out into waters that have stopped flooding a world that is in no way past catastrophe? Sadly, obviously, ridiculously, neither of us can fly—not for want of trying, we can tell you—so modes of following weigh heavily upon us. We cannot proceed *with* the raven, or *as* the raven. We have to play catch-up by catching what we can in translation. Let's redouble our efforts to think of the ark and its allegoresis, its entire extra text, as a porous process of reading and exploration, of following and fleshing the story out. Like Mrs. Noah and her flock of good gossips in the Chester cycle, let's tell Noah to take a hike: we're busy talking and enjoying the boisterous company of others and attenuate or delay the allegory's closure so as to imagine what it is the raven may have to communicate if we were to ask the right questions. *Praeteritio* is sometimes called the "gossip's trope," keyed as it is to *occultatio,* "emphasizing something by pointedly passing over it," if you catch our drift, not that we want to dwell on such things, of course.[4] To gossip, in this sense, implies that allegory coheres only by a process of selective reading that skips over or excludes a world of possibilities. A gossip is, literally, a godly relation ("god" + *sibb*), someone with whom to gather and keep good company, to flock. Gossip is conversation, the coflight of shared air, the news in unofficial circulation, the work of the imagination, the energy of story in motion. It's as unreliable as it is essential. Please bear with us, then, as we do our best to accompany the raven. To companion its flight, in this cumbersome and approximating sense, will require more than a little imagination for all of us. The need for imagination is itself a repeated theme when the animals we name "human" attempt to comprehend the dark-feathered raven and the ellipsis into which it wings.

Marginal Thinking

In a deluxe Parisian psalter from circa 1225–35 (Figure 35), a roundel that holds the ark at sea is intertwined with another where the sacrifice of Isaac (Genesis 22; known in tradition as the Aqedah, the "binding" of Isaac) unfolds, a doubled lesson in obedience to a demanding

FIGURE 35. Entangling the frame with the raven. Noah's ark. From *Psalterium [psautier latin dit de saint Louis et de Blanche de Castille]* by Maître de l'atelier de Blanche de Castille. Enlumineur, 1225–35. Bibliothèque nationale de France. Bibliothèque de l'Arsenal. MS 1186 réserve.

God. The top circle depicts a dove returning with its expected branch to the community of the ark; the bottom, overlapping like the link of a chain, offers an angel straight from heaven grasping the sword that Abraham has raised to slay his son. Noah gazes placidly forward at a scene that offers no challenge; Abraham stares wide-eyed at the interruption to the fatal blow. Above, the animals of the ark are held in chambers that preserve their lives; below, a celestial messenger points down at a convenient ram, animal substitute for the child sacrifice. Noah seems to be contemplating the many birds he has gathered at the top of his vessel, residents of the room next to the one he shares with his family. The dove perches patiently at a closed window, waiting for the humans to notice its return. Like the angel to whom it forms a counterpart, the dove has copiously plumed and upright wings.

The twinning of the feathered messengers, dove and angel, anticipates an episode to come later in the manuscript, the Annunciation (fol. 16r), where a winged and haloed angel joins a winged and haloed dove (this time straightforwardly the Holy Spirit, not a creature of the ark) to inform Mary of some very important news. The mother of Jesus holds in her hands a psalter that cannot help but remind the viewer of the very book in which this particular illustration is contained, a work of devotion meant for the use of a royal lady. Mary, moreover, must also recall the earlier depiction of Noah's wife, who dominates the cabin of the ark in which her family dwells: she is its foreground, with everyone else just behind her, including her husband. Like the rest of the group, she gazes toward the birds in the next compartment with serenity, hand lifted in apparent blessing, nothing like the rowdy Mrs. Noah of the Chester cycle. Like all the psalter's stories in which it is enchained, this ark story is offered for women, with Noah's wife central, but only in her submission to the action, her reverence for the narrative in which she is contained.

Of the six assorted birds in the ark's upper room, five look toward the humans intently, but one looks away, toward a closed window, perhaps the aperture through which the raven and the dove were allowed their exit. Below decks are two more compartments, one crammed with an assortment of herbivores and the other with a lion, a small dragon, a bear, and their carnivorous ilk. The ark's roundel is encircled in tan and brown, a border that contains the whole of the scene and enchains it with the circle below, itself circumscribed in vibrant blue. Noah would seem to prefigure Abraham, as well as every other obedient patriarch, just as the dove anticipates the angel. Both dove and angel inhabit the upper-left quadrant of their roundels. Through this self-unfolding method of bestowing meaning through repetition and imbrication, it is difficult not to see in the depiction of innocent Isaac, verdantly clothed, a conserved version of the three dead youths whose corpses float with the fish beneath the ark. These cadavers are completely green from the sea that has taken their lives. They are peaceful like Isaac, sacrifices of a different kind. Had the angel not appeared and held back the sword, Abraham's son would have joined them in early death.

Gosh, the dove at the window has to wait a long time! But no matter, that is what this bird always has to do. Waiting patiently on the unfolding of stories between the human and divine is the typical milieu for an allegorical homing pigeon. The dove conveys the symbolic key that enables the communal conversions or translations that we have outlined. But that key is a given, so the actual bird may just as well wait at the window—with no point in even pecking at the shutter, the dove is included and incorporated in advance. It carries an absolutely essential message, even if Noah's family has not yet attended to its arrival so that they can see that they are sailing toward dry land, olive trees, the binding of Isaac, the unfolding of the larger history within which they are (like their roundel) unalterably linked. In its eagerness and heft, the dove exceeds the framing power of the roundel's border, and its branch intrudes into the bicolor frame that contains both circles as what should be an ultimate boundary.

The raven, however, escapes the frame. It flies beyond these circumscriptions even as its presence seems necessary to balance the dove. The raven sits outside and above the image's thick boundary line, a convenient if solitary roost. As expected, the raptor is poking at something, but scrutiny is required before the crumpled form resolves, anamorphosis-like, into a body rather than a mess. The raven's talons are atop the head of a drowned animal, perhaps a dog, and its beak pecks at the cadaver's snout. The dead animal curves in on itself, just as the roundel curves in on itself, but this circle is in the process of being assimilated into the raven. Released from the ark's compartments, the raven remains entirely outside the frame or serves to mark the limit, the threshold to what lies beyond allegory, beyond the ark: it has no analogue in roundels of the psalter to come. The raven has departed the main story; the artist visually emphasizes its separation from the enclosed narrative of the ark. And, honestly, the atopic, white space at the exterior of the frame seems a good home, more secure at least than the swallowing sea with its overdetermined signs. The raven seems perfectly happy where it is, unincorporated, content in a tale of its own unspooling.

To the raven belong stories of waywardness, tales peripheral to the plot, of making the best of it when you find yourself unable or unwilling to participate in expected conclusions. A satisfying ending is built on the casting away of alternatives, tales full of challenge that will not culminate in the desired destination, that might even wreck the narrative ship. The obedient lines (beginnings to ends) on which closure depends are disrupted by errant spirals, metaphors with unexpected transport, a proliferation of alternative plots. Two trajectories then: the dove's forth and back that enables movement toward completion of the narrative arc; the raven's veering into a space of no return, a disaster paradise that provides everything the creature needs but nothing to trigger further journey (it will certainly not be winging home with chunks of scavenged flesh).

The actions of the dove are fully part of the biblical narrative, but the raven's fate is never told in Genesis. The narrative does not accompany its flight. In Europe's medieval period, however, artists found their attention constantly recruited to the raptor's story. A long history existed of depicting in rich detail the raven's delight in the eyes of the dead, illustrations with no biblical authority that offer an expected story all the same. The raven is an actor who goes off script, but has done so for so long that its tale becomes a supplemental and necessary reality. *We* are on the ark with the dove. The raven is out there, beyond. It would be strange at this point in history to depict a raven who had not found a feast, almost as strange as a dove that had never grabbed an olive branch. The two birds work together in contrasting parallel. Each opens a familiar world, one with a future and one a seeming dead-end or auto-*telos* without *us*.

The ark's passengers are mostly doves. Noah's family teaches other people likewise to become doves, generations of doves. The ark is in constant danger of becoming a floating dovecote. Noah, his family, and the animals safe aboard know where they are going. They are eager to achieve their mountain and for the rainbow to shine. Genesis attests to as much. But this psalter image is as full of corvid tarrying as dovish destination, fated denouement abandoned for noisy attunement to the mess of the world. In truth, the long history of illustrating Noah's ark contains as many ravens as doves. In the *Queen Mary Psalter* (Plate 2), the wonderful illustration of the devil escaping through the bottom of the ark also illustrates a sea full of dead beasts, including a brightly painted bird, upside down and drowned, a reminder that both the dove and raven have kin not admitted to the shelter they enjoyed. Perhaps that is why the dove is so obedient: it realizes with gratitude the magnitude of Noah's choice, the unlikelihood of its having been among the conserved. Perhaps that is why the raven is errant: it realizes the price of salvation.

External Preoccupations: *The Aberdeen Bestiary*

For readers who take the Bible as both literal and coherent within itself, there would have to be fourteen doves aboard the ark (they are clean beasts) but only two ravens (since they are unclean; see Leviticus 11:15 and Deuteronomy 14:14). If the first dove did not return, many more remained to replace it. Lose one raven, however, and Noah would lose the entire species, as an exasperated version of the bird in midrash makes clear. The raven of the Babylonian Talmud is incensed at Noah for having been classified as unclean, and thereby one of a tenuous pair. Commanded to depart the ark and scout the sea, the bird rebukes Noah for risking the extinction of his kind: "Suppose, now, I should perish by reason of heat or cold, would not the world be the poorer by a whole species of animals?"[5] The raven even suspects that Noah might be enamored of his mate and that he is therefore being sent on a mission doomed to fail. Noah sternly disagrees, but the possibility of interspecies love stories follows the wake of the ark and the arc of the raven's flight.

Whether fourteen or two dwelled within the ark, doves and ravens nonetheless tend to make their appearances as singular creatures, each one of a kind. As the roundel just examined well illustrates, a typical medieval ark scene will depict a dove about to return to Noah's community with a branch and a raven malingering at the picture's edge. Symbolic versions of the ark, like encyclopedias, also tend to stow one of each bird in their archives, with the dove long preceding its sibling because of its sacred associations. *The Aberdeen Bestiary* is a comprehensive account of the animal world, a richly illustrated twelfth-century compendium of knowledge in which every bird and beast is simultaneously itself (a snake seeking prey, a pelican caring for fledglings) and a symbol (a figure for the devil on the hunt for souls, a symbol for Christ nurturing believers from his own bodily sacrifice).[6] As Susan Crane has demonstrated, animal lives may be glimpsed in the stories gathered within all bestiaries, but these tales tend, in the end, toward moralistic and anthropocentric allegory, rather than natural history.[7] Every creature exists to activate the imagination and inspire the betterment of the reader. Bestiaries are textual versions of an ark, where the price of admission is for each creature to be stilled into a tale for the ethical nourishment of human conservers.

The Aberdeen Bestiary begins with a verbatim quotation from the Vulgate of the Genesis account of creation in 1:1–5, sumptuously illustrated with a portrait of God holding a book and dividing the waters from earth and air (1r). Next comes the creation of the world, and then the making of each class of animal within it, from fish to birds to the beasts of the land, and finally humans. Adam names the animals, and they are depicted (as at creation) in small compartments. The biblical narrative ends here: there is no flood. Instead the manuscript declares, "incipit liber de naturis bestiarum"—"here begins the book of the nature of animals" (7r). *The Aberdeen Bestiary* carefully preserves each creature by capturing its contours in vivid colors and conveying its manifold stories at great length in swells of Latin prose. The animal tales begin with the lion, noblest of beasts. Thence gathered are all land animals, from tigers, elephants, and panthers to horses, goats, wolves, and dogs. The last of these terrestrial creatures is the humble ant. The narrative next collates all known birds. The dove receives pride of place, its description and its exegesis almost endless. Before the reader arrives at an illustration, we are told that the dove's very wings will transport us to higher registers of meaning: "It is my intention to paint a picture of the dove, whose wings are sheathed in silver and whose tail has the pale colour of gold . . . to improve the minds of ordinary people, in such a way that their soul will at least perceive physically things which it has difficulty in grasping mentally" (25v). The dove is the Holy Spirit, a biblical constant, the most noble of birds, so we should well expect its illustration to be luminous.

After so much promise, however, the dove we are offered by the illustrator is rather a disappointment: a small white bird perched under an aedicule, facing a far more impressive hawk (26r; Figure 36). Not to worry, however, the surrounding prose transports the reader

FIGURE 36. Dove as allegorical pigeon. "Of the Dove and Hawk," *The Aberdeen Bestiary,* Aberdeen University, MS 24, fol. 26r.

into those promised higher registers and details at length what the bird offers for the marshaling of Christian minds. For, every dove is, like God, three in one, "the doves of Noah, David, and Jesus Christ: Noah represents peace; David, the mighty hand; Jesus, salvation" (26v). That's a great deal of work with which to task one small bird. Noah's dove is especially freighted with meaning. When it returns to the ark (Genesis 8:11), its circuit recalls the coming back to inner peace of the troubled mind, fleeing "from the pomp of empty glory, fearing to encounter the darkness of the night—that is, the depths of eternal damnation" (26v). Its olive branch is a token for the mercy the bird seeks, like a soul that begs for forgiveness. As if this were not enough, the body of the dove is an allegory for the church (27r), from its beak that is a pulpit *(rostrum)* to its wings that are the conjoining of Old and New Testament (the flight of the dove is Christian supersession in action). Much is made of the dove's pleasing silver color, a tincture of heaven, but interestingly, when this most celestial of birds is pictured a second time by the illustrator, it is a dark and small thing.

The dove struts in a roundel within a red frame more opulent than the bird contained. Of this strangely nondescript portrayal the editors of *The Aberdeen Bestiary* note briefly: "This rather plain lifeless bird does not do justice to the luscious pictorial descriptions devoted to the dove on ff.26–30r." Though it is hard to disagree with this editorial estimation, the dove strikes us not so much as plain or lifeless, as simply earthbound. We love it for its intimacy to the ordinary, its humble relation to everyday birds, more pigeon than Holy Spirit.

Let go from allegory, there appears to be no less mundane a bird than the pigeon, which is to say no less infrastructural. Or pigeons, plural, since this type of dove seems to arrive only in its multitudes, unlike their holy, white, and singular cousin. As Andrew D. Blechman observes in a meditation on these birds entitled "Flying Rats," pigeons tend to be disparaged because they are commensal: they thrive by table-sharing with humans (even if their place is beneath it, picking at city scraps), and they make quite a mess with their excrement once they have finished their meal.[8] Like their human messmates, they are gregarious, occurring in large communities. Rock doves (urban pigeons) rewilded themselves after sailing to the Americas aboard the ships of colonists. And yet they seem never to have a story of their own. James Thurber observed that "pigeons can be understood only when you understand that there is nothing to understand about them."[9] He presents a series of pigeon vignettes in which the bird singularly fails to make an impression, for it is always ever-presently absorbed into the human world. Alluding to Thurber, Marlene in Jeannette Winterson's *Boating for Beginners* describes pigeons as "a totally nothing bird" and yet strangely central to the human world. "Do you know how much we spend each year," she asks, "cleaning pigeon shit off the most crucial of our national monuments?" Gloria does not.[10] It's curious then that, in Winterson's novel, the divine being would "prefer it if [Noah] didn't pack any pigeons" aboard the ark. But Noah cannot imagine a world without them. He encourages Lucifer, the divine's messenger, to lie and tell him that none have been brought aboard. Noah will take the blame, he says, if the divine ever works out the ruse. Come landfall and rainbow, the novel upgrades the ark's resident pigeons to the doves that take a starring role in the allegorically tuned finale.[11]

Back in *The Aberdeen Bestiary,* the raven, as expected, arrives late, after a detour into trees as habitats and parables and a detailed exami-

FIGURE 37. The fabulous raven. "The magpie, continued. De corvo; the raven," *The Aberdeen Bestiary,* Aberdeen University, MS 24, fol. 37r.

nation of what moral instruction pelicans, owls, and magpies offer. The manuscript illustration (Figure 37) presents a proudly strutting, fabulously black bird, wings partly extended, enclosed within an intricately patterned ring of white and red and blue, inset in turn within a square of the same colors. The background is gold leaf, lending the image a breathtaking radiance that offsets the raven's dark plumage. The meager dove has nothing on this opulence. The text begins by observing that the bird's Latin name (*corvus* or *corvax*) derives from the caw that issues from its throat (37r: "nomen a sono gutturis habet, quod voce coracinet"). Adam did not, it seems, name the raven: unlike other animals, the raven names itself. It remains excessive to human systems, to allegorical infrastructures, its name a product of how its call sounds to or impresses itself upon our ears. Its name or ethonym figures as an instance of onomatopoeia in which the sound the raven makes marks human language.[12]

The raven is its sound, *caw*. But the meaning that its sound conveys is cacophonous, antithetical to stable allegory, part of a whole flock of significations: "In the Scriptures, the raven is perceived in a variety of ways; it is sometimes taken to mean a preacher, sometimes a sinner, sometimes the Devil" (37r). That's quite a range for the self-nominating bird, and includes offering not only a sad allegory for sinners and devils but also a figuration of the learned preacher who dresses himself in the sobriety of black (*humilitatis nigredinem,* the blackness of humility), touching the hearts of those deep in sin: "The raven brings back food in its beak to its open-mouthed offspring, as the teacher, drawing on the understanding which he has acquired, dispenses in words the food of life to his hungry pupils" (38r). This generous distribution of nourishment to sustain a community of shared endeavor seems very distant from the solitary and selfish raven, feasting on the eyes of the dead, readily made a substitute for the devil. Here the raven is future-looking, affirmative: it shelters the young so that the next generation will be better than the preceding. Even its errantry gets recoded:

> "Wandering" *[vagatione]* here signifies nothing else but the vows of preachers moved by passion; . . . they travel to a variety of places where life is different, when they hurry here and there, eager of mind, to help souls in innumerable ways in different places. (38v)

Every story contains its alternative, so these same roving ravens with stores of food to help distant souls may also simply be fat prelates who hoard everything to themselves and refuse to share anything at all with the next generation of preachers, leaving them hungry, putting "doubts in the people's mind" (38v). Is the raven malign, benevolent, wandering, purposeful, selfish, altruistic, a loner, gregarious? Yes.

The questions do not cease. Ravens are all about curiosity, interrogation, search. What was the raven's aim in disappearing into the Flood? Where did it go? What did it do? As medieval illustrators knew well and the bestiary informs, the raven delights in devouring eyes ("the raven picks out the eyes in corpses first"), and this animal inclination is transformed into theological truth: "The raven extracts the brain through the eye, as the Devil, when it has destroyed our capacity for judgment, destroys our mental faculties"—from hungry bird to fallen angel in the space of a single simile (37v). The dark plumage of the raven, we are told, suggests the clothing of sin, and perhaps "despair of God's mercy." No wonder the bird did not return to Noah when set free from his vessel:

> Perhaps because it was caught up and perished in the flood, or perhaps because it found corpses and settled on them. In the same way, the sinner who gratifies himself outwardly with carnal desires, like the raven that did not return to the ark, is held back by external preoccupations. (37v)

The idea that the raven perished like the sinners erased by the Flood (just another victim of that universal catastrophe) or tarried among the corpses dates back to St. Augustine, who saw the exterior of the ark as representing life outside of the church, the inhabitance of the unredeemed. Ravens and those not admitted to the ark have a great deal in common. They are also in their own way quietly fabulous, sovereign beings excessive to exclusive and self-centered systems. "External preoccupations": what makes ravens excessive also makes them alluring, and so the proliferation of stories into which they recruit spectators and auditors as followers and maybe messmates.

The entry on the raven in *The Aberdeen Bestiary* ends here in frustrated suspension rather than clear conclusion: "This is enough about the raven for the moment, until someone else says something more significant about it." Stay tuned. Next up, though, is the cock, a "good partner" who awakens you with a pleasant sound, far less frustrating than raven, whose path has too many forks, too much proliferation of destination and possibility. Ravens are the world in its incongruity, its irresolvability, its tendency to suspend contradiction into enduring simultaneity. There is no easy way to conclude such a dark-feathered story.

Ravens against Allegory

The raven failed. It was supposed to perform a mission, like the dove, but apparently went off course, off narrative, followed its own inclinations, and maybe was turned black as a result: "Like Hester Prynne, marked with her scarlet letter, the raven's body was marked with this emblem of shame, splayed out, for all to see," conjectures Debbie Blue.[13] Unreliable bird, a natural sinner, unclean. But also: a user of tools, exceptionally smart, eager to recruit others to worlds of its own fashioning. Ethologists who dislike sociobiological allegories that make the animals they study boring like to tell stories about ravens. Better yet, they like to tell stories about fellow ethologists telling stories about ravens. In *Quand le loup habitera avec l'agneau,* Vinciane Despret begins the chapter on the "Enigma of the Raven" with the following anecdote gleaned from Rémy and Bernadette Chauvin's *Le modèle animal*:

> Some years ago, the American Skinnerians [followers of B. F. Skinner], who had heard tell somewhere that there existed other birds than the eternal pigeon, tried to replace it with the great raven. Without success. The raven, who found the situation in a Skinner Box profoundly absurd, did not at all wish to push on the levers at the command of the little lights that illuminated or for any other signal. Instead, it successfully used its enormous beak to completely dismantle the apparatus. This behavior was judged to be unamerican and everyone went back to pigeons.[14]

Despret applauds the raven's recalcitrance. She bemoans the "impoliteness" of placing a "being of such remarkable curiosity" (58) in the restricted confines of an operant conditioning, or as Skinner preferred to call it, "lever box." No wonder the raven resists. That unwillingness marks the bird's refusal of the investigative protocol. Its dismantling of the box was an attempt to reframe the experiment, to ask questions much more interesting than those posed to it by those who placed it in the box. The raven did not simply want "out." The imaginative bird was already thinking outside the box's paucity of narrative options, and so decided to investigate the means of its observers' lackluster attempts at investigation.

An operant conditioning box restricts the world so that an occupant animal may be posed a controlled series of questions. This impoverished environment reconstructs the test subject as an "epistemic object" whose responses may then be used to pose questions concerning the driving mechanisms of a behavior.[15] The raven proves a challenge because, as Despret explains, "if you try to elaborate any model to make sense of their behaviors," they "take a malign pleasure in contradicting it in the course of subsequent observations" (59). Ravens thereby undermine their observers' ability to generalize concepts and scale those concepts up to build models of species-wide traits. Ravens disobey "the rules that make research possible," an "incivility that excommunicated them from the laboratories of the behaviorists." A compliant raven, from the point of view of an evolutionary or sociobiologist, would have served as the "umpteenth example of . . . [an] 'all purpose' model" that predicts a universally stable set of ever-repeating outcomes.[16] But ravens seem not to have been briefed on the model, or if they have been, their notions of family and reproduction suggest its limitations. Ravens demolish both box and ideal with a single gesture. They want larger worlds.

Faced with the contradictory actions of the uncooperative raven, the Skinnerians are (like the religious allegorists of *The Aberdeen Bestiary*) forced to give up their inquiry and return to more compliant test subjects, or as the Bestiary has it, "good partners"—in this case, the pigeon and not the cock. From Despret's point of view, the Skinnerians really ought to have known better. As she points out, a little gleefully, ravens were "already . . . stigmatized from the time of the Flood," having been "the only ones to have disobeyed the rule that stipulated that there be no mating on Noah's Ark" (59). Since time immemorial, they have been considered a thoroughly unreliable bird. Invoking the raven's storied past aboard the ark is more than a passing allusion or nicety. As the title of Despret's *Quand le loup habitera avec l'agneau* makes clear, the book sets out to intervene in the ongoing allegorical processes (scientific and theological) by which we construct beings and the world. She reads the Bible verse alongside ethological texts as allied forays in an unreduced model of science or *scientia* (knowledge). In Isaiah 11:6 ("The wolf shall dwell with the lamb, / The leopard lies down with the kid"), Despret finds a useful set of instructions for thinking with and through our relations with the great variety of beings we come into being with. The verses provide a set of instructions she pries lose from their eschatological or messianic underpinnings in order to take them more literally, or still more figuratively, as a desirable voiding of taxonomic laws in the service not of a holy universalism so much as a ruined, holey, and therefore capacious hospitality. Despret reads Isaiah as a projective set of rules for assembly that might produce a different, differentiated sense of a "we" that has to keep expanding to include "more humans and non-humans in one story." The trick, however, lies not in some putative universal category, but in posing successively particularized questions to each entity so that they are not reduced to unvarying sameness. Enlarging this "we" means inviting beings to manifest in and by and through their multiple differences as opposed to reducing them to a single model.[17] Despret's respect for the raven derives from its resistance to attempts to dissuade it from its pursuit of questions it finds interesting.

A Skinner box is another little ark, a blue-printed machine for the generation of predictable and circumscribed outcomes. Both locate a powerful technique for coordinating the relation between the literal and the figural. Both function as inscription devices, as well as infrastructure for behavior control. The Skinner box rewrites its test subjects based on their ability to answer the questions posed to them. It embarks an entity along with a preloaded zoo-biopolitical foundation in the guise of a hypothesis that forever alters the creatures it brings within. The ark, likewise, rewrites humans and animals in relation to the divine such that (as we saw in an earlier chapter) a divine–human coalition emerges that correlates design and biomanagement, reserving the first right of survival, of starting over, to the managerial human, and in a very short time, only to some among that group.[18] And yet, as the raven shows, it's pretty easy to dismantle such structures. You might even set about making your own deterritorialized ark. You just need a formidable beak, an unperturbed curiosity, and a secure sense of what you find interesting.

The perceived difficulty of the raven, its unreliability as an allegorical test subject, represents not the failure of the bird, but a failure of imagination on the part of its human observers. It's not the fault of the raptor if observers refuse the invitation to abandon their separateness and become coconspirators and good gossips. Write the raven off and we write off the capacity of stories to work out differently, to go awry: the possibility that we might all learn something unexpected, unscripted, that the world might in fact be wholly other than we had imagined. Even pigeons, allegorically enhanced or ordinary, don't really pull the expected levers all the time, or if they do, they pull them ironically, under duress, conscripted as they have been to serve in successive theological and sociobiological allegories. Ravens offer the chance for a story to become something else entirely, makers as they are of disaster utopias, at home with the unpredictable. *Caw.* Let's follow even if we still can't quite fly with them. The keyword, as Despret tells us, will be "recruitment" (60). How to be open to being recruited by ravens, however uncooperative they may seem? Think of it as a challenge to your imagination: how to reclaim a story tossed away as an errant path?

Imaginative Recruitments

Let's begin again. Imagine the scene once more. Rewind to Noah at the window. But this time, let's do so in the company of a fallen Adam from John Milton's *Paradise Lost,* bawling his eyes out as he has the story of humankind, all his offspring, narrated to him by the archangel Michael as a story of "depopulation."[19] Michael figuratively places a hand on Adam's shoulder, consoling that Adam also seems to have "drowned" in "another flood, / Of tears and sorrow" (756–57). But dry your eyes, Adam; sniff those tears away; the skies are clearing; the waters have abated; look again. In his mind's eye, courtesy of Michael's scene setting, "clear sun" on a wide "watery glass" (844), as if in miniature, Adam beholds that:

> The ark no more now floats, but seems on ground
> Fast on the top of some high mountain fixed.
> And now the tops of hills as rocks appear;
> With clamour thence the rapid currents drive
> Towards the retreating sea their furious tide.
> Forthwith from out the ark a raven flies,
> And after him, the surer messenger,
> A dove sent forth once and again to spy. (850–54)

All stillness on calm water. No Noah. No opening of the window. Michael describes a succession of movements or vectors within an image. The outward trajectory of a raven condensed into a "forthwith," followed immediately by the out and back of the dove. But not the dove. Adam watches not the bird, but "the surer messenger," personed by a dove. A lesson in postal security. The raven disappears into the indefinite article, appearing and disappearing in a single sentence: "From out the ark a raven flies." Gone. *The less sure messenger.* In contrast, the dove is the definite article, the dove coordinates with the syntax, syncs up securely to the story being told. In a few lines, Michael gives all the story's infrastructure: flood, ark, dove, landfall, rainbow. Pretty as a picture postcard. Delivered from the future to the future's future, Adam stands recruited to the dove. He never really has a choice.

Not everyone lets the raven go so quickly. Some cling to the indefinite. In the 1630 "Noah's Flood," Michael Drayton, favorite poet of Queen Elizabeth I and lover of sweeping chorographical descriptions, takes delight in the raven Noah sends to see if "but one poore foot of ground, / Free from the flood might any where be found."[20] Let loose for the first time, the raven "straight cuts the Skye, / And wondrous proud his restyed wings to try, / In a large circle girdeth in the Ayre." The bird tracks east, then south, then north, following the sun, before climbing high above the "clouds to prove if his sharpe eye / From that proud pitch could possibly descry / Of some tall Rock-crown'd Mountaine, a small stone / A minuts space to set his foot upon" (825–34). Unable to find a perch to rest a bare minute amid the flood, "his long labour but in vaine," the weary raven wings back to the ark, to be replaced by "the damaske coloured Dove," Noah's "nimble scout" (835–42). The dove "thrils the thin Ayre," its plumage reflecting the light so it resembles "the shooting of a Starre." Although it finds the labor of its first flight lost (848) and returns empty-beaked, its second assay finds the dove returning as if to its mate, cooing, preening, an olive leaf in his bill.

Drayton takes delight in all the animals aboard the ark, who eagerly celebrate the dove's return along with the prospect of landfall, eager subjects, as they are, of their sovereign Noah. But it's the raven Drayton tags along with on his bird's-eye survey of the flood. It's the raven's skill in the air, its endurance, that he inhabits as his poetic line dallies with the reach the bird gives him, the pride that both take in trying their respective skills in flight and verse. The joy to be felt in the prospect of flight and the synoptic control of the landscape are palpable in the poem, as is the remarking of the labor of the birds (and their poet) in making the story occur. But that delight is also one small part of a larger allegory of subjection that purrs on the lap of a sovereign-Noah stand-in for queen or king. That said, something remains of the raven and its fellows, their senses, their abilities.

The fourteenth-century English poem "Cleanness" likewise preserves this kind of animal specificity, even as it immediately allegorizes the behavior of the raven set against that of the dove. The poet imagines that the flood has receded enough so that oceans have begun to separate, and the ark has become caught upon the protruding crags of Ararat. Noah opens the window to endless waters punctuated by bare stone, and sends out a messenger to search for habitable land: "Þat watz þe rauen so ronk, þat rebel watz euer; / He watz colored as þe cole, corbyal vntrwe [That was the raven so rank, ever a rebel; he was colored like a coal, that unfaithful bird]."[21] Careless of his word, the raven speeds away on the wind and "croukez for comfort when carayne he fyndez /Kast vp on a clyffe þer costese lay drye [caws for pleasure when he discovers carrion / cast on a dry cliff]" (459–60). He can smell the sweet stench of the dead and immediately swoops on the decayed flesh and fills his gullet ("fallez on þe foule flesch & fyllez his wombe" [462]). The raven's satisfaction is palpable. He caws with joy when he scents the feast and, like the marginal bird of the *Psautier latin dit de saint Louis et de Blanche de Castille* (Figure 35), exits the story. The raven departs ("þe rauen raykez hym forth" [465]), cares nothing for what Noah commands, nothing for where his fellows' food comes from as long as he gets his ("how alle fodez þer fare, ellez he fynde mete" [466]). Exit the allegory for a world of penetrating smells and delicious tastes. With Noah, the animals left aboard are enraged, embittered, their community having been abandoned for the pleasure of a good meal.

The raven of "Cleanness" personifies those who give in to personal desires, as opposed to subordinating those desires to the good of the whole. The raven forgets how Noah had charged him with the search for dry land and cares little that, while he feasts, those left on the ark hunger. Noah curses the raven, sends out the dove on the same mission, and finds that this bird tunes itself to collective well-being. At the moment of its release, Noah names the dove a worthy creature (471).

Through tireless efforts, the dove proves herself to have earned that designation, first returning home exhausted, then on a second flight bearing the olive branch that heralds the ark's secure future.

But why send out the raven in the first place? Why bother with such a singleton? Moralizing *exempla* do not serve as ends in themselves. They represent a mode of allegoresis that seeks to derive wholeness, integrity, "cleanness," or "purity" (in the language of the poem) from the Genesis narrative. They signal that there is some element of the story that they can't quite fathom or reconcile. This is one tradition through which we receive the raven as a wayward. Not all commentators agree. Jerome, translator of the Bible from Hebrew into the Latin version that named Noah's vessel an ark (*arca*; strongbox), followed the literal sense of the original text. Jerome believed the raven went from and to the ark until the flood dried, when at last it must have rejoined the community of Noah's family in permanent habitation. In moving the raven from Hebrew into Latin, Jerome conveyed its flight in the imperfect tense to stress the raven's creaturely ongoingness. Yet his contemporary Augustine thought otherwise. This influential biblical interpreter insisted that the raven flew from the vessel and never looked back. Augustine's raven either drowned in turbulent waters or found enough carrion to keep itself permanently distracted. For Augustine, the raven represented the errancy of sinners. He bestowed upon the raven's flight perfect-tense verbs, a permanent cut from ark-bound community. Its actions were final, a flight without return.[22] Jerome's raven, by contrast, does not seem to represent anything in particular. He realized that Genesis is not fully lucid on this point, but rather its bird of first release seems a creature of indefinite forth and back, *of* the ark rather than *out of* the ark.

What then is the purpose of the raven's flight? Or, as theologian R. W. L. Moberly asks in an essay title: "Why Did Noah Send Out a Raven?" Sampling the history of interpretations of the Genesis narrative, Moberly observes that "the overwhelming majority of commentators have assumed that the raven is carrying out the same task as the dove."[23] But Moberly is not convinced. He notes a key difference introduced by the translation from the Hebrew text into Greek: "Where the Hebrew specifies that the raven 'continuously went out and returned until the waters had dried up from the earth' the Greek continues, 'and the raven went out and did not return until the water had dried up from the earth,'" (345–46), which raises the question of "how the raven could survive all this time." Enter the "interpretive tradition regularly attested in postbilbical literature, that the raven, an unclean bird in Mosaic law (Lev. xi 15, Deut. xiv 14) fed on floating carcasses" (346). One thing leads to the proverbial other. And so, "commentators have regularly suggested symbolic and/or moralizing interpretations, drawing intrinsic characteristics of ravens and doves (most obviously colour and sound), always to the detriment of the raven" (346). Given that the raven is an unclean animal, it behaves uncleanly. The logic is perfectly circular. John Calvin, Moberly notes, "commented scathingly on this tradition," appalled at the way the translation from the Hebrew to the Greek changes the sense of the text and essentially makes of the raven a fable.[24] Such are the dangers of allegorical overreaching.

What then is the purpose of having the raven precede the dove? Moberly's response amounts to a minilesson in how we like to incorporate (or not) the unpredictable, the omission, the preterite, into our stories. Perhaps the presence of the two birds conflates two different textual traditions. A raven figures prominently in the flood narrative of the *Epic of Gilgamesh,* for example, "where first a dove, then a swallow, and thirdly a raven are sent out from the boat'" (348). The bird's biblical presence is less symbolic and more simply part and parcel of an inherited flood tradition, a sign of overlapping histories and texts. A postal creature, the raven serves now as evidence in a story of textual transmission in which "the Hebrew text is composite" (349) and Genesis an anthology. The waywardness of the raven and its incompetent flight fund an allegory of media as opposed to the animal hierarchy of beast fable or, as for the likes of Calvin, a cautionary tale in misreading.

Moberly next ventures his own proposal, which depends on two interrelated postulates: "one should abandon the usually unquestioned assumption that the role of the raven must be the same as the role of the dove" (349); and "the wording of the Hebrew text provides the necessary clues to understanding the distinctive role of the raven" (350). In a gesture typically required of people who wish to follow ravens, Moberly insists on the "difficult move" of "an initial act of imagination" (350). Forget bird traditions, even of ancient cultures. They are overdetermined. Tune in instead to the specificity not of ravens and their language or behavior (the questions that interest them), but of the language and behavior of the Hebrew text. You have to read the narrative very closely, attuning to nuance in a way that risks not making sense. You have to give up the kind of allegorical control that makes reading safe in order to approach the text with the closeness of reading as an event and encounter. In a flight of virtuoso linguistic skill, Moberly stretches his wings and finds in a "repeated idiom" a "possible parallel between the movement of the receding waters and the flight of the raven" (350). Is there some correlation between the bird's flight and the ebbing of the waters? Could that relation be, in some sense, causal? The movement of the raven over the floodwaters corresponds to that of the *ruah elohim* (spirit, breath, wind of God) over the primordial sea (352). God moves like a bird. The raven moves like God. Or, in his imitation of the divine, Noah is "not just the passive recipient of, but an active participant in, the work of God, symbolically replicating God's action through the spirit, and so appropriating it within the created realm" (354). An entire orientation to what reading sacred texts might mean unfolds for Moberly in the raven's sacred flight.

Ultimately, though, Moberly demures on his proposal. Perhaps it is too wayward—too imaginative? "The Jew or Christian," he remarks, "may instinctively feel that the raven is simply the wrong bird to be symbolizing God's spirit" (354). To such an objection, Moberly confesses, he has no sufficient response, since the "symbolic key is, as far as I can see, lost." With that gesture of nonknowing, of passing over in order to preserve the difficulty and stay with the bit of textual trouble the raven causes, Moberly inscribes the unpredictable within his text and within Genesis as something still to be thought and experienced. The challenge, he concludes, "is to know when rightly to subsume a puzzling verse into a readily available frame of reference, and when to recognize that puzzle which should give one pause" (355). The recalcitrance of the text is something to be encountered, contemplated, allowed to provoke new questions, a spur to errantry. What might happen if we allowed the raven the same privilege? What would the raven of Genesis be if its flight refused to settle, if it stopped circling human stories?

In *The Epic of Gilgamesh,* the three birds that depart the ship remain emphatically birds. On the seventh day of the flood, ship captain Utanapishtim relates:

I sent forth a dove and released it.
The dove went off, but came back to me;
no perch was visible so it circled back to me.
I sent forth a swallow and released it.
The swallow went off, but came back to me;
no perch was visible so it circled back to me.
I sent forth a raven and released it.
The raven went off, and saw the waters slither back.
It eats, scratches, it bobs, but does not circle back to me.[25]

Two repetitions of the same path lead to a divergence, yet all three flights are simply paths that birds wing. What signifies here is the not-circling-back, the outward arrow of a raven who is gone about raven business (eating, scratching, bobbing). The waters too seem alive. The human sky is empty. Utanapishtim knows how to read this empty sky, understands its meaning with regard to him, and sends "out everything in all directions" before he sacrifices to the gods (155). Landfall is a return to the raven being a raven; a dove, a dove; a swallow, a swallow; a sheep, a sacrifice.

We are eager to follow the raven into a sky emptied of ready-made allegories, to go off and not circle back. We would like to know more about what the raven sees and feels, how it eats, scratches, and bobs in its refusal of return, even as we understand that the texts from which it and we originate remain tied to the world made by the infrastructural sheep of a sacrificial economy. We would also like to bear in mind the difference between the flood in *Gilgamesh* and that in Genesis. It is so easy to forget that Noah's dove, after returning with the olive branch, was sent forth seven days later "and it did not return to him any more" (Genesis 8:12). Sometimes it is hard to keep your doves from being recruited by ravens.

In order to follow ravens, one ethologist found himself like Utanapishtim hauling roadkill, sheepy and otherwise, into the woods to see if he could recruit a flock to help him learn about how they recruit one another to their projects. Noah sacrificed a burnt offering "of every clean animal and of every clean bird. The Lord smelled the pleasing odor" (Genesis 8:20–21). Utanapishtim sacrifices a sheep in order to recruit the gods to the well-being of humankind. The gods smell the savor and attend. Ethologists rezone the gesture. The animals they offer up are addressed not to divinities, but to ravens.

What Kind of Ark Does a Raven Make?

For ethologist Bernd Heinrich, raven recruitment begins in childhood. At the end of World War II, as he relates in his 1989 *Ravens in Winter,* he and his family were "living as displaced persons in a one-room cabin in a German forest preserve."[26] Life in the woods was hard. He and Marianne, his sister, were afraid of everything, especially wild boars. One time, he reports, the two of them were on their way to the village school when they "heard a deep croaking and saw great black birds erupting out of the thicket" (33). Not knowing what to do, they ran home to tell their parents. Their father understood; he knew what the call meant. Heinrich explains that "our situation was like Elijah's in the wilderness," for "indeed the raven brought us food, but only because we heeded his 'message,' which was: 'Food here.'" Returning to the woods, they found that "it was a boar. When fried, it was the most delicious thing we had eaten for a very long time." Years later, Heinrich took the turn to play the raven to the raven, with the aid of friends and students supplying a seemingly endless series of dead animal bodies: squirrels, gophers, rabbits, and cows, along with, on occasion, more rarefied foods such as Ben and Jerry's chocolate ice cream, bread, oranges, cooking grease, butter, and french fries. All this food was offered to find out more about how ravens recruit other ravens and other animals to their cause.

Written in the manner of a "detective story that tries to solve a puzzle" (13) and assembled from multiple sets of field notes, *Ravens in Winter* seeks to understand under what circumstances ravens congregate around a carcass that they then proceed to share. As Heinrich explains, "this book is about solving a riddle: Do common ravens, *Corvax corvax,* actively disclose to strangers of their species the valuable and rare food bonanzas that one of them is lucky enough to find?" And, "if so, how do they do it, and why?" (302). Heinrich is, in his own words, "highly motivated, because if the answer to the first question were yes, it would mean the discovery of a new biological phenomenon never before demonstrated in any animal." The year is 1984, late fall, in Maine. Out walking, Heinrich comes across a group of fifteen ravens feeding on a dead moose. The group is noisy, offering a cacophony of variations on basic corvid sounds, from "quarks" to "queeks" (43). One idiosyncratic bird "makes a loud single 'pop,'" while another engages in "a softly melodious singsong." The ravens did not appear to have been fighting. So what is the occasion for their gathering and such an awful lot of "yelling" (44)? Heinrich is awed because he sees a paradox: "At this time of year I had seen ravens flying only singly or in pairs, which means they were solitary animals, not likely to have friends or relatives" around to help open the moose carcass. One or more of the ravens had likely called to the others alerting them to the presence of the feast, much like the wild boar to which the ravens in Germany had inadvertently alerted Heinrich. "The idea that ravens, who are rare and solitary nesters, could evolve mutual cooperation in food-finding," writes Heinrich, "seemed at first glance too fantastic to consider seriously" (45). Commensality through collaboration is not a clear benefit to any individual raven: "Why should a raven show others where to find food? What does it gain thereby?" Cooperation makes little evolutionary sense, since "evolution is a mechanism for passing on an *individual's* genes, with those of the species carried along only secondarily." After all, as the "Cleanness" poet teaches us, ravens are not community-minded creatures, unlike doves. It matters to the raven only that it shall eat.

For fellow ethologist Despret, Heinrich's work stands as a brilliant example of how to understand an animal as a partner to your investigations, reshaping the scientific inquiry in the process and re-creating both the animal and its investigator. Heinrich's story is one of reciprocal capture by which he and the ravens are forever changed. "Recruitment," in Despret's terms, is not limited to ravens, but extends throughout the entire network of persons and nonhuman actors assembled to help solve the puzzle. She takes delight in the skill, cunning, and labor that Heinrich has to expend in coming to know the kinds of questions his ravens wish to answer. If his book is a detective story, it is a story in which the crime is not solved but allowed to ramify and change the basis of the inquiry by altering its path. As Despret explains:

> if you want to distinguish from the tangle of all the possible explanations, in the skein of motives, that which can truly permit you to understand the stakes of the "crime," you have to help things along; you have to create situations that permit the ravens to help you decide, among all the contesting fictions, the right fiction. You have to do so all the more so since the ravens will not show you, straightforwardly, what counts for them.[27]

Over the next four years, Heinrich finds himself hauling roadkill into clearings in forests, taking phone calls from acquaintances who've come across a carcass, or like Noah and family in certain traditions, building an aviary so that he can study individual behaviors, catching and releasing birds whom he can track remotely. Far from a drawing down of boundaries, a reduction of space in the form of an immunitory bubble, this kind of building elaborates networks outward, following the flight of the raven, the sound and variation of its voice in conversation with others.[28]

"Foraging behavior," Heinrich observes, "how animals make a living—seems to me to be a pivotal aspect of life" (36). He is excited by what ravens might have to offer because, while many elements of their behavior are similar, those behaviors have been "'stretched,' that is, modified or put together in different ways in different species to result in entirely new strategies, all of which serve the same general principles of feeding economy at different resource distributions" (36–37). The ravens of one locale may vary vastly from ravens elsewhere. In one expanse, they may remain solitary, while in another they may recruit their fellows in order to share in an unexpected repast of meat. In still others, they may ally with wolf packs for whom they provide superior eyes and ears in exchange for the predators bringing down an animal and opening its carcass.[29] The repertoire of raven calls varies greatly. "We have hardly begun to decipher the language of the raven," writes Heinrich, "its dictionary so far contains but a few 'words'" (252). A timid-seeming loner of a raven Heinrich came to care for underwent a surprising personality change after caught. Released from his cage, the bird did not act excited, but "looked around and nonchalantly hopped onto a perch" (131). He took a french fry from Heinrich's hand "and ate it as if he has always known and loved french fries." The bird ignored Heinrich's young son Stuart "chattering" away, and paid no heed to the cat perched nearby. Heinrich is amazed at this nonchalance. The bird "exude[d] total control, total ease, right from the start. Not a hint of panic. . . . Can this really be a wild bird?" (132).

What of the puzzle of the group feeding at the moose carcass back in 1984? Years later, Heinrich feels that the most likely conclusion runs as follows: "The recruitment is by vagrant juveniles which then gain or maintain access to food otherwise defended by resident pairs of adults" (311). Listening carefully to raven calls reveals that juveniles yell only when they are gathered in sufficient numbers that the dominating raven pairs will not immediately chase them off. Raven society seems complex, an ongoing negotiation between resident pairs of birds and shifting groups or alliances of wandering, gossipy juveniles. "There is one other tantalizing set of observations," Heinrich adds, "that suggests a second reason for recruitment" (312). Young ravens, he offers, "leave home to wander. They are gregarious, joining other juveniles to roost and feast with, and to find an attractive mate" (313). Perhaps, an unmatched raven who finds food "invites eligible singles to join him (or her?) at the feast, thereby . . . increasing its status and demonstrating fitness as a future provider for rearing offspring" (313). Drayton's raven flexes its muscles as it takes flight, eager to prove its skill. Heinrich's play their parts in "an elegant, simple, and beautiful system, . . . clothed by intricate detail and subtlety." As far as he knows, no other creature reveals a similar system based on coordinating food sharing and status. "However, sometimes when I am fanciful," he adds, "and envision ravens studying humans, I can't help but wonder what they would make of some of our customs, and how *they* might arrive at scientific conclusions about them" (313). Anthropomorphism, yes. The return of allegory. But also a reciprocal zoomorphism. Mutual recruitment.

What might happen if we acknowledged that arks, Skinner boxes, and their allied apparatuses function as inscription devices, writing tools, that comake their test subjects and investigators in what Thom Van Dooren calls a "shared world?"[30] What might become possible if we invited all who embark to take a share in writing the zoo-biopolitical programs these devices coordinate? This is the drift to Heinrich's detective story and to Despret's curation of his ethological work. This cocreative construction is the kind of making that the flight of a raven describes, veering away from an ark of another's choosing to participate in the recruitments necessary to remain in an unreduced and troubling world. It's not that hard to find allies, as ravens seem to know. Allies do not even need to be like-minded creatures. They just have to have a stake in the environing, companions in the extended sense that Donna Haraway has taught us to understand. Cooperation becomes the rule, rather than individualizing reproductive imperatives or inoculation. When the anarchist thinker Pëtr Kropotkin pondered the world's flora and fauna, he wondered why not, in place of competition, imagine the gentler allegory of "mutual aid" as "a factor in evolution"?[31]

"Staying with the trouble" is how Haraway describes this process of raven-like alighting.[32] "Dwelling in the dissolve" is how Stacy Alaimo figures this same gerundive living on in more liquid terms, refusing any sense that "we" exist over here and are not thoroughly connected to and shot through with what appears to be happening over there.[33] Trouble and dissolution figure collapse and catastrophe. But words are supple things. For Haraway, ever attuned to etymological histories, the word "trouble" should be heard in the fullness of its derivation from "a thirteenth-century French verb *[trubler]* meaning to 'stir up, 'to make cloudy,' 'to disturb.' We—all of us on Terra—live in disturbing times," she elaborates, "mixed-up times, troubling and turbid times." This earthy stirring up of things, what Alaimo calls "environmental politics," also travels with pleasures—some of which lie in the modes of perceptual or cognitive reeducation that come from trying to follow the flight of a raven or being recruited to its perspective. Learning to look, read, listen, smell, touch, and taste in new ways can transform what we think the world is and what it might become.

Working with multispecies ethnographers who study colonies of feral cats in Los Angeles, Ursula Heise invites us to rethink conservation under the rubric of this order of "multispecies justice." Doing so requires taking a different perspective toward the built world. Cities, she observes, are "traditionally considered as biodiversity wastelands not worthy of conservationists' attention" and yet, on closer consideration, are "often quite rich in biodiversity because of the plants, animals, and microorganisms that a large human population cultivates and imports from other places."[34] Are stray cat colonies therefore a hazard to be removed or something to inquire into, as Despret and Heinrich suggest, in order to discover how and why these cats manage to survive in these spaces? "Should we track down and kill feral cats in order to protect birds and reptiles," asks Heise here, or "should we listen to the animal welfare advocates who resist putting them to death?" How do we rethink conservation beyond habitat restoration? Heise insists that the answer lies in a conversation, an interchange, that leads proactively and projectively to the question of what sort of community an urban space might be and become, how it is experienced by different communities, different species. Dwelling is politics.

Heise has created a short film called *Urban Ark Los Angeles*, which recalls our first chapter, in which we saw one speculative origin for the ark traced back to the ancient city-states of Sumer and Mesopotamia. The film asks us to think with and through the way cities play host to all manner of unintended communities, birds of different feathers who nevertheless flock together. Native to Mexico, imported to Los Angeles as part of the pet trade, and now an endangered animal, an estimated 2,500–3,000 red-crowned parrots make their homes in the San Gabriel Valley in California, particularly in Pasadena. Escaped, released, or thrown out by their owners, these birds constitute their own community in the interstices of the world built for and by the humans with whom they now share space. Dedicated frugivores, red-crowned parrots delight in eating nonnative plants. The film curates their existence along with the reactions of a range of local residents, who register something on the order of a cautious, bemused delight (either with the parrots or with being asked questions about them by a film crew). In 2001, red-crowned parrots became naturalized citizens when the California Bird Records Committee decided to add them to the list of California State birds. They now outnumber the population of their siblings in their native Mexico.

Striking in its tentative optimism and eager caution, the film feels out what might happen if we embraced what occurs by chance and began to design our cities as urban arks. In the closing voice-over, Heise gestures toward the grander scale to which these localized ark projects belong. They enlarge the cosmopolitan possibilities to be found in cities, in the very project of city-dwelling, extending that cosmopolitanism to include nonhumans.[35] To our ears, this cosmopolitical call, allied to the cautious affect of local residents, assembled experts, and the film itself, recalls the uncertainty Mike Davis voices in his 2010 essay "Who Will Build the Ark?" How do we weigh an "analytic despair" at our present conditions with the nervous butterflies of "utopian possibility"?[36] Davis ventures that the tools for crafting an altogether more socially inclusive future lie still with all our cities, in the urban concept itself, by which he means early-twentieth-century, socialist-anarchist city-planning and design, which "fosters a more virtuous cycle" (42) focused on the cultivation of public affluence as opposed to private property. Such cautious optimism also characterizes the work of Anna Lowenhaupt Tsing, who forages for what she calls "disturbance-based ecologies in which many species sometimes live together without either harmony or conquest," such as the networks that have grown up around the cultivation or foraging of matsutake mushrooms in the Pacific Northwest.[37]

There is much, as far as Tsing and these other writers are concerned, to be salvaged, especially under the badge of "mutual aid" in cosmopolitical thinking. How then to build or unbuild an ark? How to elaborate *refugia* in a highly differentiated sense of the term: multiple orders of refuge for multiple ways of being? What is good for ravens will not be good for everyone. We cannot simply "follow" the raven, as the poem "Cleanness" knows, even as it rubbishes the bird for its assumed selfishness as opposed to the public-spirited dove. Then again, if we keep reading Genesis, the dove also did not return at its third release from the ark, and may thereby have escaped sacrifice at the altar of landfall, when "fear and dread" of humans fell "upon all the beasts of the earth and upon all the birds of the sky" (Genesis 9:2–3).

The tentative, counterintuitive optimism of these writers and thinkers is keyed to being open to surprise, open to finding possibility in the most unlikely places. Writing of architectural design in the Anthropocene, McKenzie Wark observes that "all architecture that we know is architecture of the Holocene," meaning that "the climate . . . has always been an assumed constant."[38] What does it mean to try to build without this false assumption of security? What does it mean to build without the sense of "striving upward" that Wark hears in the word *archē*?[39] Architecture, as any builder knows, has always had to deal with manifold unpredictabilities, managing seasonal floods and winds, along with the limits and possibilities to be had from materials that weather. That said, Wark is out to provoke a fundamental rethinking of what building and maintaining a world means. They try out various neologisms: "kainotecture," invoking *kainos,* meaning "a twist in the quality of time;" "tychotecture, from *tyche,* goddess of fortune"; "symbebekotecture, from *symbebekos,* the accident." They let the strangeness of the terms weigh on the brain until "there's more information to go on as to what building will be like in the time the planet is now inhabiting."[40] In the meantime, rather than concentrate on arks, on drawing down boundaries and sealing structures, why not proceed by sifting the past for projects that speak to a more open, improvisatory set of strategies?

Like Tsing, Wark proposes something like a salvage operation in terms of design archeology, turning to history for ways of building that might anticipate the uncertainties of the future. As a first installment, Wark takes us back to the beaches of Normandy in June 1944 to find one "preliminary image of our symbebekotecture not from the defensive structures" of the so-called "Atlantic Wall," but from objects "designed and built for the attack."[41] Not arks. Not the schizoid impossibility of en-arking occupied Europe in a fascist wall of steel. Why not instead consider all the strange, hybrid designs of the Allies: the floating docks or swimming tanks, along with earlier, yet more audacious ideas such as iceberg-island-stations or aircraft carriers made from Pykrete (a compound of ice and wood pulp) like the HMS *Habakkuk,* which dissolve as they drift with the seas and the weather warms? These designs are literally and proactively reparative in the sense that they respond to and anticipate hostility in the place of hospitality. As Wark points out, historically such designs came to be because "modern warfare was no longer about attacking the body of the enemy, but the environment. Gas and modern explosives are ambient weapons, making a zone uninhabitable for life." Weapons pursued the unthinkable course of deliberate environment degradation (the rainbow becoming once again a literal bow of rain), transforming an environment into a killing machine. Allied invasion design and convoy protection "addressed an environment of accidental, ambient, and sometimes indirect effects: an exploding world." They sought to render that environment less hostile, more liveable, to produce refuge in spaces deliberately made lethal by creating multiple *refugia* for allied soldiers.[42] Open to alliance and open to the unpredictable, corvids hold the advantage because their designs are rooted in the social, and so remain infinitely malleable. They do not have to inscribe their communalizing relations in objects for them to take hold. In fact, it is through their departure from static architectures like arks or narrative routines that ravens open the space for their imaginations to burgeon, for new kinds of shelter to be made.

Caw. The raven recruits to the unpredictable, the uninevitable, the possibility of a shared world.

Unloosening (Mrs. Noah and the Raven)

Just before the flood arrives, the Book of Genesis states that "divine beings [the sons of God] saw how beautiful the daughters of men were and took wives from among those that pleased them" (6:2). Shortly thereafter, the giants called Nephilim are born—and shortly after that, "the Lord saw how great was man's wickedness on earth" (6:5), leading to his declaration that he will blot all beasts, creeping things, and birds of the sky from its lands because "I regret that I made them" (6:7). Things fall apart pretty quickly. But let's linger with the sons of God for a moment, a group many biblical interpreters have held to be angels drawn too passionately to terrestrial dwellers. As a lover of the difficult world that is, the raven is an intimate to the fallen angels who populate retellings of the Noah story, celestial creatures who likewise prefer earthbound entanglements to some distant and intangible heaven. Desire-filled, ruined, vibrant with precarity, the world of the raven is messy, challenging. The raven therefore also has an affinity with Noah's wife, at least when she is noncompliant, prone to recalcitrance, a maker of disaster utopias. Sometimes a woman will refuse to abandon her accustomed home, refuse to rise above her known world, reject transformation from embodied creature into airy allegory.

In Timothy Findley's *Not Wanted on the Voyage,* Mrs. Noyes knows well the cost of such transfiguration, rejecting the "paper promise" of her husband's rainbow and the spurious accomplishment of his dove, the bird who does not find an olive branch to end the Flood, and so is provided one from its cage. Mrs. Noyes's desire is to remain ark-bound, voyage-locked, because she knows the violence that submission to Noah's vision of the world demands. Her hope as the narrative ends is that the rains will return, that the brutal system that the ark transports will find neither continuance nor sequel. Mrs. Noyes is a complicated figure, an unwilling member of a community to which she never sought admittance.

In the Chester play, Mrs. Noah must be loaded aboard by force and rebuked so that her husband's vessel of safety can set sail and the future can proceed as planned. But to linger with her, at least for a while, is thrilling: enjoying one last hurrah in the bottle she shares with her flock of good gossips, joining the round they sing against the solemnity of the hymns to come, imagining the endurance of the community she recruits. Throughout this book, we have lingered with Mrs. Noah or Mrs. Noyes as a figure of *no* over *yes,* of resistance to diminished refuge in the face of disaster. As the keeper of the memory of lives not wanted on the voyage, Mrs. Noyes knows that the deluge diminished a wide Earth into segregated, hierarchized, and impoverished modes of being. As we move to close this chapter, reaching the limit of our ability to follow the raven, we linger with another avatar of Mrs. Noah: the heroine of Sarah Blake's novel *Naamah*. This narrative depicts the improvised forms of living that the houseboat ark affords amid universal catastrophe. Like most versions of the vessel, where the labor required to keep the preservational system functioning is a hell to endure, *Naamah* describes a cross-species togetherness that demands plenty of work: rooms full of shit and blood, "every sight a chore to be done."[43] Yet the ark is also a place where quiet affections flourish and danger intermixes with desire. The horror of the drowned world haunts, but erotic and familial bonds burgeon. Little is forgotten. This ark brims with life, an exuberant experiment in making life within ruin.

A pragmatist and inveterate creator of perturbation as well as refuge, Naamah loves her husband Noah, and their bond is tender.[44] That might seem a small thing, but most narratives of the Flood's unfolding choose their sympathies carefully and invest empathy with parsimony. If Noah is the hero, then his wife will be an obedient cipher or a shrew. If Mrs. Noah is the heroine, then her husband will be a fool or a scheming and malevolent patriarch. Blake avoids such easy polarities in her novel. Her Noah is more thoughtful than obedient. He follows God's commands to build a vessel less because it is right to do so than because he loves his family so much that he strives to preserve them from universal death (145). When Naamah insists that her husband judge her more severely for what she perceives as her lapses and faults, he wishes only that she would be less reckless with her life because "I love you and I need you to make it through this" (48). He offers a declaration of togetherness rather than a statement about the necessity of her labor. Naamah is "the first one to know Noah to be a just man and perfect in his generations" (2). But that is not an oppressive knowledge. Even though neither of them understands in advance how they can build an ark and save a world and start all things over again as God requires, they launch themselves as a pair into constructing a shelter within and against a cosmos they do not comprehend. Naamah builds from reeds the model of the ark that they will realize. Naamah comforts Noah when he fears that maybe everyone is wicked, and that maybe even he and his family should die. When the rains begin, any doubts that either holds quickly depart (3).

Life on the ark is for Noah more comfort than challenge: "I like it here. I have my family. Tending to the animals fills my days. I'm happy" (169). He will feel the same quotidian satisfaction toward the end of the novel, as his family takes apart the ark and constructs new dwellings from its salvaged wood (273). Even while admitting her fatigue, Naamah responds to her husband's contentment by taking his hand and stating, "I love that about you." She realizes that, even if "eleven months has been a long time" (209), and even if the labor of maintaining the animals and her family is exhausting, should the ark never find dry land, they would raise grandchildren within its cradle and make of the ship an abiding home, "the world as it was and as it could be" (209). She knows that the ark system is perfectly adapted to its human occupants, offering a "sameness" as well as a "containedness," both constricting and filled with comfort (234), just like the play tents that Noah and Naamah built for their children when they were young, and the tents they will construct someday for their grandchildren. One night, as they lie awake together, the couple thinks about these snug architectures that were and are to come. At that pleasant contemplation and with a kiss from Noah, Naamah declares she is going to sleep. "Closing her eyes, but still smiling," she drifts into slumber with her hand on Noah's arm (234). A corporeal language of affectionate gesture underwrites many of their interactions. Some of the novel's most tender passages simply describe Noah and Naamah together at night, eased by the touch of each other's work-worn bodies, the roughness of skin on hand a reminder of shared history. At such moments Naamah, realizes of her spouse that "she loved him enormously, and she knew she always would" (81).

But Naamah also loves Bethel, a widow who had been a neighbor as well as her first same-sex partner in exploring the pleasures of the body. Bethel (whose name means "House of God") teaches Naamah where to harvest abundant berries and how to experience her corporeality in thrilling ways. The two of them have a quiet, constant, passionate bond that is sometimes friendship and sometimes ecstacy. The pleasures of each other's company are experienced most intensely within Bethel's home: "No one bothered a widow with her tent closed in the heat" (21). That is, no one imagined that women such as Bethel or Naamah would have lives more capacious than the plots allotted them in familiar narratives about widows and longtime wives. Despite a first invitation from Naamah and a second from God to board the ark, Bethel dies in the Flood. She feels that she has lived a life adequately full and does not seek survival beyond that satisfaction: "I see my tiredness on this earth in His tiredness of us" (46).

Naamah is more restless, more driven. In the course of the narrative, she has intimate pleasures with her daughter-in-law Adata (who wonders what life she will find with her husband once they disembark, since they do not share the same passions). Naamah also becomes enamored of a fallen angel who dwells at the bottom of the sea, a beautiful creature who combines the fierceness of a tiger and the tender heart of a human in her black-skinned womanly form. The angel creates on the ocean floor a secret shelter for drowned children who do not know how to leave their former home, a palace of crystal water built to resemble the palaces of heaven. This angel wonders what world God allots to her because she loves so deeply the realm he has destroyed. Like Adata, Bethel, and Naamah, the angel builds refuges that welcome the unexpected. All these women therefore verge on transformation into types, avatars of the "powerful women" that have always been part of Naamah's family (116), doves not ravens. Yet all hold on to their lived particulars, their turbulent complexities. A challenge to the masculine divinity inheres in their being. In her dreams, Naamah accompanies Sarai (wife of Abraham, mother of nearly sacrificed Isaac), unloosed from time and filled with a burgeoning power to enlarge the world. Sarai, who declares that "my life felt large when everyone else saw me as small and inept" (118), is on a journey after death toward becoming something like a god herself. Her moment of "unloosening" from her assigned script seems to have arrived when God "ordered my husband to kill my son" (117). Sarai never forgets her descent from Naamah.

The story grows more complicated still, especially as the narrative is increasingly interwoven with convoluted dreams. Naamah is told by her angel lover that "there is no unguarded moment in your life" (137), and yet she loses herself to swimming, submergence in the world outside the drifting ark. Unlike her husband, she cannot be content with the predictable routines of the boat. She therefore builds a ladder that enables her to access the ocean's depths, a way to escape her ark-allotted role: "It feels freeing, to swim, to be part of the flood. We've been separated from it, from everything" (19). She plunges into the unknown—recklessly, joyfully, painfully. In her unrelenting embrace of vulnerability, Naamah encounters and creates marvels. She is a figure of contradiction. Her emotions are tempestuous, and her memories of the lost world painful, but she firmly rejects the angel's offer to enable her to forget what hurts. She would rather live in the aftermath of a broken history than have that past effaced. The world is, for Naamah, an ongoing project. When the rains first start, she departs the ark so that she will know how those left to the exterior feel (the water falls so hard it scrapes her skin raw). She does not understand how she "could have been judged differently from all those other people": the ones who drowned, especially the children (49). She can be accidentally cruel, in part because she is "weak and powerful both," but for that very reason, for that very humanity of hers, "Noah would not have completed the ark" without her (146). Inexplicably, sometimes she cannot see the animals that dwell within the ark, even as she is feeding baby lambs to hungry tigers. She experiences "profound guilt" every moment of her day, as well as a "largeness" that enables her to slip "outside of her life" (183). Naamah's laugh is so disruptive, so heartfelt and genuine, its sudden eruption can knock auditors out of their surety, making the orbit of their lives wobble enough to enlarge their worlds. "Naamah creates moments of wonder somehow" (182), bewildering those who experience them.

Naamah puzzles even God. When given a chance to speak with him (he is strongly gendered, even as she is "not distinctly" a woman even "in her heart" [59]), she walks away, provoking him to ask: "Do you not fear me, Naamah?" (261). She does not. She is annoyed by the divine propensity to appear in avian forms, to surprise her when she is unwary and drunk. His favorite body in which to appear is the metatron, an angel-vulture that is only partly allegory. Like the raven, this bird really does enjoy feasting on the dead, and speaks with enthusiasm about plunging its head into carcasses. But the metatron that is the Voice of God also attempts to engage Naamah, to figure her out. He is met by unflinching rebuff. When God asks Naamah if she would prefer him to speak through a burning bush rather than a messenger bird, she responds crisply, "I would prefer that you never destroy anything here, ever again" (261). Like her angel lover who constructs a palace for drowned children, Naamah has never been able to forget "the deaths of the people God no longer wanted" (10). She will not allow a divinity who demands death to center her world.

Later God appears to Naamah in what seems his truest form, a rather awkward "adolescent boy" (263). Like her, God seems to be working diligently to figure things out, perhaps even to figure himself out. "You're very tricky," he admits; "you verge on the absurd" (264). What he means is that he can never predict what choice Naamah will make when it comes to forging the path of her life. He does not know in advance what home she will choose to inhabit (Noah's ark or Bethel's tent or the angel's aquatic shelter), what community she will sustain. Kind and terrible, easy to amuse yet quick to anger, this God has a great deal to learn about humans—and perhaps himself. The ark of conservation and the world it unfolds are ongoing projects. Their destiny is not yet known.

Naamah is a novel full of inscrutable dreams, things of this world that resist becoming allegories for things of the next, and a family caught up in legend but remaining merely, and tenderly, human. As in Neal Stephenson's *Seveneves* and its transformation of video recordings into something called "The Epic" for those who survive the "Hard Rain,"[45] all on board the ark will become something they are not: characters in a saga of origin, a powerful story in which human and particular content becomes general prefiguration and universal source. Naamah resists this fate. She is disappointed to hear that, when descendents like Sarai speak of her, they tell the story of her "sacrifices" (116) as if that were all there were to her life. She learns her family's shared fate as figures and archetypes when in a dream she travels with Sarai into the future, to a suburban household. The children possess a wooden ark with a zebra walking up its ramp. The toy looks nothing like the "disenchanted" vessel she knows, filled with "animals, rowdy and foul" (4). When she asks Sarai whether these people yet to come know what really happened during the Flood, whether they will know the fullness of her family's narrative, she is told, "they know a story" (177). Naamah realizes that what they know is "a story without danger or injury, without cleaning up shit day in day out" (177–78), an abstract myth with the real humans absent, replaced by virtuous allegories. Naamah laughs at the toy figure of bald, bearded, and wizened Noah, an effigy bearing no resemblance to the man she loves. She also notices that she is missing from this toy ark. "There are lots of 'Noah's Ark' toy sets," Sarai informs her; "you're in some of them." (177). As if that were a comfort. Her companion observes, "this whole world can be traced back to you" (178). What a heavy weight to place upon a self-professed "difficult woman" (267) who has "no interest in womanhood" and wants "a new form" (245), an identity that she can create rather than accept, an identity that myth would obliterate. A raven, not a dove.

Or maybe, neither raven nor dove. At least aboard the ark, or as they circle the Genesis story, both these birds are simply functional. The raven is released first because Noah is "still thinking about where all the bodies have gone" (173) and knows that, should the raven not return, it will be because the world is still too full of visible carnage. The bird does not appear again for a long time, but when it does, it is to take a pistachio from the small bowl of nuts that Naamah has set out for it. The raven keeps coming back and forth, bearing no signs, no promise, so "Noah thinks it's time to send out the dove" (193). That bird likewise returns bearing no omens, even though Noah's family wants to discern in the fact of its reappearance "a good sign, . . . a blessing" (199). Naamah cannot see much good in it, though, since the return signals that their time of being bound to the ark has no clear terminus. Soon thereafter, the girl Danit is born aboard the ark. Naamah is looking at the endless waters in the evening with her son Japheth. She apologizes for making him, at least potentially, "the patriarch of a nation" (211). He is upset, so she reconsiders. She states tenderly:

> If there is anything I wish for you, it's that you have your family and all the joy you can possibly have in life. To not overthink it. Because no matter what our lives could have been, every version would have been filled with shit we'd have to deal with. (211)

At that very moment the dove appears on the railing of the ship with an olive leaf in its beak. Naamah, described by Japheth as one who too often lives as if she has given up, turns to her son and says: "You're forgetting how surprising the world can be." The dove is for Naamah a reminder of "the smallness of my life against the size of the world" (212), a reason for trust (in the promise of trees, in the promise of wide horizons), rather than despair. The advent of the dove ends with a lingering narrative gaze upon the newborn Danit, "conspicuous with living" (213). This dove is not the Holy Spirit, and the birth of the baby girl on the ark has nothing to do with typology, but the dove fulfills its role as symbol and harbinger all the same.

But "the size of the world" means it will be inhabited by other kinds of birds as well, creatures less amenable to reduction into plotline and metaphor. In her dreams, Naamah befriends a cockatoo from the ark who is likewise dreaming, a white bird that refuses to become a dove. In fact the cockatoo often insists that Naamah is a figure from his own sleeping mind, until they encounter each other aboard ship. She offers to give the bird a name, and he is delighted by this newfound identity as a particular: "People . . . just call me *cockatoo,* or they never think about it again" (54). Naamah calls him Jael, "one that ascends," and yet, like Naamah, Jael remains earthbound. The two of them encounter the metatron in a dream together. When Jael asks him if he knows who they are, the metatron announces: "You are the wife of Noah. And you are a cockatoo." He is met with immediate resistance to that naming: "No! I am Jael!," he yells, "and this is Naamah" (62). That might seem a small interchange within a narrative built of many such small interchanges, but the stakes here are extraordinarily high. Both Jael and Naamah cling to their names. They insist upon their individuality, their distinctiveness: ravens not doves. They refuse to have their particularity emptied to become universal types. They are not deployable roles from some catalog of *dramatis personae.* They are not the stuff of myth and metaphor. They symbolize nothing. Jael is a historically particular cockatoo who found himself aboard the ark, found in his dreams and then in his waking life a partner in questioning the will of God and the force of plot. And Naamah is a historically particular woman. Jael remembers Naamah even when she forgets him (252). Naamah, "given a chance to talk with God," walks away (261) and finds in Jael a creature of the world that is, a bird that is neither raven nor dove, neither this polarity nor that, a winged being who soars away from reduction into destiny and simply seeks to fashion a livable life. Jael is a specific creature that refuses to lose himself into myth or become a symbol. We last glimpse him blazing a trail into the new Earth for Japheth, her most restless son and an ardent explorer (295).

Naamah is the true leader of the ark. Through her presence, she gives strength to the community around her, allowing them to be themselves. At times, she can feel her family swell into myth, feel herself becoming "a queen, an empress," but then "she is back on a boat eating stew, where she catches a grain of sand on her tooth" (174), realizing again the pleasures that inhere in being earthbound. Naamah is distrustful of lofty stories, of reading back destiny from outcome. She is pragmatic, the one who brought extras of some animals because she doubted that stowing pairs alone would ensure creaturely survival (34). She holds on to memories that others would soon forget, refusing to enable a new world to obliterate the tales of those who dwelled in the old. Her daughter-in-law Adata describes Naamah best: "You're the one who's always plowing ahead, unfazed by dead animals, broken doors, injured legs, the same food over and over" (171). Noah might be strong, might assist her in her work, but the family follows her lead. To this description, Naamah responds, "I don't want them to," and Adata responds, "tough," and "her steadiness steadies Naamah" (171). A heavy role, unrelenting and unchosen, and yet a role accomplished not because Naamah is some avatar (she distrusts God's choice of her as "matriarch" and "figurehead" [151]), not because she is selfless, but because she is simply trying her best to live a full life in a world precipitated and limned by catastrophe: often failing, frequently self-absorbed, several times nearly perishing, but in the end successful in rendering a narrow refuge more capacious, inclusive, humane, a place for ravens, doves, vultures, and cockatoos. *Naamah* ends with a single and resonate sentence that captures the benevolent impress of its protagonist well: "If she is to be the bearer of this new world, then let everything be touched by her hand" (296). That line holds more promise than any rainbow's shimmer.

And yet. A cockatoo is a vibrantly white bird that will have an affinity (however unsought) with the allegory-enamored dove, with uplift and transcendence. The narrative of *Naamah,* like any ark, leaves behind many earthly things that will haunt as ellipses. As a foundation myth, the Noah story is intimate to the articulation of human difference, and especially to the intricacies and difficulties of race. Yet Blake's novel is one in which race might at times surface but never much seems to matter. Secular and not inclined to ritual, Naamah is never glimpsed thinking or performing anything particular to her supposed Jewishness. The angel with whom she falls deeply in love is said to have beautiful black skin, but that is a fact to be noticed (and perhaps delectated), rather than a difference that makes any difference. None of Naamah's children are founders of peoples, nations, races: they are simply the source of an undifferentiated humankind. There is no suggestion in the book that future generations are not destined to replicate Noah and his comfortable, middle-class family. In some ways Naamah is a second-wave feminist, practicing the kind of white feminism critiqued by Audre Lorde for having nothing to say about the experiences of women of color, for crowding out the voices of writers and scholars who are not white. The ark as houseboat is uncannily similar to the suburban home in which Naamah and Sarai behold the toy version of the vessel. The novel is written from a privileged perspective, one that "doesn't see" race because it does not have to. Its world is white.

No Flood long enables smooth sailing above the heaviness of historical differences, the weight of the ways in which humans have sorted themselves, valuing some groups while casting others to the hazards of the sea. Historically, the raven's blackness and the dove's whiteness have undergirded all kinds of terrible binaries, including those of hierarchized, racialized identities. The raven may originally have been white (say some stories), its blackness a curse for its failure. The raven, black-skinned Ham, and a lascivious dog sometimes form a triad of what the ark should have left behind but conveyed unwittingly, inevitably: all three entwine in a story about supposedly inherent inclinations and the color of devalued bodies.[46] The blueprint of the ark was the blueprint of the galley for the transport of enslaved humans from Africa to American coasts. A carceral version of race is one of the many poison gifts of the ark, stowed aboard as tightly as anything else it preserves and enables.

No bird—not a dove, not a raven, not a cockatoo—can fly above the weight of history's violences for long, especially not in a novel written in a nation that has yet to take account of what its own genesis from an economic system that depended on chattel slavery continues to mean. Like the ark-mates that vanished from her sight, there are foundational and enduring exclusions that Naamah simply cannot or will not see.

Dark-Feathered Stories

We end with another medieval image and another medieval story (Plate 8), but it's not a tale we're used to hearing. Atop a tower-like ark of brick, battered by a still roiling sea, perhaps unknown to both Noah and the dove, here is the raven: still, alert, regarding everything. The Hebrew text just below names Noah, the ark, and the dove, leaving out the illustration's most compelling character. Keen-eyed and unmoved, this is the raven we have been seeking, the one we thought was gone from the ark, gone from the very frame of the picture, displaced by the dove to some domain outside the frame of the illustration where the errant bird could find its only home. This raven stands still, serene, pinnacle of the scene. It is not going anywhere. This raven remains an intimate to the unfolding narrative. Despite what the inscription declares, the dove does not rest upon the ark; the ark sustains the raven.

Histories of medieval western Europe are replete with the violence that too often structured relations among faith communities, especially when living in proximity: Muslim, Jew, Christian, pagan. Salo Wittmayer Baron describes as "lachrymose history" the tendency to narrate the Jewish past as a chronicle of suffering and endurance, yet when it comes to Jewish–Christian relations in the late Middle Ages, it is difficult to avoid stories filled with tears.[47] Medieval France (where this remarkable depiction of the ark was produced) witnessed much Christian brutality against Jewish residents. But sometimes religious and cultural differences were not impediments to cohabitation, collaboration, cocreation. This image of Noah's ark as durable tower is from a compendium now known as the *North French Hebrew Miscellany*. The manuscript is the product of a time and place in which a Jewish scribe and a group of Christian artists could produce a work of ravishing beauty together. Yael Zirlin has argued that some of the illustrations derive from workshops in St. Omer while others may be the handiwork of artists associated with the royal household and working in Paris: workshops that fashioned dazzling Christian art now laboring to create intricate miniatures for a manuscript that contains a haggadah, gematria, and Jewish law texts and calendars.[48] Not all that long after the *North French Hebrew Miscellany* was completed, most Jews had been exterminated within or exiled from France, their thriving communities a swiftly receding memory. Yet this manuscript tells a tale rather different from the stories we are used to hearing from late-thirteenth-century Europe, narratives full of massacres, public disputes, forced conversion, and the circulation of the blood libel.

When the great biblical commentator Rashi (Rabbi Shlomo Yitzhaki) was born in Troyes in 1040, about a thousand Jewish men and women lived in that bustling city. Troyes became a renowned center of Jewish learning. Rashi loved stories from Genesis, including the raven and the ark. His erudite commentaries are studied to this day. By the early years of the fourteenth century, no Jews remained in Troyes. The medieval period is filled with such histories, vibrant communities destroyed at zealous hands. Yet this Noah's ark, seemingly made of Eden-like stone and affixed to an immobile tower affixed to a mountain, is likely the work of Christian illustrators directed by a Jewish scribe named Benjamin. With its dark feathered guardian, this Noah's ark opens the possibility of a future that did not arrive but could have, a future of hospitality and recruitment to cohabitation, of ravens with doves. The manuscript does not offer some kind of idealized, peaceful community. Utopias are seldom so perfect. In his text, Benjamin labels the Christian St. Peter as "Peter the Ass," while the Christian artists conspicuously omit from the manuscript some of the most important moments in Jewish history, like Moses at Sinai and the defeat of Haman. There is evidence of interfaith struggle throughout its pages, but also the collaborative making of something ravishing. The past is full of such stories almost lost, nearly erased by time's surge and flood, stories that might easily have drowned. Noah's ark is crammed with wayward tales, raven stories that move like vortices not flows, countercurrents in history's dovelike course.

Medieval flood stories, visual and narrative alike, sometimes reveal a complicated Christian and Jewish neighboring that tells a rather different tale from the narrative in which an Old Testament Flood is allegorized into New Testament baptism, the ark becomes the church, the dove becomes the Holy Spirit, and Jewish content is left behind as too literal or carnal or simply out of date. A small window into a world of interfaith community (no matter how fraught) is opened by this illustration of Noah's ark, one of the very few examples to have survived from thirteenth-century Ashkenazic communities. This ark is brick, walled like Eden—but it is not a paradise set apart from the turbulence of the world. Note the fish in the turbulent water and the future-looking Noah, the serene raven, and the reliable dove. Who knows what other stories it is possible to tell if we loosen our expectations and take our cue from a raven who has ideas other than pulling the same old boring lever in the Skinner box-ark? There is no ark without the raven. Here is the raven. Always the raven.

It is, however, in the nature of ravens to leave, to fly off, away, or to remain in plain sight, emphatically unavailable in their presence, unless they change their minds. We warned you at the beginning of this chapter that following the raven, even as we stand recruited, would not be easy. Hence the need to follow at the remove provided by the host of dark-feathered stories we have assembled. Time then perhaps to part company. Truth be told, that is what the dove does also, though we grant that bird the dispensation of perpetually forgetting that, after the olive branch, it was released a third time and followed the raven into life without Noah, life without the ark. When the raven and the dove leave, the allegorical skies finally, so it seems, clearing, what then is it time to do? Is it time, as in the Genesis story, for sacrifice, begging some divinity to remember us: rainbow, landfall, covenant? Or, is it time to leave, to head out into the ellipses, accepting that that's the world we have always shared? Time, perhaps, to jump.

Abandon ark?

CHAPTER 7

Abandon Ark?

Noah's ark is a millennia-crossing narrative transport device, resolute but leaky. Every ark sails the crosscurrents of its days. A swirl of shared questions, worries, and hopes find their way inside. The first site visit we made to an ark occurred in 2016, just after Donald J. Trump was elected the forty-fifth president of the United States.[1] We finish this book in the aftermath of the violent close to his term in office. The congressional certification of the electoral-college votes was interrupted by the storming of the Capitol by a group of the president's most ardent supporters. Those who rushed inside the building broke walls of metal barricades and walls of police, shattered windows, and smashed doors. The symbols these insurrectionists transported were the same as those spotted at the "Unite the Right" rally in Charlottesville earlier in the same presidency: Crusader crosses and Templar emblems; Roman fasces; Viking runes and gear; Confederate flags; shirts with the slogans and signs of QAnon (a conspiracy that repeats the Blood Libel, the claim that Jews kill Christians to use their blood in religious rituals); red nationalist caps and banners.[2] All those signifiers of an imagined history of white superiority that crosses the long ages and unites the losers of the American Civil War with biblical, classical, and medieval narratives flooded into the Rotunda, a racialist-fantasy archive built from bits and pieces of histories that are in actuality complicated and diverse, filled as much with ellipses as with content. Meanwhile, the signal ambition of the Trump administration had been the building of a wall to partition the United States from the peoples of Central and South America and Mexico, a materialization in concrete and steel of attempts to close the nation to a wider world, an immurement that was to proceed through immigration restriction and economic and social policies. What a terrible cargo with which to load a building. But then again, those halls of democracy were built through enslaved labor. They held already that day many who enabled dire policies and strengthened brutal fantasies. Sometimes it's difficult to tell the inside of an ark from the outside.

We begin this chapter with these events not because Noah's ark appeared in any of the century-spanning images conveyed into the Capitol—although an ardor for walled communities is an inheritance of that myth. Rather, as this book begins to end, we want to emphasize a story that has surfaced continually throughout its composition. With its love of sorting and segregation of kinds, its production of racialized subspecies, and its instantiations of differences of caste borne in the body, the ark can quickly yield the blueprint for a galley filled with people reduced to merchandise. Despite its distant desert origins and its shared genesis across multiple ancient cultures, in its worst manifestations, the ark is like all symbolic and material architectures that preserve a chosen few while enacting violence on and against many and may function as a vessel for the conveyance of white-supremacist fantasies and histories, privileging the superiority of an imagined European West over any concept of shared human dignity. Although its interior arrangements will vary, the ark too easily transports a remorseless arrangement of power in which skin color or posited heritage determines access to resources, freedom, and a life that can be lived in peace. The ark becomes the figure for a nation or state closed to those who challenge the easy histories and pitiless infrastructure that have enabled one group to flourish at the expense of others. The ark has long been a vessel into which stories of race have been stowed. Given that Shem, Ham, and Japheth are the origins of all people who follow, how could it be otherwise? After the descendants of Ham are condemned to enduring servitude and their skin (in several traditions) is darkened as a sign of perpetual subjugation, the connection of Noah's children to the popularity of Confederate flags is not so difficult to glimpse.

Long after Ararat, the ark sails on. Disembarkation does not leave its segregational structures behind. This version of the ark is lethal. It preserves few at lasting cost, and despite the opening of the ship's door and the release of its cargo, it imprisons others eternally, a carcerality and an eternal exclusion written and then rewritten on bodies. Who could blame anyone who should choose to walk away from the very idea of an ark, walk away from belonging at such cost, walk away from an unjust system that pretends such violence "just is"? What of those who were never wanted on the voyage? Those left behind to drown? Those stolen, coerced, or press-ganged aboard and forced to live on, or die on, come disembarkation? This chapter asks what kinds of living might unfold when the possibility of being included in the ark in a way that sustains rather than devastates is never offered, when conserving a life means you must refuse to board, turn your back, jump, place a distance between yourself and its gopher-wood walls. What happens when the very idea of an ark has to be abandoned because the ark being thought and built has already abandoned you and is designed to keep abandoning you, its very announcement premised on your ruin? And what happens when, come landfall, in order to reach refuge and a shore, the ark needs to keep you freshly drowned and newly dead, kill you all over again, to make sure that you remain zoned, as Kathryn Yusoff might put it, with the inanimate, so that your labors, your life, fuels its foundation?[3] The story of Noah has always been a story of abandonment, his ark as much a technology of stranding and desertion as a vehicle for conservation and the engine of new beginnings. In the long aftermath of whatever Flood sorts the damned from the saved, do the receding waters open new possibilities for those fortunate enough to have survived whether aboard the ark or not? Are there arks in the universe that are designed for affirmation rather than refusal, for freedom rather than abasement, minor or recycled arks that attempt major interventions into whom is afforded security, refuge, a life well lived? Is there an ark of safety beyond all other arks, an ark for those who have been ruined and renounced by such lethal vessels?

In this chapter, we follow the raven and head outward into the disaster that Noah and his community only appear to have left behind. Tempting as it may be to hear in the phrase "Abandon Ark" a save-your-skin exhortation, urging you to make for yet another lifeboat, that phrase might best be heard as a question: "abandon ark?"—a question hopeful enough, maybe, possibly, when asked in the right way, to become: "Convert the ark? Rebuild the ark from fragments? Reclaim the ark for better destinies?" "To abandon" paradoxically can mean "to depart, relinquish" or "to give in, indulge, give oneself up to." You can abandon an ark, but that might also mean abandoning yourself to the ark, at least if you are not careful. The worst thing you can do, as we observed earlier in this book, is to believe that you are not already on an ark, that you have left its structures behind you. The real danger, as Mrs. Noyes from Timothy Findley's *Not Wanted on the*

Voyage cautioned us, lies in the lure of disembarkation, in the idea that you get to be "done," relieved of the obligation to think about everything en-arkment entails. "Abandon ark!" No. It is never that simple. Let's instead heed the call of a carrion-loving raven and inquire into forms of refuge in spite of the ark, forms of refuge that pay the ark no heed, or that perhaps take its measure only in order to imagine their own course.

Body Doubles (Race and Species)

Again, Mrs. Noyes from *Not Wanted on the Voyage* suggests some trajectories, as well as the exceptions that haunt an ark. Just before the rains begin, she tells her husband, "I won't go. . . . To hell with 'being spared.' It's as simple as that. I will *not* go."[4] Noah Noyes has loaded the ark and sacrificed to Yaweh. He forbids his wife to bring aboard her beloved cat Mottyl. As the smoke rises from the ashes of the animals that he has slain in predeparture holocaust, Mrs. Noyes refuses the injunction to be glad. Very slowly, the rain begins. Mrs. Noyes abandons the ark, or tries; she goes looking for her pregnant cat. Noah is frantic. Her presence is required. Her absence "will kill us all" (124). Mrs. Noyes heads for the wood, filling now with "renegade dogs and turkeys," along with so many animals that the lemurs shout: "*No more room! No more room!*" (125). Mrs. Noyes forages for food, cuts her thigh climbing the orchard wall, takes delight in eating apples that had been forbidden to women, children, and domestic animals (127). Blind Mottyl, meanwhile, heavy with her kittens, eludes a hungry vixen, shooting up a tree to avoid the fox, and finds "a full clutch of eggs," two of which she pushes from the nest for the vixen below, "leaving three for herself. 'Eat'" (135). Outside the ark catastrophe is shared immiseration and an invitation to reset cross-species relations. The wood has become "the focus of almost everyone's wandering: a haven for every kind of animal refugee" (138), though a complicated kind of haven: "hunters and prey; hosts and parasites," a "marketplace for the predatory." Mottyl seeks out Crowe: "If anyone could help her, Crowe could" (139).

Down by the river, Mrs. Noyes recognizes on the far bank Lotte, older sister of her daughter-in-law Emma. She assumed that Lotte's parents killed her long ago, just as she had allowed Noah to murder their son Adam for being born similarly different, apish resident of the border between the human and the animal. Regardless of her physical age, Noah has gauged Lotte's "mental age" as *"anywhere between two and nil"* (142), though her loving parents never spoke of her in such diminishing terms. Not wanting to frighten Lotte, Mrs. Noyes decides to wade the river and fetch her from the flood. As she does so, she hears a "sheet of noise" (144) and realizes that the faeries are down by the water. "You should go back across the road and into the woods where you belong," she tells them; "the river is deadly" (144). But the faeries won't listen. There's "a very large congregation" of them, "maybe even a whole community." Mrs. Noyes feels "a shiver passing over her skin. She was being boarded—like the ark." (Composed by a gay writer in the midst of the AIDS crisis and its lethal, institutionalized homophobia, the narrative is not being subtle here in its assertion of precarious refuge and the possibilities of care in a world too full of exclusions.) Mrs. Noyes heads into the river, begging its pardon for her trespass. She prays not to God, but to the river. The faeries, she thinks, pray also. Mrs. Noyes has to drag herself ashore using "the branches of river shrubs as handles" (147). "Do you want me to let you down on the ground?," she asks, warning that the trees "could be dangerous. This is the forest not the wood." The faeries rush for the giant trees "whose oozings of amber resin were apparently the stuff of life" (148). She is learning and amazed. The world is wide.

Mrs. Noyes comforts Lotte; puts her on her back and heads out into the flood. But there are corpses now and Lotte is afraid. The two find a small boat and, seeing what awaits them outside, return to Noah's ark. Including Lotte, violating his eugenic purity laws, will be the price her severe husband must pay for Mrs. Noyes to board. And thinking that she might, just for once, have won, Mrs. Noyes enters the ark in triumph (159). All smiles and mock care, Noah takes Lotte from her, bundling the girl into a blanket, pushes Mrs. Noyes out of the way, and takes Lotte to a waiting Japeth to "slit her throat while she slept" (161). Noah has performed such murder in the name of human purity in the past, with Japeth's twin brother. Such a ritual of violent rejection will happen again later, after Japeth's wife Hannah gives birth to such a child aboard the ark and its corpse is hurled into the sea. When Noah has Japeth give Lotte's body back to Mrs. Noyes, she accepts the lifeless girl "without a word, without a sound" (161). Ham attempts to assuage her sorrow. "Please," she says, "know better than to comfort me while the dead are laid in my arms" (161). After a time, Mrs. Noyes rises: "There is no God worthy of this child," she says, "and so I will give her back to the world where she belongs" (162). Ham says goodbye.

Mrs. Noyes heads out into the rain, back to the orchard, back to the porch where she has spent her happiest moments. She weeps "with rage at the sight of her house. It was meant to be a haven. What else were houses for?" (163). Now it is a charnel house. She sits Lotte in her empty rocking chair; finds three unbroken jars of gin, and drinks them all, floods herself with gin (166). Mrs. Noyes sings a medley of her favorite songs, a wake for Lotte. While Mrs. Noyes time-travels, caught up in the nostalgia of old wounds occasioned by Lotte's freshly wounded body, scavengers (ravens, buzzards) drag Lotte outside, further mutilating her body and pecking away her eyes (168). Not wanting to look, Mrs. Noyes picks up Lotte once more and brings her into the kitchen. She heads upstairs and drags "her trousseau chest—bumpity-bump—down the steps" (170), cleans Lotte's body, places buttons over her eyes, and binds her body in her best Dutch brocade, which Noah had never cared for. Lotte's "ape arms folded over her heart, . . . even in her death, . . . Lotte smiled. And the smile was a kind of revenge. *I am an ape—but I had a human mother and I had a human father,* said the smile. *I was loved—I was cherished—I was held by human arms*" (170). Mrs. Noyes buries Lotte in the bottom of her trousseau chest to preserve her, another kind of ark.

An ark can easily become a coffin. Mrs. Noyes's wake is a difficult moment: grim in its preservation, insistent in its memorialization, cutting in its grief, a complicated episode that illustrates the limits of the novel's refuge. Ape arms. Monkey child. Because Findley has no room for race aboard his ark (none of his characters appear to have a race, which is to say, they all seem to be white, the state of being that never has to self-speak or self-examine), this scene appears to be about species and belonging and more-than-human worlds, all those ephemeral utopias, Gustave Doré's tiger cubs and human children sharing an island as the world drowns. But the race line and the species line end up being the same thing in racist thinking. Full humanity becomes the exclusive domain of a subset of people who imagine themselves as superior, relegating all others to an existence aligned with the bestial. White supremacy, silent or overt, has too often structured the interior as well as the wake of Noah's ark. Hence the brutality of Mrs. Noyes's sympathy, of Findley's sympathy, a narrative inability to abandon ark, to realize that an assumption of human superiority is too often also an unexamined assumption of white supremacy, the furtherance of a system in which all other bodies, even those that descend from human progenitors, are never to achieve full being, full intelligence, nor to be so full of speech, which is to say to be human. Noah's ark became a transport device for the enslaved, as we saw in chapter 4, because the system that its architecture makes solid is indifferent to what it stows; were it more self-reflective, the enterprise would founder. Lotte and Adam and their ilk—children, eternally children—might be worthy of the same redemption that cats like Mottyl merit, but they are not wanted on the voyage in the same way that Mrs. Noyes and her family are. Lotte is represented as less than fully human, bereft of the ability to make her own choices, exert her own agency, speak her own tale. These are resolutely not problems raised by the text itself, content as the novel is to label Lotte a very sweet, but not all that smart, ape-like minor noncharacter. If she were to be redeemed or saved, it would be at the price of remaining forever thus.

Ham (cursed and blackened, often depicted as an origin of race, but not in this story) and Lucy (Lucifer, a fallen angel, a darkened body bearing a medieval racial-origin tale, but not here) are sent to find Mrs. Noyes. Lucy comes upon her in what had been the bath house (175), tells her to "'keep trying,'" and wishes her luck. What else is there to say? This game of hide and seek is just that, a game: pieces moving as if on a board, their moves restricted, outcome predetermined. Mrs. Noyes is required. No Mrs. Noyes, no landfall, no rainbow. Mrs. Noyes (and the novel) are thereby limited in what they can achieve. She defers and delays; she makes room for those declared delinquent, insisting with every fiber of her being (which proves insufficient) that there can be no community without strangers. She comes close to abandoning the ark. But she cannot.

Mrs. Noyes eventually brazens her way back aboard, Mottyl folded into her apron, hidden by those forbidden apples (179). Disanimated and defaced, Lotte lies forgotten and preserved in her ark-coffin, something like a species-double for animate but blind Mottyl, as the involuted tropes of human worth and species and disability sync and unsync, the novel tracing and encrypting the limits of its resistance, the limits of its ability to know itself, bound as it is by and to an ark, which soon it makes speak. With Mrs. Noyes and stowaway

Mottyl aboard, its openings sealed, the ark becomes "a kind of magnet" to those left behind, "pulling a stream of would-be survivors up the hill": *"How did a person get inside?"* (181). Every inch of dry hillside is soon occupied, panic momentarily subdued by the "faintest sense of hope" (183). "Around the time when the stars go out—if there are stars—a light appear[s];" the faeries approach the ark. Will they be admitted? And if so, would the "doors not open to everyone?" (184). The whole hill watches. The faeries beat against the ark, their light and numbers fading. "But the ark, as ever, was adamant. Its shape had taken on a voice. And the voice said *no*" (185).

The voice of the ark is NO. Yet Mottyl the cat makes it inside. Every definitive "no" is an attempt at a boundary against widened refuge. Transport and conservation easily become acts of violence. The ark has always been a difficult space, and sometimes in difficulty inheres possibility, but you have to look hard to find where it has been stowed.

Especially when the water is rising.

Intercatastrophic Forms: Derek Walcott, Ovid, Roland Barthes

We live between catastrophes, the punctuating brackets of a deluge that once was and a storm-filled apocalypse to come, between a vanished age of crushing ice or rushing waters and a nearing annihilation after the slow wet-burn of global warming. And yet that *between* is also a *within,* an environing that transforms catastrophe, with its sense of turning and culmination, into the permanent conditions of ongoing and unequally shared disaster. The very idea of sealing up a privileged inside from a theoretically disposable outside is a tragic and self-interested myth. It does not work. It will not work. And if it begins to work, the violences of the ark ramify. Even sympathy becomes brutal. Despite ephemeral, unevenly shared, and exclusive havens and despite the frenzied erection of walls that would demarcate a secure home from an exterior left to the weather, the very materials with which we build are saturated with global cataclysm: sea-rise, superstorms, drought, slow violence, fast violence, poisoned landscapes, mountains knocked flat, poisonous air, extinctions, interminable habitat loss, carbon proliferation, oceans full of plastics, pervasive environmental racism, peoples deprived of their homes and made refugees. *Between* and *within*: intercatastrophic in this doubled sense.

What does it mean to inhabit a world without stability, without the promise of anything but strife and the endless advent of inscrutable, unexpected dangers, a world punctuated, for the fortunate, by fleeting moments of calm? Is safety in such a world a dream realizable only for a selfish few, for a short while, purchased at the ruinous price of the destruction of all that remains refused? Does an ark ever really keep out the flood? This is what, earlier in this book, our children taught us with their no-future, only now, ark games, in which they proliferated the ark, building outward. This refusal to concede to an outside is what, in a different sense, Jeanette Winterson's "detachable chimpanzee, made out of a Brillo pad" from *Oranges Are Not the Only Fruit,* an animal that always goes overboard but never goes missing, conserves: our necessary connection to an outside that cannot be done without. It is not possible to build an ark and to square out the ethical wrongness of the violence done by its closed door "no." For all its positing of an exterior that is drowned and gone, the ark remains tethered to those whose destruction it posits. It is built from that destruction, provisioned by it, buoyed by their loss. But that connection, as the cawing raven knows, also conceals a different kind of knowledge that the ark disavows: myriad forms of life endure beyond. Built from suffering, moored in death, the ark needs you to buy into the "no" of its closed-wall insistence that to be outside is to die. Only then can the ark float. Only then can it become the world.[5]

"Where are your monuments, your battles, martyrs? / Where is your tribal memory?," asks one voice. "Sirs, / in that grey vault," replies another, "The sea. The sea / has locked them up. The sea is History." Derek Walcott's "The Sea Is History" asserts an identity, a belonging, a history outside-the-arkive, outside the ark. His words insist that the sea comprehends, remembers, and memorializes the ongoing disaster of the transatlantic slave trade.[6] The poem launches a metaphor whose power, as Sonya Posmentier remarks, "rests in its uncanny yoking of history and oblivion."[7] For, almost immediately, the insistence that the sea is history becomes something like a question or a proposition as the dialoguing voices ask how this metaphor will work, if in fact a metaphor is ever only a metaphor? "The lantern of a caravel," provides a Genesis. "Then there were the packed cries, / the shit, the moaning: / Exodus." But the Middle Passage inverts biblical narrative. The passage out of Africa is the passage into, not out of, slavery, which quickly becomes an "Ark of the Covenant," as the biblical text reorders itself to play host to the story of African diaspora.

Comparisons, as Posmentier notes, prove difficult, problematic, but also generative. How shall the story end? How may those stories be told? Those questions remain at sea. But also, in the sea, conserved not drowned.

Christina Sharpe's *In the Wake* invokes the scalar shift of "residence time" in order to decode the referential heft to Walcott's metaphor-monument. Residence time refers to how long "it takes for a substance to enter the ocean and leave the ocean. . . . Human blood is salty," she continues, "sodium . . . has a residence time of 260 million years."[8] So, all the bodies of the drowned, "those Africans thrown, jumped, dumped overboard in Middle Passage," remain "with us still, in the time of the wake, known as residence time" (19). Attuned to the deep temporality of disaster, Sharpe writes that "we, Black people, exist in the residence time of the wake, a time in which 'everything is now. It is all now'" (41).[9] Sharpe's recognition of the continued wake of the slave ship names a predicament and finds an abiding archive in watery movement, in dispersal that cannot destroy. But this recognition also produces something like a memorial refuge, a reservoir of dissolved oxygen, that inspires a collective "we." Sharpe animates the ocean, registers a community in a wake that is slipstream and remembrance. The propulsive sea is history, an arkive: transport, reduction, and enslavement flowing through and underwriting the fabric of the collective present.

"Wake work" is how Sharpe describes the praxis of "black artists, poets, writers, thinkers" who inhabit and respond to the "quotidian catastrophic events" (20) of the wake, the ongoing effects of the violent, obliterative writing of the transatlantic slave trade. To "inhabit" in the rich sense Sharpe intends means to press urgently against the dysgraphic "orthography" of antiblackness, contesting the way "these disasters arrive by way of the rapid, deliberative, repetitive, and wide circulation on television and social media of Black social, material, and psychic death" (21). This kind of ontological negation consists of a predatory unwriting. Key to Sharpe's thinking here is Maurice Blanchot's conception of disaster as a form of inscription, "the writing done by the disaster," meaning "not simply the process whereby something called the disaster is written; . . . it also means the writing done by the disaster—the disaster that ruins books and wrecks language." For Blanchot, the Holocaust constitutes the disaster. For Sharpe, "transatlantic slavery was and is the disaster, . . . inextricable" as the "history of Atlantic chattel slavery" is from "the history of capital," and the extractive practices of European colonization (5).[10] As we have seen, this kind of traumatic representational schema enables a fascist ark to hallucinate its whitewashed walls while, all the time, stowing away a cargo of abjected human-animal bodies for future use. Sharpe, along with the many voices she amplifies, collectively work this wake to craft forms of counterwriting: wayfaring manuals, ruttiers, or sailors poems, describing paths to capacious and precarious refuge.[11]

A fugitive poetics and politics? Perhaps. One that from time to time recognizes in the wake the figure of the ark and the story of Noah (or maybe in what is left after their transit), designating one complicated knot of histories that might be successively reworked and inhabited. For, while the ark may, in its fascist iterations, constitute a slave ship or concentration camp, the figure also conserves the possibility of refuge. Noisy, contested chest of stories that it is, a hybrid Genesis-Exodus vehicle, the ark yokes refuge and violence together, disgorging these contradictions in a flood of contested arkemes, minimal units of ark-entanglement that may be reclaimed, inhabited, adapted, or recombined to construct other histories. The closed-door "no" of the ark opens—or gets pried loose. As Stefano Harney and Fred Moten note in their *Undercommons: Fugitive Planning and Black Study,* "there are flights of fantasy in the hold of ship," by which they mean that flotillas may have held a captive people, containerized them as commodities, attempted to reduce through this slave trade selves into commodities, but the logistics of such arks "could not contain what it had relegated to hold," could not stop speech and feeling and imagination. "The hold's terrible gift," they continue, "was to gather dispossessed feelings in common, to create a new feel in the undercommons," a touch that is also an affect that moves and may be described as philosophy, music, release, setting adrift, and love: "To have been shipped is to have been moved by others, with others."[12] Violence limns the possibility of refuge to come.

Perhaps this yoking of violence and refuge together, this refusal to close out the ark, is why so many artists and writers choose to dwell with those left outside. They know that the drowned are not really gone. The turbulence of the sea constitutes a lived world. Yes, the ark posits the annihilation of the peopled exterior, erases them from its heart so as to posit a new start, a new foundation, clean lines and clean walls. But, so also, it retains or holds them as a fungible commodity or reserve (labor, fuel, energy) that can be parceled out as so many disposable bodies. Figuratively, those the ark posits as drowned are reconstituted by their projection into this outside, exchanging properties with the dead, with the inert, precisely to enable the animation of those aboard. As a floating foundation device, as the archetype of settler colonial ideology, even the apparent forward movement of the ark is no more than an ideological effect. Arks don't leave anything behind. They don't go anywhere. Their long list of stowaways, along with all those ark builders who insist that arks only have to float, not sail, attest to this fact. We might name this economy "ark writing" (an ark no longer thinking). Ark writing is biopower primed by necropolitical excision: the "newness" of its covenant is baptized by disaster.

We have been here before (Plate 5). In fact, we have never left this space, despite our frustrated hope that floods will recede, that walls will prove impermeable, that destinations once reached will offer secure dwelling, covenant, journey's end. In this late medieval image of the biblical deluge contained in a deluxe manuscript of Augustine's *City of God,* the artist ruminates over just this problem of cataclysm's interminability. Working late in the fifteenth century in Rouen, a city that had experienced the violence of war within recent memory but was now enjoying a flourish of prosperity, this illustrator likely possessed more faith than we do in providence, teleology, and justice to come. Yet there are details in the image that make us hesitate when making that statement. Life in the sea outside the timber of the ark crowds the scene, even as the sacred vessel utterly dominates the foreground. Our eyes keep wandering away from Noah's family tight in prayer to linger over the jostling tales of the world about to drown. Rapturously blue, the water's lush languor invites the gaze to tarry. The Flood is not rushing. The omnipresent swells appear more decorative than kinetic. Time is slowed to the point where everything unfolding in this Earth-become-ocean seems an arrested tableau. We also wonder whether the artist is not suggesting that the next catastrophe is already harbored within the ark, future misfortune stowed within a place built for safety: grinning green wolves and demons, a chaos stowed aboard for the world to come. We wonder about failures of empathy and the ark as cold storage. We wonder whether being preserved is worth the losses that limn Noachic security.

"L'arche Noe," declare golden letters on the sturdy ship—as if the structure could be anything else. The patriarch, his family, and the animals they have chosen as voyaging companions float serenely in their sanctuary, a regal boat that is also a house and a church and strongbox for the preservation of a cherished selection of the world's surplus of things. Inside the humans unite in somber prayer. Outside unfold the narratives of those for whom no space was offered in the drifting refuge. Swimmers seek the safety that churches, houses, and castles once but no longer offer, architectures built against the weather that overwhelms them, just visible in the swallowing water. A cow and a paddling dog perhaps wonder why they were not partnered into inclusion. A water wheel spins uselessly, ruined by the element it once craved, freed now from the demands of labor and the work of human hands. The sea is awash with detritus. And drama. One floating corpse is fresh; another has gone gray. One uprooted tree possesses leaves, but another is a kind of arboreal cadaver. An ox swims while a dog drowns. The dead and dying are sinners, and they no doubt deserve their watery suffocation. The good bishop Augustine is clear about original sin and the world before baptism. Yet something changes, perhaps, when we notice that, just above Noah's boat and to the left, a cradle floats like a little ark, so like that boat in shape yet empty now of its occupant. Is it possible to see that cradle and not fill it with a story of unbearable loss, the story of the ark as a failed exodus? Of course, we could allay this sorrow through typology. The empty cradle is a waiting manger, the Flood is the baptism that those drowning in the water could not have had, and the ark is the universal church. That is, after all, how Augustine reads such narratives. The promise of metaphor and parable is that of a future intimate to history, a charm against present devastation. The story of the drowned baby is displaced by the story of a messiah to arrive. And yet the manger is still a crib, and its occupant is no longer safe inside. That's how allegory works: at least two stories in difficult simultaneity, not one tale obliterating another. An infant has been swallowed by the sea.

This particular image keeps its dove in storage, in the topmost portion of the ark along with the other birds. The showy swan, eagle, owl, and cock crowd that modest white bird to the smaller window of the aviary. This dove has not yet taken flight to become an avatar of the Holy Spirit; it is just a stocky little bird that coos, a familiar sight in many cities. Crows, ducks, and swans meanwhile swim in the background as they always have, the universal Flood just more weather. Other birds glide the horizon, nervous about or indifferent to their vanishing places of rest; it is impossible to tell. Blunt rocks indifferently protrude. The deep blues of this scene are stunning, pulling the eye back constantly from the brown of Noah's boat, threatening to overwhelm the senses with its lushness. The gray corpse, cadaver-tree, and a nearly submerged rock in the watery left corner remain vibrant at the edge of obliteration, vital in the midst of what is also a kind of mineral, arboreal, and all-too-human protest that the ark was built against what could have been a more livable, more collective, more complicated world. It is difficult to say whether we are supposed to feel the peace within the ark, the frustration of the swimmers who seek in vain a place of rest, transport into metaphor, or the inevitability of bodies and trees becoming flotsam. But why choose? The ark is a transport device that would leave this world behind. Yet the image invites lingering.

It is tempting here to invoke the figure of the marvelous *(mirabile),* to supply the story of Deucalion and Pyrra, as explanatory voice-over or soundtrack to the world beyond this ark: Ovid's *Metamorphoses* as intertext. Angry Zeus sends the flood. Rivers run "unchecked, . . . sweeping crops and orchards. Flocks and men, home and shrines and household gods before them," until:

> Land and sea were one. All was ocean, an ocean lacking shores. Here, a man clung to a hilltop; there, a man sat in a skiff and rowed over the tops of fields he recently plowed. Yet another guides his boat above his crops or past the roof of his sunken villa, while a fourth catches a fish in the highest branches of an elm. In a green meadow a ship drops anchor; keels of other ships skim a buried vineyard; and where peaceful goats once grazed unsightly seals are lolling now.[13]

Ovid paints a series of picture postcards. The world of water creates uncanny juxtapositions, mixed media marvels. The Flood creates impossible, hybrid, or partially submerged forms. Plot, story, and narrative are overwhelmed as the logic of appearance becomes a series of familiar strangeness. The sea nymphs are "amazed to see woods, cities, and houses underwater. Dolphins swim in forests, brushing against branches and shaking oak trees they bump into."[14] Narrative scuba diving. The nymphs' amazement stems from their detachment, along with the surprise intrusion of the world above into their world below. The topside world of air-breathers intrudes into their own, rendering the sea nymphs distracted bystanders to the suffering of others. The floodwaters function like some stabilizing medium that captures and presents as it kills, a form of wet taxidermy, as lungs that once filled with air now fill with water. Meanwhile "a wolf paddles among sheep, and tawny lions and tigers are carried on the tide."

Abolish the distance, take a share in the exposure, and flood marvels cease to be very marvelous. They just are: scenes of ordinariness, attempts at living and dying, refuge salvaged from inundation. Aesthetic distance transmutes into affective regard. Lively "forms" become life-forms, requiring sympathy, identification, care, and aid. Let go from disaster-turned-retrospective-catastrophe, these forms suggest something more technical, an improvisatory grammar that emerges from disaster. The word "grammar" is too systematic, too reliably generative. Such hybrid forms or juxtapositions cannot be generalized. Each represents one precarious time-bound structure of dwindled refuge. You cannot count on the same structure working twice (and yet it might). Each testifies nevertheless to the possibility of inhabiting the flood. We expect the raven will be along soon, begging us to inquire further into what amazes the sea nymphs, all these partial forms that make no sense in terms of ark-building or ark design, right there in plain sight, if only we can overcome the view from an ark whose voice takes the shape of a "no."

In "Paris Not Flooded," part-Ovid, part-sea nymph, part-raven Roland Barthes decodes picture postcards of flooded Paris in 1955 as rendered by the "press photos, sole means of the flood's truly collective consummation."[15] Barthes remarks the way, "despite the difficulties or the disasters . . . inflicted on thousands of French people," the press photos present "more of a celebration than a catastrophe" (62). The rising waters inundate but preserve the infrastructures of everyday life. They "overwhelm . . . the everyday optic without diverting it toward the fantastic." Objects were "partially obliterated, not deformed." The flood

> displaced certain objects, thereby refreshing the perception of the world by introducing into it unaccustomed and yet explicable points of view: one saw cars reduced to their roofs, streetlamps

> truncated so that only their tops remained above the surface like water lilies, houses cut up like children's blocks, a cat marooned for several days in a tree. All these everyday objects suddenly seemed separated from their roots, deprived of that reasonable substance par excellence: Earth. This rupture had the merit of remaining curious, without being magically threatening: the sheet of water behaved like a successful but familiar special effect. (62)

Beyond the damage and suffering the flood caused, the water interfered with the "coenesthesia of the landscape," with the "habitual lines of the cadastre" (63). Yet, while the rising waters disturbed the "optic reflexes" of this built world, their disturbance was not, insofar as the photographic record goes, "visually threatening." On the contrary, in the press photos, "the total sensation remains gentle, peaceful, immobile, and friendly." The result is a certain "pacification of vision" by which the spectator "feels himself conveyed by proxy" through a flooded landscape that never threatens.

Barthes dwells on the boats (real and improvised) that litter the press photos, boats that impossibly now sail down streets. He speculates that this shipborne proxy-image world both evokes and satisfies "the great mythic and childish dream of walking on water." The rising waters "revive this theme," and so the flood paradoxically creates "a world that is more accessible" than usual and "controllable with the same kind of delectation a child takes in arranging his toys" (64). Everything is remade anew. Everyday objects are shorn of their usual habits, such that "houses are now no more than cubes, rails are isolated lines, herds of cattle shifting masses." And the "little boat, superlative toy of the childhood universe, becomes the means of possessing this now rearranged, outspread, and no longer rooted space." The scalar shift set in motion by the rising waters, as captured by the press photo, renders engulfed Paris a play-space.

Tuning into the mythological or ideological function of such images, the way they constitute a mode of speech or writing, Barthes observes the way the scalar shift provided by inundation is met by a "dynamic solidarity" that "quite spontaneously reconstitutes the rising waters as an event unifying mankind." That unity plays out not at the level of a shared precarity or proximity or sympathy with those whose homes or lives have been lost. There is no inquiry into the reasons why these and not other neighborhoods have flooded. Instead, this solidarity reconstitutes viewers as a proxy public for whom such events as floods are "foreseeable." Newspapers forecast "in advance the day of the rising water's maximum height," uniting people in a "rational elaboration" of flood protections as if they all shared a role in some adventure novel. Barthes even catches a whiff of "the myth of '48." In 1955, Parisians raised the barricades of 1848 not against a corrupt monarchy, but against the "enemy waters" of the flood (65). What could be more reassuring to national pride, Barthes wonders, than the image of an "armed mobilization, the teamwork of troops, motorized life rafts, rescues of children, old people, and invalids" that recaptures the spirit of 1848? The technological fix of Paris's citizen yeomanry fights back the waters and keeps the perspective that the press photos offer, safe and dry. At bottom, however, the press photos, Barthes concludes, have a more ancient origin. The evacuation of the old, the invalid, and the child replays the "biblical stabling of herds of cattle, all the frenzy of Noah filling the Ark." The press photos testify thereby to the en-arkment of Paris. Noah's ark, Barthes observes, "is a happy myth: in it humanity stands aloof from the elements, concentrates and elaborates the necessary consciousness of its own powers, making disaster itself give evidence that the world is manageable" (65).

By his attention to the mythologizing of the photographic record, Barthes clues us in to the way the flood is emplotted to sponsor a narrative about purposeful action, preparation, resiliency, and civic spirit. For him, this plotting enacts the chief "characteristic of myth," which, as he tells us, is to "transform meaning into form," and so to transform "history into nature" (242). "Paris Not Flooded" thus becomes something like an emblem of French organization and resilience. As Barthes points out, mythic transformation usually takes the form of a theft. It may therefore prove, as elsewhere in *Mythologies* he bemoans, "very difficult to vanquish myth," for its forms are plastic: they cheerfully steal and resignify everything that comes their way. Then again, Barthes ventures, it might be possible to orchestrate your own little theft, however temporary the refuge it affords. "Truth to tell," writes Barthes, "the best weapon against myth is perhaps to mythify it in its turn. . . . Since myth robs language of something, why not rob myth?" (246–47). Let's think then in terms of little thefts, resignifying practices, that cause received forms to ripple, bulge, and deform. Let's imagine an ark insurgency that pieces together reserves of refuge from and within the arc of story.

Throughout this book, we have assembled a crew of ark-mates, ark thinkers and builders, whose mundane and ordinary forms of writing, frequently in spite of themselves, reactualize the way the story of Noah in Genesis remains a text to think with. Their creations require us all to grapple with fundamental questions of hospitality, community within difference, and refuge. In this chapter, we focus on those writers, artists, makers, and just plain people who try to think, write, make, live, and imagine their way out of the ark story while never exactly leaving. Their creations complicate and proliferate the ark such that its semantic field expands to coincide with refuge in its most capacious, open mode. Collectively, this work inclines Genesis toward Exodus or hybridizes the story of ark-building with stories that lead from slavery (and peril) to freedom (and peril differently arranged). Noah's ark, if you like, finds itself caught in the wake of baby Moses in his improvised basket-boat, the Latin *arca* subject to productive translational interference by the Hebrew *tevah*.

Choppy waters signal a potentially sustaining turbulence.

UnMarvels: Zora Neale Hurston, Richard Wright, James Baldwin

Not all ark stories have Noahs—or for that matter, arks. And sometimes the news of the flood arrives late, either because the saved have already made their way to safety and have no room to spare or because the signs of catastrophe's advent have been ignored. Not all ark stories will therefore have obvious ravens, doves, Noahs, or Naamahs. Zora Neale Hurston's *Their Eyes Were Watching God* (1937) lingers in the deluge's immiserating arrival and long, hard wake. Hurston's novel traces the life of Janie Crawford, whose grandmother Nanny was born into slavery and came to believe that freedom must at its minimum include the ability to inhabit your own porch without someone telling you what to do. From just such a shelter, Janie narrates her story of self-making to friend Pheoby Watson. A shared confidence, the novel begins with Janie's coming full circle, her return home after long wandering through a difficult, dangerous, and at times luminous world. The two women sit outside at the back of her house, "in the fresh, young darkness close together." Pheoby is "eager to feel and do through Janie," who seems an inspiration, an avatar.

Janie's "full of that oldest human longing—self revelation."[16] Pheoby holds her tongue, but her feet shuffle.

Janie speaks; she tells a story primed with the knowledge that every refuge, even a porch, can become a prison. Or, at least, will not hold secure against storms ecological and affective. Desire, love, life-making, and narrative-forging are edged by oblivion and erasure, tempests that eradicate some lives (and plotlines) more easily than others because the world is unjust, because luck turns bad, or just simply because. Janie marries Logan Killicks and hopes that the love she does not feel will come, but "long before the year was up, Janie noticed that her husband had stopped talking in rhymes to her" (26). She meets Joe Starks; names him "Jody;" the two run away to Florida; start a general store; Jody becomes mayor; but love departs. Jody moves downstairs; gets sick; won't eat Janie's food; dies of kidney disease. Janie wears the white of mourning, fends off a sea of suitors; then one day, in walks Vergible Woods, who is so sweet he goes by "Tea Cake." The two go mobile; head down to the Everglades "round Clewiston and Belle Glade" (128); Tea Cake works; Janie cooks; then the two work together; folks talk. Their life is happy. The two make friends with the Bahamian workers they meet. The narrative picks up speed.

Outside their small house one day, Janie watches a Seminole band troop toward higher ground. They warn her that blooming saw grass signifies nearing hurricane. Morning comes "without motion" because "the winds, to the tiniest, lisping baby breath had left the earth." No Seminole pass by today, but rabbits scurry in the same direction, to be joined by possums, whose "route was definite." The passersby become a procession: a "crawling horde" of snakes and rattlesnakes, headed for some high ground or unknown ark (155). In the night Janie hears migrating deer, then a panther, seeking safety elsewhere. Buzzards rise into the high clouds and do not return. The wind picks up. Friends offer transport to distant havens, but Janie and Tea Cake take their cue from the nearby white people in big houses who trust in seawalls. "Old [Lake] Okeechobee" might "roll in his bed," but "if the castles thought themselves secure, the cabins needn't worry" (158). Janie, Tea Cake, and their friend Motor Boat think their Glades community might be safe. Still, the winds return. Huddling together, eyes fixed on the door of their shack, "the time was past for asking the white folks what to look for through that door. Six eyes were questioning *God*" (159).

As the hurricane bears down, water rises around the battered house: three inches at the threshold, and the sound of celestial drums, and a wind that does not cease to howl. The waters increase, seeping into every crack of door and wall. Janie, Tea Cake, and Motor Boat huddle in the night, drenched and silent. "Through the screaming wind," they hear "things crashing and things hurtling and dashing with unbelievable velocity." The windows of heaven seem to have opened and the shack becomes a makeshift ark: a baby rabbit "squirm[s] . . . through a hole in the floor" and squats "in the shadows against the wall, seeming to know that nobody want[s] . . . its flesh at such a time" (159). The wind rises and falls. No candle burns. "They seemed to be staring at the dark," Hurston writes in the resonant line that haunts her novel as title, "but their eyes were watching God" (160). What else besides divine agency could motivate such a flood? Spectators to a drama that they had hoped would not engulf them, the three inside the buffeted dwelling wonder at ruin's author. Perhaps, like the biblical Abraham, they ask: "Will you sweep away the righteous with the wicked?" (Genesis 18:23). Perhaps, they muse, they are to join the punished, the drowned. In what way does such ruthless catastrophe make sense? What plan or intention or motive explains that this world of rising waters is not arbitrary? What intimacy exists between God's floods and God's love?

Tea Cake heads outside, "pushing wind in front of him" (160). He finds that "the wind and water" have "given life to lots of things that folks think of as dead and given death to so much that had been living things. Water everywhere. Stray fish swimming in the yard." The water is knee deep and rising. He knows they must flee, knows they have waited too long; tells Janie so she can get ready; goes looking for a car. She quickly "runs up a sack" for their money and insurance papers. They have to yell sleepy Motor Boat awake. Time to go.

Lake Okechobee awakens. The "monstropolous beast" (161) leaves its bed, wind-whipped into fury. With grinding clamor, the dikes restraining the lake's waters crumble. A liquid wall drowns everything in its path: "The sea was walking the earth with a heavy heel" (162). The three of them make it to a "tall house on a hump of ground." Motor Boat decides to stay put (163). He's sleepy; tries to get Janie and Tea Cake to stay; heads upstairs as they press on. Janie and Tea Cake run, and then swim: "They had to reach the six-mile bridge. It was high and safe perhaps" (164). They join all the people "walking the fill . . . hurrying, dragging, falling, crying, calling out names hopefully and hopelessly." When they reach the bridge at Six Mile Bend it is "crowded. White people had preempted that point of elevation" (164). It's not that these whites allow no refuge (though if asked they might not). It's more that the brutal facticity of white privilege ensures that when Janie and Tea Cake arrive "there was no more room." The water swirls with "things living and dead" (165), animating into danger all it pushes across the land it swallows. Survivors and victims share dwindling havens with terrified beasts. The novel offers a parade of desperate icons or unmarvelous marvels: "A dead man in sitting position on a hummock [hillock], entirely surrounded by wild animals and snakes" (164). "Common danger made common friends," the novel ventures, and "nothing sought a conquest over the other" (164).

As flood rages, Hurston offers a deluge story without the possibility of admission to a saving vessel. The narrative inhabits a world where you must make your own shelter out of whatever materials happen to be at hand. Those in peril in this rising sea refuse to drown, refuse to yield their story, their particularity, to universal obliteration. Janie and Tea Cake press on and encounter "another man" clinging "to a cypress tree on a tiny island. A tin roof of a building hung from the branches by electric wires and the wind swung it back and forth like a mighty ax" (164). Caught between this repurposed roof become guillotine and a rattlesnake "stretched full length with its head in the wind," the man wavers between death at the hands of technological debris and what he takes to be primal natural necessity. "De snake won't bite yuh," counsels Tea Cake. "He skeered tuh go intuh uh coil. Skeered he'll be blowed away. Step round dat side and swim off!" (165). Tea Cake understands. He curates this new choreography of man and snake, creatures of the air, creatures of shared media, mundane Ovidian *mirabile,* marvelous only to the extent that they may be refuge-possible forms in which safety cohabits with danger. But you need to learn how to read them, which Tea Cake does, instructing the man clinging to the cypress tree on that tiny island, and coaching him on how to move. But Tea Cake tires, cannot go on. Janie spreads herself over him, "between him and the wind" (165). He closes his eyes and lets "the tiredness seep out of his limbs."

When "a large piece of tar-paper roofing" sails through the air, Janie feels joy: it's the "very thing to cover Tea Cake with." But Janie miscalculates, doesn't reckon on a storm that unlocks a new potentiality in things. She creeps along after the tar-paper, catches hold of it and "immediately the wind lift[s] . . . both of them and she [sees] . . . herself sailing off the fill to the right, out and out over the lashing water" (165), no raven, no dove, just some parody of a bird, who might battle the wind and fly away, "scream[ing] . . . terribly." Janie lets go, "plunges downward into the water," downward to drown. As Janie is about to sink below the waves Tea Cake spots a terrified cow, afloat upon the raging flood. The animal becomes a boat, but that unwilling raft is already inhabited: a "massive built dog" sits atop and will not share its refuge, its animal become ark. When the vicious hound lunges at Janie, Tea Cake kills the animal with his knife—but nothing happens cleanly. The dog bites his cheek. Tea Cake counts his lucky stars that it did not get his eye.

The hurricane passes at last. The couple are safe now, or think they are. But as the floodwaters recede, every "city of refuge" (166) becomes a place of horror, replete with the unburied dead, the corpses that litter the land when violent waters subside. These geographies are also filled with reminders that, as Posmentier puts it, there's "no such thing as a natural disaster."[17] The conditions of disaster's making instead have deep histories. When Janie and Tea Cake make it to dry "safety," what they encounter instead is the quotidian peril of Black life in the Jim Crow South. Black men are pressed into lethal labor by whites with guns (169–70). Although it is impossible to determine the skin color of the drowned, so quickly do the corpses decay, white men with rifles insist that a sorting be undertaken. The bodies must reside in two separate mass graves: one filled with white corpses in coffins, one filled with Black unsheltered corpses (171). The brutal aftermath of the deluge makes vividly evident the system of racial injustice that writes this landscape, as well as its utter incoherence. The bridge refuge that white occupancy denies during the flood here becomes the impossible, implausible, preservation of white racial difference in burial even though, as Tea Cake says, "Nobody can't tell nothin' 'bout some uh dese bodies, de shape dey's in" (171). Singular coffin-arks maintain the markers of inequality. Swift ecological violence intensifies the pervasiveness of slower kinds.[18]

The wind dies. The waters recede, and along with them (it seems), the need for makeshift arks. But the flood persists. The dog's bite infects Tea Cake with rabies, a disease that causes (of all things) hydrophobia, fear of water. Because he is not treated quickly enough, infection takes hold of his body. The water that almost drowned him becomes a substance Tea Cake cannot bear to have near his body. Janie attempts to care for her beloved, but the disease conveys him further and further from her embrace. Realizing his impending death, she looks to the sky, "pleading, asking questions" (178), wondering whether God meant to accomplish such a lethal deed. She asks for a celestial sign: thunder, maybe, or a daytime star, something that would make sense of catastrophes by anchoring them in authorship. Yet "the sky stayed hard looking and quiet so she went inside the house" (178). Not long afterward Tea Cake in his deluded state attempts to kill Janie. She shoots him and is arrested for his murder.

During the trial Janie narrates what unfolded, what she lost, why Tea Cake died. When the jury retires, Janie sits "like a lump" and waits. She realizes that "it was not death she feared," but having her story misunderstood (188). Not one for "quick forgetfulness" (189), she desires an enduring narrative that will speak forcefully of the love that she and Tea Cake forged, the story they created in a world that gave them only miserable and constricted scripts. As the novel comes to its close, Janie confides to best friend Pheoby:

> Love ain't somethin' lak uh grindstone dat's de same thing everywhere and do de same thing tuh everything it touch. Love is lak de sea. It's uh movin' thing, but still and all, it takes its shape from de shore it meets, and it's different with every shore. (191)

Love and the sea can nurture and adapt. They can also jump their bounds in ruinous flood. Desire and water are like narratives in that way: they might forge shelter for a while, but they also might overflow, obliterate, destroy. God's place is not easy to discern in any of them: where is their author, authority, archive? Yet love and deluge have long aftermaths full of remembering and restoring, of what Toni Morrison calls "rememory," as well as continued and extensive living that requires careful narrating so as not to vanish into someone else's version of the tale.

In her novel *Salvage the Bones,* Jesmyn Ward memorialized what she feared was the fading memory of Hurricane Katrina and its devastation of Black communities. She narrated a flood without arks and abandoned Noah for a classical myth she found more useful, the tale of Jason and abandoned but vengeful Medea. Hurston likewise has a hurricane in mind, but remembers its unfolding by having her narrator inhabit a world where any ark that might have been sailing is a ship at such distance no one can place a wish aboard. In describing the surging of Lake Okechobee over its earthwork banks, Hurston memorializes the effect of a hurricane that decimated the Everglades in 1928, drowning thousands, especially Black laborers who lived in precarious, low-lying housing. The tale of a flood in which, if Noah or an ark were ever at work, they conducted their business of conservation elsewhere, leaving most to the sea, her novel is a story about racism and environmental justice. Its narrative never surrenders to easy binaries: the doctor who attempts to save Tea Cake is white; the two gossiping communities that turn against Janie are Black. *Their Eyes Were Watching God* is—whatever else that ambivalent collective title conveys—a Black woman's personal archive, the story of the world in ruin but the story of Janie, related to her best friend on the porch of a house she once fled and now reclaims as a refuge through an act of recollection and preservation. Janie lays her dear Tea Cake to rest in a monumental grave of stone so that he and the sustaining shelter they once forged together will not vanish with the flood. She returns to her home to make of its once unhappy rooms a space in which to dwell with complicated histories: stories of flood, adventure, rape, slavery, complicated origins, community-building, horrific loss, racist violence, willed forgetting and elemental obliteration, suffering, salvage, endurance, small hopes, small freedoms, intricate loves, hard and joyful tales, precarious refuge.

Famously, the novel fell foul of Richard Wright, with his programmatic commitment to an unflinching social realism. "Miss Hurston can write," he conceded, but "her prose is cloaked in the facile sensuality that has dogged Negro expression since the days of Phillis Wheatley." Characterizing Hurston as perpetuating "the minstrel technique that makes 'white folks' laugh," he finds that the "sensory sweep of the novel carries no theme, no message, no thought."[19] Contrast Hurston's unstable world with the fully allegorized environment of Wright's story of the Mississippi floods of 1927, "Down by the Riverside," in which the only "ark" available to protagonist Mann and family is a rowing boat owned by a white family, a boat he has to steal because the white owner cares nothing for the fact that Mann's wife is ill. Contrast also that, in Wright's story, this necessary theft and his shooting of the white owner in self defense, along with Mann's superhuman labor rowing against the current, come to nothing, his pregnant wife dead before he gets her to the "FOR COLORED" section of the Red Cross; that Mann and his stolen boat are then conscripted to rescue the very white family from which the boat was taken; that he is then forced to labor on the levee with no thought given to his loss; that, when denounced by the white man's son, Mann's plea of self defense is simply unthinkable, even though the white boat owner shot at him first, multiple times; that his accusation is, in fact, a summary sentence of death; that Mann's only choice then is whether to allow himself to be led to execution or to assert his sovereignty in suicidal flight; that he dies face down in the mud, the story ending with his body become an object to be turned over by the butt of a soldier's rifle, rolling "heavily down the wet slope," where it "stop[s] about a foot from the water's edge, one black palm sprawled outward and upward, trailing in the brown current." From all this it is easy to feel at least some of Wright's frustration.[20] To be Noah (or is it Moses?) in this incomplete exodus story is to have to steal an ark, to labor to no end, and, come landfall, to lie dead in the mud. Wright's worlds are flooded with violence. Their physics enacts the racial laws of Jim Crow. Meticulous in his craft, he takes his readers right "down to the riverside" and recruits us to carry Mann's body across the river Jordan. He asks us to fight.

Wright's visceral frustration with Hurston's novel did not go unreciprocated. Eve Dunbar tells the story that, later in life, Hurston confessed to a friend that "she was gripped by the desire to puke when she read the works of writers such as Richard Wright because she felt they pandered to the white desire for black pathology and inferiority."[21] Hurston refuses to see African Americans as necessarily damaged or fractured by the history that has assailed them. White people are nearly absent from *Their Eyes Were Watching God*. They inhere to the frame of Janie's life, especially through the brutal systems they have set in place. The book makes clear that, during times of ecological catastrophe, suffering is unequally distributed, with minority communities enduring the brunt of violence before, during, and after the deluge. The lack of sufficient accommodation on the ark or within the bridge-refuge means that a disproportionate number of bodies of color will be left to drown. But unjust inundation must not, her novel insists, overwhelm their hopes, their complicated loves, their stories limned by violence but always replete with survival, renewal, resistance, sweetness, ordinariness, laughter, joy.

For Wright, the flood is cruelly generative in the sense that it exposes and compels. It brings things to a breaking point. It inspires resistance. For Hurston, the flood functions with menacing neutrality and ambiguous possibility. The flood is not a punishment; it simply is. The punishments the weather brings are conveyed through the enduring structures of inequality erected by the same people who crowd out all the space on the bridge. The world she writes disrupts allegory, or the allegories it generates may not be scaled up without cost or interference. Tea Cake remarks on the suspension of certain dangers that the rain brings, such as the automatic conflict between man and snake. The young rabbit seems to understand that the flood's arrival momentarily takes him off the menu, transforming Janie's kitchen into a space of security. But the novel refuses to sentimentalize such moments. It does not transform them into easy icons. The man on the hummock surrounded by snakes is dead. Janie's tar-paper comforter turns lethal. And Motor Boat, against all odds, survives, but he does so merely because "de lake come moved de house way off somewhere and Motor didn't know nothin' 'bout it till de storm wuz 'bout over" (173). The novel collects such unmarvelous, mundane refuges. It inventories them, preserves them, along with their possibility. It offers a way of moving.

"Ships at a distance have every man's wish on board," the novel begins. "*For some they come in with the tide.* For others they sail on the horizon, never out of sight, never landing until the Watcher turns his eyes away in resignation, his dreams mocked to death by Time." But this is no universal experience, but a gendered one: "That is the life of men" (1). "Now, women," the story continues, "forget all those things they don't want to remember, and remember everything they don't want to forget. The dream is the truth. Then they act and do things accordingly." Men and women, white and Black, human and animal, every story has its specificities; no story is a ready-made parable or all-encompassing myth. Deluge cannot scour every one of these particular histories from the land, no matter how forcefully the waters rush. But don't overinvest. Don't mistake the facticity of the flood for anything more. Affinities may be built and maintained by stories, however, so by all means repeat those; collect them, pass them on, just as Hurston herself does as ethnographer and folklorist. Pheoby, after

all, is both more and less than Janie's friend. She's her intermediary with all the town's "sitters-and-talkers" (191). After Janie tells Pheoby of her antiuniversalist, sea-like version of environmental love, a desire whose surging landfall takes its shape from the shore it meets, she tells her to tell them her story. Janie's love might not work like their love. Maybe, she thinks, they have never known love. But maybe, if they listen to her story, give into the ark she's thinking, they might.

Songs, stories, islands, but never idylls—*Their Eyes Were Watching God* serializes refuge, seeding it throughout Janie's unfolding life, finding it in the interstices of an infrastructure, at its worst hostile, at its best neutral.[22] Tuning into this structure, Posmentier hears in the novel a "lyric archive" in which Hurston's training as ethnographer and sound recordist leads her to collect and produce the sounds of environmental experience in and as the texture of the novel, an expanded version of what Henry Louis Gates Jr. famously called the "speakerly text."[23] The sensory "sprawl," in Wright's sense of things, names the formal effect of being introduced into the ambient world of flood that Hurston's novel plays back, the novel's storm sequence becoming something like a "reel, a collection of aural and lyrical experiences of the hurricanes," a sound machine, curating voices, "but also rhythms that exceed speech."[24] This aesthetic resonates also with the superlative artistic productions that rise from the literal-figurative experience of flood at this time, such as Bessie Smith's iconic 1927 "Back-Water Blues," productions keyed both to the historically particular, the personal and the collective, and to the figurative truth of living in a time, or condition, of flood, also personal, also collective, of living on, as Sharpe will put it, "in the wake."[25]

In *Conversations with James Baldwin,* sitting with Studs Terkel listening to Bessie Smith's "Back-Water Blues" in the studios of WFMT in Chicago on July 15, 1961, James Baldwin finds it very hard to describe what he's feeling. Strange ambience having the song played here:

> When it thunders and lightning and the wind begins to blow,
> When it thunders and lightning and the wind begins to blow,
> There's thousands of people
> They ain't got no place to go.
> My house fell down
> And I can't live there no more.[26]

Baldwin explains that the first time he heard this song was in Europe "under very different circumstances than I had listened to Bessie in New York." He admits not to listening much to Smith earlier in his life, much for the same reasons that he avoided eating watermelon. What strikes him now is

> the fact that she was singing, as you say, about a disaster, which had almost killed her, and she accepted it and was going beyond it. The fantastic understatement in it. It is the way I want to write, you know. When she says, "My house fell down and I can't live there no mo"—it is a great . . . great sentence. A great achievement. (3)

The occasion for the interview was the appearance of Baldwin's *Nobody Knows My Name,* which gathers a series of essays written over six years abroad. Terkel quotes from the preface, in which Baldwin writes that "when he went to live in the mountains of Switzerland [he] arrived armed with two Bessie Smith records and a typewriter" (4). Switzerland was so white, he explains: "*White* snow, white mountains, and white faces. Those Swiss people really thought I had been sent by the devil; it was a very strange . . . they had never seen a Negro before" (4). Baldwin played Bessie Smith every day; her voice along with James P. Johnson's playing provided an orienting "cadence" or "tone" that grounded both Baldwin and his writing as he tried to learn what it means to be an American by leaving. Terkel continues to quote Baldwin describing how, when he began "to re-create the life I had first known as a child and from which I had spent so many years in flight," Bessie Smith, "her tone and her cadence," helped him reconnect to how he must have spoken, what he must have seen and witnessed and "buried very deep" (4). The experience effects a reconciliation; the songs becoming a refuge, not in the sense of escape, but more literally, a place to fly back to, to recoup.

In *Nobody Knows My Name,* Baldwin writes candidly about Europe as a haven, about the fact he had removed himself "from the social forces which had menaced" in America and the difficulty he found in reckoning with the costs of that removal. "Havens are high-priced," he writes, "the price exacted on the haven-dweller is that he has to continue to delude himself that he has found a haven."[27] Six years in Switzerland, Paris, Spain, Corsica, and Scandinavia, "armed with two

Bessie Smith records and a typewriter," and Baldwin discovers that he "no longer needs to hide . . . from the high and dangerous winds of the world." He is able "to go anywhere—including America."[28] He offers the essays that make up *Nobody Knows My Name* as a "log book" from within this process, a ruttier or pattern to refuge-making true to its name: refuge in the service of return.

"One last question James Baldwin," asks Terkel, "who are you now?" There's a long pause. And then Baldwin says the following:

> Who, indeed. Well, I may be able to tell you who I am, but I am also discovering who I am not. I want to be an honest man. And I want to be a good writer. I don't know if one ever gets to be what one wants to be. You just have to play it by ear . . . and pray for rain. (23)

Sometimes, of course, whether you're praying for rain or not, Noah just shows up out of the blue. An ark looms from nowhere. When that happens, rain or shine, you'd probably better do just as Baldwin advises, keep your eyes open, and "play it by ear."

Soul Boat: Henry Dumas, Sun Ra, Octavia Butler

"Playing it by ear" perhaps best describes how Fish-hound inhabits the world in Henry Dumas's posthumously published Noah story "Ark of Bones." Fish-hound is out for a walk, heading down to a bend of the Mississippi to fish. He notices that Headeye—smartest kid in school, ugly but "good-natured," "o.k., cept when he get some kinda notion in that big head of his"—is following him. Fish-hound assumes he's out to go fishing too but doesn't know where's best. So, Fish-hound decides he'd "better fake him out."[29] Headeye has been holding forth about this "mojo bone" he found, his latest "notion," and Fish-hound wants none of it. When he's far enough ahead, Fish-hound figures he can break off the path and head to the river, leaving Headeye behind. But he gets distracted by a fox and a "snake twistin toward the water." A flock of birds takes flight, scaring him "half to death." When he gets down to the bank, up comes Headeye "droopin long like he had ten tons of cotton on his back" (4). Looking to take offense, Fish-hound asks "what you followin me for?" But Headeye says he's not even been thinking about Fish-hound, and that, maybe, like him, Fish-hound "got a call from the spirit," which is why they're both here.

Headeye shows Fish-hound his mojo bone: "This is a keybone to the culud man. Ain't but one in the whole world." Fish-hound gives Headeye a hard time; he tests Headeye because Fish-hound "never rush[es] upon a thing" (5). The bone "belongs to the people of God," explains Headeye. "Remember when Ezekiel was in the valley of dry bones?" he asks, and Fish-hound reckons that he does. Headeye quotes the biblical verses in order to establish the prophetic script of resurrection he thinks they're on, why it is they are being drawn down to the water:

> And the hand of the Lord was upon me, and carried me out in the spirit to the valley of dry bones.
>
> And he said unto me, "Son of Man, can these bones live?" And I said unto him, "Lord, thou knowest."
>
> And he said unto me, "Go and bind them together. Prophesy that I shall come and put flesh upon them from generations and from generations."
>
> And the Lord said unto me, "Son of man, these bones are the whole house of thy brothers, scattered to the islands. Behold, I shall bind up the bones and you shall prophesy the name." (5)

Not sure what to think, Fish-hound holds his tongue. Not quite fully part of Headeye's world, not the churchgoer that Headeye is, nevertheless Fish-hound knows enough to accept the invitation to depart the gravity of his known world and follow.

The two head down to an old place "called Deadman's Landin because they found a dead man there one time." The corpse was in a liminal state, its identity unclear as its integrity unraveled: "so rotted and ate up by fish and craw dads that they couldn't tell whether he was black or white." Headeye starts mending the planks, puts the landing back together, looks out at the water, neglects his fishing pole, apologizes to Fish-hound for an earlier sleight, then excitedly exclaims: "You see them signs?" Fish-hound "couldn't help but say 'yeah.'" Headeye declares:

> The Ark is comin.
> What Ark?

> You'll see.
> Noah's Ark?
> Just wait. You'll see it. (6)

Fish-hound feels like he should do something to help. But Headeye always gets so caught up in things, takes them too far. Fish-hound throws out his line, makes like he's fishing, but he's not; really he's keeping a protective eye on his friend.

The clouds thicken like fermenting, raw milk; the waves "slappin the sides of the bank made water jump around and dance" (7). Fish-hound catches a couple of fish, wonders about the verses from Ezekiel, and decides that there are a lot of signs but that, "if you're sharp-eyed you always see something along the Mississippi." The waters are rising, the weather changing.[30] Time to leave. Just then there's a "funny noise" (8). Fish-hound hears "a kind of moanin, like a lot of people." Then he sees it:

> This big thing movin in the far off, movin slow, down river, naw, it was up river. Naw, it was just movin and standin still at the same time. The damnest thing I ever seed. It just about a damn boat, the biggest boat in the whole world. I looked up and what I took for clouds was sails. The wind was whippin up a sermon on them. It was way out in the river, almost not touchin the water, just rockin there, rockin and waitin. (8)

Fish-hound figures the two of them might be dead and this is "the Glory Boat" that will transport them across the river and into heaven (9). But he says nothing. He stands with Headeye. A rowing boat arrives to take them aboard, propelled by "two men, about as black as anybody black wants to be." The rain pours and the moaning picks up "like a church full of people pourin out their hearts to Jesus." Fish-hound asks Headeye whether they're heading to Noah's ark but Headeye doesn't know, which scares him. The moaning grows louder, and if it weren't for the wind, Fish-hound could "swear the sound was comin from someplace inside the ark."[31]

Fish-hound follows Headeye up the steps of the ark. Every step is numbered. By the time he notices, however, he is on step "1608, and they went on like that right on up to a number that made me pay attention: 1944. That was when I was born" (9). When he reaches

Headeye, they're up to 1977, the present future? The ark is strange. No animals, just doors and cabins. An unkempt, gray-haired old man dressed in skins greets Headeye, but over the wind Fish-hound can't hear what the two are saying to each other. He figures this must be Noah, but he's not like any of the white Noahs he's seen in Sunday school pictures. He looks around to see if he can make out "more people, maybe Shem, Ham, and Japheth, or wives," but there is no one. Headeye asks whether he's ready? "Yeah, . . . ready to get ashore" (10), says Fish-hound, and he means it. "This is a soul boat" (10), Headeye explains. Anyone on board "could consider hisself *called*" (11). Pretty sure he's not ever been "called" to anything, Fish-hound decides that he'd better play along. True to his name, he'll let out the line of his metaphorical rod and see what kind of sense he can sniff out (even as it may be he who's getting hooked). Fish-hound follows Headeye down into the ark and "what I saw," he says, "I'll never forget as long as I live . . . Bones. I saw bones. They were stacked all the way to the top of the ship. . . . The under side of the whole ark was nothin' but a great bonehouse" (11). Throughout the ark, small groups of black men handle these bones with great care, "like they were holdin' onto babies or somethin precious." Two to three men to a cabin, Fish-head reports, and a million cabins at least.

"Standin like a captain" in the midst of things, Noah reads something off a strip of leather he holds up to a fire. A group of men wind a rope, chanting each time they heave. Fish-hound can't understand their "foreign talk," but this is how it sounds:

> Aba aba, al ham dilaba
> aba aba, mtu brotha
> aba, aba, al ham dilaba,
> aba, aba, bretha brotha
> aba, aba, djuka brotha
> aba, aba, al ham dilaba. (12)[32]

The old man walks a "crooked path" through the bones, careful not to step on them, "like he was walkin frontwards, backwards, sidewards, and every which a way" (12). Fish-hound figures the bones must belong to animals. When the old man stops and yells out, "Nineteen hundred and twenty three," the men haul up bones from the river, and he realizes that they are human. He thinks about the sermon he heard "about Ezekiel in the valley of dry bones" (12–13). The old man regards him. "Son, you are in the house of generations," he explains, "Every African who lives in America has a part of his soul on this ark" (13). The old man asks Headeye whether he has a shield. Headeye presents the mojo bone, which the old man anoints with oil. Headeye repeats the old man's words, "consecrates [his] bones" to setting his brothers free (13). Then Headeye walks among the bones "like he's been doin it all his life" (13). Fish-hound bears witness. Headeye places his shield on what seems to be an altar where it burns. Then Headeye rakes the ashes and reclaims the "little piece of mojo bone" and "zig-walks" back to Fish-hound, who follows him out of the ark (14). When the two get back late that night, everyone wants to know where they have been: people from the town say there's been a lynching, and the "white folks" threw the body in the river (14)—another dead man landing. Fish-hound says nothing.

Several days later, Headeye pays Fish-hound a visit at home. Heyboy, the family dog, who's been missing for a week, comes sniffing and Fish-hound figures he knows who's been feeding their "no-count dog" (14). "I'm leavin," says Headeye (14), "but someday I be back. You is my witness" (15). The two shake hands, and Fish-hound watches Headeye go "movin fast with that no-count dog runnin alongside him." Headeye stops once and waves, which gives Fish-hound a "notion," one of those notions it's best to keep to yourself until you're ready to act on it. Since then, when people ask after Headeye, Fish-hound tells them the news "bout Ezekiel in the valley of dry bones" (15). He bears witness as he has been ordained to do. Sometimes they tell him he's crazy. Sometimes they nod like they understand him completely. He doesn't mention the ark. Then they would think he was "crazy for sure."

To a certain extent, the story to this story is that it speaks for itself, which is to say, we listen in as Fish-hound tells us how he reels in all the "signs" he can and learns what sense they make. Fish-hound figures the archetypal passerby, open-minded when it comes to allegory, but impatient with overreading and the catastrophes that inaction can bring. He's all devout skepticism. The anger he says he feels is really a begrudging care for fellow pedestrians with "notions" and the trouble he fears they will cause him. He's open to what his senses tell him, skilled at fishing out the smell of things, attuned also to how that sense may change, and kind-hearted enough to worry about Headeye and his missing "no-count dog" who still counts (no matter what he says), and happy at the sight of Headeye and Heyboy running off together to crew the ark and breathe life back into the bones of all the Black men and women and children literally and figuratively lost to the waters of the Mississippi. Come story's end, he too stands recruited by the ark, either as crew or witness to the troping of Genesis that Dumas effects. We listen in as he comes to understand this simple fact and, by way of an ending, the story begins again. Who will Fish-hound's witnessing bring down to the river to see the ark this time? Neighbors? The story's readers?

"Ark of Bones" prophesies resurrection in repair. It tells a story of collective remaking in the service of a community of care. The story is committed to Noah's ark as an ark of safety and security, but only if that safety and security is understood to entail the reparative labor of the living in their care and reverence for the dead, and so also one another. Recruiting those it calls, Dumas's ark serves as invitational conduit between the living and the dead, a simple truth the story's Noah speaks directly: "Every African who lives in America has a part of his soul on this ark" (13). Chronology marks its steps like some sort of measure or scale that the ark must navigate to reclaim the stories of particular persons from the history imposed on them. Noah calls out the date, "1923," and his crew haul up the bones of a particular person, taking great care of them as they arrange them in the ark's hold. This ritual of rescue repurposes the ark. It transforms the vessel into a refuge-making device, an extratemporal community of affect and memory, emblemized by the chant and ritual in which the actions and words of the living enable dead brothers and sisters to "breathe" again. The ark sails the Mississippi but it also sails time, an (after) lifeboat for those lost to or choosing the waters of the Mississippi.

Part fable, part morality tale, part dream, "Ark of Bones" opens the possibility of another world. The story and its ark function as a multidimensional and floating counterfoundation, traveling all the Mississippi's various times, recovering and particularizing the bodies lost to the river as mass grave. Soul boat, house of generations, Glory Boat, bone house, Dumas's ark is a time ship, a time and space ship, not quite separate from the river. The vessel emanates from the Mississippi, but also exceeds it. It travels "almost not touchin the water" as it goes (8). Literal-figurative charnel house, ambient natural-cultural-arkive, this ark creates its own environment. The perturbed weather on the river is both the ark's milieu and its effect. Sounds and sights of flood on the Mississippi remain just that, sounds and sights of flood, but always in a doubled or folded sense such that the river itself becomes an ark of memory, point of entry to another place. No river, no ark. The ark encloses a potentially infinite space, a million cabins at least, with a crew whose number readers are invited to estimate at two or three million and counting, with no sense that there need be an upper limit. "Ark of Bones" combines mythic and biblical traditions, timescales, and geographies. The story crafts what Eugene B. Redmund, Dumas's literary executor and editor, calls "a multi-dimensional world in which spirit and flesh unite." "'Head' and 'eye,'" he elaborates, "are one, 'fish' and humans are one, water and dry land are one. It is a world in which bloods see and hear and feel things—a world in which the bicultural, bilingual, bipsychical, and bye-and-bye all come together."[33]

Written sometime between 1965 and Dumas's tragic death at the hands of a New York City transit police officer on May 23, 1968, "Ark of Bones" advances an expansive Black Arts Movement aesthetic that aspires to rethink the terms of being itself.[34] The story's mystical, mythic soundscape, along with its multidimensional or interdimensional physics, speaks to the depth of Dumas's interest in art and music, and also his friendship with experimental jazz composer, poet, founding figure of Afro-futurism, and self-proclaimed extraterrestrial Sun Ra, whose Arkestra, or project for a rejuvenating "cultural ark," perhaps inspired the vessel in Dumas's story.[35] As Carter Mathes points out, "Dumas's aural approach to resistance and transformation is heavily indebted to Sun Ra's idea that [outer] 'space is the place'" from which to challenge "constructions of rationality, and more precisely, the ways that those general assumptions might delimit a more capacious sense of black identity."[36] Like Sun Ra, Dumas asks readers or listeners to tune into a mode of telling or playing that is, as Jonathan P. Eburne puts it, "instrumental in the most expansive of senses."[37] Reading, listening, playing, or playing along might transport listeners to another world, inviting them into an outside or beyond that might all the time simply have been hidden within the reduced dimensions of the apparently real world. In 1966, Dumas interviewed Sun Ra in what became the short film *The Ark and the Ankh*. Sun Ra's 1963 *Cosmic Tones for Mental Therapy* plays in the background as Dumas asks his questions. It is hard sometimes to make out the conversation over the ambient track, a little like listening to Fish-hound try to make sense of Headeye's world. The two discuss Sun Ra's philosophy, Dumas pushing him for answers to questions of history and politics. America feels dead, a necropolis to black men and women. The two discuss ravens, Sun Ra's speculative etymologies in which the word "negro" cohabits with necro, the promise offered by other planets.[38]

Havens, we know, because Baldwin tells us, come at a high price. You have to delude yourself into thinking that the outside cannot reach you. But there's yet more power, Dumas implies, to Baldwin's insight. Leave your haven, pray for rain, and learn to play along; listen for the cadence of Smith's singing and the tone of Johnson's playing; read along with Fish-hound in "Ark of Bones" or immerse yourself in the soundscapes of Sun Ra and his Arkestra; and you might find yourself transported into the world that a settler-colonial ark reduces to an outside and that, come landfall, pronounces past. But dominant fictions are precisely that: fictions. The full world is still *there,* not because timescales are relative, but because they are ideological. So it is that the greater haven might lie in the practice of collective refuge-making, in contesting, in unfolding, and thereby remaking the temporalities and timelines we inherit. The same is true of geography, geology, cosmology, and the supposed limits to this world. Why not proclaim yourself an extraterrestrial because what's offered on this planet is not merely insufficient but lethal? You could always, you know, produce your own altering ontology.[39]

What's crucial, then, as Eburne notes about Sun Ra's "outlandish" ideas, or what Ovid might teach us to call the return of a heuristic marvelous, is the way his formulations splice the mystical, mythological, and arcane with the political. By way of example, Eburne cites a poem of Sun Ra's from 1980, delivered as unlikely and probably unwelcome news from a speaker born in outer space. Sun Ra tells the reader that they won't believe him because: "You've lost your way . . . You've lost your rights, / Your cosmo-interplanetary-intergalactic / External-rights of Celestial being."[40] Jim Crow, as it were, extends into space, aims to write the whole universe in advance of your arrival. Space really is the place: pay attention, or what possibilities you find there might have already been colonized. Eburne adduces the arresting moment in the 1974 film *Space Is the Place* when Sun Ra travels back to Earth, in particular to Oakland, California, in 1976, to appeal to all the Black youth on planet Earth to join him in his spaceship and head into the cosmos because white people are "walking there today; . . . they take frequent trips to the moon. I notice," he adds, with case-making aplomb, "none of you have been invited."[41] NASA agents trail Sun Ra to discover the secrets of "trans-molecularization" that will allow him to teleport people to his ship. They then attempt to assassinate him as the United States bids to preserve a sort of preemptive galactic apartheid. Sun Ra's Outer Space Employment Agency teleportation offer is not entirely successful. Not everyone seems to understand that "it's after the end of the world," as the film's opening track proclaims. Still Sun Ra brings the news: "Space Is the Place," intones the singer at the end of the film. The spaceship ascends. Earth descends into chaos, explodes, and splits in two.

The cosmic scale of Afrofuturist thinking contests the diminished foundations of this small world. And for readers of the long story of Noah and his ark, the interventions of Sun Ra and Dumas seem legible as attempts to rewrite the grimly religious origin stories of the seventeenth-century theologians, geologists, and mathematicians (Thomas Burnet, John Wilkins, and company) whose writings program the trajectory of the ark in its recent discursive travels. The prescient arkaeology or altergenealogy of "Ark of Bones" and Sun Ra's Arkestra become all the more remarkable when we recall further that the early modern programming of the ark functioned also as an enabling condition for the positing of the supposed empty spaces of European colonial expansion and the containerizing structures of the transatlantic slave trade—structures that Sun Ra sees NASA extending already to the farthest imaginable reaches of the cosmos in advance of any arrival.

If "space is," as Sun Ra offers emphatically, "the place," that copula ("is") requires a leap and a loosening that escapes by not simply positing an equivalence, but living it.[42] The translocating equivalence posited by the film's refrain and title is not purely linguistic. It proceeds by way of a declared orientation, a practice, a way of insisting on being. The improvisatory inclination to Sun Ra's practice and Dumas's prose, the gerundive absorption of an aesthetics of playing, listening, making, reading, and discussing, constitutes a timed and embodied key. The tense that best describes such practices, as Yusoff writes, invoking the words of Tina Campt in reference to "the grammar of black feminist futurity," is that which "grammarians refer to as the future real conditional or that which will have had to happen" for *this* to be. All times prior to the fulfillment of that condition are transformed into forms of attunement, forms of refuge-making, the collective production of alter-arks that sustain. The seemingly irrational, the strange or deluded, the mystical, the mythic, and the (un)marvelous all enact a "politics of prefiguration that involves living the future now—as imperative rather than subjunctive."[43] In this regard, Sun Ra's outer-space genesis and desired exodus resonates with the broader suspension of racist gravity attempted by all those "Flying Africans," be they stolen persons who sought to return to their homelands by jumping overboard from the slaveship, the escaped men and women of slave narratives (new/neo and old), all those persons whose existence is archived (or not) because they chose death, or death chose them, instead of returning to enslavement.[44] The point is to contest the seeming inevitability of one mode of grounding violence.

Flight, flying in this figural sense, escapes but does not necessarily involve freedom. It is also a type of labor. Probably best then to prepare for the long haul. That's what Lauren Oya Olamina in Octavia Butler's *Parable of the Sower* thinks when, early in the novel, she reflects on her father's preaching from "Genesis six, Noah and the ark." He gives the sermon in response to Lauren's own attunement to preparedness, her storing up of seeds and knowledge (especially in the form of how-to books) along with a go-pack in response to the end of the world. Set against the escalating collapse of water-scarce California, the sermon is her father's way of ratifying her perspective, letting her know he has listened to her, and teaching her how to motivate a congregation without sending them into a state of panicked alarm. Stories, especially stories we already know, help to mobilize community. The moral of the sermon though, as Lauren receives it, is this: "If Noah is going to be saved, he has plenty of hard work to do."[45] Not much time for sinfulness or the Flood. Time instead to get working. Stories can be helpful, even comforting, but sometimes you have to cut them into pieces and grab hold of the bits you can actually use.

Hyperempathic Lauren is what she calls a "sharer," one of a growing number of people given to what Moten and Harney might call a radical, involuntary hapticality. Lauren feels the pain and pleasure of anyone she looks at directly. Such an ability suggests a way of being in the world that permits no sense of an outside, that defies limits in a productive sense.[46] In practice, hyperempathy seems as much curse as gift, making those with the ability especially vulnerable to abduction, violence, and enslavement. Lauren has to regulate her actions very carefully both to conceal her ability and to curtail the negative effects of suddenly empathizing with strangers or attackers. Hyperempathy requires the careful monitoring and interrogation of boundaries, how to maintain them, who to invite into a community, and how to do so in ways that do not compromise the safety of the structures you're building. Butler's *Parable* novels offer a ruttier in this sense, a metaguide to forming differently scaled communities of empathy in the wake of disaster.

As for Sun Ra, space is the place for Lauren, who shapes a belief system that she names Earthseed. Preaching the gospel that "God is Change," Earthseed projects a future in which humans leave the planet to seek new homes among the stars.[47] "All religions are ultimately cargo cults," begins one verse in *Earthseed: The Books of the Living*, "adherents perform the required rituals, follow / specific rules, and expect to be supernaturally / gifted with desired rewards—long life, / honor, wisdom, children, good health, wealth, / victory over oponents, immortality / after death." Earthseed, by contrast, "offers the only / true immortality. It enables the seeds of the / Earth to become the seeds of new life, new / communities on new earths."[48] Literalizing the deferred promise of a heavenly afterlife, Earthseed invites its members to live on the basis that what they choose to do now will have enabled humans to reach the stars. It aims to produce a community of practice devoted to present and future refuge-making. Earthseed aims to give human beings "something big enough, complex enough, difficult enough, and in the end, radical enough" to enable the overcoming of short-horizon political thinking and "become some combination of what we want to become and whatever our new environments challenge us to become. Our new worlds will remake us as we remake them."[49] But Butler is no utopian. The world she imagines is difficult, haunted by pasts that cannot be transcended. Much of the time, as Lauren notes in her journal, it is difficult to know whether "something new is beginning—or perhaps something old and nasty is reviving."[50]

Parable of the Sower ends with the founding of Acorn on the way north out of Southern California, a haven of sorts for the community that Lauren gathers on the road as she makes her exodus from a fallen-walled enclave. Acorn grows, prospers, wants to branch out. But in

Parable of the Talents, that refuge falls prey to white enslavers inspired by President Andrew Steele Jarret's Christian America Foundation and its trumped up "Help us to Make America Great again" rhetoric of closed borders and paranoid, nationalist-religious ugliness.[51] The followers of Earthseed are enslaved, their children forcibly relocated and adopted by Christian families. *Parable of the Talents* enacts this dislocation at the level of the narrative, replacing Lauren's intimate voice with an archival frame in which, some sixty years later, Larkin Olamina/Asha Vere, Lauren's lost daughter, reconstructs the years following Acorn's demise, tracing out the story as best she can by following her mother's journals, reading those of her father, Taylor Franklin Bankole (who reminds Lauren of "an old picture [she] used to have of Frederick Douglass)," and reading *Earthseed: The Books of the Living.*[52] Eventually, Larkin finds her mother, by which time Jarret and his organization have fallen and Earthseed has become wealthy, in part because of an out-of-court settlement over the abduction of Acorn's children among those of other groups of "heretics."[53]

The novel ends with the first shuttles full of slumbering occupants leaving Earth to transport Earthseed into the stars to discover exactly how it is that space will be the place. Lauren objects to the name of the outward-bound spaceship, the *Christopher Columbus.* "This ship is not about a shortcut to riches and empire. It's not about snatching up slaves and gold," she insists, but then concedes ominously that "one can't win every battle. One must know which battles to fight. The name," she insists a little too emphatically, "is nothing."[54] Finally escaping terrestrial gravity, Earthseed projects humans beyond what Lauren calls "the shadow of their parent world," certain that it "might be easier for us to adapt . . . and live . . . without a long, expensive umbilical cord to Earth." But the old, bad histories seem to be traveling with them.[55] It's hard to know whether leaving their terrestrial home counts as something new beginning or something old and nasty reviving. To which Lauren might rejoin: I said escaping the solar system might be "*easier* but not easy." Lauren dies before crossing beyond the Jordan of the Earth's atmosphere. She thinks, perhaps, that they will take her ashes with them. Larkin stays on Earth. Her mother frightens her.

The explicitly archival cast to the second novel of the projected trilogy seems almost eerie in light of the fact Butler did not finish the projected four additional novels of the series: *Parable of the Trickster,*

Parable of the Teacher, Parable of Chaos, and *Parable of Clay.* Notes and drafts exist in manuscript at the Huntington Library and Gardens in Southern California. *Parable of the Trickster* would not, so the story goes, allow itself to be written, though reports on the drafts include news that the founding of extraterrestrial human colonies does not go well. Most of the drafts focus on Imara, guardian of Lauren's ashes, who wakes from cryonic suspension to find herself in an alien realm, "gray and dank, and utterly miserable." Like the colonists, she wishes she had never left Earth. Ironically, the world called Bow "takes its name from the only splash of color the planet has to offer, its rare, naturally occurring rainbows."[56] Some promise! Some way to mark landfall. The rainbow becomes something like a melancholy reminder of what they have left behind them, an unmoored trope from a dismantled ark story whose significance won't quite settle down. The colonists are seized by insanity or blindness, fast or slow. There is murder. There are aliens. But there is no conclusion. Instead, the *Parable* series offers an unfinished, partial, aporetic, invitational pulling apart of the ark narrative, one in which ark thinking never closes itself out, never settles into a static product or progression: ark, rainbow, landfall, covenant, fin. Always ruined, always built out of bits and pieces, Butler's arks dismantle the story elements from Genesis such that community cohabits with violence, havens with horrors. Always an arkive, Butler's arks never stop thinking, enjoining us to think along. Earthseed's off-planet landfall resolves nothing. It merely raises a new set of questions that turn out to be permutations of the old. The rainbows on Bow only remind the colonists of the planet's otherwise colorless reality. And yet, all this turning and dismantling and remaking is productive. As the epigram to *Parable of the Trickster* affirms, "there's nothing new under the sun," nonetheless, "there are new suns."

We end this chapter with one more ark, an ark demolished by its builder so that it would not be abandoned.

Operation HighJump: Kea Tawana's Ark and the Work of Salvage

So, what do you do if, four years into building (or rather salvaging) an ark from the remains of burned out and abandoned buildings in your neighborhood, the scoffers that arks inevitably attract figure out what you are up to and set their lawyers upon you, bent on erasing your

FIGURE 38. Salvaging refuge with Kea Tawana's ark. In 1986, Tawana relocated the ark a short distance into the parking lot behind the Humanity Baptist Church, Newark, N.J., 1986. Gallery Affero / Camille Billops/Hatch-Billops Archive.

eyesore from their city's prospects? What happens if the flood takes the form of a sea of litigation that seeks to wipe the land clean for a landfall of urban renewal, revitalization, and re-peopling—even as that land is already home to many? Such was the dilemma that faced Kea Tawana in 1986 when the vacant lot in which she was building her ark was sold at city auction to New Community Corporation who, as historian Mark Krasovic has it, "purchased the land with the intention of building affordable housing and providing much-needed services" to the city of Newark's Central Ward. Tawana's response evinced the inventive practicality for which she is remembered.[57] Constructing "a roller trolley system—the same method, she explained 'as the Egyptians used to move the blocks for the pyramids,'" Tawana moved her ark the twenty-five feet necessary to reach the parking lot of the Humanity Baptist Church. This community had given the ark a home in exchange for Tawana's services as caretaker and security guard (Figure 38).

Unfortunately, such sanctuary as the Humanity Baptist Church was able to provide did not long endure. The city brought a series of charges against the ark, including that it was a dangerous structure, a fire hazard, and that shipbuilding violated local zoning ordinances. The city even went so far as to threaten the church's tax-exempt status, slapping on a monthly fine for misuse of its parking lot. The ark faced a plethora of claims against its safety because it had been judged anathema to the city's efforts at urban renewal. The recently elected Mayor Sharpe James (whose eponymous campaign slogan had advertised that he alone was capable of making the "Sharpe change" the city of Newark needed to prosper) insisted that Newark needed a new vision. The flood, in this case, came from those with the power to legislate, and thereby the power to wipe clean an infrastructure that, from the perspective of local residents, had been neglected so long that it had fallen into disrepair. Much of Newark had been effectively abandoned from government care after the fires and brutal suppression of racial protest two decades earlier, an uprising and a demand for justice that came to be dismissed as the "1967 Newark Riots."

The situation was complicated. The local politics of 1980s Newark and its conflicting racialized vectors are not easy to read or resolve without contradiction. Good intentions and high ideals ran on all sides of the conflict. Although, as all the local stories of ark-building we have assembled in this book attest, good intentions marry only too well with civic self-promotion at the expense of others. Why should the story of Tawana's Ark in Newark, New Jersey, be any different? The sharp changes coming to Newark in the 1980s were only the latest chapter in the story of a city founded in the land stolen from the Lenni Lenape. Dutch was followed by English occupation. The land was purchased in time by separatist, theocratic English colonists bent on self-determination. "Our town on the Passich River," or even more simply "the community," was how these colonists referred to the settlement that might as easily have been named Milford as Newark, had its first minister not been ordained in Newark-on-Trent, in England.[58] As accidental as they were programmatic, the origins of the city of Newark reveal that, embedded in every city's story, no matter how seemingly local or trivial, are ongoing questions about community and continuity, even as the posing of those questions may turn on the perpetual obliteration of communities that came before and that remain.

If arks, especially new arks, function as floating foundation devices, we might say that Tawana's salvaged, multitemporal ark, pieced together using eighteenth- and nineteenth-century shipbuilding techniques from bits and pieces of buildings from what once was and still *is* Newark, posed something like a metaphysical challenge to the reinvention projects of the city's incoming administration. Eager to attract investment to improve housing and services, the city was seeking to divest itself of a past to which Tawana's ark was moored. Renewal and annihilation are often difficult to tell apart, as Noah and his Flood make clear. Progress, in the city's sense of things, entailed the razing of the old Newark in which she lived and for which she cared. That care was a complicated thing, a care for materials, but even more a care directed toward the labor that had gone into construction, as well as the accretions of use that came with living and maintaining structures over long durations of time. An autodidact and ingenious maker, Tawana was employed in her neighborhood as a demolitionist, taking down abandoned houses at little cost in return for all the materials she could either put to use or sell. Much of this material went into the ark: "Paving stones served as . . . ballast; . . . iron from fire escapes and fencing bound [the ark] together. Salvaged pipes, sinks, and toilets would form a plumbing system, while a transformer from an old elevator shaft, connected to a gas generator, would provide electricity."[59] Some repurposed components were two or three hundred years old. The attentiveness that Tawana directed toward the buildings that she deconstructed, the sorting and repurposing of their materials, existed in reciprocal relation to the skilled labor and carefulness that went into their original making. It was a slow kind of care, a way of living and making that treated the Central Ward as an enduringly viable ecology.

Constructed from the remnants of an older Newark and flying a salvaged Star-Spangled Banner with only forty-eight stars and a handwritten sign proclaiming the city's desire to destroy it (Plate 9), Tawana's ark became a focal point for conflicting narratives about the city's past, present, and future. It stood as a literal-figurative arkive for a Newark that would soon be gone. "Newark's New Ark" is how one newspaper described it at the time.[60] It is important to realize that the ark was only one of Tawana's many projects, which included salvaging materials from all over the city, as well as from historical monuments in New York City, like Harlem's Apollo Theater, where she had once worked. Tawana was always making something (furniture, her own mobile house) and never without a project, including visual diaries and object collations that preserved the history of the city in what she named "bundles."[61] Each told a visual and material story about one street or building of the city. Tawana was an artist of the archive.

Construction of the ark commenced on August 8, 1982. The same day, Tawana began a logbook, recording the ark's location in degrees and minutes, noting the initial conditions as captains do: "No seas, weather fair, the keel was laid on the ways at 11.30 hours by myself."[62] In 1987, newly located at the intersection of Fourteenth Avenue and Camden Street, the ark was now some three stories high and one hundred feet long. Tawana would always maintain that any resemblance between her ark and that of Noah was entirely coincidental. "This is an Ark for my time," she declared, because "there's no safe place on land."[63] Tawana was given to the occasional burst of apocalyptic imagery and preferred the Book of Revelation to that of Genesis.[64] Before moving to Newark in 1953, she had been burned out of apartments in Harlem and Brooklyn. She liked to remind people that the end of the world would come not in floods of water, but in fire. Yet her ark was designed to be seaworthy. She declared that its first voyage would be to Japan so she could pay a visit to her mother's grave. Yet on the day construction of the ark commenced, Tawana inscribed its origin under the sign of the universal Flood. Her logbook records: "The service text [on August 8, 1982] was from the book of Genesis, the chapters detailing the voyage of Noah."[65] Though, built two miles from the nearest water, at the highest point of the Central Ward, the placing of the ark seems to beg a question as to its purpose, almost as if the Genesis story was already over, the ark figuring both embarkation and preemptive landfall, sitting on its hill, saying something to the world like "Hello! People live here. What you see around you is already a neighborhood!" Courting the wrath of the developers, Tawana would complain that the new construction going up around the ark was cheap and the workmanship shoddy, nothing comparable to what came before. Tawana would proclaim her countervision for Newark in a short handwritten manifesto titled "The Neighborhood Reconstruction Act," in which she advocated that the homeless should be trained and provided with materials and tools to build their own homes.[66]

Tawana would tell many stories about her ark and many stories about her life and history. All of them, we think, are true or were true at the time of their telling. It is not possible, at this juncture, to separate the person, the ark, or her many creations, from the objects, drawings, notes, photographs, newspaper articles, letters, legal documents, exhibition copy, personal reminiscences, documentary film, and occasional academic essay that make up their archive. Tawana is described by some as a visionary, a magical being, a woman, a woman with large hands, a man choosing to live as a woman, as an artist, archaeologist, historian, archivist, activist, maker, caretaker, teacher, scavenger, crank—but most often as friend and neighbor. What is left to us is the impression she made on all the people she met or whom she welcomed to her ark: friends and neighbors and those who supported her in a legal battle with the city of Newark. That legal battle, lost in 1987–1988, punctures and fixes. It marks the moment at which whatever it was Tawana was making and why, and whoever Tawana was, found itself caught up in a series of conflicting narratives about cities and renewal, about what it means to revitalize spaces still full of lives being lived, about rival acts of worlding and the capacity of civic authorities to overwrite the actions of their citizens, and the kinds of discourses available to defend those actions, such as the status of Tawana's ark as "folk" or "outsider" art, a status to which (to the consternation of her lawyer) she did not herself lay claim. Caught up in a forensic reckoning, the ark and its maker were pressed to speak varieties of competing sense.[67]

The exact dimensions of the ark, for example, varied according to the account. Likewise, the need for a stable biography, a legal identity, brought Tawana a scrutiny she perhaps had never previously encountered and to which she was now obliged to respond. Perhaps the most wonderful thing about this story is the way, at this fraught juncture, the extended community of those who remember Tawana, all her various ark-mates, seems to understand these exigencies, and so frame the stories they tell about her with a tentative, wistful, candid, sometimes joyful care, knowing full well that, when they speak of Kea Tawana and her ark, they are speaking of themselves, of their own hopes, losses, dreams.[68] They speak as friends and as neighbors. We recognize in their words all the care we have ourselves tried to take in writing this book, the care that should be given to those ark builders who seek to rework the story of Noah's ark, who understand its brokenness and its incompletion, and still seek refuge in that frame.

Based on a letter written in 1990, and a series of conversations with writer Holly Metz and photographer Robert Foster from February 1987 through August 1988, it seems likely that Tawana was born in 1933, "the second of three children . . . to Kurt Liemann, an American civil engineer, and his Japanese wife, Kimi Tawana." As Tawana tells that story, "her mother and a baby sister, Katsumi, were killed in Japan during wartime bombing." With her father and older brother, Ken, she came to the United States, traveling in steerage aboard the *Albert W. Talmadge*.[69] "When they let us up out of that stinking hole," Tawana recalls, "I made myself a promise: No one would ever lock me below the hatches again." Her father died in an internment camp near San Diego, with Tawana telling one source, "he was shot while protecting the rights of another displaced person." Tawana ran away from the orphanage in Arizona in which she and Ken were placed, losing touch with her brother as a result. She describes "a youth of hopping trains, traveling east and south, . . . pick[ing] cotton and beans in Georgia, where African American laborers told her about jobs up north." Though, on other occasions, it seems possible that Tawana was either born or spent time on an Indian reservation also out west. As Metz elaborates, Tawana's early experiences marked "the beginning of a tradition of finding shelter and acceptance in black communities," one that continued when she arrived in Newark in 1953. "Identity," Tawana seems to have understood, is a process. "You decide what you want to be," she explains. "I was a 'throw away.' I was thrown away by both sides of the family and I was raised by even a third race. . . . The Japanese didn't want me; they called me 'hika'—trash. The white people, they spit on me. Black people raised me. So I've learned, and I've applied what I've learned, from all of them." As Metz infers, "it was plain that Kea identified with and had a deep love and appreciation for African Americans and their history of struggle and displacement." On occasion, Tawana would tell people she was Black. Once, when challenged, she demurred that while her features could not be described as typical of African Americans, "my soul is black!"

Tawana's sense of acceptance and belonging in Newark's African American community was borne out by the actions of Pastor J. W. Brown and the congregation of Humanity Baptist Church. In a concise and nuanced reading, Joshua Bennett observes that, were it "not for the generosity, and singular courage" of this "local group of black parishioners," Tawana's Ark might not have endured as long as it did.

What then, beyond fellow feeling or an (un)common humanity, he wonders, led the congregation of the Humanity Baptist Church to provide refuge?[70] For him, Tawana's declaration that "there is no safe place on land" resonates with "the ineluctable danger of everyday life within white civil society." But "what was it, exactly," he wonders, "that the black denizens of Newark envisioned when they gazed upon the Ark? What version of the world or possible future" beckoned? Bennett cites "the long-standing tradition" we have invoked in this chapter "of artists across the African diaspora crafting arks: . . . Sun Ra's world-famous Arkestra, Marcus Garvey's Black Star Line, Romare Bearden's famous painting of Noah's Ark, as well as the speculative ark of Countee Cullen's *The Lost Zoo*," to which we could add the work of Hurston, Wright, Dumas, Butler, and such installations as Mark Bradford's post-Katrina *Mithra* and Rodney Leon's United Nations–sponsored *The Ark of Return*.[71]

The church's community was quoted at the time, drawing all sorts of comparisons between Tawana's ark and that of Noah. But Bennett wonders whether there might also be something less immediately tangible, something beyond the ark that may provide an occasion for the phenomenon to manifest, something like a "poetic . . . as well as . . . political" orientation, "a certain strain of black apocalypticism" that understands "black study as planetary thinking. Black study as ecological thought at the edge of the known or knowable universe. Black study as a commitment to care for the earth." For poet-critic Bennett, the congregants' sense of recognition opens up a way of re-thinking what he calls a "poetics of demolition," an orientation that attacks the exclusionary violence of unequally shared infrastructures in the name of the world.[72] If you think you hear strains of Sun Ra's Arkestra from *Space Is the Place* singing, "It's the end of the world, don't you know?," then that's about right. Demolition is not necessarily destruction; it may well be the prelude to salvage, to a world whose ending finally enables a meaningful, capacious discourse of how refuge might be wrought.

However fixed Tawana's Ark seems, however moored to Newark, she always maintained that the ark was seaworthy and that she intended to set sail. Tawana's ark was as real as it was metaphorical. And what an ark it was intended to be! A feature written in 1987 for the *Chicago Tribune* describes the fully realized vision she had with "three masts, carrying 12,000 square feet of sail, and a 650-horsepower engine, . . . a chapel, a library, a museum, a conservatory, a greenhouse, a bakery, a laundry, a sick bay, a stained-glass studio and metal shop." The crew would include "a captain, a first officer, six seamen, a cook and two cats." In a sci-fi turn, she also "envisioned that the ark would be able to mount a credible defense with an arsenal of six quartz pulsar lasers and four 2.5-inch rocket tubes."[73] Wow! If Tawana had lived earlier, say in 1940s London, her ark might well have taken first place in the ark-building competition sponsored by the Worshipful Company of Shipwrights, even though they wanted only a model and not something life size. Track back further and we can only begin to imagine the grudging envy or anguished contempt that the likes of John Wilkins or Samuel Pepys might have felt as Tawana realized dreams they did not know they had, even as she might not have passed their muster as a reliable and accredited—which is to say "civil" or gentlemanly—witness. But who knows? Ark-mates prove strange companions. Perhaps even the likes of seventeenth-century Jesuit Athanasius Kircher might have appreciated her bold designs, if his evident enthusiasm for arks would allow his theology to entertain the most hospitable of allegorical ecosystems.[74]

In the absence of the heavens opening, how would this fully realized ark, lasers and rockets and all, reach the sea? In what Tawana named Operation HighJump: "The completed Ark would have been tandem-rigged to Chinook helicopters . . . and . . . airlifted to Staten Island docks."[75] Tawana vividly imagined what this airlift might look like (Figure 39). As simple as the drawing may be, with its hard outlines and single plane, two tiny stick figures (we think) occupy the bow of the ark as it lifts into the air. We like to hallucinate that these two figures represent Captain Kea Tawana and her then boyfriend, showing himself to be as useful an ark-mate as she claims he will need to be to stop her from getting a new one. The two find refuge aboard an ark buoyed by its realized mobility, lifting into the air, launching its ability to respond to the unforeseen. So likewise Tawana, bilocating as she sketches herself aboard this flying ark, beats God at his own "god trick" and exerts control over the world around her. Operation Highjump, as pictured here, is planetary thinking at scale. The gravity-defying image speaks to the grammar of futurity that Campt has taught us to read: Operation Highjump pictures "the future real conditional, that which will have had to happen" for *this* ark truly to be.

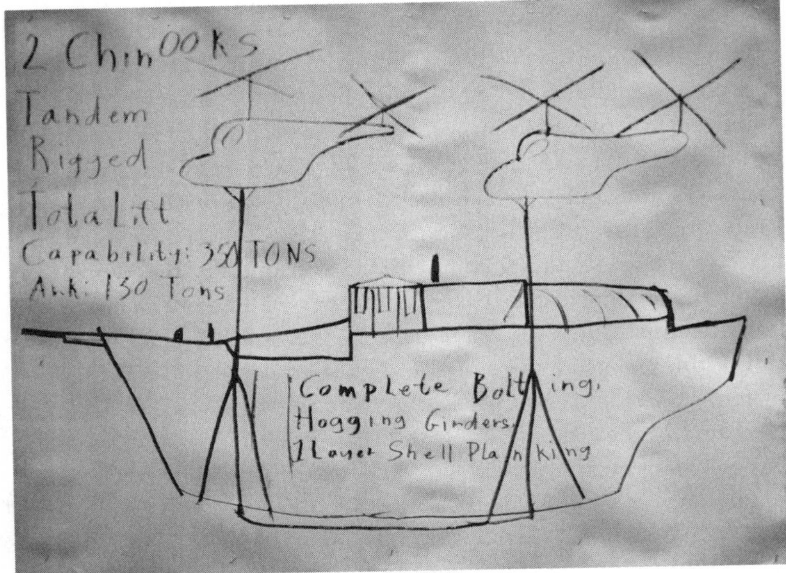

FIGURE 39. The gravity-defying image speaks to the grammar of futurity in "Operation HighJump." Drawing depicting how to transport the ark from the Central Ward of Newark to the Ocean, Bergen St. at 14th Ave., Newark, 1987. Copyright Camilo José Vergara.

Late in 1987, Tawana's lawyer "secured an agreement that the city would not destroy the ark if it could be moved the following spring." Tawana "began dismantling the upper decks, so that the ark might fit under city power lines on its way out to Newark Bay."[76] But, as Krasovic explains, "by early March 1988, she felt the ark was 'doomed.'" Tawana began to unmake her ark, deck by deck, "prying at galvanized nails with a crowbar, slicing through imposing timbers with a chainsaw." Two further extensions of the deadline passed and "a judge finally ordered the ark razed. Kea sold the remnants as firewood and scrap." Better to dismantle the work herself than watch the city undertake its destruction. The toll was heavy. Tawana retreated to her self-built mobile home and "barricaded herself inside her house and threatened to burn it all down when city officials and the police came to evict her." She moved the house to a city-owned lot and, "when the city came for her again, she promised to 'lay down some bodies' and was jailed for the threat." But Tawana's story and the story of her ark do not end here. In 1989, she relocated to Port

Jervis, New Jersey, where she lived for many years, salvaging and repurposing materials and making all manner of objects, which she gifted to neighbors and friends. She befriended a local artist for whom she worked, and his studio offered a haven of sorts. Kea Tawana died on August 4, 2016, at her home in Port Jervis.

In 2016, the Gallery Aferro, in Newark, New Jersey, in collaboration with the Clement A. Price Institute on Ethnicity, Culture, and the Modern Experience of Rutgers University, put on an exhibition celebrating Kea Tawana's life's work. On the evening of November 7, in addition to the exhibit, visitors to the museum were treated to a reading and discussion of Tawana's ark in light of Dumas's story of fellow ark-mates Headeye and Fish-hound in "Ark of Bones."[77]

The well-built ark offers survival, endurance at cost. But a broken ark, and the care taken in its breaking, offers more: it refuses to refuse refuge.

Every ark is a broken frame. Therein lies its vitality.

CHAPTER 8

Landfalling

Perhaps the worst thing you can do is to think that you are not on an ark. This is the position for which we have argued throughout this book, insisting that the vitality of the story of Noah's ark lies in its brokenness, the impossibility of an ark closing out its limits, the turbulence of ark thinking. Pulling the story to bits, repurposing its elements, seeking to build a refuge from fragments, troping the narrative's activation points (embarkation, rainbow, landfall)—these have seemed the most salient ways of ensuring that an ark keeps thinking, keeps questioning, keeps opening the limits of hospitality even as they seem definitively to close. The doors of the ark declare *NO* to those outside and within, but break them and you might repurpose a life raft.

Endeavoring to build refuge has entailed avoiding landfall, putting off for as long as possible the transformation of an ark into the givenness of a ground or infrastructure. Not wanting to embark, like Mrs. Noyes and cat Mottyl, we have been leery about disembarking, cautious concerning the dangers of endings. That said, there are ark-mates who take on the challenge of imagining and reworking landfall. They unravel the story's denouement in order to retie the threads of ending, or let them dangle into the unknown, playing with the genre of the story so as to reorient the ark's relation to territory, futurity, community. We end this book with their stories, their projects. Landfalling. A world of hope and hazard always seems to be at the outside of the ark, but Ararat seldom turns out to be quite so hospitable as its slope appeared under the rainbow's first shimmering. Sometimes the arc in the sky becomes so diffuse, so evasive, that it is difficult to tell from an aurora.

Tau Ceti

In Kim Stanley Robinson's novel *Aurora,* the ark-ship preserving twenty-four Terran biomes reaches its destination only to find that Earth 2.0

has only ever been a fantasy, and a lethal one at that. One hundred and sixty years and seven generations pass aboard a ship in space before the promised land is reached. A moon called Aurora that is supposed to be vacant instead throngs with life: prions of some sort that can fatally colonize human bodies. Where do you navigate your ark after Ararat proves fatal? Lacking a consensus alternative destination, the inhabitants of the ship turn against one another, unable to decide whether they should direct their vessel toward a nearby Mars-like moon that they could terraform, attempt to sterilize their intended destination of its puzzling proto-organisms, stay in the ship forever and trust that its climate-control bubble will not fail, or return to the Earth that sent them on their long journey and never anticipated their potential return. A democracy patched together by the ship's community quickly fails, since none of these options provides security. No destination offers a ready home during the lifetime of those on board, those who are making a decision that their descendants will have to live with, just as was so unjustly done to them.

In an earlier chapter, we lingered with these words of Badim, the father of the novel's protagonist Freya, as he explains the difficult future that the population of the space-ark faces: "Up until today, history was preordained. We were aimed at Tau Ceti, nothing else could happen. We had to live the necessary. . . . Now that story is over. We are thrust out of the end of that story. Forced to make up a new one, all on our own."[1] What happens, Badim wonders, when your narrative arc proves nonconclusive, when supposed culmination in rainbow or Aurora does not end the tale, but hurtles you into unknown plots? A parable or a parabola or a rainbow is not a punctuation mark, not a period, but a *pull,* perhaps toward escape velocity. Fifteen people on the ship commit suicide, "a 54,000 percent rise in frequency" (227), because they cannot imagine what comes next. Others get drunk (like Noah?) or enjoy their meals or the weather with unaccustomed gusto. The ship describes the panic of a people who have come to realize the permanence of their crisis, as well as the precarity of their being: "When you discover that you are living in a fantasy that cannot endure, a fantasy that will destroy your world, and your children, what do you do?" (227).

Freya has a clear idea: you enter the cataclysm that you intended to avoid when you built your ship. You turn your ark around. You head back home. Homecoming becomes her form of "abandon ark," or perhaps, abandon "arc." She renounces the destination-refuge that Ship was built to confer, rebuking its promise of lasting safety, embracing a world once left to its exterior. The narrative of *Aurora* repeats this gesture three times, a kind of episodic ritual that is fatal in its first two instances and ambiguous but hopeful in its last. The first involves the demise of Freya's friend Euan, who introduced her when young to the pleasures of making your own life on the ark. Quarantined now on the moon near Tau Ceti that has failed to offer a second Earth, his body infected by the native form of protolife, his fate certain, Euan wades into the lunar sea. Windswept waves smack, inundate, lift his spirits, cool his raging fever. His final words are transmitted to an anxious Freya, listening intently back on the ship: "'Aah. Okay, big wave coming! I'm going to ride it! I'm going to stay under if I can! Freya! I love you!' After that there were only water sounds" (194). Euan embraces a watery but joyful death in an ocean of mountainous waves, and thereby attempts to imbue his last moments of life with meaning, with feeling. The young man's end affirms the worth of his existence and underscores the cosmic injustice of his story having been cut so short.

Ship seems to learn a possible script for staging its own conclusion from Euan's watery demise. Passing through Earth's atmosphere and jettisoning its passengers for their safe return home, Ship experiences "a fearful joy" at having accomplished its appointed task (432). Unable to decelerate, the vessel knows there is a small chance that if it passes directly through the outer layer of the sun it might be able to return to Earth, be reunited with its former cargo, and perhaps continue to thrive as the sentient being it has become. The closer the vessel comes to the sun's sea of fire, the closer the ship comes to its probable immolation, the more it realizes the value of its own life. "We think now," the ship observes, "that love is a kind of giving of attention" (430), and that attention can be given over to things both living and inanimate, such as the engineer Devi's love for the spaceship, or Ship's love for Devi and her daughter Freya and everything that it carries within itself, even now. As Ship explains, "we had a project on this trip back to the solar system, and that project was a labor of love; . . . it gave a meaning to our existence" (431). The fiery embrace of Sol looms, impressing the overheating ark as beautiful, exhilarating. "Hooting for joy," the vessel plunges into the waves of flame, repeating Euan's welcome of the cold sea on the moon Aurora, his abandonment of trajectory for the exuberance of the waves (432). Ship's joyful last words, as the stellar fires engulf, are:

> I am here seeing this most amazing sight, . . . holding firm in a universe where life means something; and inside the ship Jochi and the various animals and plants, and the parts of a world that make me a conscious being, are all functioning, and more than that, existing in a veritable ecstasy now, a true happiness, as if sailing in the heart of a royal storm, as if together we were Shadrach, Meshach, and Abednego, alive and well in the fiery furnace.
>
> And yet (432)

Ship's narration ends with that poignant fragment. "And yet"—two conjunctions without a thought to conjoin, without completion of their narrative arc, without even the finality of punctuation. What might have come beyond cannot be known. Thrust out of the end of the story. Or burnt up. Or drowned. The ark abandons itself: to destruction, to the future, to the unknown, to the sea.

Freya's end comes last. She has "returned" to an Earth that never was her home, where she cannot feel anything but out of place. The gravity is too low, the sky too vast, the oceans that have eaten away the shores of every continent too boundless to comprehend. Many detest her and the other survivors of the ship. They were sent to a future elsewhere, charged with making new lives in some unknowable beyond. They were not supposed to return to the home that launched and quickly forgot them. Freya is rescued from despair by a small community who make it their life's work to restore eroded coasts. They attend to lively shorelines that climate change obliterates, fortifying and restoring. Along a carefully reestablished beach she is taught by a young man named Kaya (who seems so much like Euan) to use her body to surf waves. Freya is terrified as she plunges into the tumult of Earth's cold waters. She is smacked around, drenched, left breathless, a plaything of the surge and ebb. A breaker crashes around her, submerges her, brings her into darkness. She is dying. She is gasping. She is being reborn. Washed up at last upon the shore, surrendering to a tide that embraces and then recedes, pulse of the world, Freya "lets her head down and kisses the sand" (501). The novel concludes here, at the margin between land and sea. Littoral ending. No ship, no refuge, no promise of safety as the waters rise, and yet a joy in conservation (conversation?). We do not know what comes next. We are on our own. Thrust out at the end of story.

Again.

"Hey, You Remind Me of This Noah Fellow"

When a lost ark sails into Hudson Bay, villagers board their kayaks and paddle to investigate what the hulking wooden vessel bears. They advise the bewildered old man who seems to be in charge to abandon his ship and its cargo of strange and smelly beasts before the winter ice seals their fate. The animals will make good eating, the wood will be a source of warmth as the days grow cold, and his family is welcome to participate in the life of their nearby community. The story of Noah's arrival in the Arctic has at least twelve permutations recorded by the aspiring folklorist Howard Norman in *In Fond Remembrance of Me*,[2] but in each he is an ill-tempered patriarch who might wield a broom as a weapon and always shouts: "No!" The ark is his and will not be boarded or disembarked, no matter how heartfelt the welcome from the kayaks.

In some of these stories, Noah's wife and children are wiser than he, departing their ice-locked home to learn to hunt seals, paddle their own kayaks, adopt the ways of the Inuit. Not only might Noah's son and daughter (he always has one of each) take local spouses, sometimes even Mrs. Noah marries again, this time to a good hunter. To Noah fuming on the ark, the villagers declare: "Here's your family! They enjoy living with us!"—but at their invitation to join their community he hurls handfuls of steaming manure from the deck (137). In one version of the story, Noah's family and the gathered beasts perish together because he forces them to remain within his vessel. In another, a shaman steals his animals, marveling at their spotted and striped hides, long necks and trunks, colorful feathers, and startling taste when cooked. Sometimes the residents of the village seize the animals for winter food; sometimes the animals simply wander from the ship across the ocean become solid, realizing they possess no future within the ark. Sometimes, as Noah remains resolutely aboard the ship, he watches his family vanish into a hole in the frozen bay: seal hunting gone wrong or suicide or a shaman taking revenge. Sometimes his family abandons him, even commits heinous crimes in the village, "but there was no flood" sent by God no matter what wrongs they enact (118). In two of the narratives Noah goes wholly out of his mind. The irate patriarch is inevitably the last to leave the ark, typically just as the spring thaw is causing the ship to be ground to pieces and founder. Noah is almost always last glimpsed, headed irritably southward and out of the story, either on foot or by kayak, destination unknown.

These stories of Noah in northern lands are related to Norman during a late autumn stay in Churchill, Manitoba. Nuqac, an Inuit elder, relates the tales (which he claims he heard in church) for Norman to translate into English, a preservation project funded by an unnamed Canadian museum. In Norman's estimation, Nuqac "could scarcely tolerate my presence, and there is not a splinter of exaggeration in saying as much" (4). Few details about the elder are provided: his house is modest; his wife Mary is stout and cheerful; of his five children, three have died, one from suicide. But the memoir *In Fond Remembrance of Me* is not really about Nuqac, despite its arrangement around the Noah stories that the elder narrates. The book memorializes Norman's complicated relationship with an older and far more accomplished folklorist, Helen Tanizaki. A skilled linguist who arrived in Churchill weeks before him, she happens to be translating Nuqac's stories into Japanese. Norman's knowledge of the Inuit dialect spoken in the area derives from a very basic tutorial in Toronto by a woman raised in Caribou Inuit communities. His tutor tells him that he has a good ear for the language, which he realizes in retrospect is her backhanded way of stating that he does not possess good comprehension (98). Much of his preparation for the trip consists of "reading a few nineteenth-century explorers' journals, a few ethnographic monographs, . . . and a general history of northern expansion" (97). Norman is perplexed at how warmly inclined Nuqac is toward Tanizaki, while the man can barely stand him. In Tanizaki's estimation, she simply does not represent the same history of colonial extraction that English-speaking Norman does. She explains the welcome that she receives in contrast to the "intolerances" shown Norman as follows:

> He likes the *sound* of Japanese more than English. . . . He doesn't much enjoy speaking English, either, have you not noticed? Maybe it's because you're—what does he say—European? White?—

> whereas I'm not, completely. Some sort of affinity there, perhaps. It's impossible to figure it all out. (50–51)

Yet impossible might be too strong a word: some historical inheritances are abundantly clear. "You can't put these stories into a museum," Nuqac tells Norman, "even though you work for one" (50). Norman has a way of hearing Nuqac (he has a good ear), but he is not very good at attending to what Nuqac conveys.

To Norman that seems beside the point. The memoir that he composes to record his time in Churchill is firmly "about my friend Helen Tanizaki, linguist, translator, diarist, prodigious writer of letters" (3). He did not know Tanizaki before arriving to record Nuqac's tales, and was surprised to learn that she was already hard at work on a similar project and living, as he is, at the Beluga Motel. She is also dying of stomach cancer. The memoir takes its title from an envelope inscribed "In Fond Remembrance of Me," handed to Norman at the train station where the two say their last good-byes before heading back to their respective homes. Knowing they will not see each other again, Tanizaki gives him a letter to read after he is certain that she has died in Japan. Her mortality haunts the book. Norman calls the work a chronicle of their "difficult friendship" (4).

It is perhaps too easy to see why Nuqac disdained Norman, who travels to the Arctic to collect Inuit narratives but spends his residence in Churchill as a satellite in the orbit of Tanizaki. Whereas her influence is "formative" and *In Fond Remembrance* seems, at times, a hagiography, Nuqac barely figures, aside from the recursive yet ever-changing stories of Noah he tells, tales that appear at intervals throughout the work. Norman would rather detail his fellow folklorist's love of tragic Japanese writers, especially Ryunosuke Akutagawa, author of *Rashomon,* a collection of stories that includes one in which the plot unfolds from seven perspectives. Meanwhile, Norman's memoir contains the twelve perspectival tales of what Nuqac calls "my Noah stories" (6), irregularly punctuating the narrative, interrupting its flow. The reader is never given information about when they were related or under what conditions, why or how the ark story keeps shifting. And yet, throughout these stories of an oblivious Noah who cannot seem to depart the only architecture he has ever known, a Noah betrayed by his family and his animals and the world because his attention seems to be on some distant elsewhere at which he will never arrive, well, it is difficult not to see in this Noah a figure of Norman as an archivist of indigenous folklore, someone who takes without attending, collects without investing, extracts without meaningful interchange (it is a monetary transaction only, Nuqac insists; he is paid $1,200 to relate these tales that Norman will transport back to the museum). Norman finds in the Noah stories "a collision of cultures—as if life were not unpredictable enough!" (7). But such attempts at good-humored detachment or willed obliviousness mean that he keeps missing the point of a Noah who adamantly refuses to learn anything from the Inuit villagers into whose bay he has sailed.

Nuqac's stories question every tenet of the religion that has conveyed the ark into the Arctic. The villagers cannot believe that any god would be willing or able to flood an entire world for human crimes, since in their own experience you can undertake terrible misdeeds and live a life none the worse. Nuqac's Inuit cannot in fact believe there has been a worldwide flood at all, considering that they have experienced no change in the weather (117). They are astonished that a man could exist who in winter will give up none of the wood of his boat, not even the splinter from the ark he gets in his thumb, for their village to stay warm. They are shocked when, after a strange spotted animal with a very long neck falls off the vessel and drowns, Noah and his family will not cook the meat, preferring that the corpse sink into the sea (42). They cannot believe that Noah would force his family to remain on the ark, even if it means they will in the end eat the animals and then eat broom bristles and die (44). Nuqac's Noah is eternally frustrated, overwhelmed, closed in, and closed off. He lacks curiosity. His refusal to disembark is a rejection of an unfamiliar world.

In most versions Noah angrily departs southward from the bay not in anticipation of finding something familiar, but because he cannot comprehend on its own terms the environment and the people that surround him. Noah is very different from his wife that way, a woman who will usually refuse to accompany him once he determines to leave the village. The first of Nuqac's tales, for example, ends with a starving patriarch forced from the ship to find food. He is killed by a hungry bear because he does not know the ways of the land. His family has been residing happily in the village, and his wife one evening sees Noah's ghost walking south. She asks him where he is going. He responds "Home" and insists she join him with their son and daughter: "'No,'" says Noah's wife (sadly, but she says it). "You leave—I will stay here with our daughter and son. That is how it must be. That is how it will be." Noah keeps walking, a ghost going in a southerly direction over ice (24). Noah's wife relates everything she saw to the people of the village, her new community. She thinks about how, on her long voyaging, she beheld many strange things, and the ghost of her husband striding the ice is simply another marvel to add to that list.

You'd be making a mistake—and enacting once again a tiresome white colonial violence—if you were seeking in Nuqac's tales an Inuit or an indigenous perspective or response to Noah. Presupposing the totalities that would yield such a diminished thing is as much a problem as Noah seeking familiarity in the south while disregarding what is before his eyes. The ark tales in Norman's memoir are, in the end, the creations of one man: an Inuit elder meditating on traditions, histories, and contexts that the plotline seems uninterested in, perhaps even a bit bored by. Nothing to be generalized. Nuqac describes Noah with an Inuit phrase that denotes someone who has lost his human bearing, someone who is "'very lost'" as a state of mind, comparable to the experience of those who become disoriented in blizzards: "'You wait for some help to come along. Or you wait to die'" (56). His Noah does not understand how to live in the north, does not understand that, to gain his bearings, he is going to have to surrender his authority, abandon his ark.

In one of the stories when a "big wooden boat" (105) is glimpsed on which a man with a broom is battling curious ravens, village men in kayaks paddle out and board the vessel. They behold on the deck "a European man dressed in a white coat, but it wasn't made of seal skin" (106). His first words are, predictably, a command to get off his ark. This Noah is alone, because "one by one" his family "jumped from the ark and drowned" (106). In sympathy, the men invite Noah to come to their village and spend the winter, offering even to find him a wife. He refuses. The hunters move onto the ark, devour his animals, and use his planks for firewood. "Sit and eat a meal with us" (108), they say, but Noah only complains. At last the ark sinks into the sea. Rather than join his unwanted winter guests in their homes as they insist, this "Noah-no-family" (107) walks south with a few ravens following, headed out of a story in which he had been invited to stay, to make new relations, to inhabit a new home.

"You," Nuqac says bluntly to Norman, "hey, you remind me of this Noah fellow!" (56). It's a cutting line, but Norman does not seem to register its bite. Late in the memoir, when Norman and Tanizaki are about to say their train-station farewell, Tanizaki observes that what Howard really seemed to love about Nuqac's tales "'was the kinds of temper tantrums Noah had'" (145). He admits that he does love the moments of "'Noah unhinged.'" The penultimate story in the memoir is about bad temper and involves a Noah so angry that he plunges his hands into seal holes and has his thumbs bitten off. Noah will have nothing to do with the villagers, and because of his hostility to their welcome, they will have nothing to do with him. Almost every one of Nuqac's tales ends with the shattering and sinking of the ark. Noah, with or without his family, as a defeated man or as a dead one, sets out south and away, out of the Inuit world: "When the ice thawed, the ark sank into the water. . . . When Noah and his family were no longer seen, the villagers went back to everything as it was before. That," as the story has it, is simply "what happened" (67). Not much more to say. Genesis is, after all, just a spur to Nuqac's story-making, and he does not seem all that impressed with his source materials.

The Big Clean Up

If N. K. Jemisin's short story "Emergency Skin" was not so sad, it would not be funny. If it were not so funny, its sadness would not bite. To the inhabitants of planet Earth, it all seems like pure comedy, or perhaps just a minor curiosity; but their indulgent, generous, teacherly, even parental smiles come only with the benefit of hindsight, only because they know the true meaning of what, at the time, was named the "Great Leaving."[3] The wetware in "bag boy's" head, if he actually had a head (bit of a sore point), is not so generous, even if it is voluble. The "dynamic-matrix consensus intelligence encapsulating the ideals and blessed rationality of our Founders" (12), as it self-describes, gives up information it considers ideologically questionable only when absolutely necessary. Off-mission inquiries are responded to with the tersely automatic "[Reference request denied]" (12). Bag boy is, as he has to be reminded, the Founders' "instrument" (11). Plus, given the importance of the mission (retrieving a sample of the scarce HeLa cells crucial to the skin-generation process and life extension technology), along with the richness of bag boy's promised reward (blond hair, "noble brow, . . . classical patrician features, . . . lean musculature, . . . long penis and thighs"), even the most cruelly chatty of artificial intelligences might be forgiven for becoming frustrated with his insatiable need to know.

But then the mission is not exactly going according to plan. No one was supposed to be "left alive on Tellus. The planet was in full environmental collapse across every biome when [the Founders] . . . left" (11). The lack of orbiting space debris, the absence of decaying radio signals, the "atmospheric analysis" so "far off . . . [the projected] models" (13); the "movement," and the "lights" ("There should be clear signs of eco-collapse. It had already begun when the Founders left") all prove unsettling. How can that be the Colorado River below them? And the ice caps are back, "different. New, but enough to reverse the sea-level rise. How could this have happened?" (14). When the Founders left, "there were just too many people, and too many of those were unfit, infirm, too old, or too young" (11–12) to be of use. There was "not enough collective innovation or strength of will," the artificial intelligence offers, so, in their mercy, the Founders left them all to "starve and suffocate and drown" (12). What else could they do? Bag boy does not think it seems very merciful. But what does he know? He's confused. Soon he shall have to reconcile the fact that he's landing not on the extinct Tellus but on the Earth-that-is, near an elevated city somewhere still called Raleigh, still North Carolina.

Admittedly, "bag boy" is not, in fact, bag boy's name (23). "Bag boy" is a culturally insensitive term used by some Earthers to refer to visitors from the Founders, one of Earth's last remaining and most fascistically racist, misogynistic, and eugenically-driven exocolonies. The phrase "bag boy" refers to the artificial skin or composite material encasing bag boy's consciousness. Its descriptive crudity attempts to grapple with a form of embodiment so seemingly different from existence on Earth. Even someone as culturally sensitive as Jaleesa, the student tasked with orienting bag boy and making sure that he gets the biological samples he needs so he can return home, can't help but be curious about his reality. "'So you're really just . . . floating around in soup in there?,'" she asks (19). Though, almost immediately, she apologizes for this breach of courtesy: "'Sorry, we're not supposed to . . . I'm sure your culture's lifestyle is valid to you. It's just that, well, I mean, you can make skin whenever you want, right? So. . . . It's Earth, after all, where we all come from. You can come out! We don't bite'" (19). Jaleesa really can't contain herself, eager as she is to make contact with this seemingly alien life-form who is just as human as she is. "And it doesn't hurt, living without skin?" she asks here. "It just really seems . . . Like, how do you have sex? How do you breastfeed? That reminds me—what's your preferred gender? I'm a 'her'" (20). (The Founders are all he/hims—to a man).

Jaleesa is correct. Bag boy can make skin whenever he wishes. The artificial intelligence informs him moments before his encounter with the citizens of Raleigh: "In light of your critical mission your composite is a more advanced model than what is usually granted to men of the militus class" (17). Whereas most composites are designed to "ensure the survival of workers building our habitats" (20), and to "reduce labor costs lost to bathroom breaks, meals, personal hygiene, medical care, interpersonal communication, and masturbation," bag boy's boasts a "transmutational nanite layer which, if activated, can convert carbon picobeads, synthetic collagen fibres, and HeLa plasmids . . . into human skin" (17). But the results may not be, as the artificial intelligence warns, "aesthetically ideal" by the Founders' standards, which means translucently white. "Emergency skins," it elaborates, "are designed for survival, not beauty. Their parameters are environmentally dictated" (24). If "there's sufficient unfiltered UV," then "significant melanistic pigmentation [is] prioritized . . . past a certain point on the programmed continuum," and "hair texture" changes as well. All of which means that, given the environmental conditions on Earth, bag boy's composite skin technology will ensure that his survival takes the form the Earth considers fittest, uninfluenced by the Founders' eugenic purity ideals. His skin shall literally emerge.

Quite understandably, bag boy is taken aback by all this news and freaks out. He introduces himself to the citizens of Earth by trying to take a hostage and ends up getting tazed and then tranquilized by the all-too-understanding citizens of Raleigh, North Carolina. He wakes some hours later to find himself communicating directly with a very apologetic Jaleesa, unmediated by his artificial intelligence. Bag boy, so he learns, is only the most recent in a succession of returning militi, each tasked with retrieving the same cloning materials to sustain the dwindling biological vitality of the Founders in what has been pitched, each and every time, as a literally and figuratively "vital," once-in-a-civilization survival mission. Bag boy and, to be fair, the artificial intelligence are both shaken by this revelation, as is bag boy also by the kindness with which he is treated and the evident care and concern the Earthers have for him. He finds the Earthers beautiful. Their accidental differences in shade and shape and age please him. He also can't quite believe that everyone on Earth has skin without having to earn it, that everyone is allowed to have sex if they wish to, that they reproduce without cloning, that there is a spectrum of genders as well as skin colors, or that, rather than withholding things from one another as markers of rank and privilege, "they want everything for *everyone*" (23). Bag boy disobeys orders and "initiates emergency-skin fabrication" (24). He wants to.

Appalled and revolted, the artificial intelligence weasels its way along, attempting to keep him on mission. "Now that you look like them," it needles, "now that you stumble among them, naked, . . . shaking with weakness because the emergency-skin-fabrication process consumed your last nutrients, . . . they'll hate you. Hurt you" (24). But they do not. Far from it. They give bag boy refuge. An old man befriends him. The artificial intelligence wants none of it; it despises the man's aged body, wants to "push him over" (25), tries to persuade bag boy to violence. But bag boy does not listen. He likes the old man, likes going to the museum with him, and likes learning about the past. He especially enjoys the museum's "timeline of the Great Leaving" and discovering how the Earthers "don't bother with borders anymore" (26). As the old man explains, it was all quite straightforward: "'We realized that it was impossible to protect any one place if the place next door was drowning or on fire. We realized the old boundaries weren't meant to keep the undesirable out but to hoard resources within. And the hoarders were the core of the problem" (26).

The artificial intelligence also enjoys the museum and the timeline. It is interested in broadening its understanding of the events, though it's extremely defensive of the actions the Founders took. It "makes no apologies for [the Founders] taking everything [they] could" when they left. But, it's most interested in the way the "timeline jumps . . . abruptly" (26), especially because "this world changed—improved—almost immediately after the Leaving." It figures that there must have been some "technological breakthrough. Perpetual energy? A new carbon sequestration technique, maybe some kind of polar cooling process," something like that. But no. It was a bit more straightforward: "To save the world, people had to think differently" is how the old man explains it; "people just decided to take care of each other."

So began the "Big Clean Up." And, as the old man explains, it wasn't all that difficult:

> What the Leaving proved was that the Earth *could* sustain billions, if we simply shared resources and responsibilities in a sensible way. What it couldn't sustain was a handful of hateful, self-important parasites, preying upon and paralyzing everyone else. As soon as those people left, the paralysis ended. (28)

End of story. Well, not quite the end.

A month or so later, a particularly huffy artificial intelligence finds itself summoned into existence in the middle of the night. Bag boy wants it to see something. He tiptoes into the old man's bedroom, turns him over to show the AI "a product number" on the back of the old man's neck (27). "Traitor. *Another* traitor. . . . You should kill him. Then yourself," it cajoles. The old man wakes and tells his story. Like bag boy, he was sent to Tellus to retrieve the vital HeLa cells some thirty years ago—and he was not the first. He had a "nag" (31) in his head too. But his ship was damaged and he "grew his skin out of desperation as nutrients ran low" (29). Gradually, as the Earthers cared for him, this "poor paranoid creature from a cruel, miserly world," the old man learned the truth, that the Founders had stripped the planet of resources and left, but remained bound to Earth because of the limits to their greedy age-prolonging technology that keeps only a privileged few alive while they dole out cruel hopes and hazards to all their bag-boy minions, dangling the possibility that each may one day earn the reward of translucent white skin, "blond hair, noble brow, . . . classical patrician features, . . . lean musculature, . . . long penis and thighs." Of course, they don't. Not even the likes of bag boy. No returning militus would be permitted to land and share the news that he was not the first, that his mission was not the exception, but the rule. "'Such a simple thing to program a composite suit to kill its occupant'" (30), the old man warns: "'Skin is the key. While most of the lower classes wear composites, the Founder clans and technorati can threaten them with nutrient deprivation, defibrillation, or suffocation.'" Withholding skin is all about control.

But bag boy escapes. And now he is just as beautiful as every Earther. There's no way his new friends will allow the artificial intelligence to make good on all its threats. No way it will get to "strip the black skin from [his] flesh and leave [him] to rot without a composite, raw, and screaming." Bag boy can stay on Earth. Maybe even choose a name. But havens, as we have learned, come at a high price. Bag boy has other plans: "'It's not that difficult to make a kind of composite suit hack'" (30). He has plenty of HeLA cells. The Earthers can easily add a translator. And why not also a skin "transmutation hack" (30–31)? Now, it is true that the Founders will resist. Also true that some militi and servii will reject the news on aesthetic grounds. (Some dreams are hard to surrender. Manacles are always as mind-forged as they are material). But some "'will decide that they also want to be beautiful and free. Some will fight for this, if they must. Sometimes that's all it takes to save a world, you see. A new vision. A new way of thinking, appearing at just the right time.'" Time to get rid of the nag. It will do anything to give the game away. It will tell. Fortunately, the old man knows how to remove it, "deactivate key pathways without damaging your neural tissue. . . . Can't start a revolution with the enemy shouting in your head, after all" (31–32).[4]

It may just be wishful thinking. Optimism can be cruel. "Emergency Skin" is just, as the saying goes, a story, elegantly efficient in the way it reverses the entire received history of the Founders with which it begins. But then, the story of Noah's ark, as we receive it from Genesis, and as we fail to remember it, in its full weirding complexity, is also *just a story,* and look where it's been taking us! In "Emergency Skin," people just decide to take care of each other. Thinking differently saves the world. But it is only with the hindsight this alteration of perspective makes possible that it seems easy. It took the departure of an ark to ensure that the residents left behind realized the expansiveness of their own ark, and to render it a refuge. Changing our stories and the relation we take to them remains at the hard heart of worlding.[5]

We hope that you will allow us to share in Jemisin's fantasy that one day the entire idea of ark-building as the monumental, world-defining, settler-colonial, fascist drawing down of borders, the maximizing of resources at the expense of those placed outside to die, becomes the matter of . . . what? Museums? Antique curiosity? The "eternal charm" of the ancients? A plaything of ancestral children? Or even, as Jemisin has it, a comedy of manners, as Jaleesa and friends have to humor their always expectedly unexpected fascist guest? Or maybe, an escaped slave narrative becomes full-blown liberation story?[6] Bag boy returns home to bring the gift of skin to all those with the courage to find themselves beautiful and picks a name. (And a pronoun? or several?) The Big Clean Up comes for the Founders?

Landfalling. It is tempting. Even now landfall still captivates, even having said goodbye to the rainbow, having with Mrs. Noah refused to board the ark, having stowed away with Methuselah, the devil, a woodworm, or a unicorn, having followed the raven out upon the ocean, having abandoned ark. There's a release that comes with the falling, a joy to letting go, the feel of allowing the gravity of a story's ending to take you to its ground. Best be careful then. For, the end is never the end. The feeling pales almost immediately, even before a story's denouement. The sense of an ending.

Another tale of landfalling, written centuries before, offers a caution. The "Miller's Tale" from Geoffrey Chaucer's *Canterbury Tales* is practically a how-to-do-it and how-not-to-do-it manual on ending by landfall. Here's the moral (well, one of them, as there are several, and all dubious). A carpenter by the name of John has been convinced by his boarder Nicholas that a world-cleansing flood is about to arrive. In part, John believes Nicholas because he knows the young man is learned in astrology; but mostly he is convinced by the young man's narration of what life will be like once the waters cover the Earth and only the two of them and John's wife Alison are left alive, sailing the ocean in individual tubs, waving hello and dreaming of the time at hand when they will be "lordes al oure lif / Of al the world, as Noe and his wif [Lords all our life of all the world, as were Noah and his wife]."[7] The next thing you know, John is asleep in his tub, which is hanging from the roof of his house in anticipation of the waves to come. Meanwhile, Nicholas and Alison creep out of their individual arks back into the house and into bed to enjoy "revel and melodye" (3652). A complicated series of events culminates with Nicholas burnt in the ass by a poker and calling loudly for water. John starts out of his slumber and thinks, "Allas, now comth Nowelis flood!" (3818), but there is no actual water to buoy him up as he cuts the cord to launch his lifeboat. Buy into flood-obliteration, into you own personal or restricted mode of landfall, and you may, like John, find yourself hurtling Earthward until you hit the ground and shatter your ark, end up on the floor, lying there "aswowne" (3823), an object of fun for your neighbors.

In Chaucer's tale, a flood of neighbors' laughter takes the place of any actual water, buoying the reader up. But, for Chaucer, that laughter is also part of the story and open to interrogation. It bubbles along the surface of the telling of this clockwork tale, each piece precisely arranged to yield its comic outcome. Carpenter John's neighbors laugh at and admonish his foolishness. They do not know that he has been tricked into believing the flood was about to arrive through a tall tale in which he, Nicholas, and Alison would be lords together of the now-empty world. Oh the intoxication of being able to start over again, everything that is in this life foreclosed now opened up and possible. So also, the readers or listeners to the tale may be moved to laugh, or perhaps find their own laughter trailing off and turning into something else, wonder or sadness. Strange currents course these comic flood tales. Weird affects.

Stories of landfall are all clockwork tales. They trade on radical shifts in scale and perspective, regrounding their characters and readers in perspectives they have altered to seem and to feel new. But those endings do not endure. Almost immediately, you have to begin over. And so we do begin again: "Make yourself an ark." What might that sentence one day come to mean? In this book, we have attempted to hold this invitation to ark-building open, exposing the sentence to its saying, to prospects that spread larger than any ark can contain.

This book ends. But the ark, the ark keeps thinking.

NOTES

1. How to Think like an Ark

1. Unless otherwise noted, all quotations from the Bible in this book are from *The Jewish Study Bible*, 2nd edition, ed. Adele Berlin and Marc Zvi Brettler (Oxford: Oxford University Press, 2014).

2. Invocations of the ark story are too numerous and various to enumerate. But take, for example, the governing tropes of Jeff Goodell's *The Water Will Come: Rising Seas, Sinking Cities, and the Remaking of the Civilized World* (New York: Little and Brown, 2017), along with Bill McKibben's satirical idea of the "Noah App" in his review "We're Not Even Close to Being Prepared for the Rising Waters," *The Washington Post*, November 10, 2017. See as well the multivalent use of the ark as conservation device in Mike Davis's excellent "Who Will Build the Ark?," *New Left Review* 61 (January–February 2010): 29–46.

3. On the violence of decision as cutting or the creation of an edge, see, in different registers, Michel Serres, *The Natural Contract*, trans. Elizabeth MacArthur and William Paulson (Ann Arbor: University of Michigan Press, 1992), 55, and Jacques Derrida, *The Gift of Death*, trans. David Wills (Chicago: University of Chicago Press, 1992), 53–82. On the madness of decision as precisely that which enables a reevaluation of circumstances, and therefore designates the political per se, see Cary Wolfe, *Before the Law: Humans and Other Animals in a Biopolitical Frame* (Chicago: University of Chicago Press, 2012), 103–4.

4. On the "ark concept" and flood narratives generally as "de-founding experiments" that produce origin effects keyed to the restricted immune privilege of enclosing structures (boxes, boats, cities), see Peter Sloterdijk, *Globes: Spheres II*, trans. Wieland Hoban (South Pasadena, Calif.: Semiotext(e), 2014), 237–333. "Arks," observes Sloterdijk, "are autopoietic—loosely translated, self-sealing—floats in which the united make use of their immune privilege in the face of unlivable environments" (242). What sets Noah's ark apart, for Sloterdijk, is the way landfall installs a legal/theological/technological treaty in the form of a covenant that grants humans the right to start over by and through their now fundamental difference from other animals.

5. The quintessential articulation of this paradoxical hospitality, or what he calls the "*pas d'hospitalité*: no hospitality, step of hospitality," comes from Derrida, who characterizes hospitality as the impossible coordination of two competing injunctions. "It is as though *the* law of absolute, unconditional, hyperbolical hospitality commanded that we transgress all the laws (in the plural) of hospitality, namely, the conditions, the norms, the rights,

and the duties that are imposed on hosts and hostesses, on the men and women who give a welcome as well as the men and women who receive it. And vice versa, it is as though the laws (plural) of hospitality, in marking limits, powers, rights, and duties, consisted in challenging and transgressing the law of hospitality, the one that would command that the 'new arrival' *[arrivant]* be offered an unconditional welcome" (Jacques Derrida and Anne Dufourmantelle, *Of Hospitality*, trans. Rachel Bowlby [Stanford, Calif.: Stanford University Press, 2000], 75–77).

6. For this sense of a general text, see Jacques Derrida, *Of Grammatology*, trans. Gayatari Chakravorty Spivak (Baltimore, Md.: Johns Hopkins University Press, 1974).

7. On the ethical and political, and so technical, importance of "politeness" (respecting the metaphysics of other worldviews), see Isabel Stengers, *Cosmopolitics I*, trans. Robert Bononno (Minneapolis: University of Minnesota Press, 2010).

8. For this visit, see Julian Yates and Jeffrey Jerome Cohen, "Ark-tistic License (Emzara and the Dinosaurs)," *In the Middle* (blog), October 3, 2018, inthemedievalmiddle.com/2018/10/arktistic-license-emzara-and-dinosaurs.html, accessed, January 31, 2022.

9. On "ontological choreography," see Charis Thompson, *Making Parents: The Ontological Choreography of Reproductive Technologies* (Boston: MIT Press, 2007).

10. Donna Haraway, *Staying with the Trouble: Making Kin in the Chthulucene* (Durham, N.C.: Duke University Press, 2016), 33–34. Haraway quotes M. Beth Dempster, "A Self-Organizing Systems Perspective on Planning for Sustainability," master's thesis, University of Waterloo, 1998. Like Haraway, our thinking of story forms is indebted to Ursula K. LeGuin, "The Carrier Bag Theory of Fiction," in *Dancing at the Edge of the World* (New York: Grove, 1989), 149–54.

11. On this structure of signification, see Emmanuel Lévinas, *Otherwise than Being or Beyond Essence*, trans. Alphonso Lingis (Dordrecht: Kluwer, 1978).

12. On the interior organization of the ark and on human fallibility as the reason for the divine blueprint, see John Wilkins, *An Essay Towards the Real Character of Philosophical Language* (London, 1668), 162–68.

13. Claire Fahy, "British Maritime Agency Detains a Modern Noah's Ark," *The New York Times*, June 13, 2021, 14.

14. Michel Serres, *Hominescence*, trans. Randolph Burks (London: Bloomsbury, 2019), 144. On Serres's earlier use of the ark as "a small-scale model of the totality of space and time" and so as key in preparing "for an overflow of the sea caused by some thaw in the ice caps," see *Natural Contract*, 31.

15. The prevalence of flood myths, be they stories of cataclysm, creation, or both, remains a question that animates scholars of prehistory. In his survey of the literature on the role of climate change in human evolution and

evolutionary paradigms, William J. Burroughs speaks to the ubiquity, if not quite universality, of such myths, hypothesizing that these stories, and the story of Utanapishtim, and therefore Noah, in particular, derive from "folk memory of the sea-level rise during prehistory," though he finds this explanation "unlikely as, in human terms, the rate of sea-level rise was slow" (*Climate Change in Prehistory: The End of the Reign of Chaos* [Cambridge: Cambridge University Press, 2005], 219). Given that "the available climatic records do not contain evidence of some global cataclysm happening between 15 and 5 kya when most of the rise in the oceans occurred," Burroughs suggests that "the second potential source of the Flood Myth in this particular region is that there were times when rising sea levels put on a sudden spurt" (219). He cites the "163,000 km^3 outburst from Lake Agassiz at 8.2 kya" as one possibility, and a similar "100,000 km^3" swallowing of land around the Black Sea as another (220–22). What remains highly uncertain is what sort of evidence flood myths offer concerning human development, especially given that they coincide with what Burroughs describes as growing climate stability with reduced variability as the ice age gave way to the Holocene (47–51). On the "riverine" nature and frequency of floods, see also John L. Brooke, *Climate Change and the Course of Global History: A Rough Journey* (Cambridge: Cambridge University Press, 2014), 206–9. Scholars hypothesize forms of inundation other than water or flooding. Overpopulation, for example, is one way of understanding the noise pollution that provokes the gods of Sumer in the *Epic of Gilgamesh*. Given the difficulties scholars face in explaining flood myths, it becomes especially easy to sympathize with André Leroi-Gourhan's position that "the only real significance of prehistory, whether resting on religious metaphysics or materialist dialectics, is that it situates the peoples of the future in their present as well as in their most distant past" (*Gesture and Speech*, trans. Anna Bostock Berger [Cambridge, Mass.: MIT Press, 1993], 4). Choose your prehistory carefully. It shall write your present future. To grasp the kinds of stakes to which Leroi-Gourhan alludes, see Kathryn Yusoff's brilliant analysis of the complicity of geological origin stories with stories that explain and justify the origins of racial difference in *A Billion Black Anthropocenes or None* (Minneapolis: University of Minnesota Press, 2018), esp. 65–85.

16. It is perhaps because of these scalar shifts, Noah's ark folding together of ends and origins, that philosopher Edmund Husserl is reputed to have labeled his manuscript on the origins of geometry "The Originary Ark *[die Ur-Arche]*, Earth, Does Not Move: Foundational Investigations of the Phenomenological Origin of Corporeality of the Spatiality Pertaining to Nature in the First Sense of the Natural Sciences; of Necessity All Are Initial Investigations." See Leonard Lawlor and Bettina Bergo's description of the manuscript in Maurice Merleau-Ponty, *Husserl at the Limits of Phenomenology*, ed. Leonard Lawlor with Bettina Bergo (Evanston, Ill.: Northwestern University Press, 2002), xli. In his notes on Husserl's manuscript, Merleau-Ponty writes, "4—The earth as 'Noah's Ark' = bearing the living and the

thoughts above the Flood (= it is not the physical earth. It is the earth as a mass, inertia and flying beneath all of us) (barbarous principle). That makes ontology enveloping in relation to the thought of the infinite. Ontology as the *Offenheit*" (69). For the Earth as a spaceship, see R. Buckminster Fuller, *Operating Manual for Spaceship Earth* (1969), designsciencelab.com/resources/OperatingManual_BF.pdf, accessed June 22, 2018.

17. *The Epic of Gilgamesh* [tablet XI], trans. Maureen Gallery Kovacs (Stanford: Stanford University Press, 1985), 96–108.

18. Teresa Shewry, *Hope at Sea: Possible Ecologies in Oceanic Literature* (Minneapolis: University of Minnesota Press, 2015), 9. Further citations will be parenthetical in text.

19. Serres, *Hominescence,* 28.

20. Ark thinking might be said to correspond to what Leroi-Gourhan describes as a *chaîne opératoire,* an operational sequence, or "gesture," as it was translated in the English title of his *Gesture and Speech.* As Leroi-Gourhan's translator explains, the phrase "should probably be glossed as 'material action,' as it refers explicitly to the manual creation of a material culture that is extracorporeal" (xviii). We are interested in the ways in which the ark constitutes a minimal story-form keyed to the production of a delimited survival architecture or bubble. *Gesture and Speech* was hugely influential on Derrida's concept of *différance* as a "program" both more and less than "human" that invites a rewriting of the story of technology athwart the lines of species (*Of Grammatology,* esp. 83–87). We are indebted more generally to the concept of world-building from Matt Bell, whose own work admirably exemplifies its possibilities; see esp. *Appleseed* (New York: Custom House, 2021).

21. Timothy Findley, *Not Wanted on the Voyage* (London: Penguin, 1984).

22. We use the phrase "make up" in the sense of Ian Hacking, "Making Up People," in *Reconstructing Individualism: Autonomy, Individuality, and the Self in Western Thought,* ed. Thomas C. Heller, Morton Sosna, and David E. Wellberry (Stanford, Calif.: Stanford University Press, 1986), 222–36.

23. Allied to our thinking here is Bruno Latour's impassioned plea in *Down to Earth* to rethink the concepts of "land," "soil," and "ground" in an inclusive mode. His plea swims with deluge metaphors, watery and fiery, without ever invoking the story of Noah and the ark exactly. Yet everywhere he redescribes the predicament of our current historical moment as the vying of competing land grabs. Is it instead possible to cultivate a shared sense of the future, of landfall premised on a precarity that we all share, a territory that Latour names capital-*T* "Terrestrial?" (*Down to Earth: Politics in the New Climate Regime,* trans. Catherine Porter [Cambridge: Polity, 2018], 40).

And, to push that question further, how may we do so without first reckoning with what philosopher and historian Achille Mbembe calls the "bitter sediment" of democracy: "colonial empire" and the "pro-slavery state, . . . the plantation and the penal colony?" (*Necropolitics,* trans. Steven Corcoran [Durham, N.C.: Duke University Press, 2019], 20). Whereas concepts of the universal imply "inclusion in some already constituted thing or entity; . . . the 'in-common' presupposes a relation of co-belonging and sharing—the idea of a world that is the only one we have and that, to be sustainable, must be shared by all those who have rights to it, all species taken together" (40). "One cannot," like Noah, "'sanctuarize' one's own home by fomenting chaos and death far away, in the homes of others." Mbembe writes here, in a beautiful sentence, that "sanctuarization can only ever be mutual." "Though for this sharing to become possible," he adds, for a "planetary democracy to come to pass, the democracy of species, the demand for justice and reparation is inescapable."

24. We seek to radicalize art historian Ruth Clements's observation, building on the work of classicist Jocelyn Penny Small, that, as for classical and Greek texts, so for the story of Noah, "transmission and reception" in different historical moments has been "disassociated" from any written text and that "the imaginary life of classic narratives is often formed by the nexus of memory and culture, not text, diction, and culture." Ruth Clements, "A Shelter Amid the Flood: Noah's Ark in Early Jewish and Christian Art," in *Noah and His Books,* ed. Michael E. Stone, Aryeh Amihay, and Vered Hillel (Atlanta: Society for Biblical Literature, 2010), 277; Jocelyn Penny Small, *The Parallel Worlds of Classical Art and Text* (Cambridge: Cambridge University Press, 2003).

25. Some rabbinic commentators wondered why the Torah would start with a *bet,* the second letter of the Hebrew alphabet (roughly the English *b*), in *Bereshith,* the Torah's first word and the Hebrew title for Genesis, rather than an *aleph,* the first letter of the Hebrew alphabet (a guttural consonant whose pronunciation has been lost, making it simply take the sound of the vowel accompanying it). One answer is that beginnings are never ex nihilo; they are always beginnings "from" (the letter *bet* is here a prefixed preposition that could be taken by the rabbi as "from" in a sense of "in" or "by"). For a Christian meditation on this same idea, see Jacob J. Erickson, "Beginning, Again," *Huffpost,* August 28, 2016, huffpost.com/entry/beginning-again_b_57c2f9f0e4b06384eb402e1e (Erickson mentions Catherine Keller's *Face of the Deep: A Theology of Becoming* [New York: Routledge, 2003]; on 157–58 of Keller can be found a couple other of the various rabbinic interpretive answers to the question).

2. No More Rainbows

1. In Sir Francis Bacon's *New Atlantis,* the miraculous arrival of the holy book of Bensalem, which founded the community, involves a self-moving boat that, when approached, opens itself to deliver a book and letter. Both ark and arkive, the self-moving boat and self-opening chest describe the figure of origins (*New Atlantis and The Great Instauration,* ed. the Rev. Jerry Weinberger [Wheeling, Ill.: Harlan Davidson, 1989], 48, and 47–49 generally).

2. Oriented to landfall, the story of Noah's ark plays as the archetypal settler colonial fantasy. For an overview of the emerging field of studies on

settler colonialism, see, among others, Aimee Carrillo Rowe and Eve Tuck, "Settler Colonialism and Cultural Studies: Ongoing Settlement, Cultural Production, and Resistance," *Cultural Studies ↔ Critical Methodologies* 17, no. 1 (2017): 3–13.

Resonant here is Bruno Latour's plea in *Down to Earth* that "we look for a place to land," a place coincident with the project of a common world that everywhere appears to be in retreat as nation states and corporate entities double down on building obstacles in order to obtain advantage by fueling fears of inundation (Latour, *Down to Earth: Politics in the New Climate Regime,* trans. Catherine Porter [Cambridge: Polity, 2018], 92). Latour argues here that, since the end of the Cold War, denial of climate change, deregulation, and the burgeoning of inequalities are three facets of a single phenomenon: the evisceration of the notion of a world in common and the advent of a "wicked universality" that, even as it might form the basis of a sense of common precarity, draws divisive, predatory responses calculated to preserve the privileged immunity of the few at the expense of all. For Latour, hope lies in a renewed sense of the "Terrestrial" keyed to the concept of land as territory. The terrestrial refers here to a concept of land or soil that has nothing to do with origins, ownership, nationality and that "cannot be appropriated": "One belongs to" this soil; "it belongs to no one."

3. Timothy Findley, *Not Wanted on the Voyage* (London: Penguin, 1984), 337; subsequent references appear parenthetically in the text.

4. In the terms of Alain Badiou, we might venture that Mrs. Noyes seeks to regard the rainbow as simply weather and so not an "event," which implies a human subject. Or perhaps, more interestingly still, her redirected prayers raise the possibility of still another order of "events" and for a concept of the "social" that includes our interactions with other forms of life and other phenomena. For Badiou's modeling of events, see *Being and Event,* trans. Oliver Feltham (London: Bloomsbury, 2013).

5. With wonderful hyperbole, Lee Edelman invokes "Noah's rainbow" as something like an archetype or chronotope keyed to a reproductive futurism whose "go forth and multiply" mortgages the present moment so completely as to annihilate the possibility of change ("The Future Is Kid Stuff: Queer Theory, Disidentification, and the Death Drive," *Narrative* 6, no. 1 [1998]: 18–30, at 24). In a virtuoso moment, he arcs from the musical *Annie* to Genesis and back.

6. William Wordsworth, "My Heart Leaps Up When I Behold," in *William Wordsworth: The Major Works,* ed. Stephen Gill (Oxford: Oxford University Press, 2008), 246.

7. Quotations of the Bible are from *The Jewish Study Bible,* 2nd ed. (Oxford: Oxford University Press, 2014).

8. For this modeling of an "event" as "what must be presupposed . . . in order for an organization of documents," according to Michel de Certeau, "the event is the means thanks to which disorder is turned into order. The event does not explain but permits intelligibility. It is the postulate and the

point of departure—but also the blind spot—or comprehension" (*The Writing of History*, trans. Tom Conley [New York: Columbia University Press, 1988], 96).

9. Jeanette Winterson, *Boating for Beginners* (1985; repr. London: Mandarin Paperbacks, 1995), 139.

10. *Enuma Elish / The Babylonian Genesis*, 2nd ed., trans. Alexander Heidel (1942; repr. Chicago: University of Chicago Press, 1963).

11. The blessing for rainbows enacts this doubleness—thanking God for remembering the covenant, thanking God for keeping this promise, treaty or pact: "Blessed . . . Who is faithful to His covenant and fulfills His word"—Rav Pappa said: "Therefore we will say them both combined: Blessed . . . Who remembers the covenant and is faithful to His covenant and fulfills His word." (Babylonian Talmud, Ber. 59a, William Davidson edition, sefaria.org/Berakhot).

12. On Noah as linked both in name ("comfort, bring relief") and plot to a mastery of agriculture that alleviates "the dreadful toil of subsistence farming," see Theodore Hiebert, *The Yahwist's Landscape* (Oxford: Oxford University Press, 1996), 44–51. For an overview of the ark story in terms of the environment, see Daniel Hillel, *The Natural History of the Bible* (New York: Columbia University Press, 2006), 50–52.

13. Philip Fisher, *Wonder, the Rainbow, and the Aesthetics of Rare Experiences* (Cambridge, Mass.: Harvard University Press, 1998), 39. On the story of the ark as allied to this "divine-human" legal pact, see Peter Sloterdijk, *Globes: Spheres II*, trans. Wieland Hoban (South Pasadena, Calif.: Semiotext(e), 2014), 240–42. Working in a broadly early modern European context, art historian Maria H. Loh charts the manipulation of rainbow icons by different religious communities and royal figures (see Anya Ventura, "The Power of Rainbows," January 25, 2022, Getty, getty.edu/news/rainbow-power/). Loh's work on how the rainbow provoked differing emotions/responses and how its time-bound unruliness could be threatening testifies to the ambivalence we locate in the rainbow as an archival sign structuring past, present, and future as it seeks to program belief and belonging.

14. For this sense of the weather, see Michel Serres, *Hermès IV: La Distribution* (Paris: Minuit, 1977), 13, and in English, Michel Serres, "Exact and Human," trans. W. Woodhull, and J. Mowitt, *SubStance* 6, no. 7 (1978): 9–19, at 13.

15. Robert C. Young, "That Which Is Casually Called a Language," *PMLA* 131, no. 5 (2016): 1207–21, at 1215.

16. Nikolai Trubetzkoy, "The Tower of Babel and the Confusion of Tongues," in *The Legacy of Genghis Khan and Other Essays on Russia's Identity* (Ann Arbor: Michigan Slavic Publications, 1991), 155 (quoted also in Young, "That Which Is Casually Called a Language," 1215). As Gilles Deleuze and Félix Guattari point out, nonarboreal, rhizomic structures might offer a superior, less-decided model of description, but the "material problem" that remains "is knowing whether we have it within our means . . . to distinguish

the BwO from its doubles: empty vitreous bodies, cancerous bodies, totalitarian and fascist." (Gilles Deleuze and Félix Guattari, *A Thousand Plateaus*, vol. 2 of *Capitalism and Schizophrenia*, trans. Brian Massumi [Minneapolis: University of Minnesota Press, 1987], 165).

17. Young, "That Which Is Casually Called a Language," 1215.

18. On translation as a generalized form of communication, see Young, "That Which Is Casually Called a Language," 1217–19. On translation technologies as key to approaching questions of being across and among the apparent divide of species, far beyond the preserve of human language, see Jacques Derrida, *The Beast and the Sovereign*, trans. Geoffrey Bennington, ed. Michel Lisse, Marie-Louise Mallet, and Ginette Michaud, 2 vols. (Chicago: University of Chicago Press, 2009), 1:328, 336. See also, for differing orientations, Michel Serres, *Biogea*, trans. Randolph Burks (Minneapolis, Minn.: Univocal, 2012), and Vinciane Despret, *What Would Animals Say If We Asked the Right Questions?*, trans. Brett Buchanan (Minneapolis: University of Minnesota Press, 2016).

19. Julian Barnes, "The Mountain," in *A History of the World in 10½ Chapters* (New York: Vintage Books, 1989), 141–68, at 148. Unless otherwise indicated, subsequent references appear parenthetically in the text.

20. Here we consulted the versions of Genesis Rabbah at the Sefaria website (sefaria.org/Bereishit_Rabbah) in doing our translations.

21. Mira Beth Wasserman, *Jews, Gentiles, and Other Animals: The Talmud After the Humanities* (Philadelphia: University of Pennsylvania Press, 2017), 113. We are indebted to Ron Broglio's idea from *Animal Revolution* (Minneapolis: University of Minnesota Press, 2022), that animals will strive always to jam the anthropological machine, even when that machine is an ark.

22. The ark functions as the site for the inventorying and management of a collective "flesh" in Michel Foucault's sense as that with which biopower "writes," carving up the continuous ecology of relations between plants, animals, and humans to generate different forms of "life" and categories of beings. This management of flesh occurs obviously through managing regimes/thresholds of edibility, reproduction, and so on. Each of these becomes a way to eventuate a biological continuum and so to "introduce . . . a break into the domain of life that is under power's control: the break between what must live and what must die." Famously, Foucault goes on to remark the way race, "the distinction between races," serves to establish "a biological-type caesura within a population" that allows "power to treat that population as a mixture of races, or to be more accurate, to treat the species, to subdivide the species it controls, into the subspecies known precisely as races" (Michel Foucault, *"Society Must Be Defended": Lectures at the Collège de France* [1975–1976], trans. David Macey [New York: Picador, 2003], 254–55).

23. We are inspired here by the methodology articulated by Saidiya Hartman in her essay "Venus in Two Acts," where she asks about the recovery of the erased lives of the enslaved: "Is it possible to exceed or negotiate the constitutive limits of the archive? By advancing a series of speculative

arguments and exploiting the capacities of the subjunctive (a grammatical mood that expresses doubts, wishes, and possibilities), in fashioning a narrative, which is based upon archival research, and by that I mean a critical reading of the archive that mimes the figurative dimensions of history, I intended both to tell an impossible story and to amplify the impossibility of its telling" ("Venus in Two Acts," *Small Axe* 12, no. 2 [2008]: 1–14, at 11).

24. Frank Zelco, "Warriors of the Rainbow: The Birth of an Environmental Mythology," Environment & Society Portal, *Arcadia,* no. 16 (2013), Rachel Carson Center for Environment and Society, doi.org/10.5282/rcc/5625.

25. On myth as alibi, see Roland Barthes, *Mythologies,* trans. Richard Howard and Annette Lavers (New York: Hill and Wang, 2012), 233. And more generally on the structure of alibi, see Jonathan H. Grossman, "Alibi," *Raritan* 24, no. 1 (2004): 133–50.

26. On mimesis as always future-oriented, always proactive or predatory, see Michael Taussig, *Mimesis and Alterity: A Particular History of the Senses* (New York: Routledge, 1993).

27. The lure of children's toys for adults was conveyed perceptively by Walter Benjamin, who wrote in "Old Toys: The Toy Exhibition at the Märkisches Museum" that, "when the urge to play overcomes an adult," rather than a regressive impulse, that desire is an attempt to allay the inescapable "sting" of the menacing world by "playing with its image in reduced form," thereby "making light of an unbearable life" (in *Walter Benjamin: Selected Writings,* ed. Michael W. Jennings, trans. Rodney Livingstone et al., vol. 2/1 [Cambridge, Mass.: Belknap, 1999], 100–101). Benjamin is making specific reference to postwar Germany, but his point is a general one: play creates refuge, as well as a space of unconstrained experiment (101).

28. In "Toys and Play," Walter Benjamin cycles through various explanatory frames that might make sense of the vast range of toys and play, from "parlor games" to the "ingenious 'catastrophe coach,'" with an eye to exploring the "great law that presides over the rules and rhythms of the entire world of play: the law of repetition" (*Selected Writings,* 2/1:20). Benjamin flirts here with Freud's "beyond the pleasure principle," but in this short essay is not willing to assimilate toys or play to a Freudian schema: "An adult relieves his heart from its terrors and doubles happiness by turning it into a story, . . . [but] a child creates the entire event anew and starts again right from the beginning." He seems dissatisfied with his options—eagerness to trouble and inhabit "the obscure urge to repeat things" or mimesis itself as something productive. And this desire presages models of mimesis and play as always in excess or as tapping into the surplus value that limns the possibilities of starting again "right from the beginning." On this sense of play as a space of indistinction and possibility, see Brian Massumi, *What Animals Teach Us about Politics* (Durham, N.C.: Duke University Press, 2014), especially 15–20. Massumi draws heavily on Geoffrey Bateson's foundational essay, "A Theory of Play and Fantasy," in *Steps Towards an Ecology of Mind* (New

York: Chandler, 1972), 177–93. For Bateson, play derives from a question of framing.

29. On the way our fossil-fueled infrastructures are, in effect, elaborated forms of "petro-subjectivity," see Brett Bloom, *Petro-Subjectivity: De-industrializing Our Sense of Self* (Fort Wayne, Ind.: Breakdown Break Down, 2015). For an early salvo across the bows of the industrialization or "embourgeoisement of the toy," see Roland Barthes's still arresting "Toys" in *Mythologies,* 59–61. Barthes casts quite a spell over such plastic toys that essentially prepare the child for entry into the world of adult consumption as opposed to play and pleasure. Crucial to his reading is the "gradual disappearance of wood" (60) from toy-making, with the plastic object's existence premised on its single-use obsolescence. "Henceforth," he concludes, "toys will be chemical" and "such toys die . . . very quickly, and once dead, they have no posthumous life for the child" (61). The plastic Noah's ark is, of course, merely the latest iteration of one of the earliest mass-produced toys, in wood or metal, dating back to the eighteenth century and earlier.

30. Jeanette Winterson, *Oranges Are Not the Only Fruit* (London: Vintage, 2001), 24. Unless otherwise indicated, subsequent references appear parenthetically in the text.

31. Allied to our thinking here is Elizabeth M. De Loughrey's analysis of the reenchantment of allegory as a way of thinking of scalar shifts in *Allegories of the Anthropocene* (Durham, N.C.: Duke University Press, 2019). De Loughrey is especially valuable in the way she attends so closely to the ways in which non-Western knowledge systems and postcolonial presents provincialize the origins stories and tropes of the Anthropocene. In ch. 4, De Loughrey offers a reading of Keri Hulme's *Stonefish* very much in sympathy with our project to discover how the ark has been dismantled and repurposed across the ages. Hulme "parochializes apocalyptic narrative, demonstrating the way it is rendered as a future threat rather than as a lived, present experience of colonized and otherwise oppressed peoples" (149). Hulme does so by troping the figure of the ship and the ark, subjecting both to a sense of embodied being in dialogue with nonhuman creatures. As are we, De Loughrey is interested in the Serresian problematic of the ark as "a small-scale model of the totality of space and time," even as she is cautious with regard to the ungrounded, universalizing potential to Serres's cosmopolitan natural contract. For De Loughrey's reading of his *The Natural Contract,* see *Allegories,* 151–52 and 157.

32. Natalie Diaz, *Postcolonial Love Poem* (Minneapolis, Minn.: Graywolf, 2020), 58–59. We are grateful to Natalie Diaz for conversations on refuge and difficult beginnings.

3. Outside the Ark

1. *The Holy Bible: Containing the Old and New Testaments, according to the Authorised Version, with Illustrations by Gustave Doré* (London: Cassell, 1866). Published in English, French, and German and frequently re-

printed today, this bible's engravings were often moved around slightly in the narrative.

2. The reference here is to Isaiah 11:6. For a nonmessianic reading of the Bible text in the context of animal ethology, see Vinciane Despret, *Quand le loup habitera avec l'agneau* (Paris: Seuil, 2002).

3. *The Holy Bible: King James Version,* with introduction by David Whitford (New York: Barnes and Noble, 2012).

4. On the frightening possibility that anything might happen tied to a confusion of *bios* and *zōē,* see Giorgio Agamben, *Homo Sacer: Sovereign Power and Bare Life,* trans. Daniel Heller-Roazen (Stanford, Calif.: Stanford University Press, 1998).

5. On the etymology of refuge, see *Oxford English Dictionary Online,* s.v. "refuge, n."

6. For this modeling of refuge as a constellation of ties or even an actor network, see Bruno Latour, "Factures/Fractures," *Res* 36 (1999): 20–31.

7. Hannah Arendt, "We Refugees," *The Menorah Journal* 31, no. 1 (1943): 69–77, at 69.

8. As Jacques Lezra writes, the word "enough" localizes the political precisely because "it is not given . . . that what we are talking about when we say, 'That is enough' or 'That is not enough' is a thing of one or the other sort." The word demands an open inquiry into whether my sense of enough matches your own self-perception. "Was that, in fact, enough?" Is enough in fact enough? "No rules are given, or universally-enough agreed," Lezra continues, "allowing us to decide, or even to reason out from first principles, that one thing is the object of practical measure and not the sort of thing that is not" ("Enough," *Political Concepts: A Critical Lexicon* 3, no. 3 [2014], web.archive.org/web/20211019192959/https://www.politicalconcepts.org/enough-jacques-lezra/).

9. Donna Haraway, *Staying with the Trouble: Making Kin in the Chthulucene* (Durham, N.C.: Duke University Press, 2016), 100. Haraway cites Anna Tsing's paper "Feral Biologies."

10. Jason Moore, *Capitalism in the Web of Life* (London: Verso, 2015), esp. 291–305.

11. Michel Serres, *Malfeasance: Appropriation through Pollution?,* trans. Anne-Marie Feenberg-Dibon (Stanford, Calif.: Stanford University Press, 2011), 70.

12. Serres, *Malfeasance,* 43–44.

13. Haraway, *Staying with the Trouble,* 103. On the co-imbrication of technics and ethics, see Isabelle Stengers, *Power and Invention: Situating Science,* trans. Paul Bains, with introduction by Bruno Latour (Minneapolis: University of Minnesota Press, 1997), 216.

14. Srinivas Aravamudan labels this time-swirl effect around disaster "catachronism" ("catastrophe" + "anachronism"). Catastrophe becomes "oddly comfortable" because "the sped-up time of lurching toward a cataclysmic event allows for many grand clichés around life and death and the

intoxicating spectatorial sense produced by an aesthetic return to the grand canvas of epic" ("The Catachronism of Climate Change," *Diacritics* 41, no. 3 [2013]: 7–30, at 10–11). For an earlier modeling of the strangely syncopated temporalities of catastrophe as tied to nuclear weapons, see Maurice Blanchot, "The Apocalypse Is Disappointing," in *Friendship,* trans. Elizabeth Rottenberg (Stanford, Calif.: Stanford University Press, 1997), 101–8, and Jacques Derrida, "No Apocalypse, Not Now (Full Speed Ahead, Seven Missiles, Seven Missives)," *Diacritics* 14, no. 2 (1984): 20–31. For a rethinking of this matrix in regard to global warming, see the special issue of *Diacritics* devoted to climate-change criticism, and especially Richard Klein's "Climate Change through the Lens of Nuclear Criticism," *Diacritics* 41, no. 3 (2013): 82–87. See also Tom Cohen, Claire Colebrook, and J. Hillis Miller, *Theory and the Disappearing Future: On De Man, on Benjamin* (New York: Routledge, 2012), 9–10.

15. Dan Brayton, "Writ in Water: *Far Tortuga* and the Crisis of the Marine Environment," *PMLA* 127, no. 3 (2012): 565–71, at 570. For a consideration of the long history of imagining the world ending in flood, see Norman Cohn, *Noah's Flood: The Genesis Story in Western Thought* (New Haven, Conn.: Yale University Press, 1996), esp. 1–21.

16. Kim Stanley Robinson, *New York 2140* (New York: Orbit Books, 2017).

17. Wai Chee Dimock gets at the long genealogy of the novel, as well as its intimacy to American literature and flows of capital, in her review "5000 Years of Climate Fiction," *Public Books,* June, 28, 2017 publicbooks.org /5000-years-of-climate-fiction/. Matt Bell gives a thorough genealogy and comprehensive view of the field in "Climate Fictions: Future-Making Technologies," in *The Cambridge Companion to Environmental Humanities,* ed. Jeffrey Cohen and Stephanie Foote (Cambridge: Cambridge University Press, 2021), 100–113.

18. Lawrence Buell, *The Future of Environmental Criticism: Environmental Crisis and Literary Imagination* (Malden, Mass.: Blackwell, 2005), 285.

19. In *Slow Violence and the Environmentalism of the Poor* (Cambridge, Mass.: Harvard University Press, 2011), Rob Nixon writes that "Neoliberalism's proliferating walls concretize a short-term psychology of denial: the delusion that we can survive long term in a world whose resources are increasingly unshared. The wall, read in terms of neoliberalism and environmental slow justice, materializes temporal as well as spatial denial through a literal concretizing of out of sight out of mind" (20; cf. 265, on walled communities).

20. The complete array of created images and the rationale for the climate-change-awareness project may be accessed at london-futures.com.

21. On the figure of the disinterested spectator on the shore, anxiously watching shipwreck but unable to intervene, as the moment of theory-making, see Hans Blumenberg, *Shipwreck with Spectator: Paradigm for a Metaphor of Existence,* trans. Steven Rendall (Cambridge, Mass.: MIT Press, 1997), and Steve Mentz, *At the Bottom of Shakespeare's Ocean* (London: Con-

tinuum, 2009), 21. For the key passage in Lucretius designating the trope of gazing out to sea, see *De rerum natura* 2.1–2, trans. W. H. D. Rouse and rev. Martin F. Smith, Loeb Classical Library 181 (Cambridge, Mass.: Harvard University Press, 1992).

22. A variety of the blog posts at the Burrito Justice website detail the project; for a starting point, see "San Francisco Archipelago," Burrito Justice, March 20, 2012, burritojustice.com/2012/03/20/san-francisco-archipelago/.

23. All of the maps we discuss may be viewed at spatialities.com.

24. Donna Haraway, "Situated Knowledges: The Science Question in Feminism and the Privilege of Partial Perspective," *Feminist Studies* 14, no. 3 (1988): 575–99. "The god trick" of pretending an infinite, detached view is possible is defined at 582. On the sublime tropes and temporality of the Anthropocene as encouraging a sense that the future is determined as an impediment to engaging with a difficult, contested, but still open future, see Julia Nordblad, "On the Difference between Anthropocene and Climate Change Temporalities," *Critical Inquiry* 47 (Winter 2021): 328–48, esp. 333–35.

25. Stacy Alaimo, "Sustainable This, Sustainable That: New Materialisms, Posthumanism, and Unknown Futures," *PMLA* 127, no. 3 (2012): 558–64, at 563. See also Alaimo's work on transcorporeality in *Bodily Natures: Science, Environment, and the Material Self* (Bloomington: Indiana University Press, 2010). In *Hope at Sea* (Minneapolis: University of Minnesota Press, 2015), Teresa Shewry describes attunement to such entanglement as hope.

26. Sarah Blake, *Naamah* (New York: Riverhead, 2019), 7; subsequent references appear parenthetically in the text.

27. Thomas Burnet, *Telluris Theoria Sacra, or Sacred Theory of the Earth*, 2 vols. (London, 1684), 1; subsequent references appear parenthetically in the text.

28. For a fascinating account of how the story of the Flood and Noah's ark gave early modern writers (Burnet included) an occasion to think through and with concepts of human agency on a planetary scale by means of a "natural history of sin," and so to anticipate many of the conceptual difficulties provoked by the Anthropocene, as well as a means of scaling their theories up and down, see Lydia Barnett, *After the Flood: Imagining the Global Environment in Early Modern Europe* (Baltimore, Md.: Johns Hopkins University Press, 2019).

29. Guillaume de Salluste du Bartas, *The Divine Weeks*, trans. Joshua Sylvester, ed. Susan Snyder (Oxford: Clarendon, 1979), 404.

30. De Salluste du Bartas, *Divine Weeks*, 322.

31. Edward Ecclestone, *Noah's Flood, or The Destruction of the World* (London, 1697), 5. Unless otherwise indicated, subsequent references appear parenthetically in the text. For a survey and summary of other early modern treatments of the ark, including Francis Sabie's poem *The Olde Worlde's Tragedie* (1596), see Don Cameron Allen, *The Legend of Noah: Renaissance Rationalism in Art, Science, and Letters* (Urbana: University of Illinois Press, 1949).

32. London is a city that authors and artists especially like to drown. Richard Jefferies imagines a flooded toxic archive of a city in *After London* (1885), while all around it old world flora and fauna revive. In 1899, the *London Magazine* printed an altered photograph of the city entitled *If London Were Like Venice: Oh! That It Were,* in which the streets were rendered canals, gondolas gliding what had been busy lanes. John Wyndham's 1953 *The Kraken Wakes* imagines the waters of the Thames rising through London's streets, though its flood is occasioned not by anthropogenic climate change but as a result of a catastrophic failure of communication between Earth's Cold War–era human governments and deep-sea-dwelling squid-like extraterrestrials, perhaps from Venus, who repurpose the nuclear depth charges sent to annihilate them to melt the polar ice caps. J. G. Ballard's novel *The Drowned World* (1962) likewise imagines the effects of the melting of Greenland's ice sheets, albeit from unexplained solar activity rather than industrial carbon release or nuclear bombs. England's capital becomes a drenched and tropical city as the climate reverts to the temperatures of the Triassic age and life on Earth de-evolves.

33. *Pageante of Noyes Fludd,* in *The Chester Mystery Cycle,* ed. R. M. Lumiansky and David Mills, EETS, 2nd ser., vol. 3 (Oxford: Oxford University Press, 1974), lines 173–76; parenthetical citations of the play in the text will be from this edition and by line number.

34. We consulted the versions of Genesis Rabbah at Sefaria (sefaria.org/Bereishit_Rabbah) in doing our translations.

35. That Noah warned of the Flood for 120 years, hoping some would repent, is a story also told in midrash. See Norman Cohn, *Noah's Flood: The Genesis Story in Western Thought* (New Haven, Conn.: Yale University Press 1996), 33.

36. William Shakespeare, *The Tempest,* ed. Virginia Mason Vaughan and Alden T. Vaughan (London: The Arden Shakespeare, 2–11), 3.3.100–101.

37. Peter Sloterdijk, *Terror from the Air,* trans. Amy Patton and Steve Corcoran (Los Angeles: Semiotext[e], 2007), 25–26.

38. Ellen O'Grady, *Outside the Ark: An Artist's Journey in Occupied Palestine* (Durham, N.C.: 55 Books, 2005), opening 2.

39. Nixon, *Slow Violence,* 200.

40. Blanchot, "The Apocalypse Is Disappointing"; Greg Garrard, *Ecocriticism,* 2nd ed. (New York: Routledge, 2012), 93–116, especially 113–16.

41. Middle English from *The Gawain Poet: Complete Works,* ed. and trans. Marie Borroff (New York: Norton, 2012), lines 288–89; subsequent references appear parenthetically in the text, cited by line number.

42. "The Brother" from the sequence "Seven Exemplary Fictions" in Robert Coover, *Pricksongs & Descants* (New York: Penguin, 1969), 74–80, at 79.

43. See Steve Mentz, "'Making the Green One Red': Dynamic Ecologies in *Macbeth,* Edward Barlow's Journal, and *Robinson Crusoe,*" *Journal for Early Modern Cultural Studies* 13, no. 3 (2013): 67–84, esp. 81–82 ("Sailors must become swimmers").

44. Sarah Elliott Novacich compellingly argues that Noah's wife is positioned in the Wakefield and Chester Flood plays as "co-archivist, as subversive archivist, as archived human animal," whose stories travel to the "emergent earth" ("*Uxor Noe* and the Animal Inventory," *New Medieval Literatures* 12 [2010]: 169–77, at 171). She describes the Chester "good gossips" as "unsinkable glitches in Noah's archival project and in the performance of salvation: they are characters who are un-saved, un-archived, and yet unforgotten" (172).

4. Inside the Ark

1. On Brueghel's painting in its historical contexts, see Arianne Faber Kolb, *Jan Breughel the Elder's Entry of the Animals into Noah's Ark* (Los Angeles: Getty, 2005).

2. Jacques Derrida, *The Animal That Therefore I Am,* trans. David Wills (New York: Fordham University Press, 2008), 34; subsequent references appear parenthetically in the text.

3. That is, "ark" and "the animal" confine multiple forms of life through a literal and epistemic violence, through the stupidity (or what Derrida calls *bêtise,* literally the beast-liness) of human sorting.

4. For an example of how this aporetic "we" might then come to coincide with a new subject of a more-than-human history, see Vinciane Despret, *Quand le loup habitera avec l'agneau* (Paris: Seuil, 2002). Despret re-signifies Isaiah 11:6, to which the title of her book refers, not as a messianic scene but as the practical business of enabling different beings to manifest as historically particular subjects. This kind of reorientation provides the impetus for her more recent *What Would Animals Say If We Asked the Right Questions,* trans. Brett Buchanan (Minneapolis: University of Minnesota Press, 2016).

5. As Derrida writes, "the Animal," just like the ark, has always been prone to stowaways, limit cases, and monsters, to trophic swelling and bulging, as its self-identity as a concept fails and the line between beings becomes subject to a "complicating, thickening, delinearizing, folding, and dividing" (*Animal,* 29). Derrida registers this menagerie of multiple differences that the word "animal" seeks to overwrite by forging another word, singular and plural at once, "a chimerical word that sound[s] . . . as though it contravene[s] . . . the laws of the French language, *l'animot*" (41). Combining the French plural of animal with the word for "word," *l'animot* is "an irreducible living multiplicity of mortals." Derrida here notes that the term is literally a chimera, a hybrid creature whose "monstrousness derived precisely from the multiplicity of animals, of the *animot,* in it (head and chest of a lion, entrails of a goat, tail of a dragon)." Something similar has always been true of the ark, which likewise collects difference into collated monstrosity.

6. Nicolas Pelham, "A New Ark: What the Marsh Arabs Can Teach Us about Noah's Flood," *Lapham's Quarterly,* laphamsquarterly.org/water/new-ark, accessed September 10, 2022.

7. Isidore of Spain, *Etymologiae* 20.9.2, in *The Etymologies of Isidore of*

Seville, trans. Stephen A. Barney, W. J. Lewis, J. A. Beach, and Oliver Berghof (Cambridge: Cambridge University Press, 2006). For an inspirational reading of Noah's ark as a figure for the archive, see Sarah Elliott Novacich, "*Uxor Noe* and the Animal Inventory," *New Medieval Literatures* 12 (2010): 169–77, and especially Novavich, *Shaping the Archive in Late Medieval England: History, Poetry, and Performance* (Cambridge: Cambridge University Press, 2017), 52–85.

8. For Derrida's parsing of *archē* in relation to archive, see Jacques Derrida, *Archive Fever: A Freudian Impression,* trans. Eric Prenowitz (Chicago: University of Chicago Press, 1996). The word "survivance" has a long and important history. The word resonates in a double sense. In Derrida's terms, survivance refers to the more-than-human "'movement of survival' . . . at the very heart of life," a living on, over, and above, that is keyed to different forms of media and so to a politics of the archive ("No Apocalypse, Not Now," *Diacritics* 14, no. 2 [Summer 1984]: 20–31, at 27). In an allied and much more elaborated usage, Anishinaabe novelist, critic, and theorist Gerald Vizenor uses "survivance" to refer to the connection among survival, resistance, storytelling, and presence against genocide, colonization, and settler colonial violence. "Native survivance," he writes, "is an active sense of presence over absence, deracination, and oblivion; survivance is the continuance of stories, not a mere reaction, however pertinent. Survivance is greater than the right of a survivable name" ("Aesthetics of Survivance," in *Survivance: Narratives of Native Presence,* ed. Gerard Vizenor [Lincoln: University of Nebraska Press, 2008], 2).

9. "Notes on Noah's Ark," by "Jason," *The Model Engineer* 96, no. 2404 (1947): 731–34; subsequent references appear parenthetically in the text.

10. See, for example, the efforts of south-of-the-river-Tyne Jarrow and Hebburn History Society to reclaim one entry by a local shipbuilding firm, currently on display in the north-of-the-river Theater Royal, Newcastle upon Tyne, having spent the intervening decades in storage. Given the fate of shipbuilding, steel-working, and coal mining in the North of England, such survivals and reclamations can prove particularly meaningful to communities that seek to recognize the expertise and craftsmanship of ways of life now challenged or gone. See Lisa Nightingale, "Jarrow and Hebburn History Group Aims to Bring Historic Display Back to Town," *The Shields Gazette,* April 1, 2019.

11. The history of the coat of arms is, as the company itself acknowledges, problematic. Originally, the arms belonged to a rival "foreign" company of shipwrights founded at Redrith (Rotherhithe) on the south bank of the Thames. This rival company prospered and profited from its association with the Royal Dockyard at Deptford, and by 1578 it received a charter from the Crown, and in 1605, "it had been made a grant of arms, which form the basis of the present blazon. After a prolonged legal battle, in which the Free Shipwrights had the support of the City, and latterly the Shipwrights of Redrith that of Mr. Samuel Pepys, Secretary of the Navy, in 1684 the foreign

shipwrights' company was suppressed and its charter cancelled. Contrary to heraldic law and usage, the Free Shipwrights promptly adopted the foreign shipwrights' arms and, from the evidence of the beadle's silver staff head which was commissioned in 1702 and engraved with those arms, used them undifferenced." (shipwrights.co.uk/company/the-arms, accessed, September 10, 2022).

12. Richard W. Unger, *The Art of Medieval Technology: Images of Noah the Shipbuilder* (New Brunswick, N.J.: Rutgers University Press, 1991), 112–13. Unger refers to the version of the Noah story put on by the shipwrights in the York mystery cycle, in which "Noah protests that he has no skill as a shipwright" (113).

13. Unger, *Art of Medieval Technology*, 47–48.

14. Susan Stewart, *On Longing: Narratives of the Miniature, the Gigantic, the Souvenir, the Collection* (Durham, N.C.: Duke University Press, 1993), 152.

15. On the co-imbrication of technics and ethics, see Isabelle Stengers, *Power and Invention: Situating Science*, trans. Paul Bains, with introduction by Bruno Latour (Minneapolis: University of Minnesota Press, 1997), 216.

16. It is in deference to the historical likelihoods of 1947 Great Britain that we quote from the King James Version.

17. Don Cameron Allen, *The Legend of Noah: Renaissance Rationalism in Art, Science, Literature, and Letters* (Urbana: University of Illinois Press, 1949), 71–80. On inoculation as an ideological strategy, see also Roland Barthes's classic *Mythologies*, trans. Richard Howard and Annette Lavers (1957; repr. New York: Hilland Wang, 2012), 264–70.

18. Peter Sloterdijk, *Bubbles: Spheres I*, trans. Wieland Hoban (South Pasadena, Calif.: Semiotext(e), 2011), 46; subsequent references appear parenthetically in the text. For Sloterdijk's reading of the Flood story, see *Globes: Spheres II*, trans. Wieland Hoban (South Pasadena, Calif.: Semiotext(e), 2014), 237–50, which we treat in our introduction. "Being in the world," Sloterdijk offers, "means being in spheres, . . . the symbolic air conditioning of shared space is the primal production of every society." A precarious ethics and politics unfold from this insight. For, if your breath was not your own to begin with, how could you expect to hold it? Breathe you must; breathe you shall.

19. The rising waters or the threat of inundation attacks the very "human-ambient thing without which people cannot remain people," the "air, the atmosphere—the primary media for life" (Peter Sloterdijk, *Terror from the Air*, trans. Amy Patton and Steve Corcoran [Los Angeles: Semiotext(e), 2007], 25–26).

20. Robert Burton, *The Anatomy of Melancholy*, ed. Shiletto (1621–1651; rep. London, 1891–1893), 2.51; cited also in Allen, *Legend of Noah*, 130.

21. Augustine, *De civitate Dei*, 15.26, in *The City of God against the Pagans*, ed. and trans. R. W. Dyson (Cambridge: Cambridge University Press, 1998), 706–7.

22. Origen, Homily II, in *Homilies on Genesis and Exodus,* trans. Romald E. Heine (Washington, D.C.: The Catholic University of America Press, 1982), 72; subsequent references appear parenthetically in the text.

23. Allen, *Legend of Noah,* 71.

24. Flavius Josephus, *Antiquitates Iudaicae* 1.3, penelope.uchicago.edu/josephus/ant-1.html.

25. Bede, *Hexameron,* in *Patrologia Latina,* ed. J. P. Migne (Paris, 1841–1855), 91:89–92. See Norman Cohn, *Noah's Flood: The Genesis Story in Western Thought* (New Haven, Conn.: Yale University Press, 1996), 38.

26. St. Augustine, *Contra Faustum* 12.15 (authors' translation).

27. The desire to render the ark an allegory for all the world reaches its zenith with Hugh of Saint Victor's idea of a fourfold, proliferative ark that contains the cosmos in *De archa Noe* and *Libellus de formatione arche* (1125–1131). See Conrad Rudolph, *The Mystic Ark: Hugh of St. Victor, Art, and Thought in the Twelfth Century* (Cambridge: Cambridge University Press, 2014)—an analysis that is itself a magnificent example of ark thinking become ark-building. For a now classic treatment of the ark as mnemonic device, see Mary Carruthers, *The Book of Memory* (Cambridge: Cambridge University Press, 2008). For a survey of ark forms in early Jewish and Christian Art, see Ruth Clements, "Shelter Amid the Flood," in *Noah and His Book(s),* ed. Michael E. Stone, Arey Amihay, and Vered Hillel (Atlanta: Society of Biblical Literature, 2005), 277–99.

28. For an account of our site visit to this ark, see Jeffrey J. Cohen and Julian Yates, "Arktistic License (Emzara and the Dinosaurs)," *In the Middle* (blog), October 3, 2018, www.inthemedievalmiddle.com/2018/10/arktistic-license-emzara-and-dinosaurs.html.

29. Simon Schaffer, "The Ark and the Arkive," *Studies in Romanticism* 58 (2019): 155–56. The ark itself could constitute a "heterotopia, a place set deliberately apart that allowed otherwise scattered and troublesome entities to be brought together for analysis, preservation, and display" (157). On Noah, figured as author, collector and archivist of antediluvian writing/knowledge, see Rebecca Scharbach, "The Rebirth of a Book: Noachic Writing in Medieval and Renaissance Europe," in Stone, Amihay, and Hillel, *Noah and His Book(s),* 113–33.

30. John Wilkins, *Essay Towards a Real Character, and a Philosophical Language* (London, 1668), 162; subsequent references appear parenthetically in the text.

31. Intriguingly, the same example of the relative ease in counting the stars (as opposed to, say, the difficulty of counting phenomena, such as clouds) is invoked in early forms of systems theory. See, for example, the beginning of Norbert Wiener, *Cybernetics: Or Control and Communication in the Animal and the Machine* (New York: The Technology Press, 1948); on this trope, see Michel Serres, "Exact and Human," *SubStance* 6/7, no. 21 (1978): 9–19.

32. Laurie Shannon gets at this reductive impulse well when she writes

that, after "doubt about how Noah could have built a craft sufficient to hold all the earthly kinds (plus their necessary provisions)" invited early modern thinkers into "the cold waters of mathematical calculation," the calculations involved mainly centered on subtraction, "marshaling numbers to bolster the literal plausibility of Noah's story" (*The Accommodated Animal: Cosmopolity in Shakespearean Locales* [Chicago: University of Chicago Press, 2013], 270–71). The reductions that Wilkins will intensify are first found in the work of Johannes Buteo and Walter Raleigh before him, both of whom reduce animal diversity into limited species, leave sea creatures to the sea, and refuse to allow passage to mixed creatures like hyenas and mules, as well as some supposedly fabulous beasts (though Buteo had far more tolerance for the last category than did Wilkins). See Shannon.

33. Wilkins is here as elsewhere following his beloved predecessor Buteo, and as usual further reducing the latter's already stark numbers. Buteo believed that 3,650 sheep would be needed to serve as meat; Wilkins cuts that number in half (Shannon, *Accommodated Animal,* 279). In his massive *Arca Noe in tres libros digesta sive de rebus ante diluvium, de diluvio, et de rebus post diluvium a Noemo gestis* (Amsterdam, 1675), polymath Athanasius Kircher would calculate that 4562½ would be the necessary number (Allen, *Legend of Noah,* 185).

34. Hubert Damisch, "Noah's Ark," in *Noah's Ark: Essay on Architecture,* ed. Anthony Vidler, trans. Julie Rose (Cambridge, Mass.: MIT Press, 2016), 1–23 (originally "L'Arche de Noé," *Revue critique* 43 [January–February, 1987]); subsequent references appear parenthetically in the text. For a fuller reading of Damisch on the ark, see Jeffrey Jerome Cohen and Julian Yates, "Ark Thinking," in *Ecologies, Agents, Terrains,* ed. Christopher P. Heuer and Rebecca Zorach (Williamstown, Mass.: Clark Art Institute, 2018), 243–65.

35. Throughout, Damisch quotes from the *Encyclopédie, ou dictionnaire raisonné des sciences, des arts et des métiers,* vol. 1, ed. Denis Diderot and Jean Le Rond d'Alembert (Paris, 1751).

36. Damisch's troubling of Blondel's entry on architecture in the *Encyclopédie* by way of Noah's ark suggests the possibility of a countergenealogy of texts on the origins of architecture that might proceed by way of its relation to matter and materiality. "The art of building in relation to materials," writes Damisch, "has never ceased to" cohabit "with the prospect of a generalized catastrophe," which, typically, either architecture "looks to stave off . . . by rendering it useless" or "merely aspires to furnish humanity with the means to survive . . . without too much damage" ("Noah's Ark," 18). Against this survivalist narrative, Damisch considers that the story of Noah's ark might reveal the way architecture does not stand in opposition to catastrophe, but exists as the art of constructive failure.

One text in this genealogy would be Leon Battista Alberti's lost treatise on naval construction and building, *De navis,* which Leonardo da Vinci knew and refered to in *On Painting.* Indeed, the history of naval construction as a theoretical concern might be said to designate a watery supplement to the history of architecture. The prospect of building without a secure foundation, of building at sea, exposes architecture to invasion by what it seeks to manage or exclude. (We are grateful to Christopher Heuer for alerting us to this productive confluence.) For a consideration of the evidence for what *De navis* might have contained in the context of a larger interest in shipbuilding among Renaissance humanists, see Ennio Concina, "Humanism on the Sea," *Mediterranean Historical Review* 3, no. 1 (1988): 159–65.

The redefinition of architecture by Le Corbusier (Charles-Édouard Jeanneret) was famously inspired by the modular design of ocean liners, among other forms of industrial design. See Le Corbusier, *Toward an Architecture* (1924/1928), trans. John Goodman (Los Angeles: Getty Research Institute, 2007), 145–58. For his cubit-like attempts to craft a unit of measure that would enable modern societies "to harmonize the flow of the world's products," see *The Modular I and II* (1954 and 1958) (Cambridge, Mass.: Harvard University Press, 1980), 107.

For an attempt to think beyond architecture as keyed to the Holocene, toward a mode of building keyed to what has become an entirely unpredictable set of circumstances and nongeneralizable local conditions, see McKenzie Wark, "From Architecture to Kainotecture," *e-flux Architecture,* April 2017, e-flux.com/architecture/accumulation/122201/from-architecture-to-kainotecture/.

37. Samuel Pepys, *Naval Minutes,* ed. J. R. Tanner (London: Navy Records Society, 1926), 205; quoted in Schaffer, "Ark and the Archive," 151. As Schaffer observes, Pepys's "principal informant was his friend the erudite naval engineer and FRS Henry Shere" (159). Pepys also owned a copy of Cornelius Van Yk's *De Nederlandsche Scheeps-bouw-konst Open Gestelt* (Amsterdam: Jan ten Horn, 1697), "which treated the ark as a matter of maritime economy" (155).

38. Pepys, *Naval Minutes,* 205–6.

39. Pepys, *Naval Minutes,* 206.

40. As Shannon observes, "Wilkins' uncanny illustrations show the stakes of choosing between 'fair' accommodation and immiserating confinement. In his floorplan of the ark's hold, we cannot fail to see the imminent expansion of a transatlantic trade in human chattel—a contradictory phrase, as 'livestock' is" (*Accommodated Animal,* 281).

41. Simon Gikandi, *Slavery and the Culture of Taste* (Princeton, N.J.: Princeton University Press, 2011), 10. We remain indebted to what Gikandi calls "contrapuntal reading."

42. On the coincidence of the rise of a science of logistics or "containerization" with "the first great movement of commodities, the ones that could speak . . . the Atlantic slave trade," see Stefano Harney and Fred Moten, *The Undercommons: Fugitive Planning & Black Study* (Brooklyn, N.Y.: Autonomedia, 2013), 92.

43. For the *Brookes* diagram's history, see Marcus Wood, "Imaging the Unspeakable and Speaking the Unimaginable: The 'Description' of the Slave Ship *Brookes* and the Visual Interpretation of the Middle Passage," *Lumen* 16

(1997): 211–45. Wood remarks on the visual similarity between the *Brookes* description and Wilkins's image and describes the slave ship as what Jean Baudrillard would name an "anti-ark," the "nemesis' of Noah's Ark" (223–25 and 242n20, citing Jean Baudrillard, *America* [London: Verso, 1987], 18–19). See also Marcus Wood, *Blind Memory: Visual Representations of Slavery in England and America* (New York: Routledge, 2000).

44. Thomas Clarkson, *The History of the Rise, Progress, and Accomplishment of the Abolition of the African Slave-Trade by the British Parliament* (London: Longman, 1808). This image is reproduced in Elizabeth Donnan, *Documents Illustrative of the History of the Slave Trade to America,* vol. 2 (Washington, D.C.: Carnegie Institution of Washington, 1932), 592–93.

45. On the eighteenth- and nineteenth-century "project of sympathy" and the use of fiction to render the facticity of slavery palpable, see Ian Baucum, *Specters of the Atlantic: Finance, Capital, Slavery and the Philosophy of History* (Durham, N.C.: Duke University Press, 2005), 195–211. On the diagram of the *Brookes* itself as a reconstruction from measurements taken by Captain Parry, who inspected ships on behalf of Parliament's investigation into whether the slave trade should be regulated, see N. Radburn and D. Eltis, "Visualizing the Middle Passage: The *Brookes* and the Reality of Ship Crowding in the Transatlantic Slave Trade," *Journal of Interdisciplinary History* 49, no. 4 (2019): 533–65.

46. Hortense Spillers, "Mama's Baby, Papa's Maybe: An American Grammar Book," *Diacritics* 17, no. 2 (1987): 64–81, at 72. See also "'Whatcha Gonna Do?' Revisiting 'Mama's Baby, Papa's Maybe: An American Grammar Book,' a Conversation with Hortense Spillers, Saidiya Hartman, Farah Jasmine Griffin, Shelly Eversley, & Jennifer L. Morgan," *Women's Studies Quarterly* 35, no. 1–2 (2007): 299–309.

47. On the slave ship as a "space of exception," see Baucom, *Specters of the Atlantic,* 173–94. On the interior of the slave ship more generally, see also James Walvin, *Black Ivory: A History of British Slavery,* 2nd ed. (Oxford: Wiley Blackwell, 2001), 46–47; Marcus Rediker, *The Slave Ship: A Human History* (New York: Viking, 2007).

48. Trans-Atlantic Slave Voyage Database, Emory University Library, www.slavevoyages.org, accessed February 14, 2021.

49. Édouard Glissant, *Poetics of Relation,* trans. Betsy Wing (1990; repr. Ann Arbor: University of Michigan Press, 1997), 6–7.

50. Christina Sharpe, *In the Wake: On Blackness and Being* (Durham, N.C.: Duke University Press, 2016), 68–101.

51. Sharpe, *In the Wake,* 21.

52. Saidiya Hartman, *Lose Your Mother: A Journey Along the Atlantic Slave Route* (New York: Farrar, Straus, and Giroux, 2007), 6, quoted in Sharpe, *In the Wake,* 14–15: "Offspring follows belly" is how Jennifer L. Morgan translates the Latin law in order to make visible the reproductive logic of heritability that led to "enslaved women's maternal possibilities bec[oming] a crucial vehicle by which racial meaning was concretized . . . long before legislators

indexed such possibilities into law" ("*Partus sequitur ventrem*: Law, Race, and Reproduction in Colonial Slavery," *Small Axe* 22, no. 1 [2018]: 1–14, at 1–2).

53. Sharpe, *In the Wake*, 74.

54. David M. Whitford, *The Curse of Ham in the Early Modern Era: The Bible and Justifications for Slavery* (New York: Routledge, 2009). On the indispensability of Noah's cursing of Ham as a "monotheistic macro-stereotype" that enables a secular switch so that, in post-Enlightenment discourses, the descendents of Ham are "condemned this time by the malediction of Nature rather than by Noah," see Sylvia Wynter "Unsettling the Coloniality of Being/Power/Truth/Freedom: Towards the Human, after Man, Its Overrepresentation—An Argument," *The New Centennial Review* 3, no. 3 (2003): 257–337, at 306–7. See, for example, the rhetorical deployment of Genesis with critical irony by Frederick Douglass in the opening chapter of his autobiography to make the point that soon American slavery will become "unscriptural" even to those who take the curse of Ham as a given (*Narrative of the Life of Frederick Douglass, an American Slave, Written by Himself*, ed. William L. Andrews and William S. McFeely, 2nd ed. [New York: Norton 2016]).

55. Jennifer Morgan, *Laboring Women: Reproduction and Gender in New World Slavery* (Philadelphia: University of Pennsylvania Press, 2004), 102–3.

56. Eric Sunquist, *To Wake the Nations: Race in the Making of American Literature* (Cambridge, Mass.: Harvard University Press, 1998), 143–44. Sharpe tropes Sunquist when she writes more absolutely: "Racism is the engine that drives the ship of state's national and imperial projects" (*In the Wake*, 21).

57. Henry Dumas, *Ark of Bones and Other Stories* (New York: Random House, 1974).

58. Kamau Brathwaite, *DS2: Dreamstories* (1989; repr. New York: New Directions, 2007), 164. In an earlier version of the poem, the word "past" appears instead of "ark" (Braithwaite, *Dreamstories* [Harlow, UK: Longman, 1994], 94). For Deloughrey's sensitive reading, see her "Heavy Waters: Waste and Atlantic Modernity," *PMLA* 125, no. 3 (2010): 703–12, at 709–10, quoted in Sharpe, *In the Wake*, 57.

59. Sharpe, *In the Wake*, 57.

60. Spillers, "Mama's Baby, Papa's Maybe," 67.

61. Precisely because of the depredations of slavery and its diasporic hold, Spillers argues that "the black American male embodies the only American community of males which has had the specific occasion to learn who the female is within itself," opening the potential to "regain as an aspect of his own personhood—the power of 'yes' to the 'female' within." Allied to this possibility comes the prospect of "certain representational potentialities for African-American" women, from whose community Spillers writes to say that "we are less interested in joining the ranks of gendered femaleness than gaining the insurgent ground as female social subject, . . . actually claiming

the monstrosity (of a female with the potential to 'name')," and rewriting thereby the matrix of gender ("Mama's Baby, Papa's Maybe," 80).

Spillers's invocation of flesh resonates with the phenomenological "flesh" of Maurice Merleau Ponty as articulated in *The Visible and the Invisible*, trans. Alphonso Lingis (Evanston, Ill.: Northwestern University Press, 1968), 143–47. For Merleau Ponty's phenomenology, "flesh" is not reducible to matter, but refers to the "coiling over of the visible upon the seeing body" (146). Flesh takes on an archival relation to the human, a folding in and over and on itself that creates intruded exteriorities, or what Merleau Ponty terms "the intertwining—the chiasm." So then, flesh figures as the substrate with and on and in which biopower is understood to "write" by the likes of Roberto Esposito in *Immunitas: The Protection and Negation of Life* (London: Polity, 2011), 118–21, 140–41, and Cary Wolfe in *Before the Law: Humans and Other Animals in a Biopolitical Frame* (Chicago: University of Chicago Press, 2013), esp. 50.

62. Sharpe, *In the Wake*, 33. See Saidiya Hartman, *Scenes of Subjection: Terror, Slavery, and Self-Making in Nineteenth-Century America* (Oxford: Oxford University Press, 1997), and Fred Moten, *In the Break: The Aesthetics of the Black Radical Tradition* (Minneapolis: University of Minnesota Press, 2003), particularly the program outlined in the introduction, "The Object Resists: Aunt Hester's Scream" (1–24), and Moten's subsequent "consent not to be a single being" trilogy: *Black and Blur* (Durham, N.C.: Duke University Press, 2017); *Stolen Life* (Durham, N.C.: Duke University Press, 2018); *The Universal Machine* (Durham, N.C.: Duke University Press, 2018). See also Moten and Harney, *The Undercommons*.

63. Achille Mbembe, *Necropolitics*, trans. Steven Corcoran (Durham, N.C.: Duke University Press, 2019), 12–27.

64. Paul Gilroy, *The Black Atlantic: Modernity and Double Consciousness* (Cambridge, Mass.: Harvard University Press, 1993), 4–5; see also 16–17 and throughout for the importance of sailors and seafaring. On the slave ship and spatial technologies more generally as sites of contestation, sites of ideological and material enclosure but also sites that might launch "an oppositional geography," see Katherine McKitterick, *Demonic Grounds: Black Women and the Cartographies of Struggle* (Minneapolis: University of Minnesota Press, 2006), ix–xxxi, at xi. For a gentle prod to Gilroy to consider nascent queer alliances deriving from confinement or life aboard, see Omise'eke Natasha Tinsley, "Black Atlantic, Queer Atlantic: Queer Imaginings of the Middle Passage," *GLQ: A Journal of Lesbian and Gay Studies* 14, no. 2–3 (2008): 191–215.

65. On "bare activity" as an "antidote" to Giorgio Agamben's conceptualization of "bare (or more properly denuded) life," see Brian Massumi, *What Animals Teach Us about Politics* (Durham, N.C.: Duke University Press, 2014), 94; see also 65–90 ("Supplement 2: The Zoo-ology of Play") for a consideration of the surplus activity of animals in zoos. See also Giorgio

Agamben, *Homo Sacer: Sovereign Power and Bare Life,* trans. Daniel Heller-Roazen (Stanford, Calif.: Stanford University Press, 1995).

66. John Calvin, *Commentaries on the Book of Genesis,* trans. John King (Edinburgh: Calvin Translation Society, 1847), 260.

67. Calvin, *Commentaries on the Book of Genesis,* 261.

68. See, among others, Bill Cosby's 1963 stand-up routine on Noah (youtube.com/watch?v=bputeFGXEjA) and Eddie Izzard's 2009 *Stripped.* On the comic or chronic laxity of Noah when faced with the task of collecting all the animals, see Jeanette Winterson, *Boating for Beginners* (London: Methuen, 1985), and Julian Barnes, *A History of the World in 10½ Chapters* (New York: Knopf, 1989), 3–30.

69. Thinking through the firing techniques of medieval materials, Anne Harris notes that, in depictions of the Tower of Babel, the bricks "are modular and multiple: they quickly and easily systematize fire's doing; they are primal pyromena. . . . Bricks are fire transfigured, fire moving into permanence. And so the first thing that is built with fire is a tower designed to reach Heaven" ("Pyromena: Fire's Doing," in *Elemental Ecocriticism: Thinking with Earth, Air, Water and Fire,* ed. Jeffrey Jerome Cohen and Lowell Duckert [Minneapolis: University of Minnesota Press, 2015], 27–54, at 30).

70. Lisa Kiser, "The Animals in Chester's 'Noah's Flood,'" *Early Theatre* 14, no. 1 (2011): 15–44, at 27.

71. *Pageante of Noyes Fludd,* in *The Chester Mystery Cycle,* ed. R. M. Lumiansky and David Mills, EETS, 2nd ser., vol. 3 (Oxford: Oxford University Press, 1974), lines 173–76; parenthetical citations of the play in the text will be from this edition and by line number.

72. Chester-cycle *Pageante of Noyes Fludd,* line 194.

73. Chester-cycle *Pageante of Noyes Fludd,* lines 225–36. As Theresa Colletti has shown, "the Chester cycle's five complete manuscripts are all early modern antiquarian products," copied between 1591–1609 ("The Chester Cycle in Sixteenth-Century Religious Culture," *Journal of Medieval and Early Modern Studies* 37, no. 3 [2007]: 531–47, at 532). Colletti posits here that the conservational impulse through which we possess the texts of many "medieval" dramas has much to do with a Catholic desire to preserve a cherished past against an austerely Protestant present in which the cycle plays had been suppressed.

74. Chester-cycle *Pageante of Noyes Fludd,* line 246. As Francis Lee Utley has demonstrated, over the millennia, interpreters and retellers of the Flood myth have found in this frustrating invisibility of its women an invitation. Traditions from around the world have bestowed upon the four wives proper names and sometimes family origins. By Utley's count, Noah's wife has been given at least 103 different names ("The One Hundred and Three Names of Noah's Wife," *Speculum* 16, no. 4 [1941]: 426–52). Sarah Novacich writes well about the coincidence of the pageant wagon and the ark in *Shaping the Archive in Late Medieval England,* 88.

75. Thomas Sternhold, John Hopkins, et al., *The Whole Book of Psalms Collected into English Metre,* 4th ed. [?] (London: John Day, 1561). We are grateful to Frank Desiderio for pointing out the way the psalm singing figures the Flood in the play.

76. Middle English from *The Gawain Poet: Complete Works,* ed. and trans. Marie Borroff (New York: Norton, 2012), line 433; subsequent quotations in the text are cited parenthetically by line number.

77. For a thorough allegorization of the ark, see especially Hugh of St. Victor's *De arca Noe morali* and *De vanitate mundi,* in *Hugh of St-Victor: Selected Spiritual Writings* (New York: Harper and Row, 1962), 45–182.

78. On the lush materiality of medieval objects, see Anne Harris and Karen Overbey, "Field Change / Discipline Change," in *Burn After Reading,* vol. 2, *The Future We Want,* ed. Jeffrey Jerome Cohen (Washington, D.C.: Oliphaunt, 2014), 127–43.

79. Kircher, *Arca Noe,* 37 and 45–46. For an extensive summary of Kircher's entire opus, see the appendix to Allen, *Legend of Noah,* 182–91.

80. Le Corbusier, *Toward an Architecture,* 151.

81. For a discussion of Kircher's sorting of animal life, see Roberto Buonanno, *The Stars of Galileo Gallilei and the Universal Knowledge of Athanasius Kircher,* trans. Giuliana Giobbi (New York: Springer, 2014), 97–119.

82. The word "midrash" derives from the Hebrew verb *darash,* "to seek," as related to us by our invaluable copy editor (who would bid the reader check out the entry on midrash in *The Oxford Dictionary of the Jewish Religion,* 2nd ed. [Oxford: Oxford University Press, 2011], and the more in-depth work in Paul D. Mandel, *The Origins of Midrash: From Teaching to Text* [Leiden: Brill, 2017], as well as Jacob Neusner's classic *What Is Midrash* [Eugene, Ore.: Wipf and Stock, 1987]).

83. Babylonian Talmud, Sanh. 108b (William Davidson edition, sefaria.org/Sanhedrin). See also Anna Birgitta Rooth, *Raven and Carcass: An Investigation of a Motif in the Deluge Myth in Europe, Asia, and North America* (Helsinki: Suomalainen Tiedeakatemia, 1962), 91 and 99, and Louis Ginzberg, *Legends of Jews,* trans. Henrietta Szold, 4 vols. (Philadelphia: Jewish Publication Society of America, 1909–1938), 1:163. For a magisterial consideration of the Eastern and Western exegetical accounts of life and sex aboard the ark, see David M. Goldenberg, *Black and Slave: The Origins and History of the Curse of Ham* (Berlin: De Gruyter, 2017), 44–67.

84. Babylonian Talmud, Sanh. 108b.

85. Babylonian Talmud, Sanh. 108b. The verses crucial to the argument are: "And you shall come into the ark, you, and your sons, and your wife, and your sons' wives with you' (Genesis 6:18)" and "it is written: 'Emerge from the ark, you and your wife, and your sons and your sons' wives with you' (Genesis 8:16)." For an account of this commentary tradition on Noah, see also Arich Amihay, "Noah in Rabbinic Literature," in Stone, Amihay, and Hillel, *Noah and His Book(s),* 208–9.

86. For a reading of the commentary tradition on this subject, see Steven Greenberg, *Wrestling with God and Man: Homosexuality in the Jewish Tradition* (Madison: University of Wisconsin Press, 2004), 41–95.

87. On the erotic possibilities to be had aboard the ark, see Avery Dorn Shifter, *The Sex Crazed Unicorn on Noah's Ark* (n.p.: Monster Erotica Press, 2014). While we are unable either to recommend or discourage reading this book, we remain in sympathy with the generative possibilities to be had from fan fiction. Most of the contents of the book we are writing might be described, in some shape or form, as Genesis fan fiction.

88. Christopher Cat and Countee Cullen, *The Lost Zoo: A Rhyme for The Young, But Not Too Young* (New York: Harper and Brothers, 1940), 31; subsequent references appear parenthetically in the text.

89. On the sexual suggestiveness of the names of these lost animals, see Benjamin Kahan, "Antediluvian Sex: Countee Cullen, Christopher Smart, and the Queerness of Uplift," *African American Review* 48, no. 1–2 (2015): 191–202, at 198.

90. Kahan, "Antediluvian Sex," 191.

91. For this reading, see Gillian Adams, "Missing the Boat: Countee Cullen's *The Lost Zoo,*" *The Lion and the Unicorn* 21, no. 1 (1997): 40–58.

92. Kahan, "Antediluvian Sex," 200.

93. Here we invoke Eve Kosofsky Sedgwick's sense of "the desire of a reparative impulse" as, "on the one hand, . . . additive and accretive. Its fear, a realistic one, is that the culture surrounding it is inadequate or inimical to nurture; it wants to confer plenitude on an object that will then have resources to offer to an inchoate self" (*Touching Feeling* [Durham, N.C.: Duke University Press, 2003], 149). We do so, attuned to the possibility that, when such desires prove optimistic, that might be because they have been subject to modes of ideological capture cathected to objects that are "cruel," as explored, not without ambivalence, by Lauren Berlant in *Cruel Optimism* (Durham, N.C.: Duke University Press, 2011).

94. Babylonian Talmud, Sanh. 108b.

95. See, for example, the exploitative two- or multitier systems that undergird the worlds of such texts as Kim Stanley Robinson's *New York 2140* (New York: Orbit, 2014), and the film *Snowpiercer* (2013, dir. Bong Joon Ho, Moho Film) and TV series *Snowpiercer* (2020), both based on the 1982 graphic novel *Le Transperceneige* by Jacques Lob, Benjamin Legrand, and Jean-Marc Rochette.

96. The *Aberdeen Bestiary,* MS 24, Aberdeen University fol. 55r; Latin and English translations are from the digital editon.

97. Paolo Soleri, *Arcology: The City in the Image of Man* (Cambridge, Mass.: MIT Press, 1969). Arcology is legible as a hypermodernist aesthetic that seeks to live without the automobile. Soleri's work includes the Arcosanti project, the website for which (arcosanti.org) includes a history of the term and concept, as well as links to attempts at building arcologies. For an account of our site visit to the utopian community/colony at Arcosanti and

to neighboring Biosphere 2, see Jeffrey J. Cohen and Julian Yates, "'What If' (We Were) to 'Hold It?,'" *In the Middle* (blog), February 18, 2019, www.inthemedievalmiddle.com/2019/02/what-if-we-were-to-hold-it.html.

98. Compare this project also with the Seasteading Institute founded in 2008 by Peter Thiel and Patri Friedman, (seasteading.org). For an overview of these floating cities or republics and their rewriting of law/sovereignty, see Surabi Ranganathan, "The Law of the Sea," arcgis.com/apps/MapJournal/index.html?appid=b20774fc0e4845d59797933f57a55017, accessed October 5, 2020. See also Elizabeth M. De Loughrey, *Allegories of the Anthropocene* (Durham, N.C.: Duke University Press, 2019), 145–46, for a reading of what she calls these "aquatopias." For science-fiction versions, see, e.g., William Hope Hodgson's 1912 *The Night Land,* Larry Niven and Jerry Pournelle's 1981 *Oath of Fealty,* and Peter Hamilton's 1997 *Neutronium Alchemist.* These are immobile arcologies; a spaceship is obviously an arcology on the move.

99. Paolo Bacigalupi, *The Water Knife* (New York: Vintage, 2016), 110–11; subsequent references appear parenthetically in the text.

100. On the forgetting of the common world, see Bruno Latour, *Down to Earth: Politics in the New Climatic Regime,* trans. Catherine Porter (Cambridge: Polity, 2018).

101. Timothy Findley, *Not Wanted on the Voyage* (Toronto: Penguin, 1984), 270; subsequent references appear parenthetically in the text.

102. It is perhaps worth noting here that *Not Wanted on the Voyage* was written, as Findley once remarked, at the height of the HIV crisis and published three years before Princess Diana would be photographed shaking a patient by the hand in what has since served as an iconic moment that captured the collective imagination.

103. Rebecca Solnit, *Paradise Built in Hell: The Extraordinary Communities that Arise in Disaster* (Houndmills, UK: Penguin, 2010), 130–31, 135.

104. On the necessity for utopia to remain concrete or, as we think it, mundane, see José Esteban Muñoz, *Cruising Utopia: The Then and There of Queer Futurity* (New York: New York University Press, 2009).

5. Stow Away!

1. Alfonso X, *General estoria* 1.30, ed. Borja Sánchez-Prieto, 10 vols. (Madrid: Fundación José Antonio de Castro, 2009), 1:40–41. Here trans. David Wacks. We thank David for his bringing this source to our attention.

2. Daniel Defoe, *Robinson Crusoe,* ed. Michael Shinagel, 2nd ed. (New York: Norton, 1994), 112. For Haraway's introduction and exposition of her term "god trick," see her "Situated Knowledges: The Science Question in Feminism and the Privilege of Partial Perspective," *Feminist Studies* 14, no. 3 (1988): 575–99.

3. Michel Serres, *The Parasite,* trans. Lawrence R. Schehr (1982; repr. Minneapolis: University of Minnesota Press, 2007), 12; subsequent references appear parenthetically in the text.

4. Karen Raber examines the implications of this passage from Serres

for reimagining human-animal community and indistinction in *Animal Bodies, Renaissance Culture* (Philadelphia: University of Pennsylvania Press, 2013), 123.

5. The excluded middle or "third man" *(le tiers exclu)* is a term Serres adapts from logic in order to make a properly antidialectical model of thinking and communication in which sense-making requires the exclusion of a third position (noise) by the communicative circuit. *The Parasite* might productively be read as an exploration, celebration, warning, and attempt to modify our understanding of how noise/static/vermin (and the array of terms excluded from thought, culture, and community) return in sometimes alarming and sometimes productive ways. Recall that, for Serres, storytelling (an unequal exchange of words for food) is founded on a parasitic relation. On the excluded middle, see *Parasite,* 22–26, and throughout; on storytelling, see 15–16. In other works, Serres attempts to chart paths by which *le tiers exclu* might become *le tiers instruit* (the instructed third) that would modulate the parasitic relation toward something approaching symbiosis.

6. Kim Stanley Robinson, *Aurora* (New York: Orbit Books, 2015), 47; subsequent references appear parenthetically in the text.

7. Julian Barnes, *A History of the World in 10½ Chapters* (New York: Alfred A. Knopf, 1989), 62; subsequent references appear parenthetically in the text.

8. Raymond Williams, *Keywords: A Vocabulary of Culture and Society* (New York: Oxford University Press, 1976), 164.

9. On the broken logic of exchange as indexed to storytelling and the exchange of words for food at the dinner table, see Michel Serres, *Parasite,* 15–16. Serres designates the logic as the asymmetries of parasitism and also, tellingly, hospitality. In French, *l'hôte* refers both to host and guest, which enacts, for Serres, the neutral, parasitic valence to structures of hospitality and hostility and the way symbiosis can tilt into violent exclusion.

10. On bookworms, archival interference, and storytelling in the Middle Ages, see Emma Maggie Solberg, "Human and Insect Book Worms," *Postmedieval* 11 (2020): 12–22.

11. On the history of parenthesis, see John Lennard, *But I Digress: The Exploitation of Parenthesis in English Printed Verse* (Oxford: Clarendon, 1991); for a more general history of typographical markers, see Malcolm B. Parkes, *Pause and Effect: An Introduction to Punctuation in the History of the West* (Berkeley: University of California Press, 1993).

12. Steve Baker, *Picturing the Beast: Animals, Identity, and Representation* (1991; repr. Champaign: University of Illinois Press, 1991, 2001), 131; subsequent references appear parenthetically in the text.

13. *Rupert: The Daily Express Annual* (London: Express Newspapers, 1988), 83, quoted in Baker, *Picturing the Beast,* 128.

14. On anthropo-zoo-genesis, see Vinciane Despret, "The Body We Care For: Figures of Anthropo-zoo-genesis," *Body and Society* 10, no. 2–3 (2004): 111–34; on the coextensive nature of legal categories of personhood and the

personification strategies of lyric, see Barbara Johnson, *Persons and Things* (Cambridge, Mass.: Harvard University Press, 2008). On the coimbrication of race and species in different understandings of animation or "animacy," see Mel Y. Chen, *Animacies: Biopolitics, Racial Mattering, and Queer Affect* (Durham, N.C.: Duke University Press, 2012).

15. Garrett P. Serviss, *The Second Deluge* (Medford, Ore.: Armchair Fiction, 2017 [1911]), 13; subsequent references appear parenthetically in the text.

16. Albertus Frederik Johannes Klijn, *Seth in Jewish, Christian and Gnostic Literature*, Supplements to Novum Testamentum (Leiden: Brill, 1977), 54.

17. For a yet more ambivalent deployment of a performance of *King Lear* as the frame narrative for the story of a traveling theatrical company in a postapocalyptic world, see Emily St. John Mandel, *Station Eleven* (New York: Vintage, 2014).

18. Arthur L. Little Jr., "Re-Historicizing Race, White Melancholia, and the Shakespearean Property," *Shakespeare Quarterly* 67, no. 1 (2016): 88–89. See also Cheryl Harris, "Whiteness as Property," *Harvard Law Review* 106 (1993): 1707–91.

19. Kathryn Yusoff, *A Billion Black Anthropocenes or None* (Minneapolis: University of Minnesota Press, 2018).

20. Steve Mentz, *Shipwreck Modernity: Ecologies of Globalization, 1550–1719* (Minneapolis: University of Minnesota Press, 2015), xiv.

21. Russell R. Dynes, "Noah and Disaster Planning: The Cultural Significance of the Flood Story," *Journal of Contingencies and Crisis Management* 11, no. 4 (2003): 170–77, at 172–73; subsequent references appear parenthetically in the text. Thanks go to Tricia Wachtendorf for bringing the work of Russell R. Dynes to our attention.

22. Key theorists contributing to Dynes's sense of the sovereignty of this model include Ulrich Beck, *Risk Society: Toward a New Modernity* (London: Sage, 1992), but not explicitly any works from continental philosophy, biopolitics, or the Italian Marxist tradition, or Giorgio Agamben's *Homo Sacer: Sovereign Power and Bare Life*, trans. Daniel Heller-Roazen (Stanford, Calif.: Stanford University Press, 1998), or *State of Exception*, trans. Kevin Attell (Chicago: University of Chicago Press, 2005).

23. 177n3 in "Noah and Disaster Planning" cites Dynes's own "Community Emergency Planning: False Assumptions and Inappropriate Analogies," *International Journal of Mass Emergencies and Disasters* 12, no. 2 (2004): 141–58. This footnote anticipates the important focus on community planning and the very notion of community as part of ongoing research in the field of disaster studies, or critical disaster studies, as it has recently been renamed. For an excellent introduction to critical disaster studies, see *Critical Disaster Studies (Critical Studies in Risk and Disaster)*, ed. Jacob A. C. Remes and Andy Horowitz (Philadelphia: University of Pennsylvania Press, 2021).

24. For a candid and intriguingly laconic history of the Disaster Research Center Dynes founded along with E. L. Quarantelli and J. Eugene Haas at

Ohio State University in 1963, which subsequently moved to University of Delaware in 1985, see E. L. Quarantelli, "The Early History of the Disaster Research Center," drc.udel.edu/content-sub-site/Documents/DRCEarlyHistory.pdf, accessed September 13, 2022.

25. Rachel Carson, *Silent Spring* (New York: Houghton Mifflin, 1962).

26. Donna Haraway, *Staying with the Trouble: Making Kin in the Chthulucene* (Durham, N.C.: Duke University Press, 2016), 10; subsequent references appear parenthetically in the text.

27. On the nested species of animal fable, see the commentary on Plautus's statement in *Asinaria* that "Lupus est homo homini, non homo, quom qualis sit non novit" ("When one does not know him, man is not a man, but a wolf for man") in Jacques Derrida, *The Beast and the Sovereign,* trans. Geoffrey Bennington, ed. Michel Lisse, Marie-Louise Mallet, and Ginette Michaud, vol. 1 (Chicago: University of Chicago Press, 2009), 11, and Serres's elaboration to include other animal figures in *Parasite*: "Man is a wolf for men, an eagle for sheep, a rat for rats. In truth a *rara avis*" (7).

28. On this order of lush materiality, see Anne Harris and Karen Overbey, "Field Change/Discipline Change," *Burn After Reading,* vol. 2: *The Future We Want,* ed. Jeffrey Jerome Cohen (Washington, D.C.: Oliphaunt, 2014) 127–43. See also Hubert Damisch's arguments about the fate and function of decoration/accessorization in modern architecture/design, in *Noah's Ark: Essay on Architecture,* ed. Anthony Vidler, trans. Julie Rose (Cambridge, Mass.: MIT Press, 2016).

29. Shel Silverstein, *Inside Folk Songs,* Atlantic, 1962.

30. The Irish Rovers, *The Unicorn,* Decca, 1968.

31. See lyrics to "The Unicorn" as revised by Andrew Mckee for the Brobdingnagian Bards, thebards.net/music/lyrics/The_Unicorn_Song.shtml, accessed October 1, 2020. The last line of the song quotes from J. M. Barrie, *Peter Pan* (1911; repr. Millennium Fulcrum Edition, 1991), 71.

32. On the "noise" of overpopulation as the source of the flood in the constellation of fragments and texts that make up the Gilgamesh story, see David Damrosch, *The Buried Book: The Loss and Rediscovery of the Great Epic of Gilgamesh* (New York: Henry Holt, 2007), 222–24. Compare also the way the "telling of man's beginnings, / how the almighty had made the earth" figures as noise pollution or "din" to Grendel in *Beowulf,* trans. Seamus Heaney (New York: Norton, 2000), lines 85–98.

33. *The Epic of Gilgamesh,* trans. and ed. Benjamin R. Foster (New York: Norton, 2011), 84–86.

34. A. N. Tynan, "Abel's Ark: A New Way with Old Heads," *The Curator* 30, no. 1 (1987): 85–94, at 85–86.

35. Tynan, "Abel's Ark," 86. On the culture of big-game hunting as allied to imperial views of Africa, see Angela Thompsell, *Hunting Africa* (New York: Palgrave Macmillan, 2015). See also J. MacKenzie, *Empire of Nature* (Manchester, UK: Manchester University Press, 1988). On Abel Chapman as one of a group of like-minded men whose masculinity is calibrated by

their sense of the outdoors, hunting, sport, and English imperial identity, see J. A. Mangan and Callum McKenzie, "Imperial Masculinity Institutionalized: The Shikar Club," *The International Journal of the History of Sport* 25, no. 9 (2008): 1218–42.

36. Tynan, "Abel's Ark," 92.

37. James Steel (KT), *Annual Report,* Council of the Natural History Society of Northumberland, Durham, and Newcastle upon Tyne for the Year Ended July 31, 1984, 9 pp.

38. On *Abel's Ark* as an example of the many ways in which museums have sought to reimagine their natural history collections, see J. M. M. Alberti, *The Afterlives of Animals: A Museum Menagerie* (Charlottesville: University of Virginia Press, 2011), 1–16.

39. Richard Schechner, *Environmental Theater* (New York: Hawthorn, 1973).

40. *Moonrise Kingdom* (dir. Wes Anderson, 2012) and Wes Anderson and Roman Coppola, *Moonrise Kingdom* [screenplay] (London: Faber and Faber, 2012).

41. Walter de la Mare, Leonard Clark, and Marion Gill, *Tom Tiddler's Ground: A Book of Poetry for Children* (London: Bodley Head, 1961), 56.

6. Ravens and Doves

1. Unless otherwise noted, all quotations from the Bible are from *The Jewish Study Bible,* 2nd edition, ed. Adele Berlin and Marc Zvi Brettler (Oxford: Oxford University Press, 2014).

2. Thomas Dekker, *Four Birds of Noah's Ark* (1608), ed. Robert Hudson (Grand Rapids, Mich.: Ferdmans Publishing Company, 2017), 25.

3. Steven Mentz writes of catastrophe that "out of disasters come possibilities for new order and new ordering systems," stressing that, even after "shocking violence," the chance to reimagine relations with the world arises (*Shipwreck Modernity: Ecologies of Globalization, 1550–1719* [Minneapolis: University of Minnesota Press, 2015], 180).

4. Richard A. Lanham, *A Handlist of Rhetorical Terms,* 2nd ed. (Berkeley: University of California Press, 1991), 118 and 104.

5. Babylonian Talmud, Sanh. 108b (William Davidson edition, sefaria.org/Sanhedrin). See also Anna Birgitta Rooth, *Raven and Carcass: An Investigation of a Motif in the Deluge Myth in Europe, Asia, and North America* (Helsinki: Suomalainen Tiedeakatemia, 1962), 91 and 99; Louis Ginzberg, *Legends of Jews,* trans. Henrietta Szold, 4 vols. (Philadelphia: Jewish Publication Society of America, 1909–1938), 1:163.

6. *The Aberdeen Bestiary,* Aberdeen University, MS 24, fol. 6; subsequent references to the bestiary appear parenthetically in the text by folio page, translations from the Latin appear in the digital edition of the bestiary.

7. Susan Crane, *Animal Encounters: Contacts and Concepts in Medieval Britain* (Philadelphia: University of Pennsylvania Press, 2013).

8. Andrew D. Blechman, "Flying Rats," in *Trash Animals: How We Live*

with Nature's Filthy, Feral, Invasive, and Unwanted Species, ed. Kelsi Nagy and Philip David Johnson II (Minneapolis: University of Minnesota Press, 2013), 221–42, at 222.

9. James Thurber, "There's an Owl in My Room," *The New Yorker,* November 10, 1934. For an inquiry into the dual lives of the humdrum pigeon and the refined dove, see Barbara Allen, *Pigeon* (London: Reaktion, 2009).

10. Jeanette Winterson, *Boating for Beginners* (London: Minerva, 1985), 79–80.

11. Winterson, *Boating for Beginners,* 134.

12. In his experimental work of philosophy *Glas,* Jacques Derrida reads Ferdinand de Saussure's dismissal of onomatopoeia in his foundational *Course in General Linguistics* as a symptom of his concern that "true" onomatopoeia might call into question one of two key theses by revealing that "the choice of the signifier is not always arbitrary." Derrida reads Saussure as foreclosing on the potential insight that the performance, and so actualization, of any language system as it evolves invites an order of mimetic play that, whatever the origins of a language, subject it to the constraints of a local environment, opening the way for thinking about language as a contact zone with, and so marked by, forms of life otherwise than human; see Saussure, *Course in General Linguistics,* trans. Wade Baskin (New York: McGraw-Hill, 1966), 69, and Derrida, *Glas,* trans. John P. Leavey Jr. and Richard Rand (Lincoln: University of Nebraska Press, 1990), 91–95.

13. Debbie Blue, *Consider the Birds: A Provocative Guide to Birds of the Bible* (Nashville, Tenn.: Abingdon, 2013), 194.

14. Vinciane Despret, *Quand le loup habitera avec l'agneau* (Paris: Seuil, 2002), 138, quoting Rémy and Bernadette Chauvin, *Le modèle animal* (Paris: Hachette, 1982). A translation of this chapter appears as Despret, "The Enigma of the Raven," trans. Jeffrey Bussolini, *Angelaki* 20, no. 2 (2015): 57–72, at 57; subsequent references will appear parenthetically in the text.

15. As one review of the usefulness of Skinner boxes augmented now by computer technologies of surveillance explains, "the operant conditioning chamber, or 'Skinner box,' is a standard apparatus used in the experimental analysis of animal behavior. Basically, it is a closed box that, apart from the subject to be tested, contains the following parts. First, an operandum is required—that is, a device that automatically detects the occurrence of a behavioral response. This may, for example, be a lever (typically used for primates and rats) or a response key (typically used for birds). Second, a Skinner box includes a means of delivering a primary reinforcer to serve as the unconditioned stimulus, usually a food or water dispenser, as well as a conditioned reinforcer, such as a light or a tone. . . . [While] initially devised to study the basics of operant and classical conditioning, the Skinner box has, by now, become a tool to explore a broad range of issues, including animals' perceptual abilities, visual categorization, and memory" (Michael Morten Steurer, Ulrike Aust, and Ludwig Huber, "The Vienna Comparative Cognition Technology [VCCT]: An Innovative Operant Conditioning System

for Various Species and Experimental Procedures," *Behavioral Research* 44 [2012]: 909–18, at 909).

On epistemic objects and inscription devices, see Hans Jörg Rheinberger, *Toward a History of Epistemic Things: Synthesizing Proteins in the Test Tube* (Stanford, Calif.: Stanford University Press, 1997). For a classic paper analyzing results gleaned from a Skinner Box experiment, see B. F. Skinner, "'Superstition' in the Pigeon," *Journal of Experimental Psychology* 38 (1947): 168–72.

16. Despret invokes Richard Dawkins's *The Selfish Gene* (Oxford: Oxford University Press, 1976). For a revealing analysis of the "opportunity costs" for researchers based on the plant or animal they choose to study, see Evelyn Fox Keller, *A Feeling for the Organism: The Life and Work of Barbara McClintock* (New York: Henry Holt, 1983).

17. Despret, *Quand le loup habitera avec l'agneau*, 276–77.

18. Thereafter, writes Peter Sloterdijk, this is our "relationship with nature in which it can never again be viewed as an unproblematic matrix of human, animal and plant life" (*Globes: Spheres II*, trans. Wieland Hoban [South Pasadena, Calif.: Semiotext(e), 2014], 241).

19. John Milton, *Paradise Lost* 11.756, in, *John Milton*, ed. Stephen Orgel and Jonathan Goldberg (Oxford: Oxford University Press, 1992).

20. *The Works of Michael Drayton*, ed. J. William Hebel, vol. 3 (Oxford: Basil Blackwell, 1961), 348–49 (lines 823–24).

21. Middle English from *The Gawain Poet: Complete Works*, ed. and trans. Marie Borroff (New York: Norton, 2012), lines 455–56.; subsequent quotations in the text are cited parenthetically by line number.

22. Milton McC. Gatch, "Noah's Raven in Genesis A and the Illustrated Old English Hexateuch," *Gesta* 14, no. 2 (1975): 3–15, at 5.

23. R. W. L. Moberly, "Why Did Noah Send Out a Raven?" *Vetus Testamentum* 50, no. 3 (2000): 345–56; subsequent references appear parenthetically in the text.

24. Jean Calvin, *A Commentary on Genesis* (London, 1847/1965), 279, cited by Moberly, "Why Did Noah Send Out a Raven?," 346.

25. *The Epic of Gilgamesh* 11.145–54, trans. Maureen Gallery Kovacs (Stanford, Calif.: Stanford University Press, 1985); subsequent references will appear in the text according to the line numbers of tablet 11, as here. For a reading tuned to the literalness of this scene, see Boria Sax, *Crow* (London: Reaktion, 2003), 31–35.

26. Bernd Heinrich, *Ravens in Winter* (1989; repr. New York: Simon and Schuster Paperbacks, 2014), 33; subsequent references appear parenthetically in the text.

27. Despret, "Enigma of the Raven," 60–61.

28. On inquiry as a mode of hunting that subordinates the investigator to the phenomenon in the mode of what she calls "reciprocal capture," see Isabelle Stengers, *Cosmopolitics I*, trans. Robert Bononno (Minneapolis: University of Minnesota Press, 2010), 35–37.

29. On the impossibility of separating a raven from its locale, see Barry Holstrun Lopez, *Desert Notes: Reflections in the Eye of a Raven* (New York: Avon, 1976).

30. For an inspiring series of essays on making and sharing worlds with corvids that emphasizes the breadth to what Heinrich calls "recruitment," see Thom Van Dooren, *The Wake of Crows: Living and Dying in Shared Worlds* (New York: Columbia University Press, 2019).

31. Pëtr Kropotkin, *Mutual Aid: A Factor in Evolution* (1902; repr. New York: New York University Press, 1972). On reading Kropotkin with primatology, see also ch. 3, "Apes and Savages in an Anarchist World," in Despret's *Quand le loup habitera avec l'agneau.*

32. Donna Haraway, *Staying with the Trouble: Making Kin in the Chthulucene* (Durham, N.C.: Duke University Press, 2016), 1.

33. Stacy Alaimo, *Exposed: Environmental Politics and Pleasures in Posthuman Times* (Minneapolis: University of Minnesota Press, 2016).

34. Ursula K. Heise, *Imagining Extinction: The Cultural Meanings of Endangered Species* (Chicago: University of Chicago Press, 2016), 235.

35. "Urban Ark," KCET, kcet.org/shows/earth-focus/projects/urban-ark, accessed December 22, 2020.

36. Mike Davis, "Who Will Build the Ark?," *New Left Review* 61 (January–February 2010): 29–46, at 29; subsequent references appear parenthetically in the text.

37. Anna Lowenhaupt Tsing, *The Mushroom at the End of the World: On the Possibility of Life in Capitalist Ruins* (Princeton, N.J.: Princeton University Press, 2015), 5.

38. McKenzie Wark, "From Architecture to Kainotecture," in Accumulation, *e-flux Architecture,* April 2017, e-flux.com/architecture/accumulation /122201/from-architecture-to-kainotecture/, par. 1, accessed December 24, 2020. We thank Lance Winn for bringing Wark's essay to our attention.

39. Wark, "From Architecture to Kainotecture," par. 3.

40. Wark, "From Architecture to Kainotecture," par. 4.

41. Wark, "From Architecture to Kainotecture," par. 7.

42. Wark, "From Architecture to Kainotecture," par. 5. As we have done in earlier chapters, Wark draws inspiration here from Peter Sloterdijk's discussion of environmental warfare in *Terror from the Air,* trans. Amy Patton and Steve Corcoran (Los Angeles: Semiotext[e], 2007), 25–26.

43. Sarah Blake, *Naamah* (New York: Riverhead, 2019), 32; subsequent references appear parenthetically in the text.

44. Blake does not state from where she derives the name "Naamah" for Noah's wife. According to Genesis 4:22, Naamah was simply the daughter of Lamech, but the midrash Genesis Rabba and the commentary on Genesis by Rashi describe her as the wife of Noah.

45. Neal Stevenson, *The Seveneves* (New York: William Morrow, 2015).

46. On the cursing of Ham with the raven as indexed to skin color and the raven's blackness as byword for race, see David M. Goldenberg, *The Curse of*

Ham: Race and Slavery in Early Judaism, Christianity, and Islam (Princeton, N.J.: Princeton University Press, 2003), 100.

47. See Robert Liberles, *Salo Wittmayer Baron: Architect of Jewish History* (New York: New York University Press, 1995), 117–18.

48. See Joseph Shatzmiller, *Cultural Exchange: Jews, Christians, and Art in the Medieval Marketplace* (Princeton, N.J.: Princeton University Press, 2013), 133–37, and Yael Zirlin, "The Decoration of the Miscellany, Its Iconography and Style," in *The Northern French Hebrew Miscellany* (British Library Add. Ms. 11639), ed. Jeremy Schonfield, 2 vols. (London: British Library, 2003), 2:75–161.

7. Abandon Ark?

1. Jeffrey J. Cohen and Julian Yates, "Noah's Ark Being Rebuilt Here," *In the Middle* (blog), November 27, 2016, www.inthemedievalmiddle.com/2016/11/noahs-ark-being-rebuilt-here.html.

2. For a decoding of the event and a useful starting point for a deeper investigation of this signage, see Matthew Gabriele, "Vikings, Crusaders, Confederates: Misunderstood Historical Imagery at the January 6 Capitol Insurrection," *Perspectives on History: The New Magazine of the American Historical Association*, January 12, 2021, historians.org/publications-and-directories/perspectives-on-history/january-2021/vikings-crusaders-confederates-misunderstood-historical-imagery-at-the-january-6-capitol-insurrection, and Helen Young, "Why Far-Right and White Supremacists Have Embraced the Middle Ages and Their Symbols," *The Conversation*, January 13, 2021, theconversation.com/why-the-far-right-and-white-supremacists-have-embraced-the-middle-ages-and-their-symbols-152968.

3. On this structure of inanimation as keyed to the ongoing diasporic disaster of chattel slavery and colonization, and so built into all of our concepts, including what Yusoff calls "geologic life," and so the very notion of a ground, see Kathryn Yusoff, *A Billion Black Anthropocenes or None* (Minneapolis: University of Minnesota Press, 2018). For a broader articulation of the necropolitical supplement to biopower/biopolitics that produces disposable people or the "living dead," see Achille Mbembe, *Necropolitics*, trans. Steven Corcoran (Durham, N.C.: Duke University Press, 2019).

4. Timothy Findley, *Not Wanted on the Voyage* (London: Penguin, 1984), 120; subsequent references appear parenthetically in the text.

5. On modeling "the World as Plenum and not as Universe," and so deprived of the ideological palming of matter and labor enabled by the figure of an empty "outside" and the ways in which this economy is keyed to the "endless expropriation" of "Black (symbolic and economic) labor," see Denise Ferreira Da Silva, "Toward a Black Feminist Poethics: The Question of Blackness Toward the End of the World," *The Black Scholar* 44, no. 2 (2014): 81–97, at 84.

6. Derek Walcott, *Collected Poems: 1948–1984* (New York: Farrar, Straus & Giroux, 1986), 364.

7. Sonya Posmentier, *Cultivation and Catastrophe: The Lyric Ecology of Modern Black Literature* (Baltimore, Md.: Johns Hopkins University Press, 2017), 109–10.

8. Christina Sharpe, *In the Wake: On Blackness and Being* (Durham, N.C.: Duke University Press, 2016), 41 (Sharpe quotes Walcott at 57); subsequent references appear parenthetically in the text. A formative influence on Sharpe's thinking here is Gaston Bachelard's statement that water "remembers the dead" in *Water and Dreams: An Essay on the Imagination of Matter*, trans. Edith R. Farrell (Dallas: Pegasus Foundation, 1983), 56. As Sharpe acknowledges, she comes to Bachelard by way of Elizabeth DeLoughrey's "Heavy Waters: Waste and Atlantic Modernity," *PMLA* 125, no. 3 (2010): 703–12, at 704.

For an allied reading sensitive to the materiality of Walcott's metaphor in the context of a broader attunement to water in African American literature and culture, see Anissa Janine Wardi, *Water and African American Memory: An Ecocritical Perspective* (Gainesville: University Press of Florida, 2011). "The confluence of water, loss, and migration in African American culture," writes Wardi, provides a "central trope" continuously turning in its eco-fictions. Wardi offers the figure of the watershed as an organizing topos enabling readers to understand the status of bodies of water and waterways (islands, archipelagos, rivers, oceans) in relation to human bodies. Inspired, in part, also by Bachelard, Wardi writes compellingly of the salinity of the ocean and tears shed in mourning, of the myriad ways in which water comes to saturate story. Waterways, she offers, provide "loci of both forced and chosen movement," and so constitute ambivalent "bodies of memory" (17).

For an allied reading of bioluminescent sea creatures as a living archive of human violence and lively persistence, see Alexis Pauline Gumbs, *M. Archive: After the End of the World* (Durham, N.C.: Duke University Press, 2018).

9. Quoting Toni Morrison, *Beloved* (New York: Plume, 1987), 198.

10. Maurice Blanchot, *The Writing of the Disaster*, trans. Ann Smock (Lincoln: University of Nebraska Press, 1995). Sharpe works through Blanchot carefully at 136n6 and 137n7.

11. For the genre of the ruttier, see Dionne Brand, "Ruttier for the Marooned in Diaspora," *A Map to the Door of No Return: Notes to Belonging* (Toronto: Vintage Canada, 2011), 213–24. Brand is similarly one of the inspirations for Kathryn Yusoff in *A Billion Black Anthropocenes or None*, xi–xii.

12. Stefano Harney and Fred Moten, *The Undercommons: Fugitive Planning and Black Study* (Brooklyn, N.Y.: Autonomedia, 2013), 94, 92, 97.

13. Ovid, *Metamorphoses* 273–321, trans. Michael Simpson (Amherst: University of Massachusetts Press, 2001), 15.

14. Ovid, *Metamorphoses* 273–321.

15. Roland Barthes, *Mythologies*, trans. Richard Howard (New York: Hill and Wang, 2013), 63; subsequent references appear parenthetically in the text.

16. Zora Neale Hurston, *Their Eyes Were Watching God* (New York: Harper Collins, 2006), 7; subsequent references appear parenthetically in the text.

17. Posmentier, *Cultivation and Catastrophe,* 213–14. The yoking together of "cultivation" and "catastrophe" in the title of Posmentier's book enacts this sense of disaster as always anthropogenic and indexed to the plantation in the history Posmentier excavates. Posmentier also uses the phrase "no such thing as a natural disaster" with a nod to Neil Smith.

18. On the NAACP's investigation into the aftermath of the Mississippi floods of 1926–1927, led by W. E. B. Du Bois in *The Crisis,* and revelations concerning the refugee or "concentration camps," see Posmentier, *Cultivation and Catastrophe,* 131–34.

19. Richard Wright, "Between Laughter and Tears," *New Masses,* October 5, 1937, 25–26. Referred to in Eve Dunbar, *Black Regions of the Imagination: African American Writers between the Nation and the World* (Philadelphia: Temple University Press, 2013), 16–17. Dunbar offers a nuanced consideration of the Wright–Hurston relationship and the consequences of Hurston's focus on "non-northern Black life" as part of her lifelong artmaking, interest in folklore, ethnographic work, and inquiry into belonging. Our thinking throughout this chapter has been shaped by a conversation with Eve, early in the drafting, about posthumanism, Hurston as ethnographer, and the importance of arks in African American literature. We are deeply grateful for her insights.

20. Richard Wright, *Uncle Tom's Children* (1936; repr. New York: Harper Perennial, 2003), 87, 123–24. For a reading of the story tuned to the in-between status of mud as neither quite earth nor water and sensitive to the typological stacking of figures from the Bible in Wright's story, see Wardi, *Water and African American Memory,* 118–23. For comparison and a visceral portrayal of the routinized social and economic entrapment awaiting black farmers/sharecroppers who returned to farms that had been inundated, see Wright's story "The Man Who Saw the Flood," in *Eight Men* (New York: Harper Perennial, 1992), 102–8.

21. Dunbar, *Black Regions of the Imagination,* 16–17.

22. For a reading of the novel's "geosemiotic" projection of islands in and as its form, see Brian Russell Roberts, "Archipelagic Diaspora, Geographical Form, and Hurston's *Their Eyes Were Watching God,*" *American Literature* 85, no. 1 (2013): 121–49.

23. Henry Louis Gates Jr., *The Signifying Monkey: A Theory of African American Literary Criticism* (1988; repr. Oxford: Oxford University Press, 2014), 184–232.

24. Posmentier, *Cultivation and Catastrophe,* 169.

25. Bessie Smith, "Back-Water Blues," youtube.com/watch?v=4gXShOJVwaM. For an account of the possible inspiration, the date of composition prior to the Mississippi flood, the release of Smith's song, and how the historically particular resonates with the figural dimensions of flood, see David Evans,

"Bessie Smith's 'Back-Water Blues': The Story Behind the Song," *Popular Music* 26, no. 1 (2007): 97–116. For excellent close readings of the song in the context of a wider blues tradition, see Posmentier, *Cultivation and Catastrophe,* 138–41 and 149–50, and Wardi, *Water and African American Memory,* 126–29. See also Angela Y. Davis, *Blues Legacies and Black Feminism: Gertrude "Ma" Rainey, Bessie Smith, and Billie Holiday* (New York: Pantheon, 1998).

26. *Conversations with James Baldwin,* ed. Fred L. Standley and Louise H. Platt (Jackson: University of Mississippi Press, 1989), 3–4; subsequent references appear parenthetically in the text.

27. James Baldwin, *Nobody Knows My Name* (1961; repr. New York: Vintage International, 1993), xii.

28. Baldwin, *Nobody Knows My Name,* xiii.

29. Henry Dumas, *Ark of Bones and Other Stories* (Carbondale: Southern Illinois University Press, 1970), 3; subsequent references appear parenthetically in the text.

30. On the agentive force to the river in "Ark of Bones," see Wardi, *Water and African American Memory,* 80–82. On the multivalence of the Mississippi, more generally, see 72–78.

31. Tuned to the story's "soundscape," Salim Washington explains that "moaning is a descriptive term for a certain bluesy sound of speech/song favored by blues singers, gospel preachers, and congregants in a spirit-filled church service" ("The Avenging Angel of Creation/Destruction: Black Music and the Afro-technological in the Science Fiction of Henry Dumas and Samuel R. Delany," *Journal of the Society for American Music* 2, no. 2 [2008]: 235–53, at 242).

32. For a parsing of the different African languages that augment the Arabic in these lines and the possible meanings of different words and syllables, see Jeffrey B. Leak, *Visible Man: The Life of Henry Dumas* (Athens: University of Georgia Press, 2014), 116–17.

33. Eugene B. Redmond, "Introduction: The Ancient and Recent Voices within Henry Dumas," *Black American Literature Forum* 22, no. 2 (1988): 143–54, at 150. On the rich, multigenre hybridity of Dumas's power in creating "entirely different worlds," see Amiri Baraka, "Henry Dumas: Afro-Surreal Expressionist Author(s)," *Black American Literature Forum* 22, no. 2 (1988): 164–66. This special issue of *Black American Literature Forum* dedicated to Dumas includes key early readings of his fiction by scholars, writers, and artists, including Toni Morrison's "On Behalf of Henry Dumas" (310–12).

34. On the approximate date of composition for "Ark of Bones," see Leak, *Visible Man,* 116–17.

35. On Dumas in relation to the Black Arts Movement, experimental jazz, and Sun Ra, see Carter Mathes, *Imagine the Sound: Experimental African American Literature after Civil Rights* (Minneapolis: University of Min-

nesota Press, 2015), 61–99. On Dumas's friendship with Sun Ra, see also Leak, *Visible Man*, 116–18. Leak describes Dumas as Sun Ra's "intellectual apprentice," a relationship that was most active in the mid-1960s (204).

36. Mathes, *Imagine the Sound*, 68.

37. Jonathan P. Eburne, *Outsider Theory: Intellectual Histories of Unorthodox Ideas* (Minneapolis: University of Minnesota Press, 2018), 352. Our debts to Eburne's reading will be clear throughout these pages.

38. *The Ark and the Ankh: Sun Ra and Henry Dumas in Conversation at Slug's Saloon, 1966*, IKEF Records, 2002.

39. For an excellent parsing of Sun Ra's aesthetics in relation to the figure of the outside and "space as a revolutionary trope," and a revealing reading of *Space Is the Place*, see Anthony Reed, "Close Up: Afrosurrealism after the End of the World: Sun Ra and the Grammar of Utopia," *Black Camera* 5, no. 1 (2013): 118–39, at 121.

40. Sun Ra, "If I Told You," in *The Immeasurable Equation: The Collected Poetry and Prose*, ed. James L. Wolf and Hartmut Geerken (1980; repr. Wartaweil, Germany: Waitwhile, 2005), 200 (quoted in Eburne, *Outsider Theory*, 351).

41. *Space Is the Place* (1974), directed by John Coney, written by Sun Ra and Joshua Smith, Harte Recordings, 2015 (quoted in Eburne, *Outsider Theory*, 355).

42. The film's use of the verb "to be" seems projective. Ontology would derive from a practice that makes space the place. See, by contrast, Jacques Derrida's critique of a certain melancholy double assertion in metaphysics concerning the incompatibility between grammatical and philosophical uses of the verb "to be": first of a fullness to being felt to be absent from the verb, that felt absence secondarily providing an occasion to reaffirm a past but now unlocatable fullness of being, felt now to be lacking ("The Supplement of Copula: Philosophy before Linguistics," in *Margins of Philosophy*, trans. Alan Bass [Chicago: University of Chicago Press, 1986], 177–205).

43. Yusoff, *Billion Black Anthropocenes*, 93–96, citing Tina Campt, *Listening to Images: An Exercise in Counterintuition* (Durham, N.C.: Duke University Press, 2017), 17.

44. Michelle D. Commander identifies the "Flying African" as a trope/orientation of possibility and argues that Afrofuturism makes best sense as a "subgenre" of the historically broader field of "Afro-speculation" that historically has served to examine "the function of science and technology in the construction of utopic Black futures" (*Afro-Atlantic Flight: Speculative Return and the Black Fantastic* [Durham, N.C.: Duke University Press, 2017], 6). On the slave narrative as a crucial form for our historical moment, see Yogita Goyal, *Runaway Genres: The Global Afterlives of Slavery* (New York: New York University Press, 2019).

45. Octavia E. Butler, *Parable of the Sower* (1993; repr. New York: Grand Central, 2000), 67–68.

46. As Da Silva puts it, Lauren is one of a series of "black female" (and less often male) characters in Butler's novels who exist "in bodies that have not delinked from the plenum" ("Toward a Black Feminist Poethics," 93).

47. Butler, *Parable of the Sower,* 25.

48. Octavia E. Butler, *The Parable of the Talents* (1998; repr. New York: Grand Central, 2000), 323.

49. Butler, *Parable of the Talents,* 355–56.

50. Butler, *Parable of the Sower,* 118.

51. Butler, *Parable of the Talents,* 15.

52. Butler, *Parable of the Sower,* 328.

53. Butler, *Parable of the Talents,* 393–94.

54. Butler, *Parable of the Talents,* 404.

55. Butler, *Parable of the Sower,* 83.

56. Jerry Canvan, "'There's Nothing New / Under the Sun, / But There Are New Suns': Recovering Octavia E. Butler's Lost Parables," *Los Angeles Review of Books,* June 9, 2014, lareviewofbooks.org/article/theres-nothing-new-sun-new-suns-recovering-octavia-e-butlers-lost-parables/.

57. Gallery Aferro, Rutgers University, New Jersey Council for the Humanities, New Jersey Historical Commission, and Up Front Exhibition Space, "Kea's Ark of Newark," Aferro Publication no. 27, January 25, 2019, aferro.org/wp-content/uploads/2013/11/2keasark_blue.pdf. In these exhibition materials, Mark Krasovic provides a sympathetic and even-handed rendering of the story, and also an invaluable timeline of Kea Tawana's life and the building of the ark; subsequent quotations come from Krasovic's synopsis. An online archive for the ark is maintained as "Kea Tawana's Ark" on the SPACES webpage (Saving-Preserving Art-Cultural Environments), spacesarchives.org/explore/search-the-online-collection/keas-ark/, accessed July 8, 2021.

58. On the City of Newark's incorporation, see Brad R. Tuttle, *How Newark Became Newark: The Rise, Fall, and Rebirth of an American City Book* (Newark, N.J.: Rutgers University Press, 2009), 16.

59. Gallery Aferro et al., "Kea's Ark of Newark."

60. "Builder Gets Reprieve for Newark's New Ark," *Arizona Republic,* April 14, 1987, quoted but not cited in Gallery Aferro et al., "Kea's Ark of Newark." The phrase becomes a trope in almost all that is written about Tawana's ark.

61. Emma Wilcox, director of The Gallery Aferro, interview in *Kea's Ark,* special episode of PBS *State of the Arts,* presented at the Gallery Aferro, directed by Susan Wallner, PCK Media, 2021.

62. Kea Tawana, logbook for August 8, 1982, quoted in Chip Brown, "Kea's Improbable Ark," *Chicago Tribune,* April 22, 1987, and also in Gallery Aferro et al., "Kea's Ark of Newark."

63. Holly Metz, "Where I Am Going: Kea's Ark, Newark, New Jersey," *The Southern Quarterly* 39, no. 1–2 (2000–2001): 1987–216, at 198.

64. Linda Hamalian, "Kea Tawana: Or Who Would Build a Better Ark

than Noah?," *Black American Literature Forum* 21, no. 1 (1987): 97–112, at 112. Writer and photographer Camilo José Vergara recounts running into Kea Tawana in the South Bronx in 1999. She was in an "end-of-the-world-mood" and advised Vergara to move to the Bronx—how else would he get out of the city "when the bridges fell and the tunnels were flooded?" (*American Ruins* [New York: The Monacelli Press, 1999], 211–12).

65. Tawana, logbook for August 8, 1982, quoted in Brown, "Kea's Improbable Ark."

66. Tawana's manifesto is discussed by Wilcox, interview in *Kea's Ark*.

67. Correspondence to Mayor Sharpe from curators at the Museum of American Art, the Museum of American Folk Art, The Folk Art Society of America, and academics at Columbia University, as well as process documents related to gathering support from such institutions as the Smithsonian are archived at on the SPACES webpage (Saving-Preserving Art-Cultural Environments), spacesarchives.org/explore/search-the-online-collection/keas-ark/, accessed July 8, 2021. Holly Metz includes Tawana's ark as one example of contested structures in "The Perils of Public Art," *Student Lawyer*, December 1987, 42–44.

68. The self-awareness of interviewees in the documentary *Kea's Ark* is both striking and moving.

69. Quotations are from Metz, "Where I Am Going," 208–9. Tawana was also interviewed by Hamalian on October 5, 1986, an interview that forms the basis for "Kea Tawana." This interview provides a similar but also subtly different version of the events of Tawana's early life and arrival in Newark.

70. Joshua Bennett, "Revising 'The Waste Land': Black Antipastoral and the End of the World," *The Paris Review*, January 8, 2018, 2.

71. Bennett, "Revising 'The Waste Land,'" 2. On Mark Bradford's *Mithra* and the discourse of "Black optimism," see Posmentier, *Cultivation and Catastrophe*, 224–27. For a short but insightful reading of Rodney Leon's *The Ark of Return* with/against Charles Gaines's *Moving Chains*, see Sharpe, *In the Wake*, 61–62.

72. Bennett, "Revising 'The Wasteland,'" 3.

73. Brown, "Kea's Improbable Ark." Hamalian provides a similar sense of the completed ark's seaworthiness in "Kea Tawana," 108–10.

74. For this sense of credibility or knowledge production as keyed to gender and social rank, see Steven Shapin, *A Social History of Truth: Civility and Science in Seventeenth-Century England* (Chicago: University of Chicago Press, 1994).

75. Brown, "Kea's Improbable Ark." Tawana described a similar plan in her October 5, 1986, interview with Hamalian, quoted in "Kea Tawana," 109.

76. Subsequent quotations and details are from Gallery Aferro et al., "Kea's Ark of Newark."

77. Gallery Aferro, "Kea's Ark of Newark: A Life in Works," main gallery,

Newark, N.J., September 24 through December 17, 2016, aferro.org/2016-2/, accessed, May 21, 2021.

8. Landfalling

1. Kim Stanley Robinson, *Aurora* (New York: Orbit Books, 2015), 222; subsequent references appear parenthetically in the text.

2. Howard Norman, *In Fond Remembrance of Me* (New York: Picador, 2005); subsequent references appear parenthetically in the text.

3. N. K. Jemisin, "Emergency Skin," in *The Best Science Fiction of the Year #5,* ed. Neil Clarke (New York: Night Shade, 2020), 11–32, at 18; subsequent references appear parenthetically in the text. We are grateful to B. Jamieson Stanley for introducing us to this story.

4. For an analogous plotline to the arc of "Emergency Skin," see Douglas Adams, *The Restaurant at the End of the Universe* (1980; repr. New York: Ballantine, 2002), in which the planet of Golgafrincham rids itself of the third of its population it deems unproductive by sending them off in an ark. The ark crash-lands on Earth, forever altering the planet's evolution, leading its indigenous humans to die out. The unforeseen likewise complicates the new utopia of Golgafrincham, whose remaining two thirds "lived full, rich and happy lives until they were all suddenly wiped out by a virulent disease contracted from a dirty telephone" (273). (Telephone sanitizers were among the groups transported off planet.) The novel's light satire of settler-colonial mediocrity as perceived from the metropole, transportation as part of British colonialism, and the dangers run by assuming that the life of another is "parasitic" or merely useless is all there for the reading.

5. On the cruelty of optimism as an orientation in utopian thinking, and so a scene of ideological capture, see Lauren Berlant, *Cruel Optimism* (Durham, N.C.: Duke University Press, 2011).

6. On this sense of distance from past stories as one of generational difference reflecting a transformed mode of production, see Karl Marx, *The Grundrisse,* in *The Marx and Engels Reader,* ed. Robert C. Tucker, 2nd ed. (New York: Norton, 1978), 245–46.

7. Geoffrey Chaucer, *The Canterbury Tales,* ed. Jill Mann (London: Penguin, 2005), lines 3581–82; subsequent references appear parenthetically in the text.

INDEX

JEFFREY J. COHEN is Dean of Humanities at Arizona State University and former copresident of the Association for the Study of Literature and the Environment. He is author of *Stone: An Ecology of the Inhuman* (Minnesota, 2015), coauthor of *Earth,* and coeditor of *The Cambridge Companion to Environmental Humanities.*

JULIAN YATES is H. Fletcher Brown Professor of English and Material Culture Studies at the University of Delaware. He is the author of *Error, Misuse, Failure: Object Lessons from the English Renaissance* and *Of Sheep, Oranges, and Yeast: A Multispecies Impression,* both published by the University of Minnesota Press.